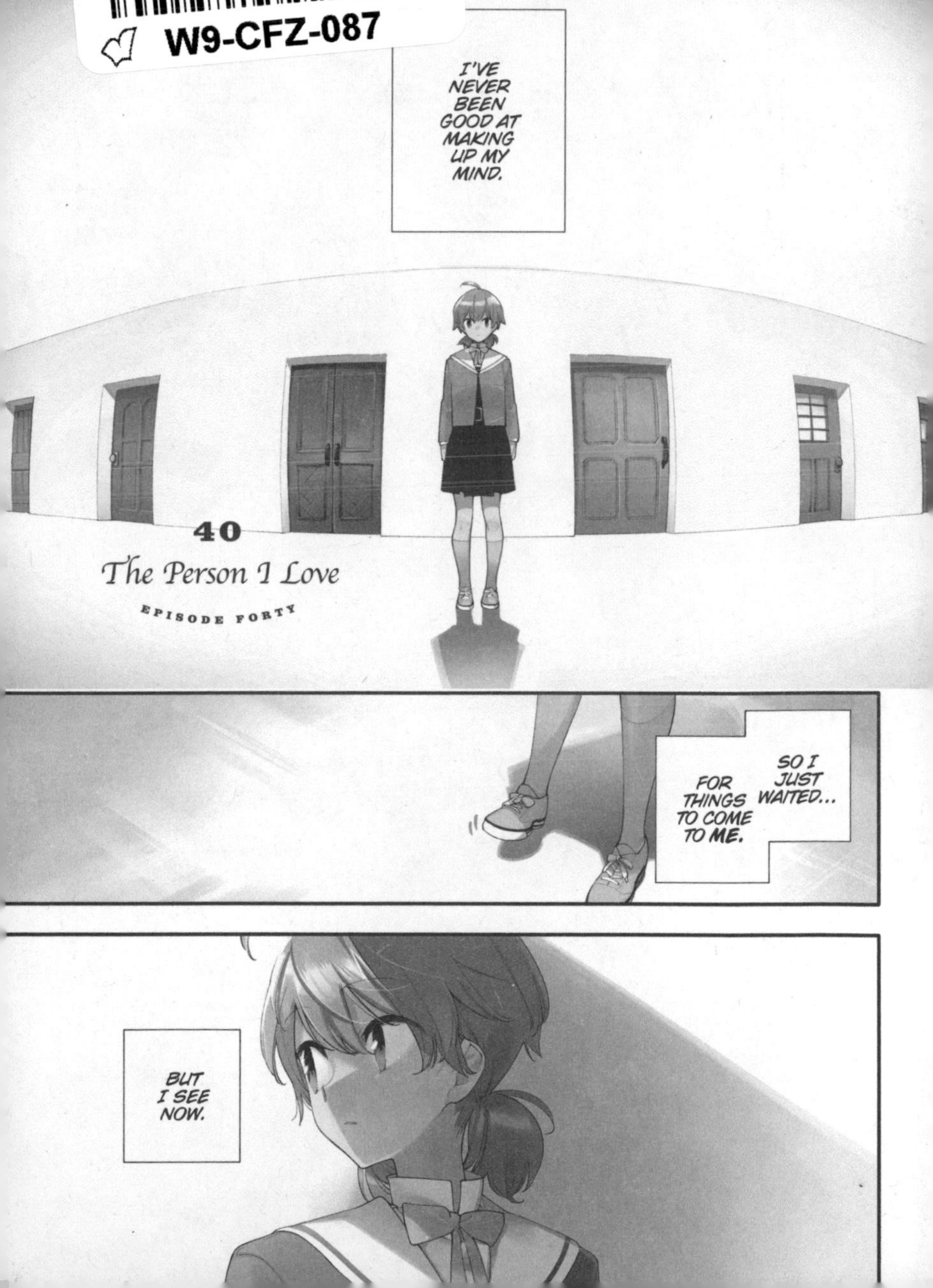
I'VE NEVER BEEN GOOD AT MAKING UP MY MIND.
40
The Person I Love
EPISODE FORTY
SO I JUST WAITED...
FOR THINGS TO COME TO ME.
BUT I SEE NOW.

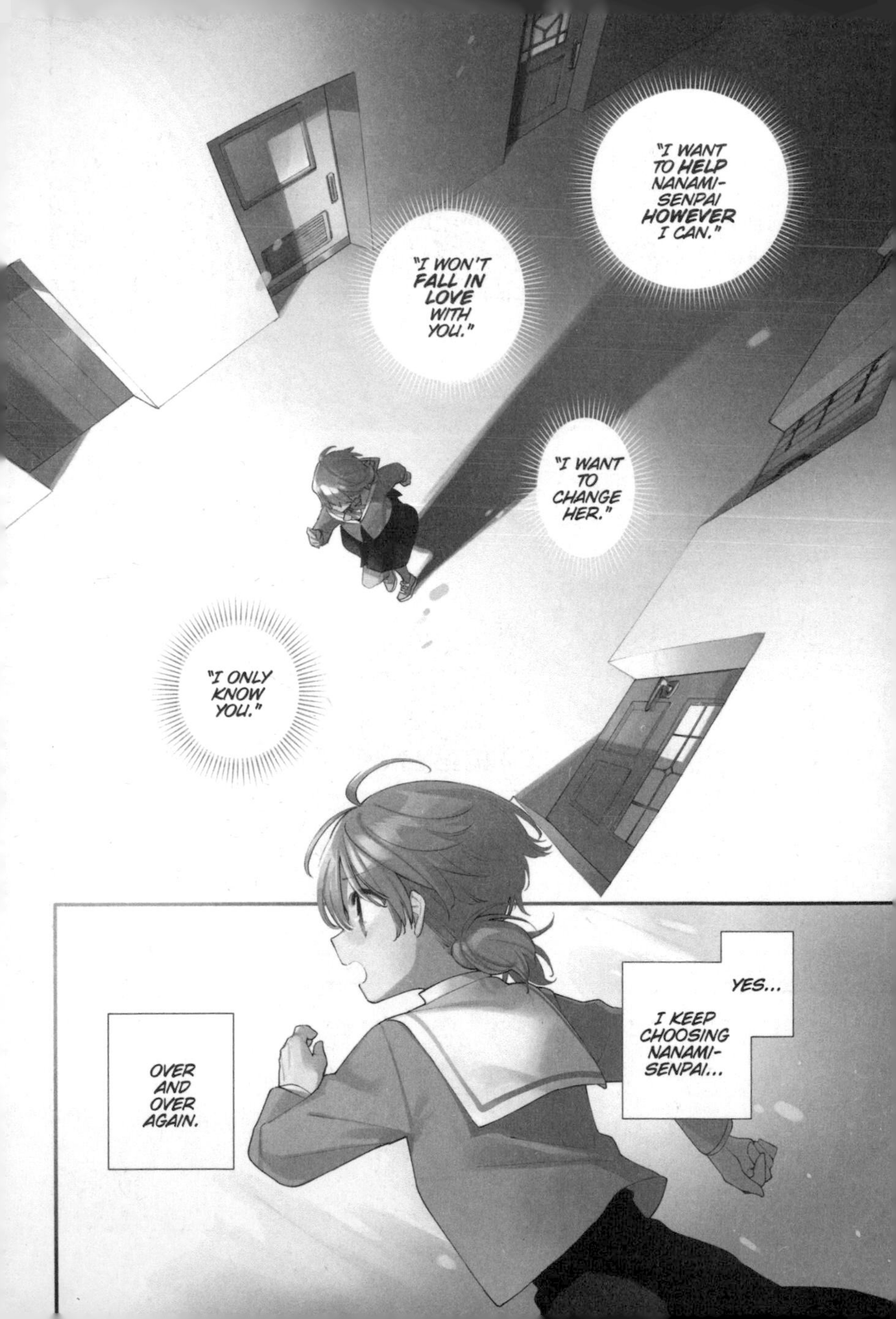
"I WANT TO HELP NANAMI-SENPAI HOWEVER I CAN."
"I WON'T FALL IN LOVE WITH YOU."
"I WANT TO CHANGE HER."
"I ONLY KNOW YOU."
YES...
I KEEP CHOOSING NANAMI-SENPAI...
OVER AND OVER AGAIN.

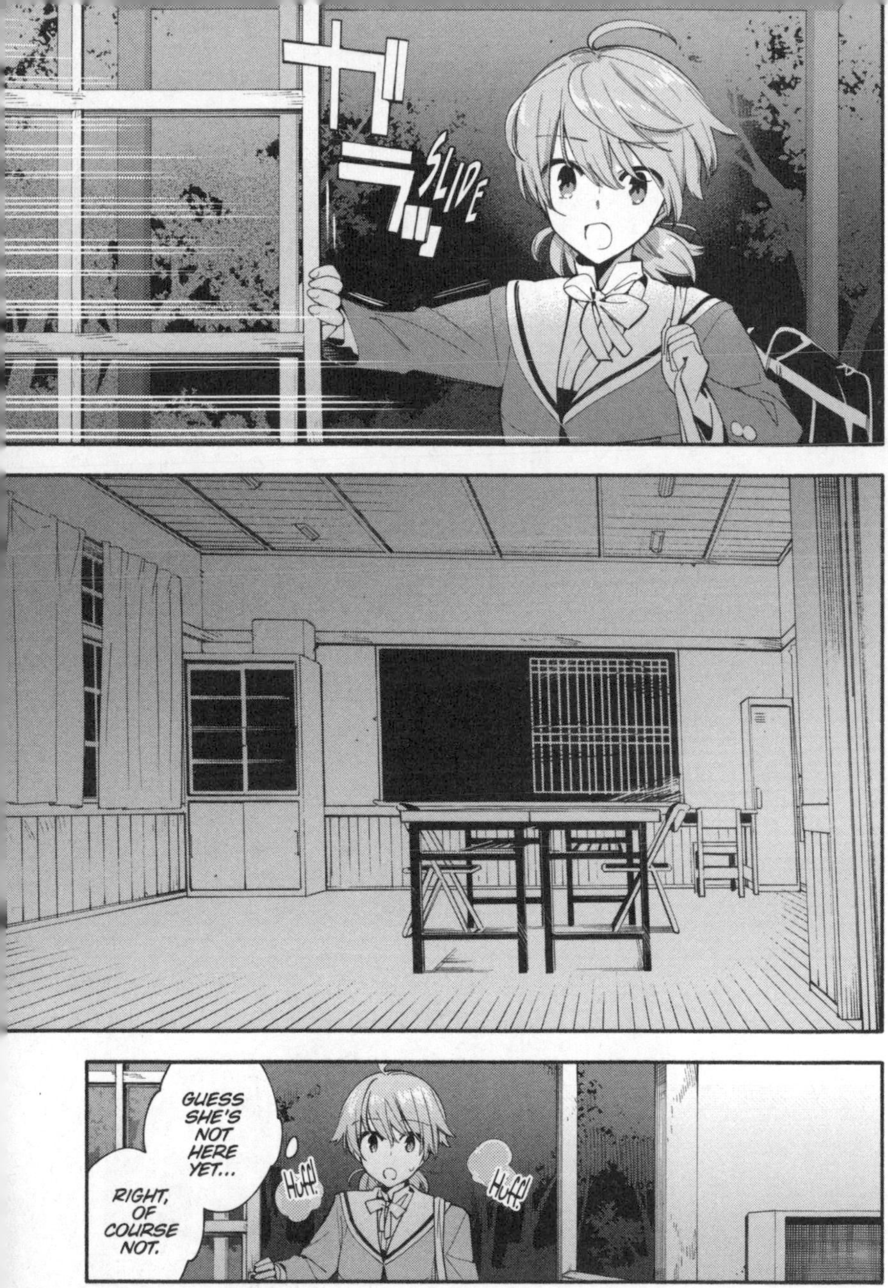
ガラッ
SLIDE
GUESS SHE'S NOT HERE YET...
RIGHT, OF COURSE NOT.
HUFF!
HUFF!

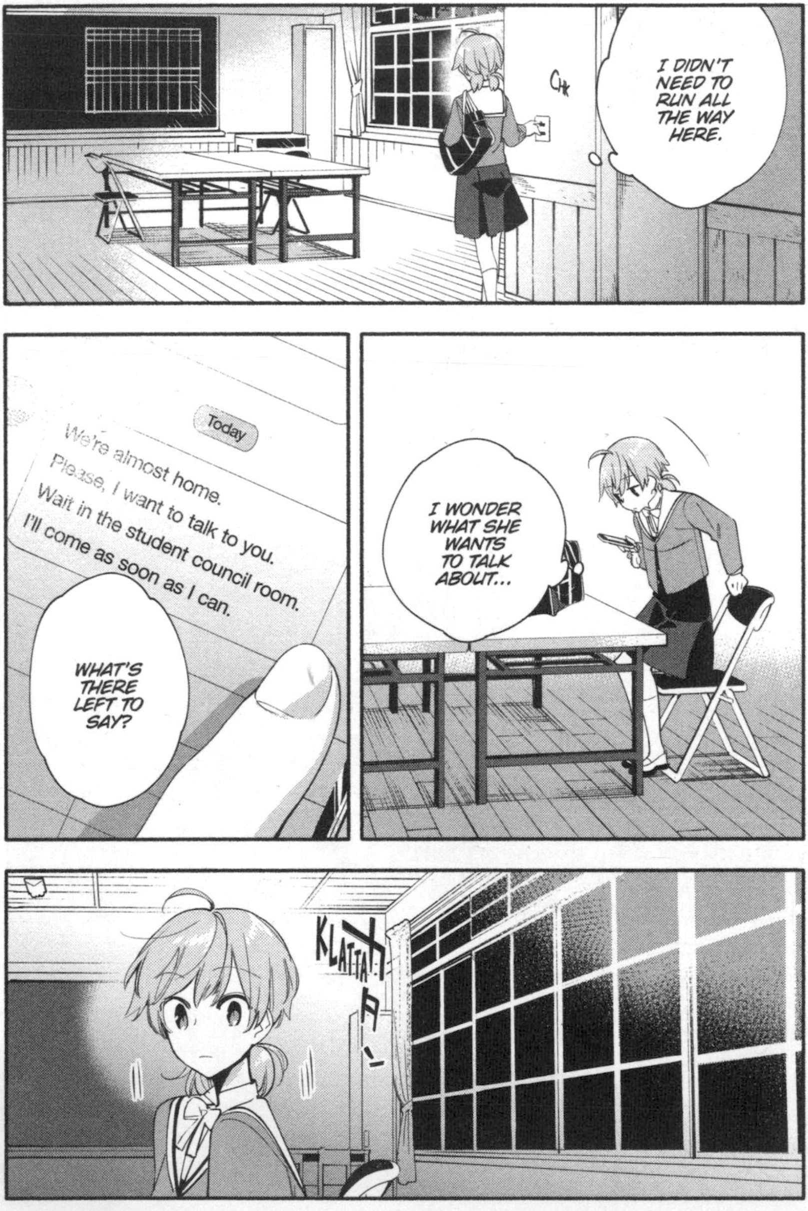
CHK
I DIDN'T NEED TO RUN ALL THE WAY HERE.
I WONDER WHAT SHE WANTS TO TALK ABOUT...
Today
We're almost home.
Please, I want to talk to you.
Wait in the student council room.
I'll come as soon as I can.
WHAT'S THERE LEFT TO SAY?
KLATTA!

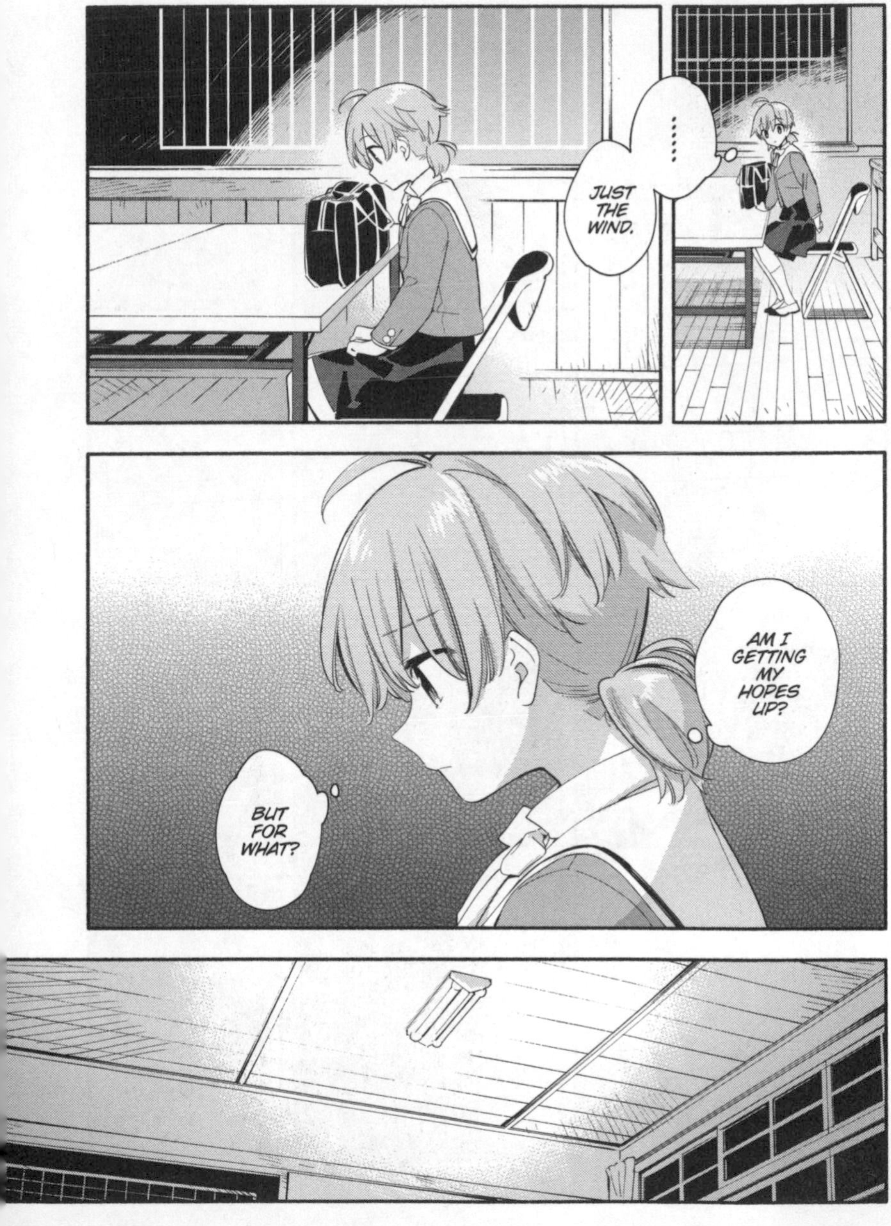
......
JUST THE WIND.
AM I GETTING MY HOPES UP?
BUT FOR WHAT?

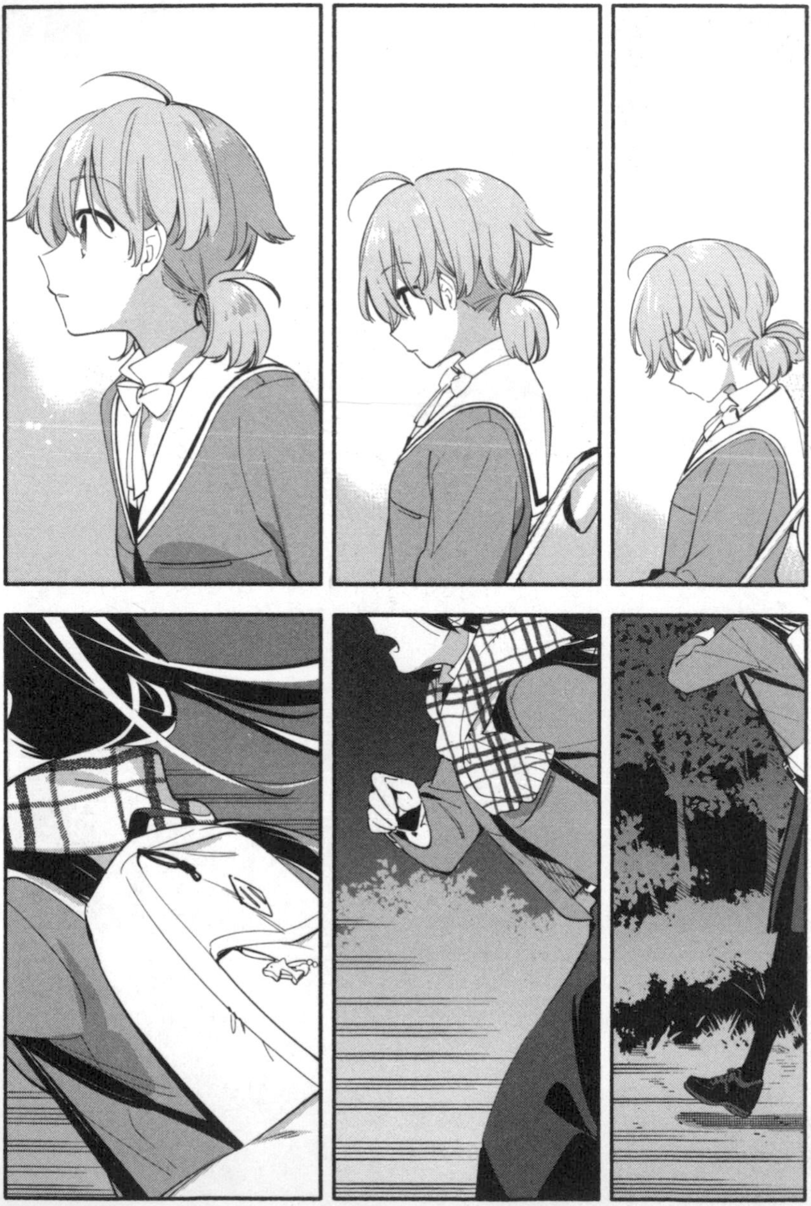

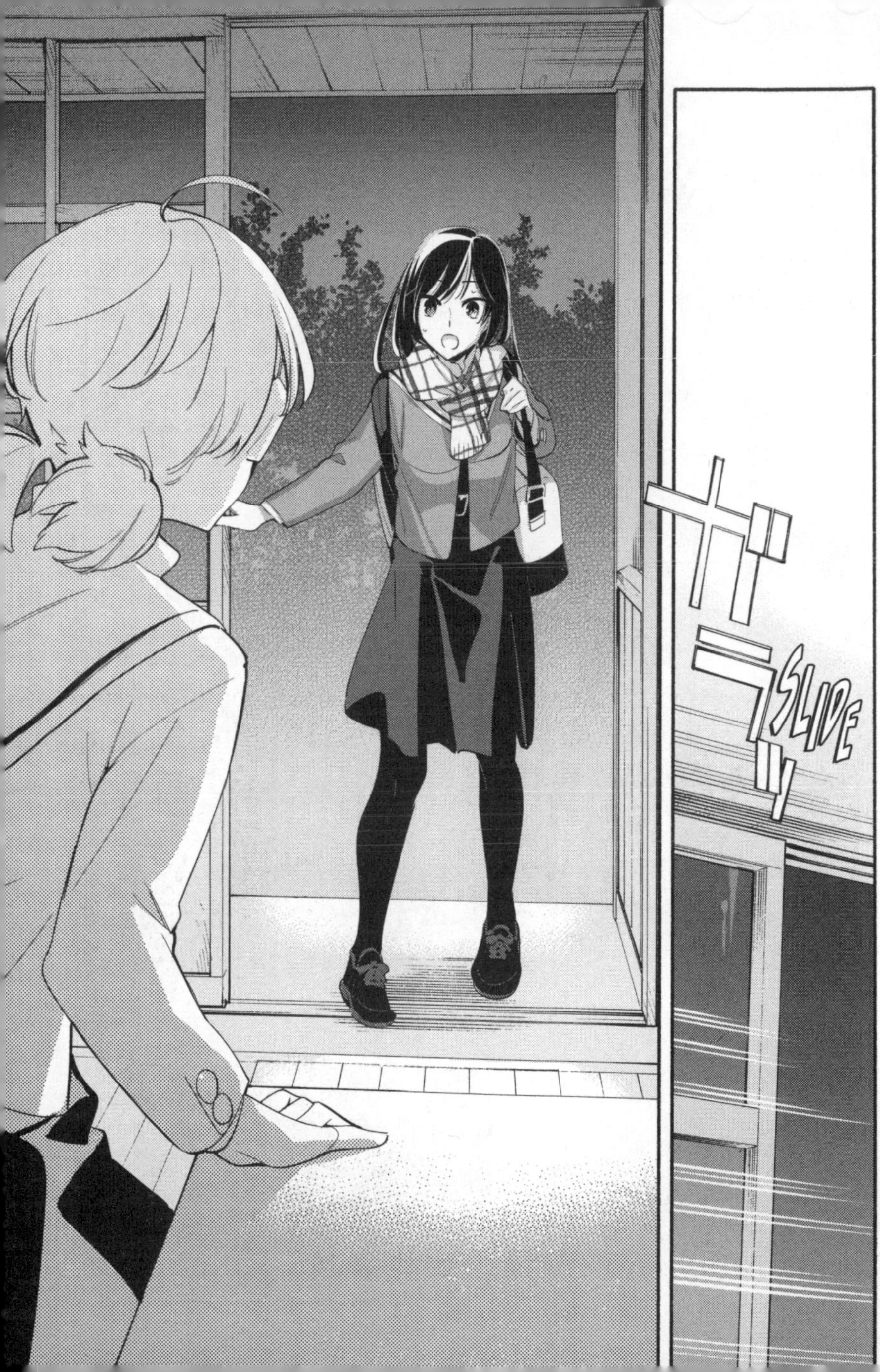
ガラッ
SLIDE

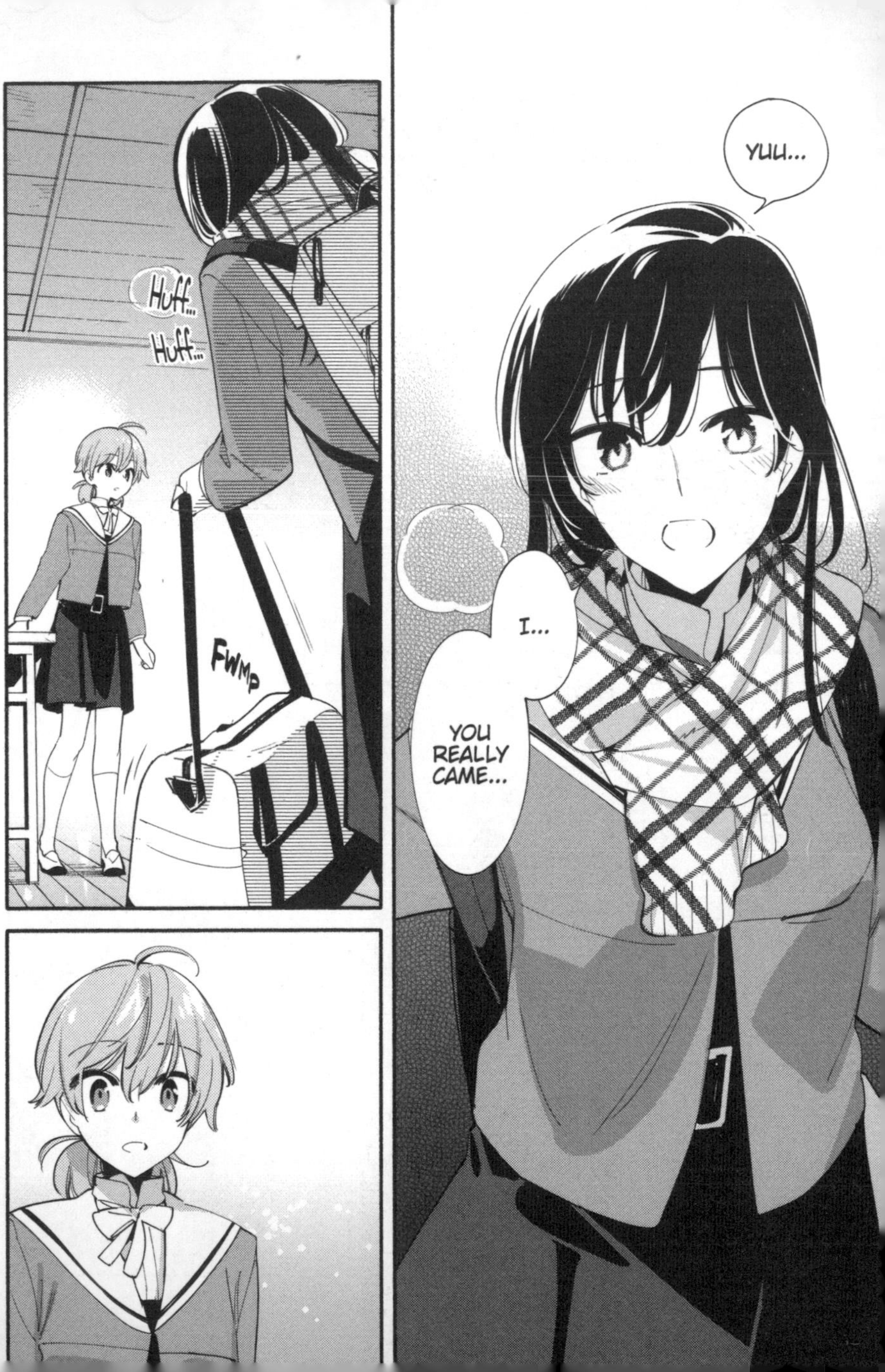
YUU...
I...
YOU REALLY CAME...
Huff... Huff...
FWMP

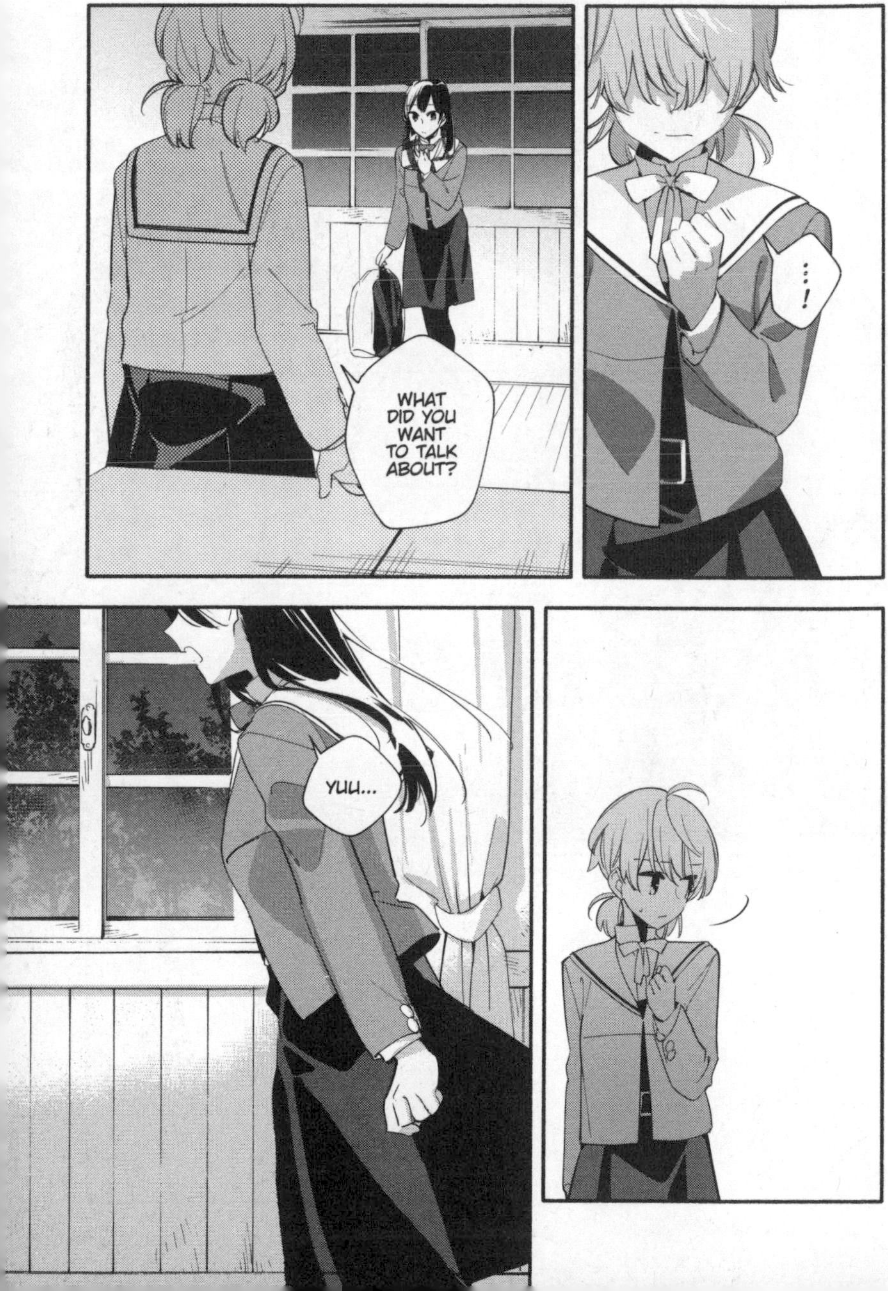
...!
WHAT DID YOU WANT TO TALK ABOUT?
YUU...

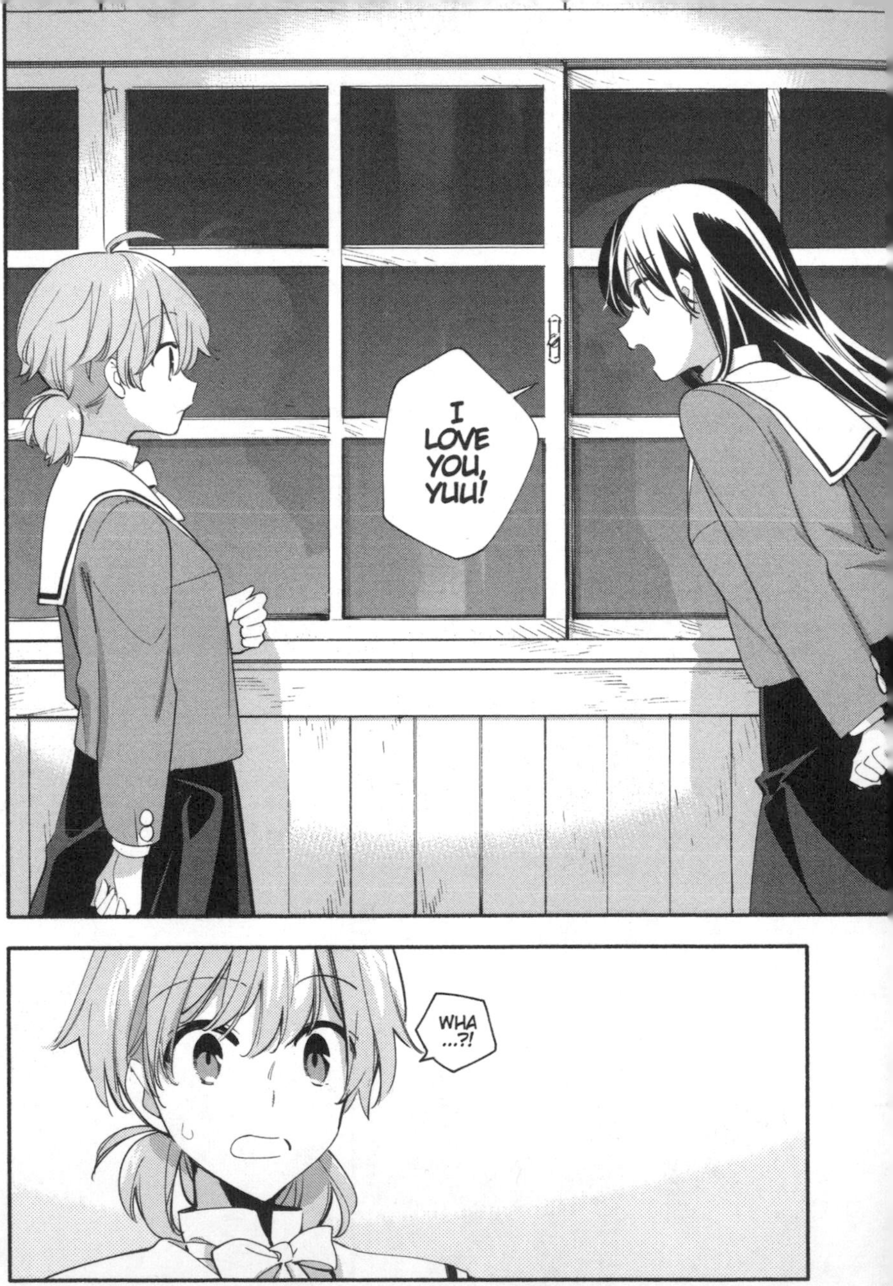
I LOVE YOU, YUU!
WHA ...?!

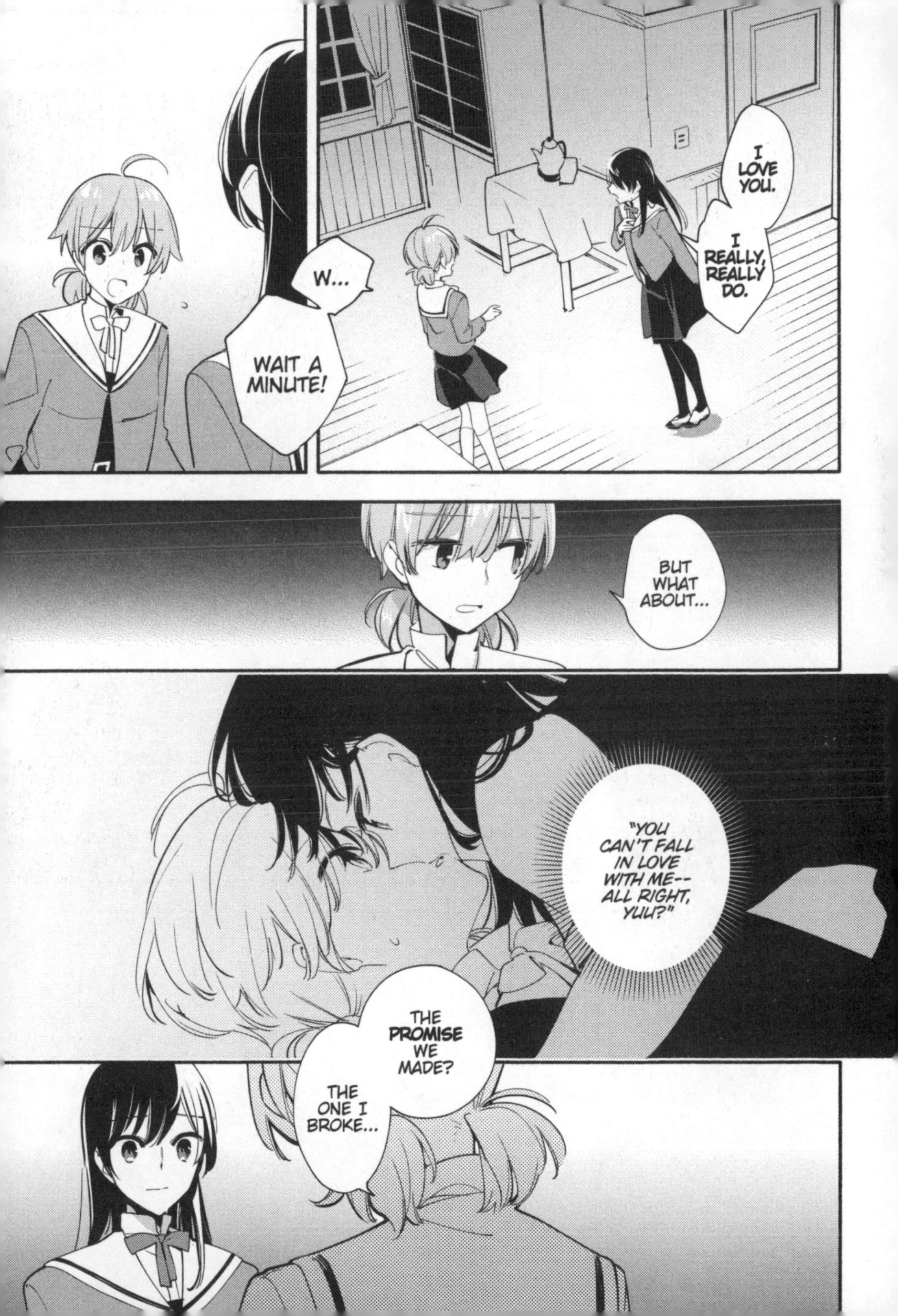
I LOVE YOU.
I REALLY, REALLY DO.
W...
WAIT A MINUTE!
BUT WHAT ABOUT...
"YOU CAN'T FALL IN LOVE WITH ME-- ALL RIGHT, YUU?"
THE PROMISE WE MADE?
THE ONE I BROKE...

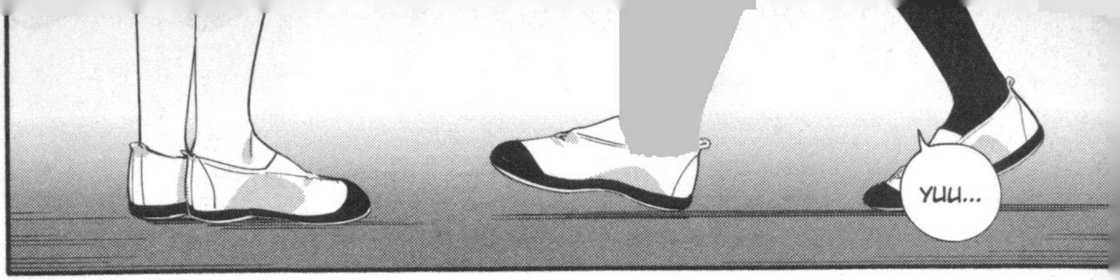
YUU...
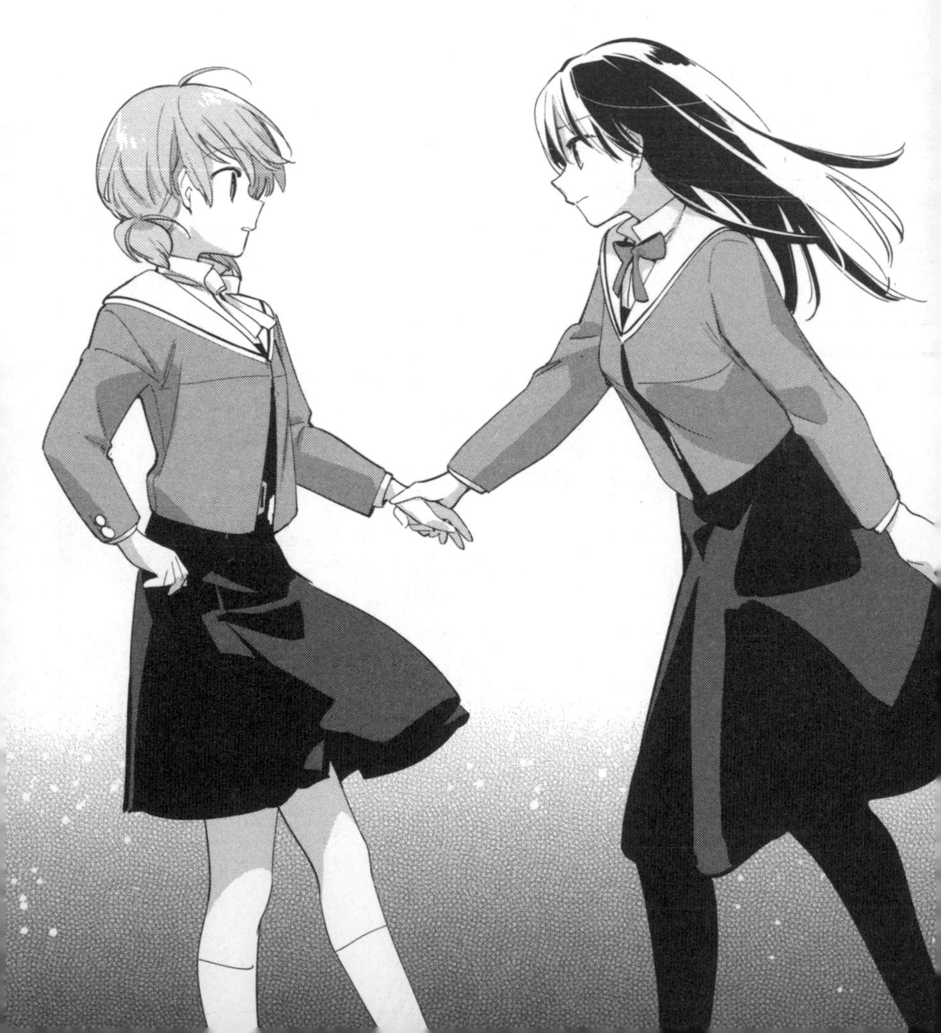

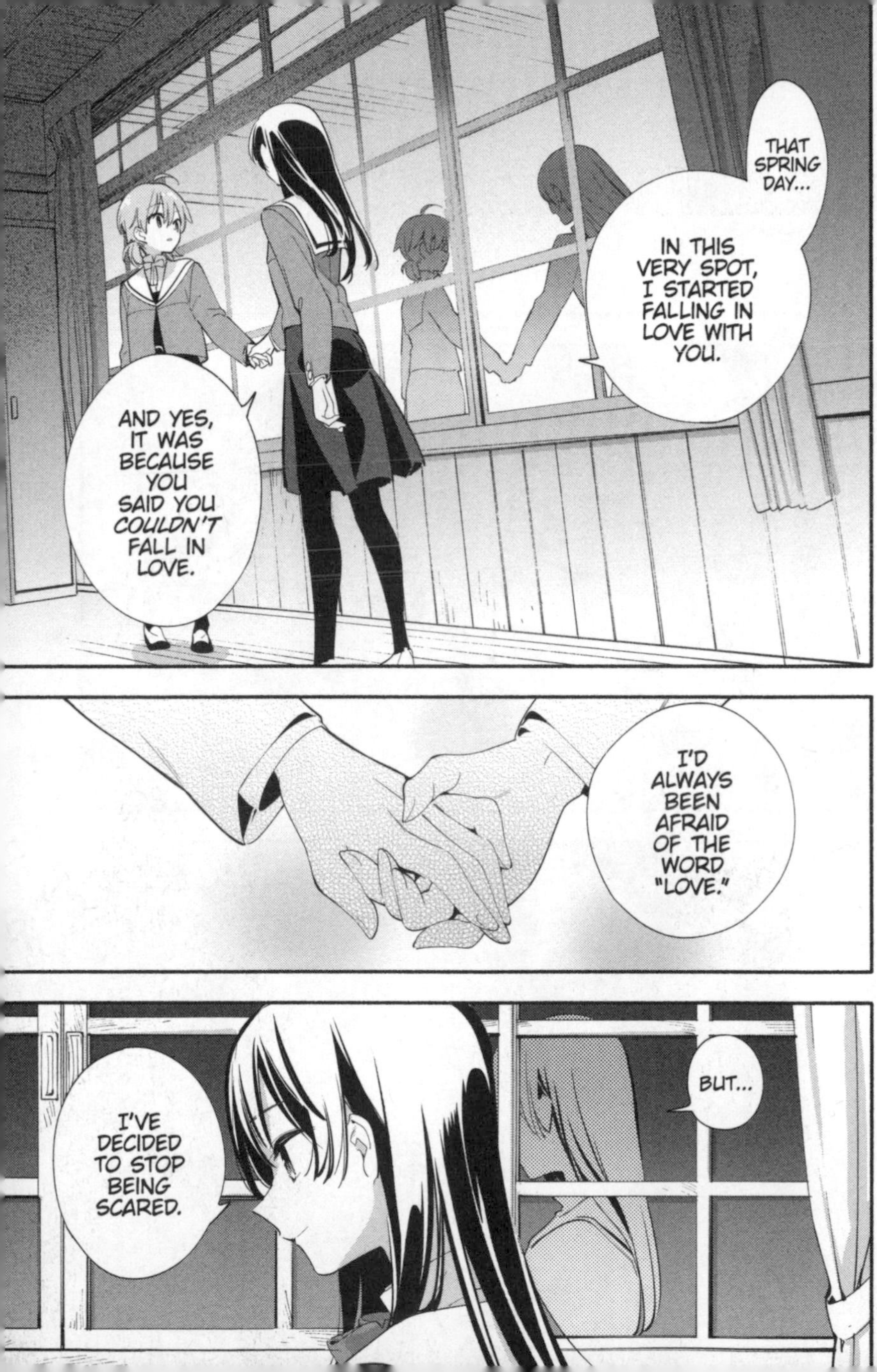
THAT SPRING DAY...
IN THIS VERY SPOT, I STARTED FALLING IN LOVE WITH YOU.
AND YES, IT WAS BECAUSE YOU SAID YOU COULDN'T FALL IN LOVE.
I'D ALWAYS BEEN AFRAID OF THE WORD "LOVE."
BUT...
I'VE DECIDED TO STOP BEING SCARED.

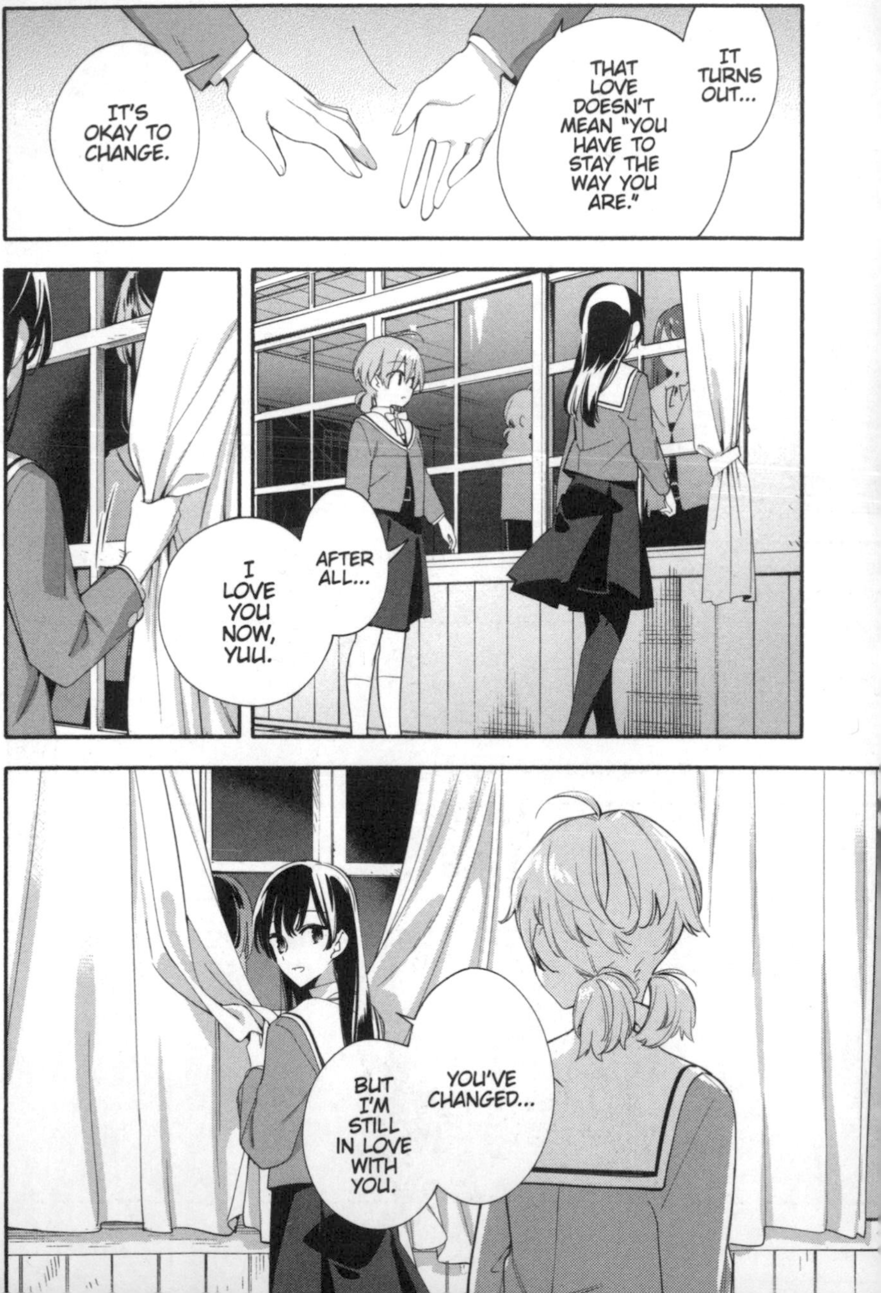
IT TURNS OUT...
THAT LOVE DOESN'T MEAN "YOU HAVE TO STAY THE WAY YOU ARE."
IT'S OKAY TO CHANGE.
AFTER ALL...
I LOVE YOU NOW, YUU.
YOU'VE CHANGED...
BUT I'M STILL IN LOVE WITH YOU.

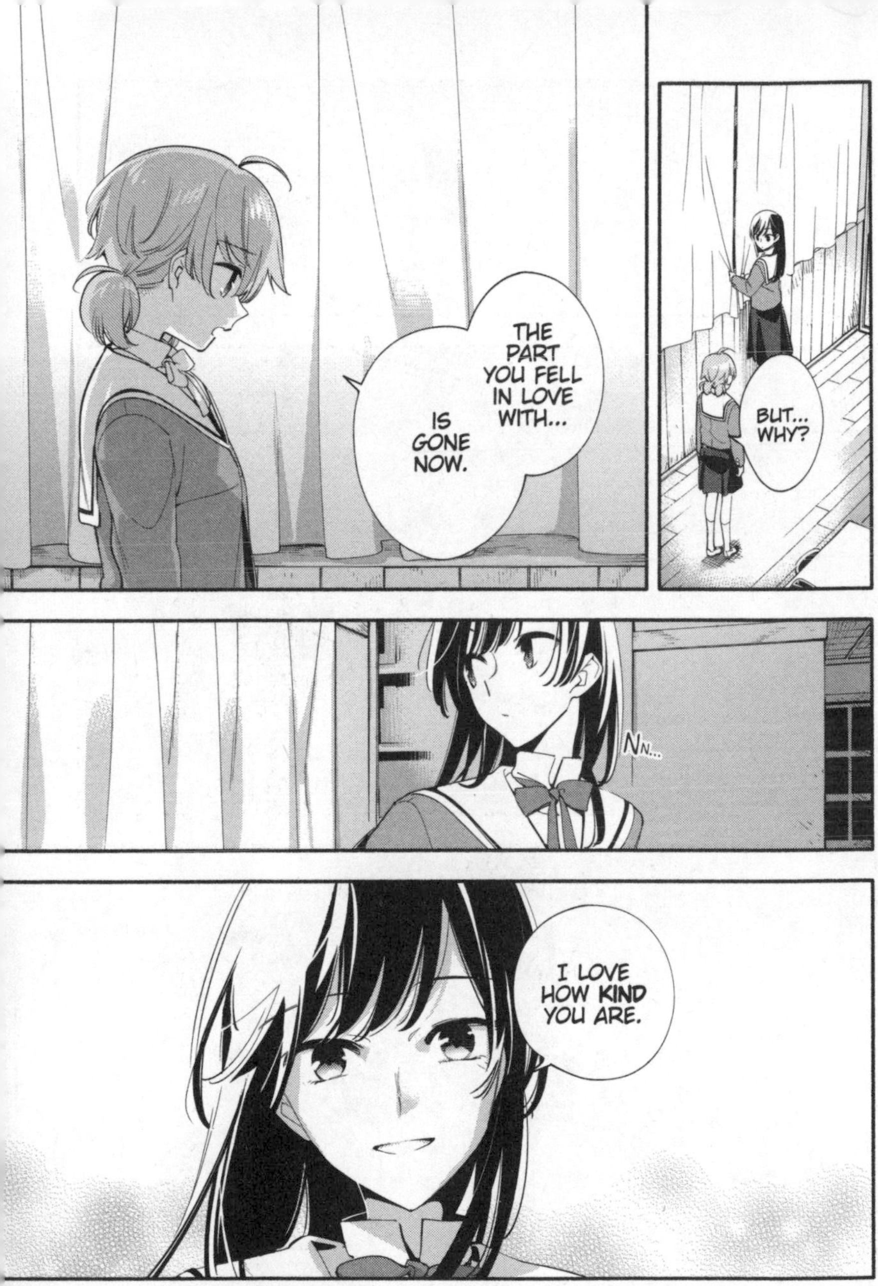
BUT... WHY?
THE PART YOU FELL IN LOVE WITH...
IS GONE NOW.
Nn...
I LOVE HOW KIND YOU ARE.

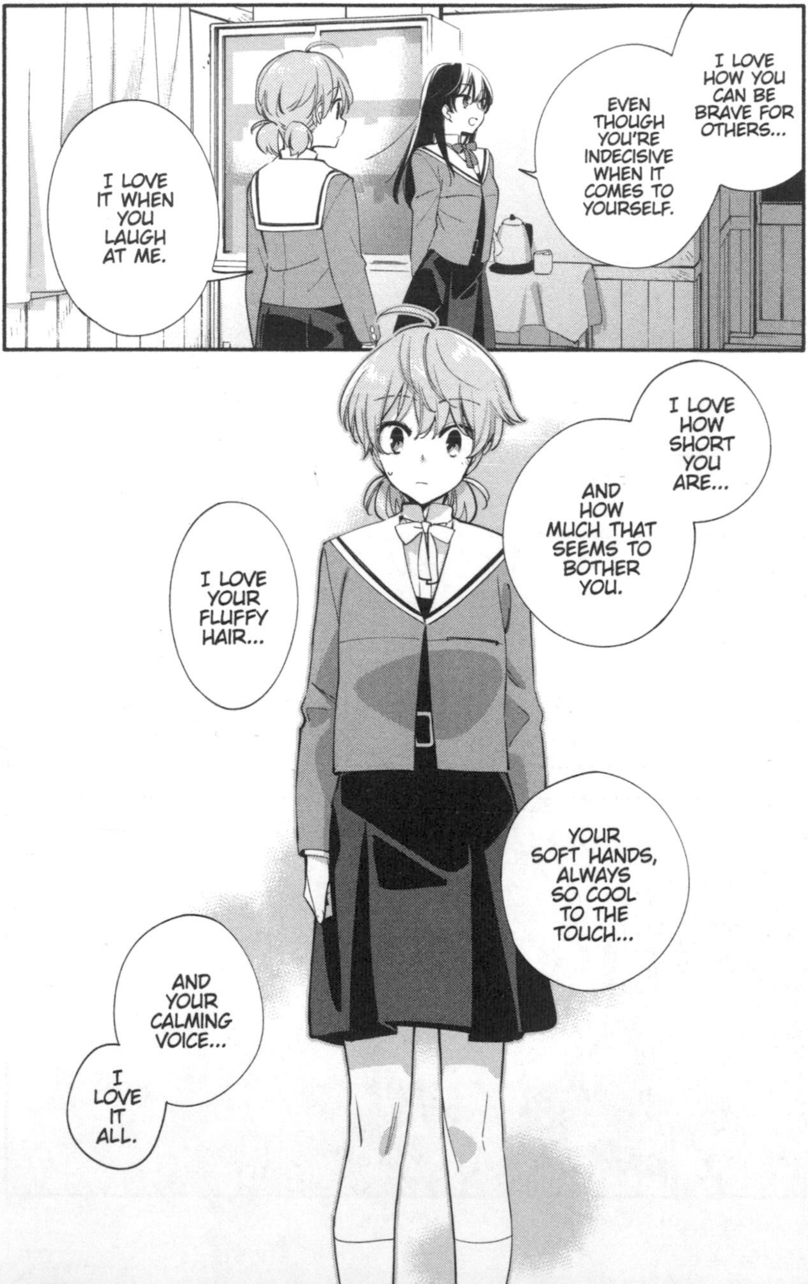
I LOVE HOW YOU CAN BE BRAVE FOR OTHERS...
EVEN THOUGH YOU'RE INDECISIVE WHEN IT COMES TO YOURSELF.
I LOVE IT WHEN YOU LAUGH AT ME.
I LOVE HOW SHORT YOU ARE...
AND HOW MUCH THAT SEEMS TO BOTHER YOU.
I LOVE YOUR FLUFFY HAIR...
YOUR SOFT HANDS, ALWAYS SO COOL TO THE TOUCH...
AND YOUR CALMING VOICE...
I LOVE IT ALL.

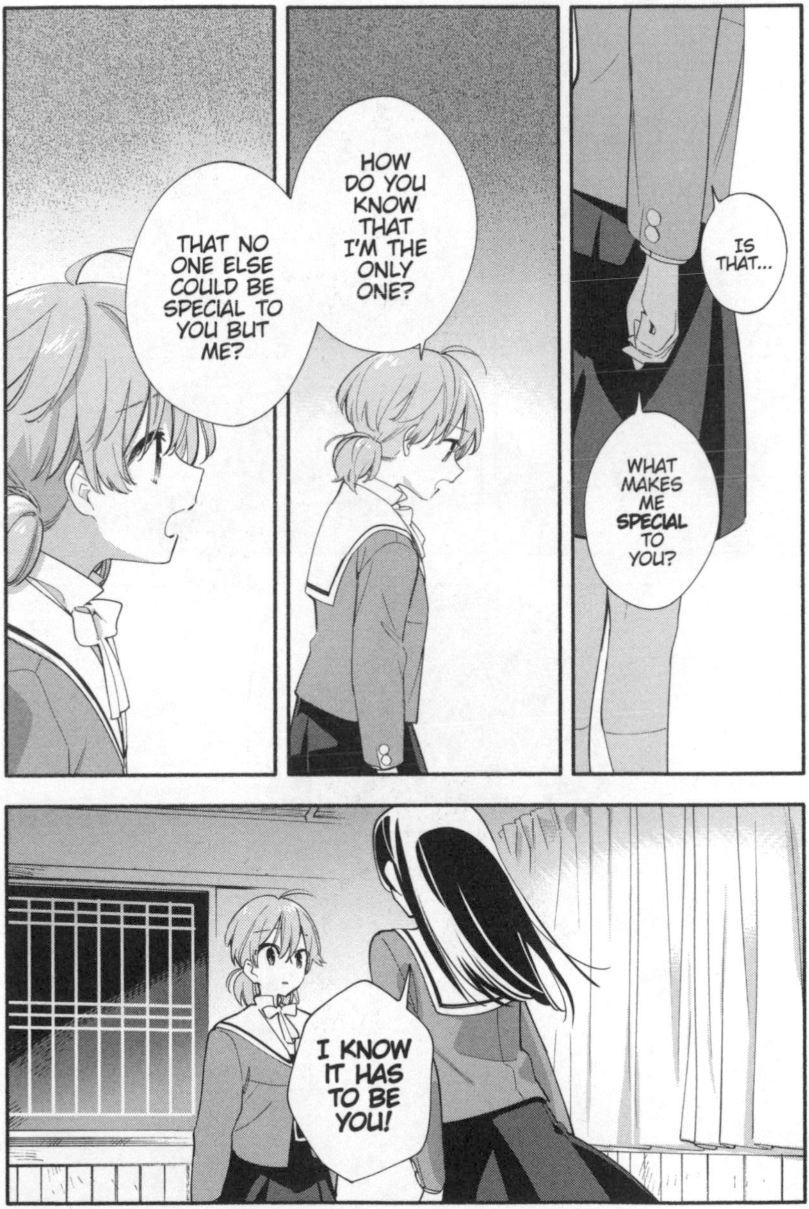
IS THAT...
WHAT MAKES ME SPECIAL TO YOU?
HOW DO YOU KNOW THAT I'M THE ONLY ONE?
THAT NO ONE ELSE COULD BE SPECIAL TO YOU BUT ME?
I KNOW IT HAS TO BE YOU!

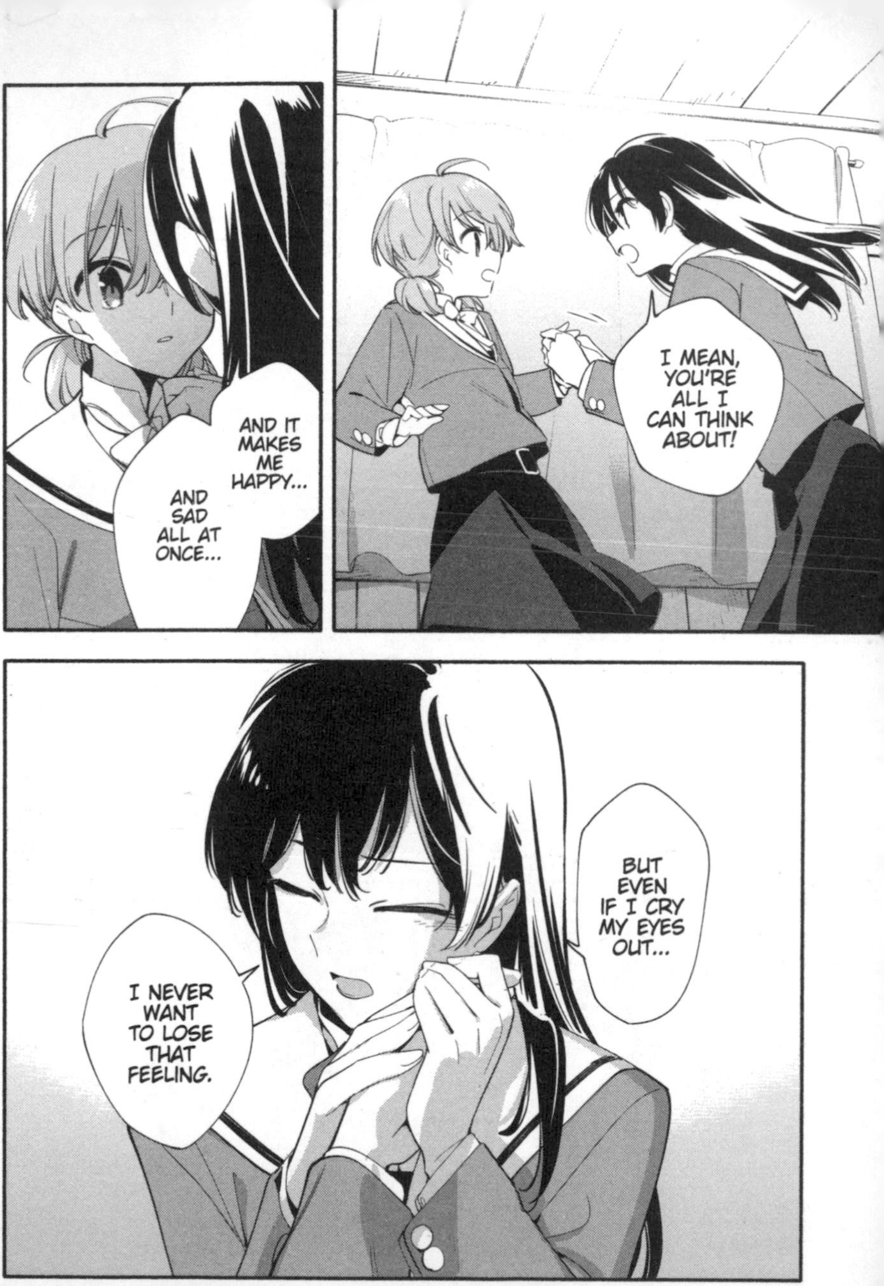
I MEAN, YOU'RE ALL I CAN THINK ABOUT!
AND IT MAKES ME HAPPY...
AND SAD ALL AT ONCE...
BUT EVEN IF I CRY MY EYES OUT...
I NEVER WANT TO LOSE THAT FEELING.

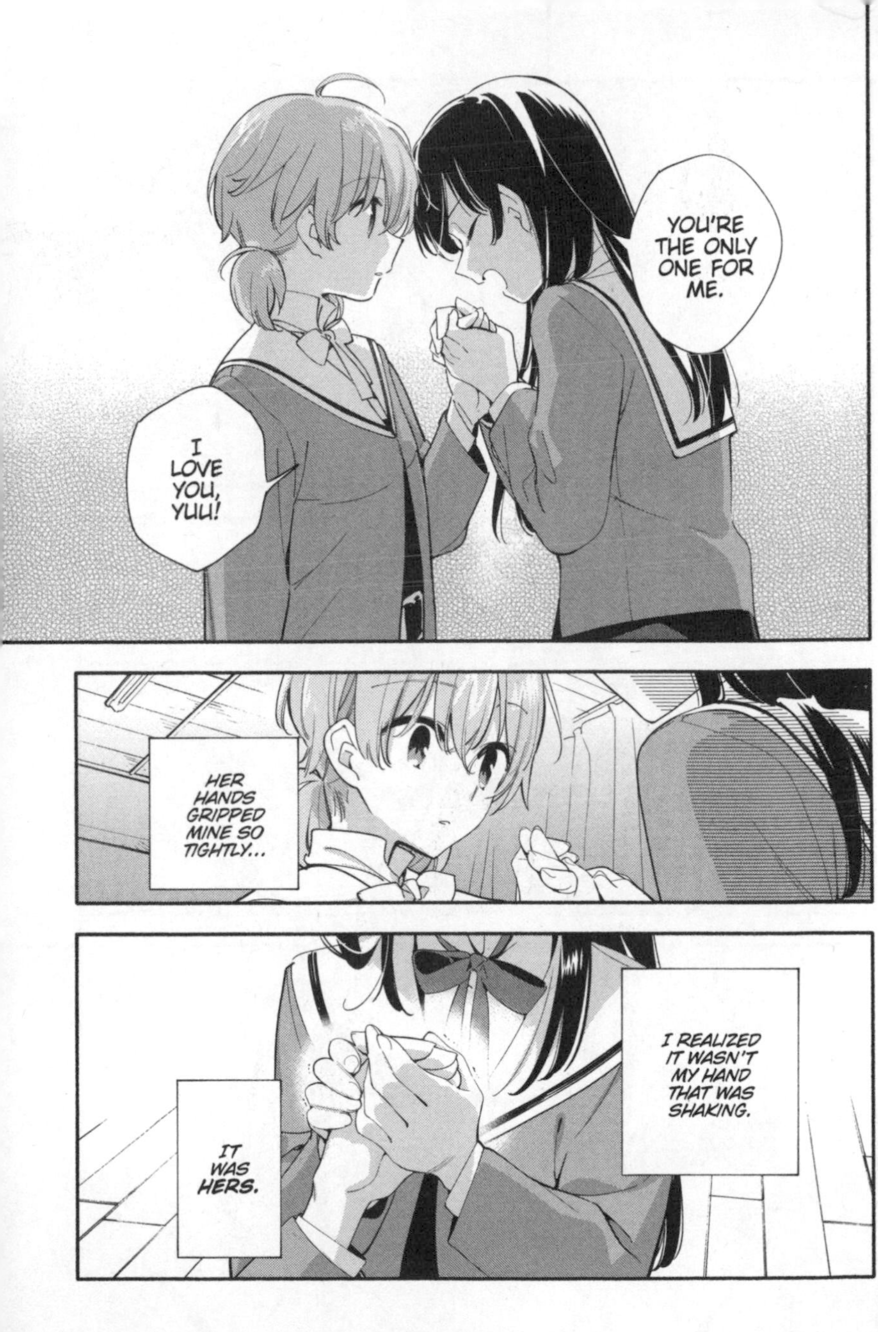
YOU'RE THE ONLY ONE FOR ME.
I LOVE YOU, YUU!
HER HANDS GRIPPED MINE SO TIGHTLY...
I REALIZED IT WASN'T MY HAND THAT WAS SHAKING.
IT WAS HERS.

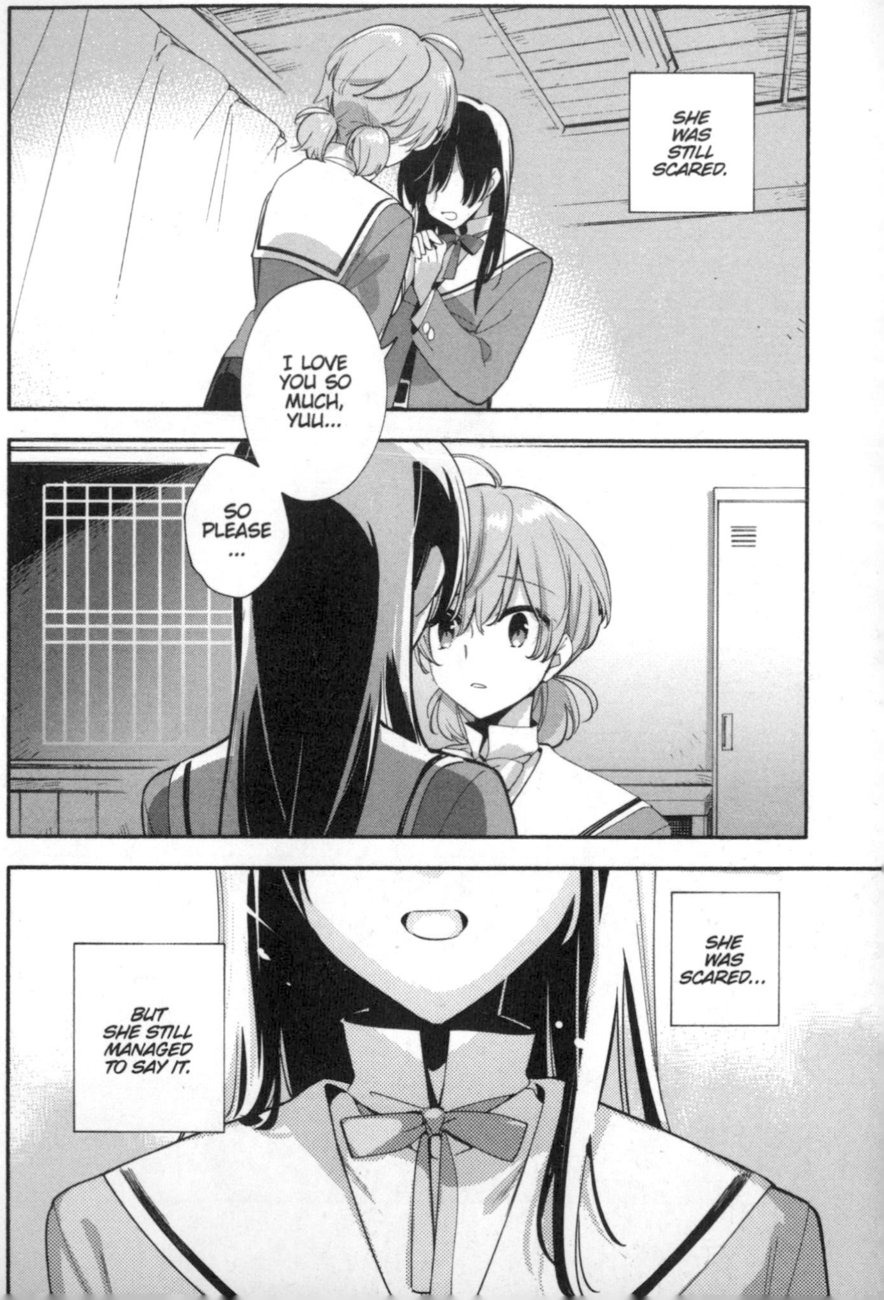
SHE WAS STILL SCARED.
I LOVE YOU SO MUCH, YUU...
SO PLEASE ...
SHE WAS SCARED...
BUT SHE STILL MANAGED TO SAY IT.

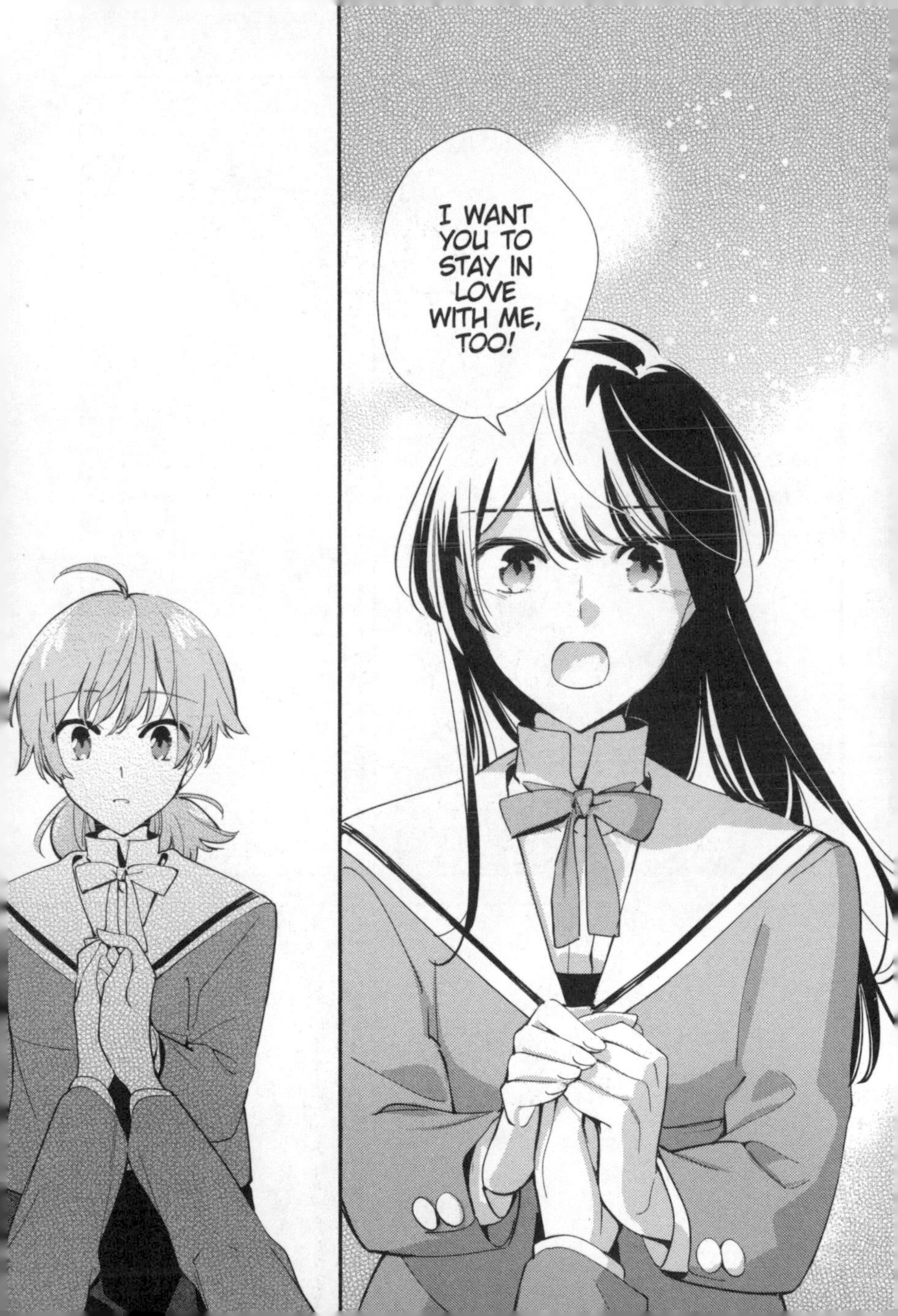
I WANT YOU TO STAY IN LOVE WITH ME, TOO!

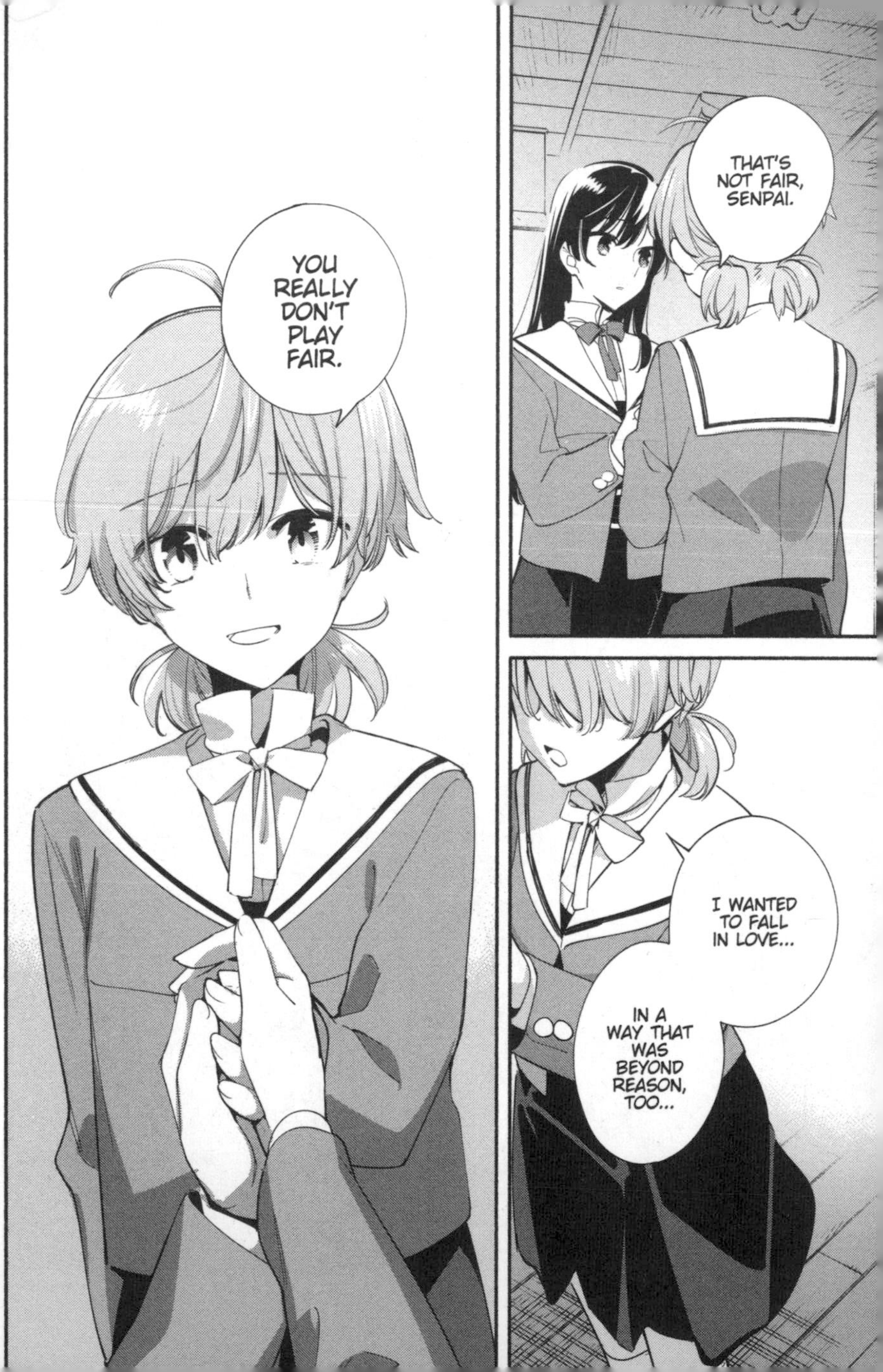
THAT'S NOT FAIR, SENPAI.
I WANTED TO FALL IN LOVE...
IN A WAY THAT WAS BEYOND REASON, TOO...
YOU REALLY DON'T PLAY FAIR.

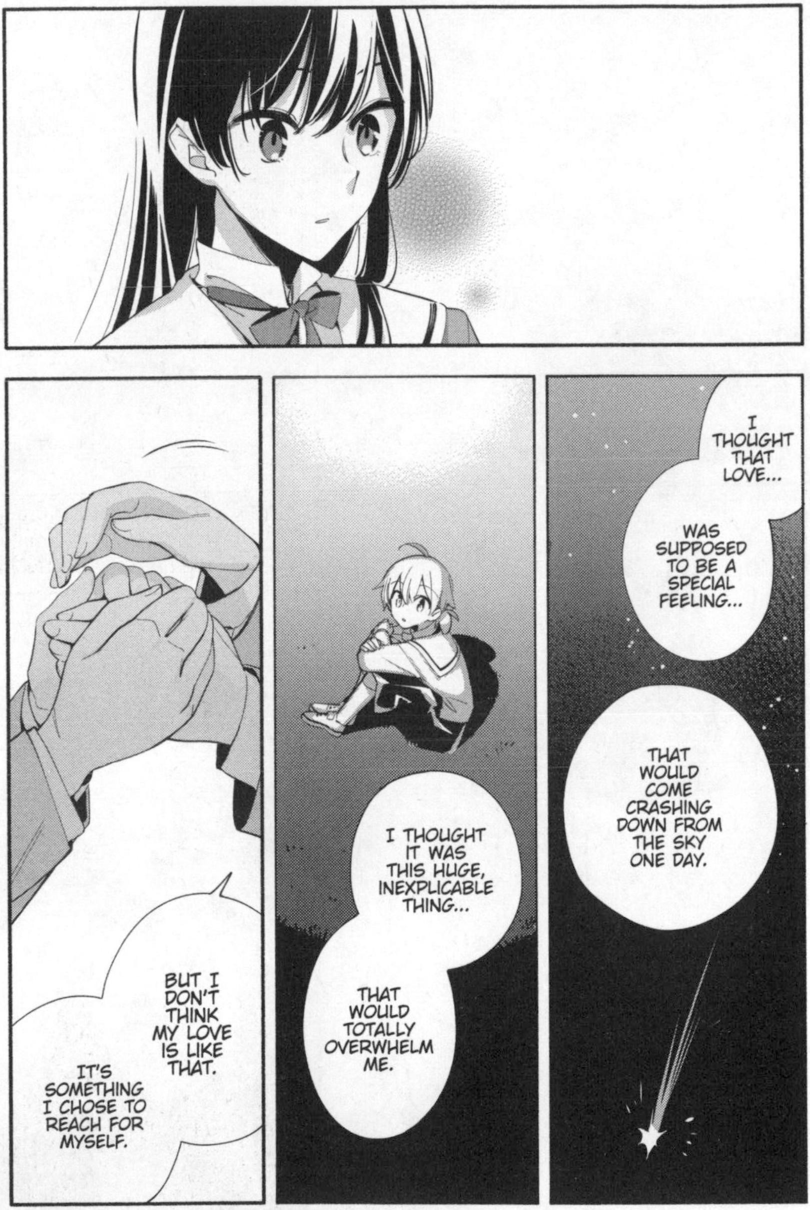
I THOUGHT THAT LOVE...
WAS SUPPOSED TO BE A SPECIAL FEELING...
THAT WOULD COME CRASHING DOWN FROM THE SKY ONE DAY.
I THOUGHT IT WAS THIS HUGE, INEXPLICABLE THING...
THAT WOULD TOTALLY OVERWHELM ME.
BUT I DON'T THINK MY LOVE IS LIKE THAT.
IT'S SOMETHING I CHOSE TO REACH FOR MYSELF.

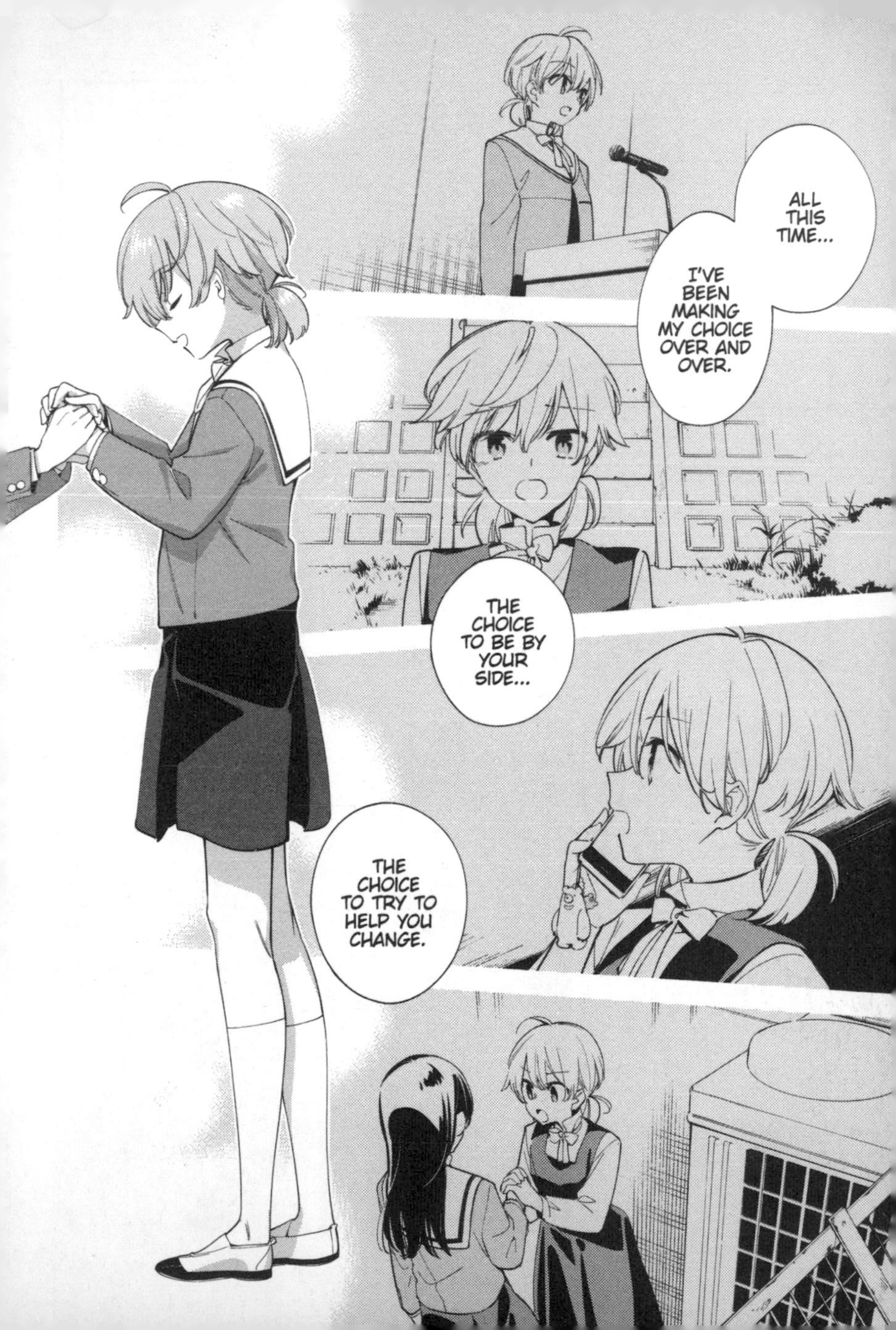
ALL THIS TIME...
I'VE BEEN MAKING MY CHOICE OVER AND OVER.
THE CHOICE TO BE BY YOUR SIDE...
THE CHOICE TO TRY TO HELP YOU CHANGE.

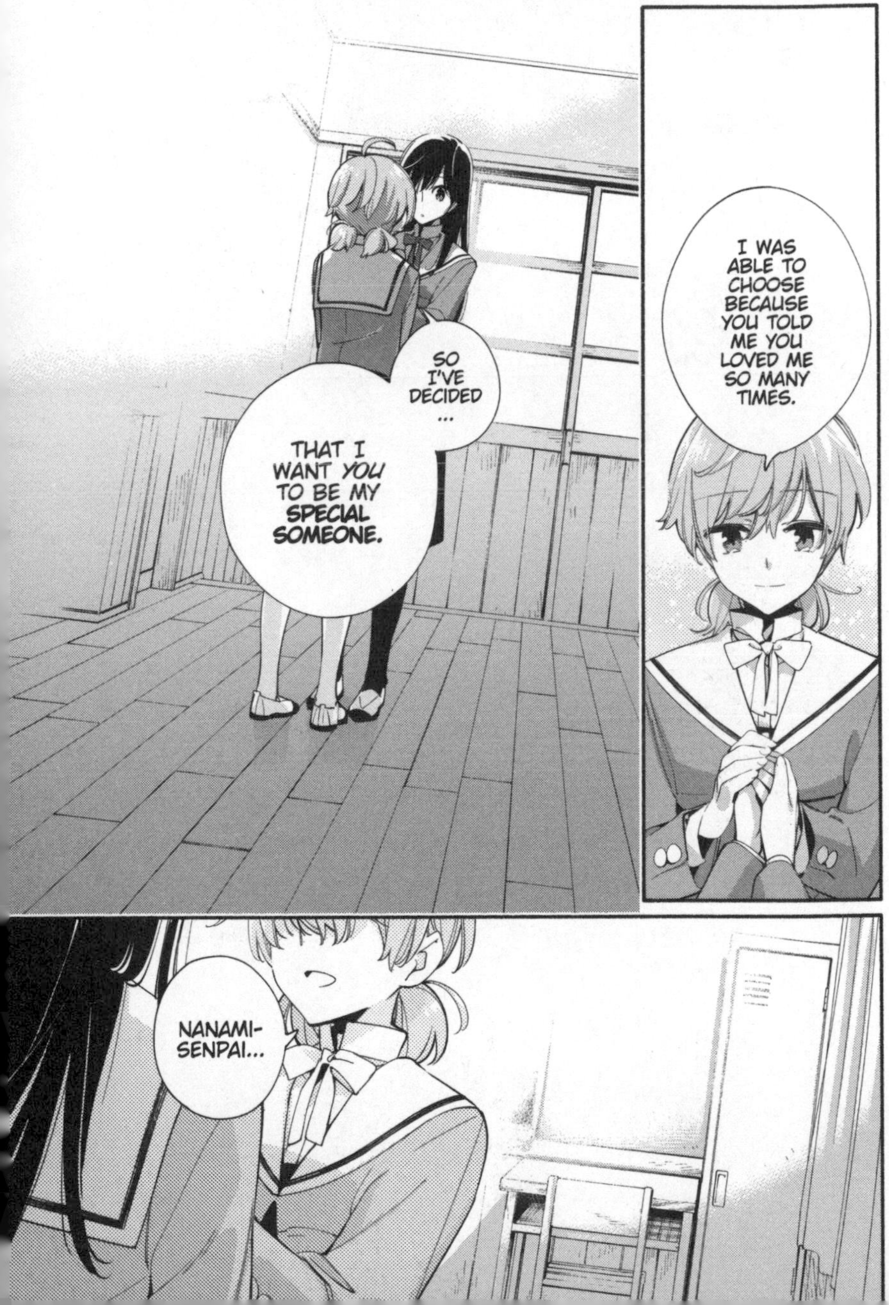
I WAS ABLE TO CHOOSE BECAUSE YOU TOLD ME YOU LOVED ME SO MANY TIMES.
SO I'VE DECIDED ...
THAT I WANT YOU TO BE MY SPECIAL SOMEONE.
NANAMI-SENPAI...

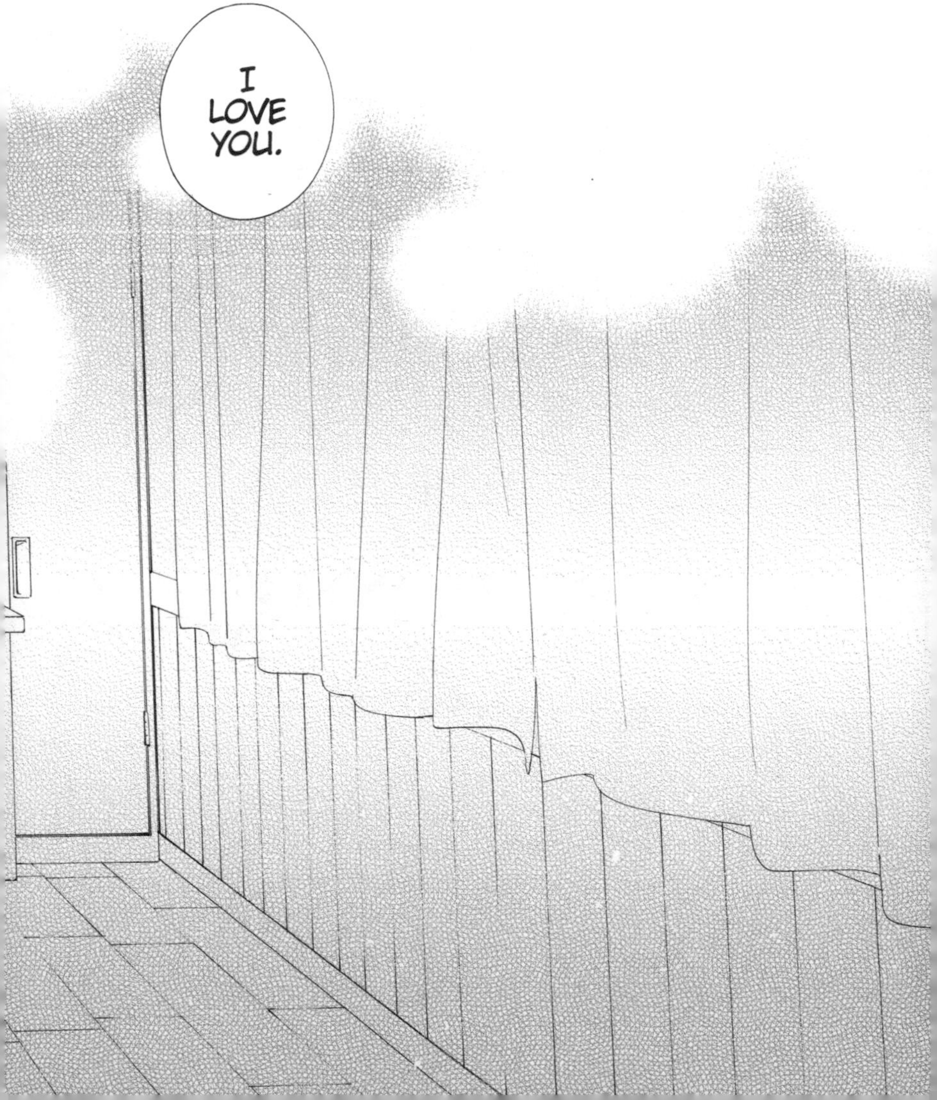
I LOVE YOU.

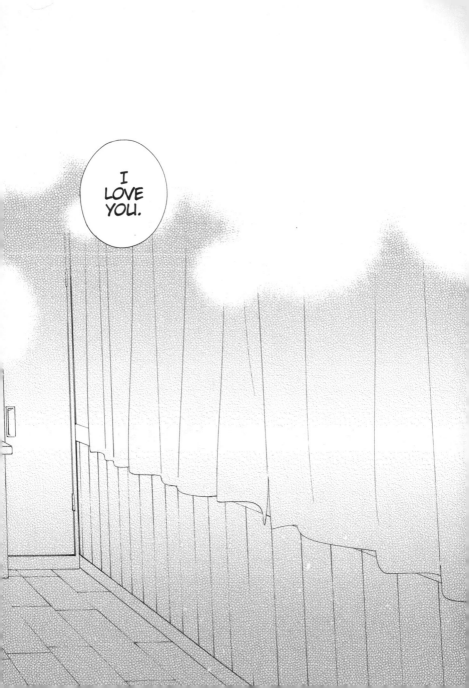

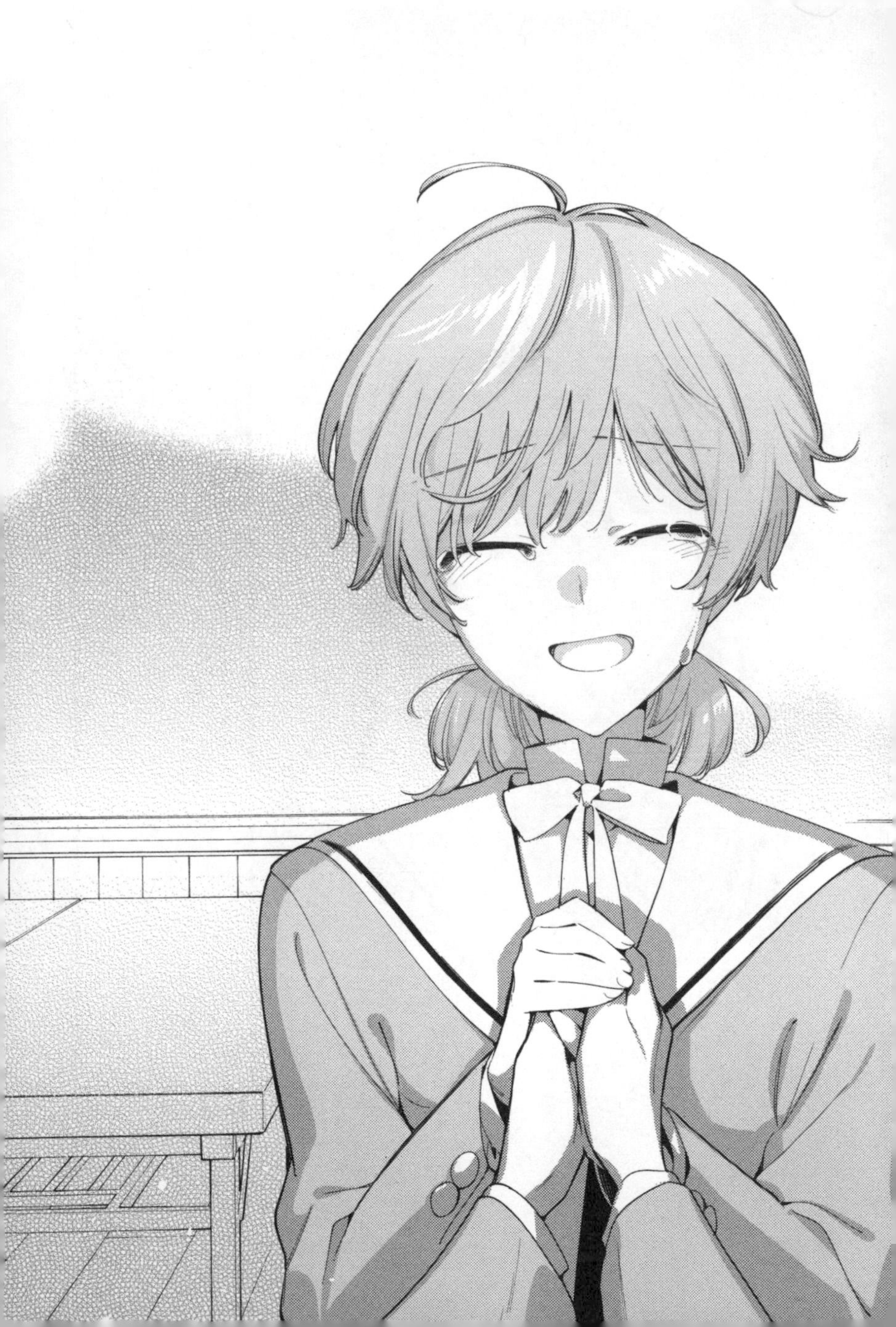

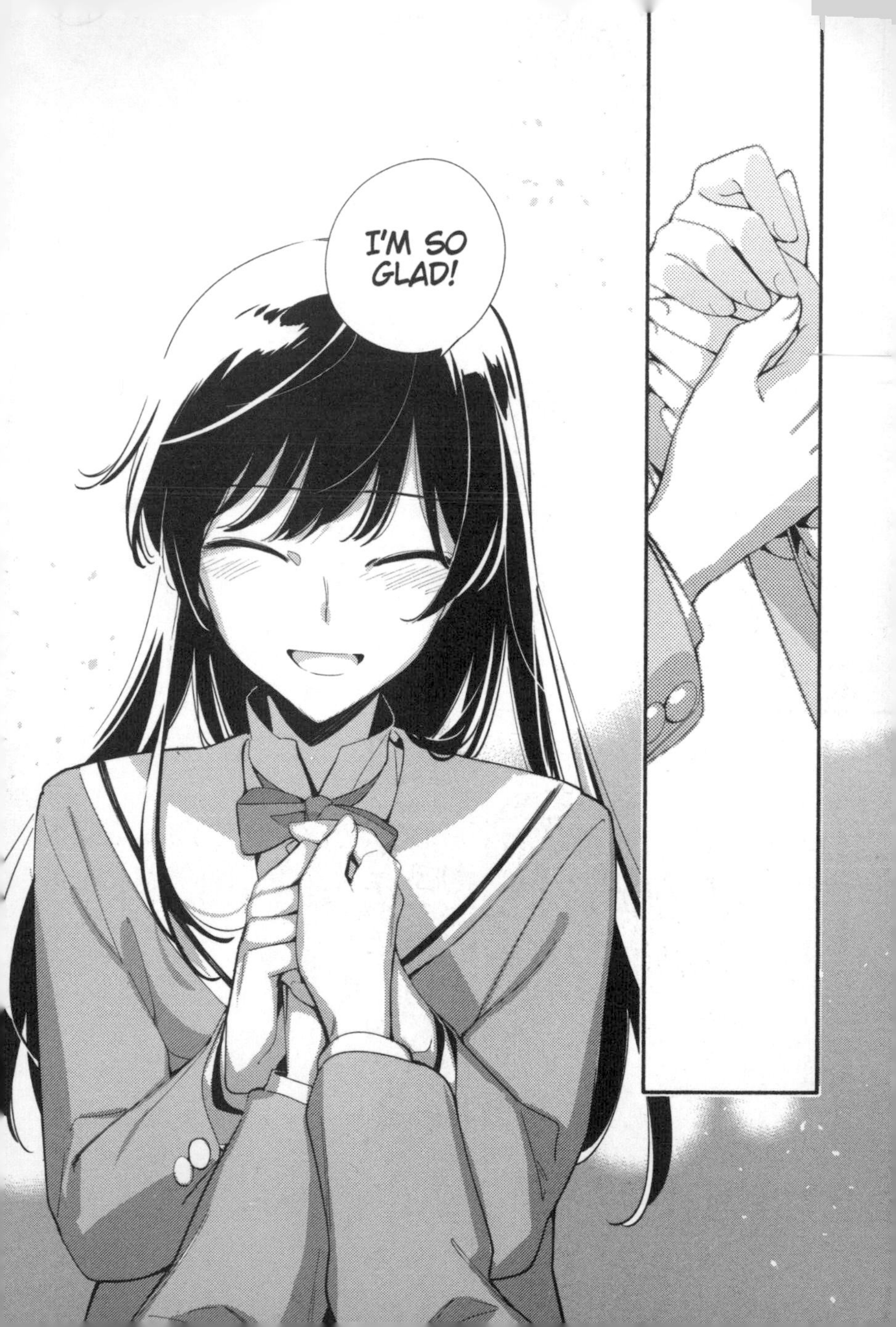
I'M SO GLAD!

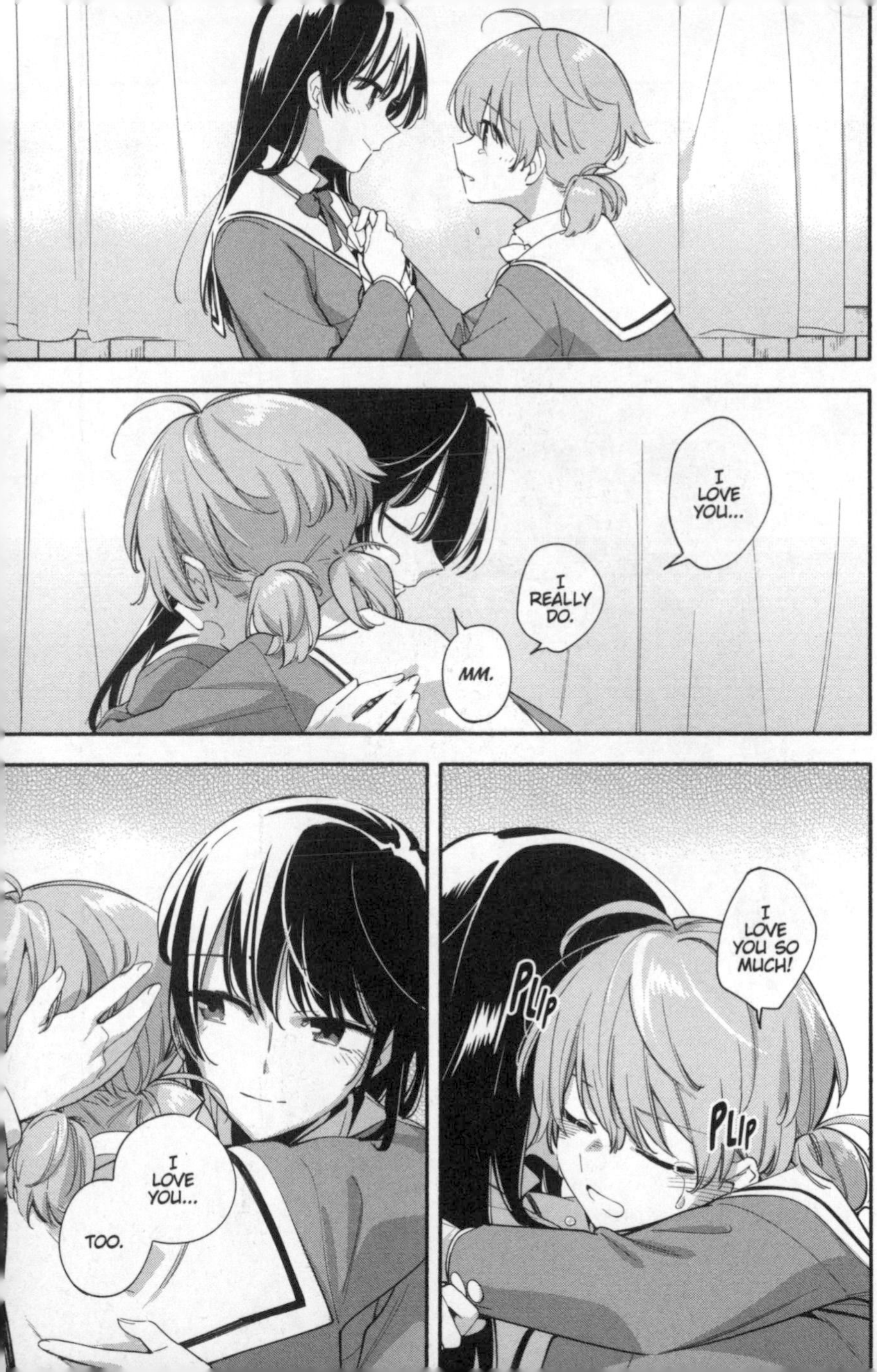
I LOVE YOU...
I REALLY DO.
MM.
I LOVE YOU SO MUCH!
PLIP
PLIP
I LOVE YOU...
TOO.

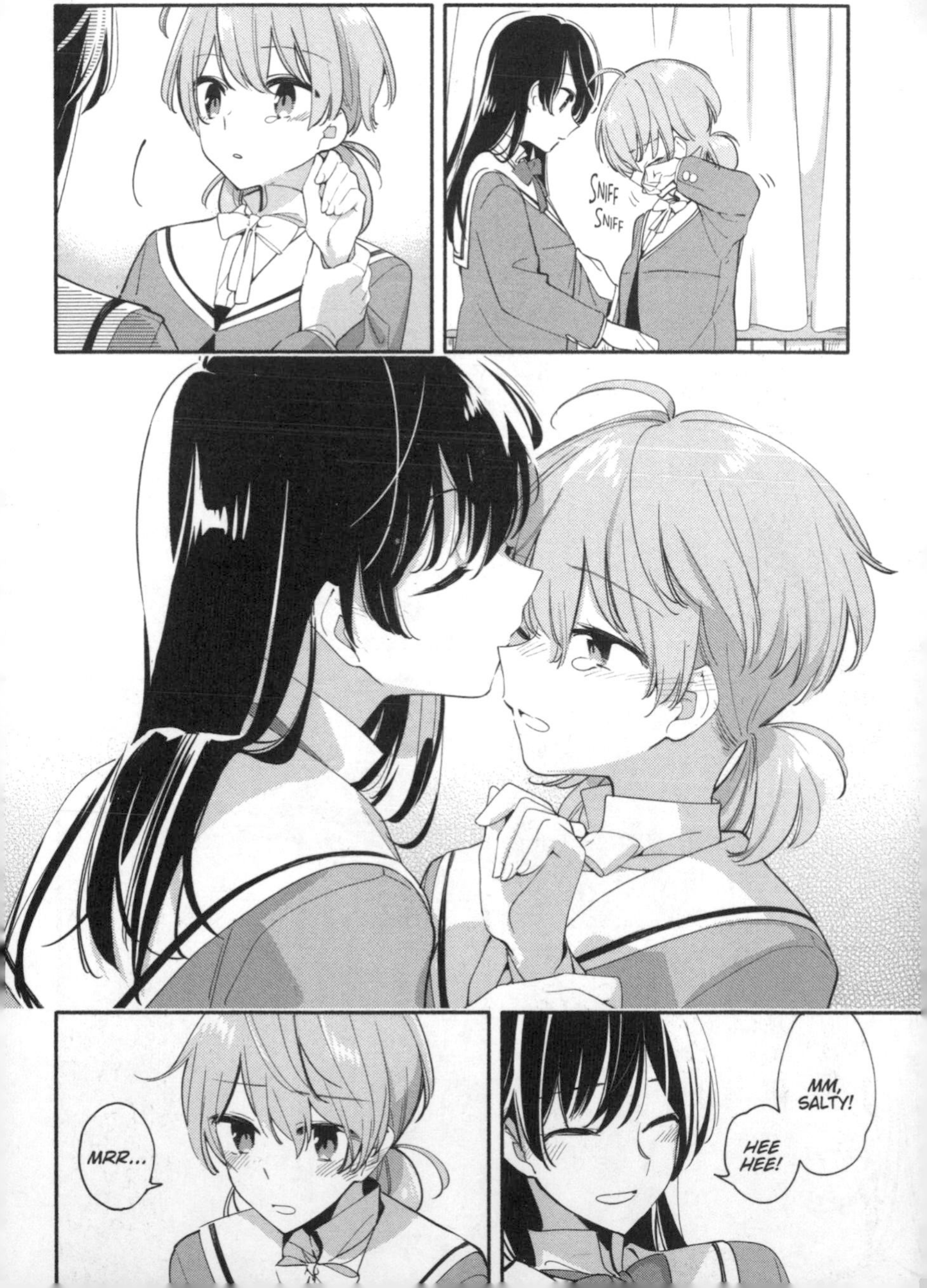
SNIFF
SNIFF
MM, SALTY!
HEE HEE!
MRR...

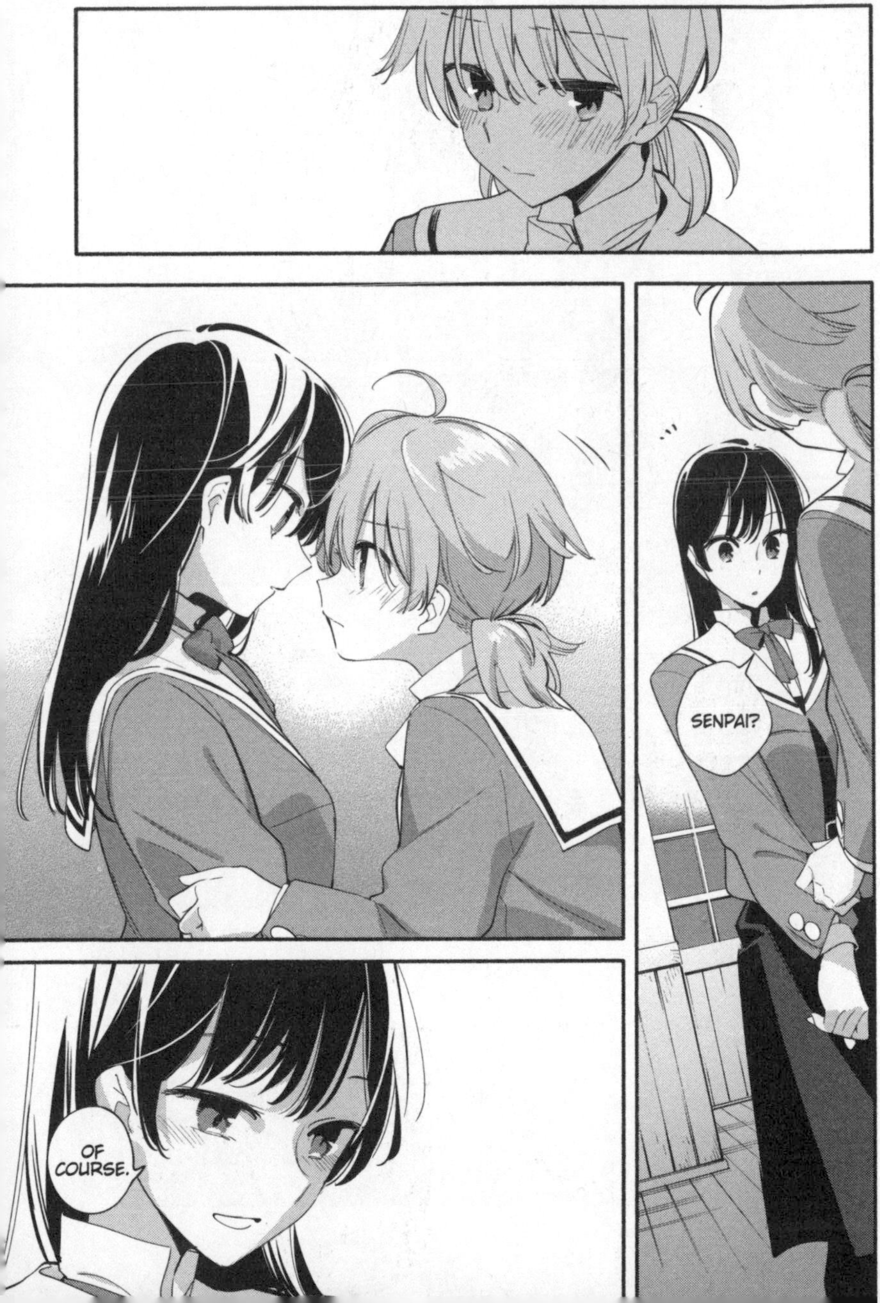
SENPAI?
OF COURSE.

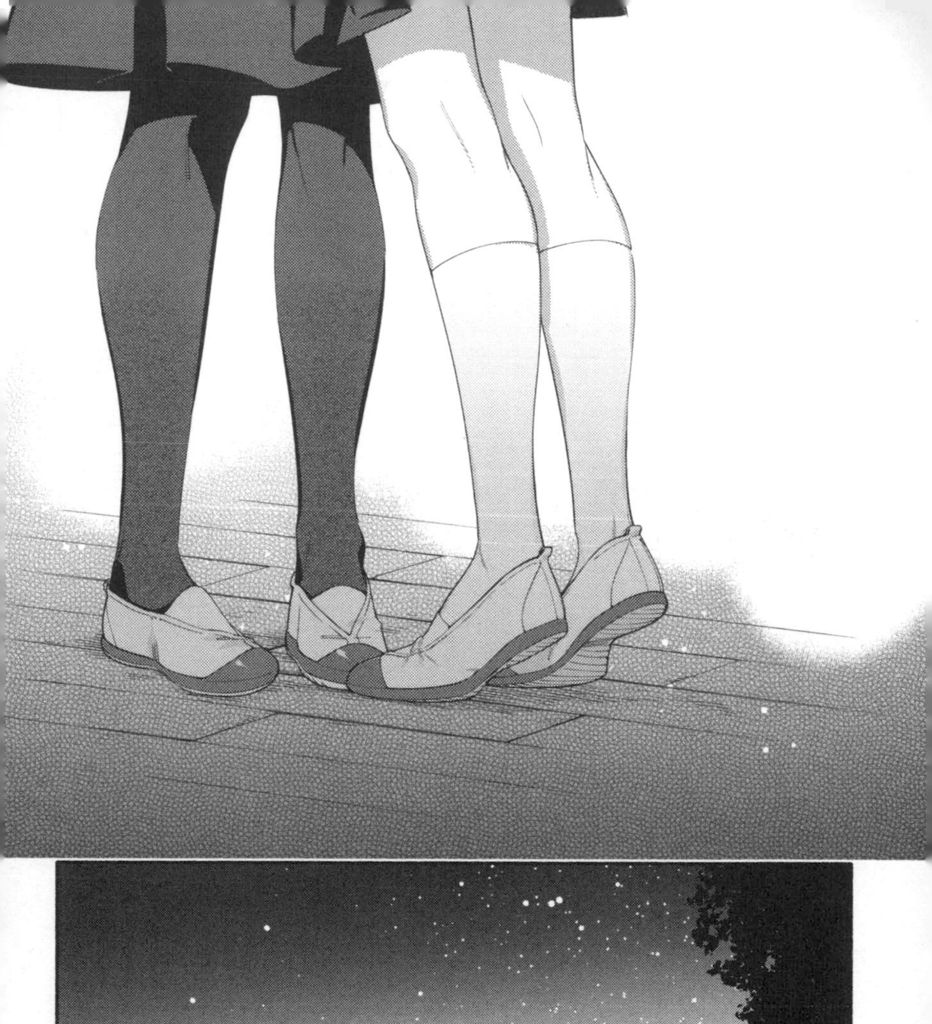
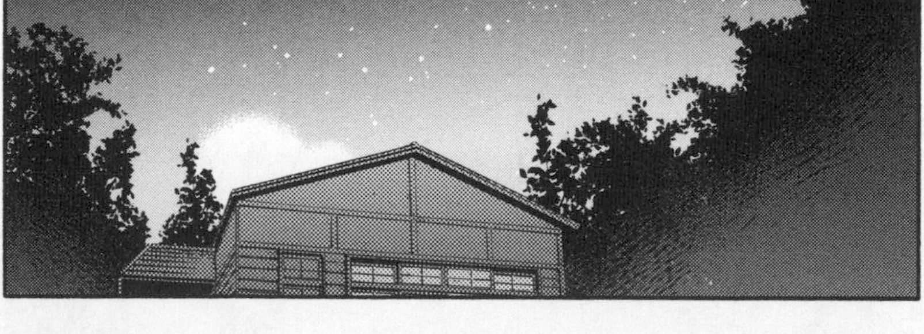

(Bloom Into You)

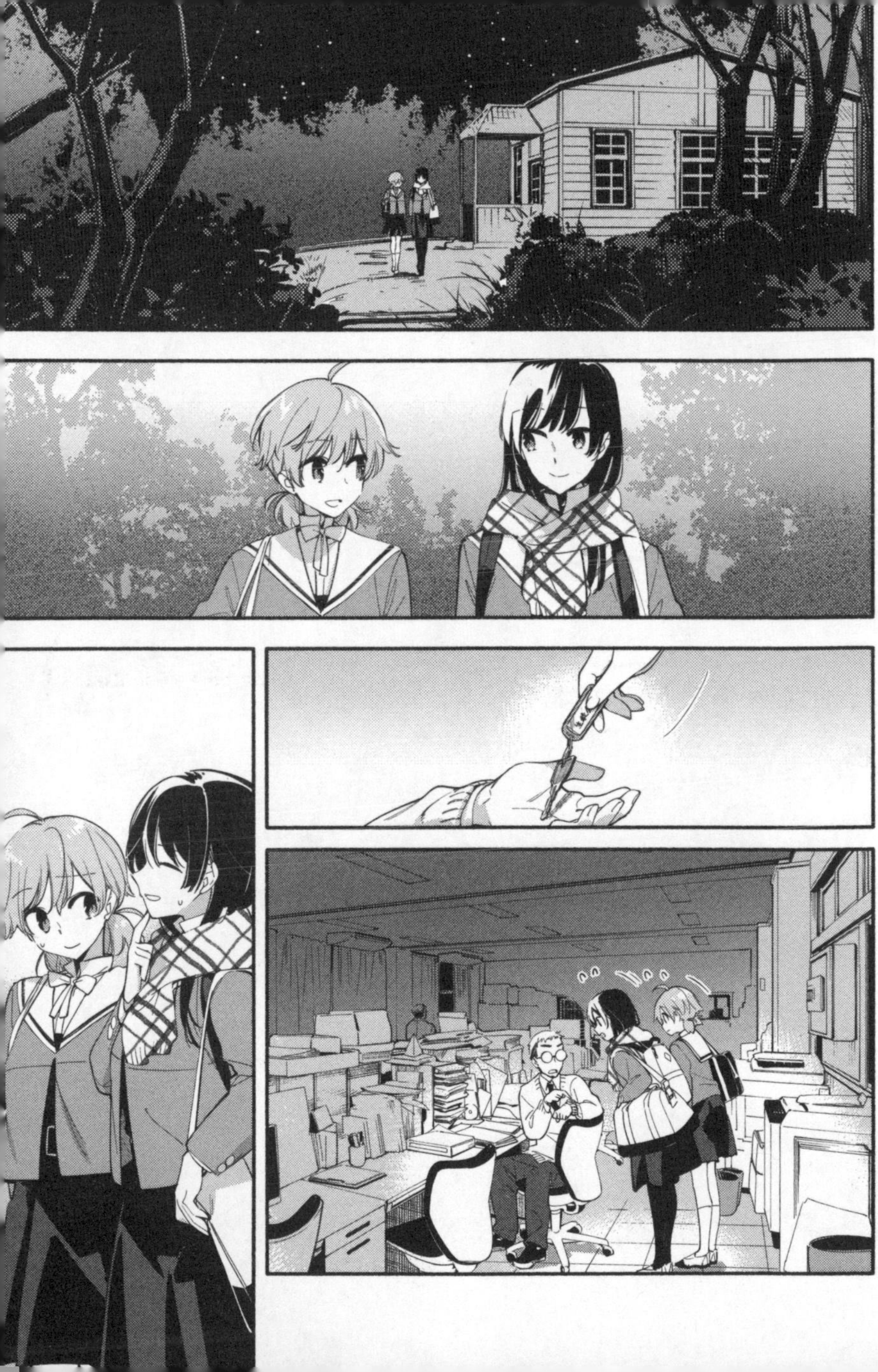

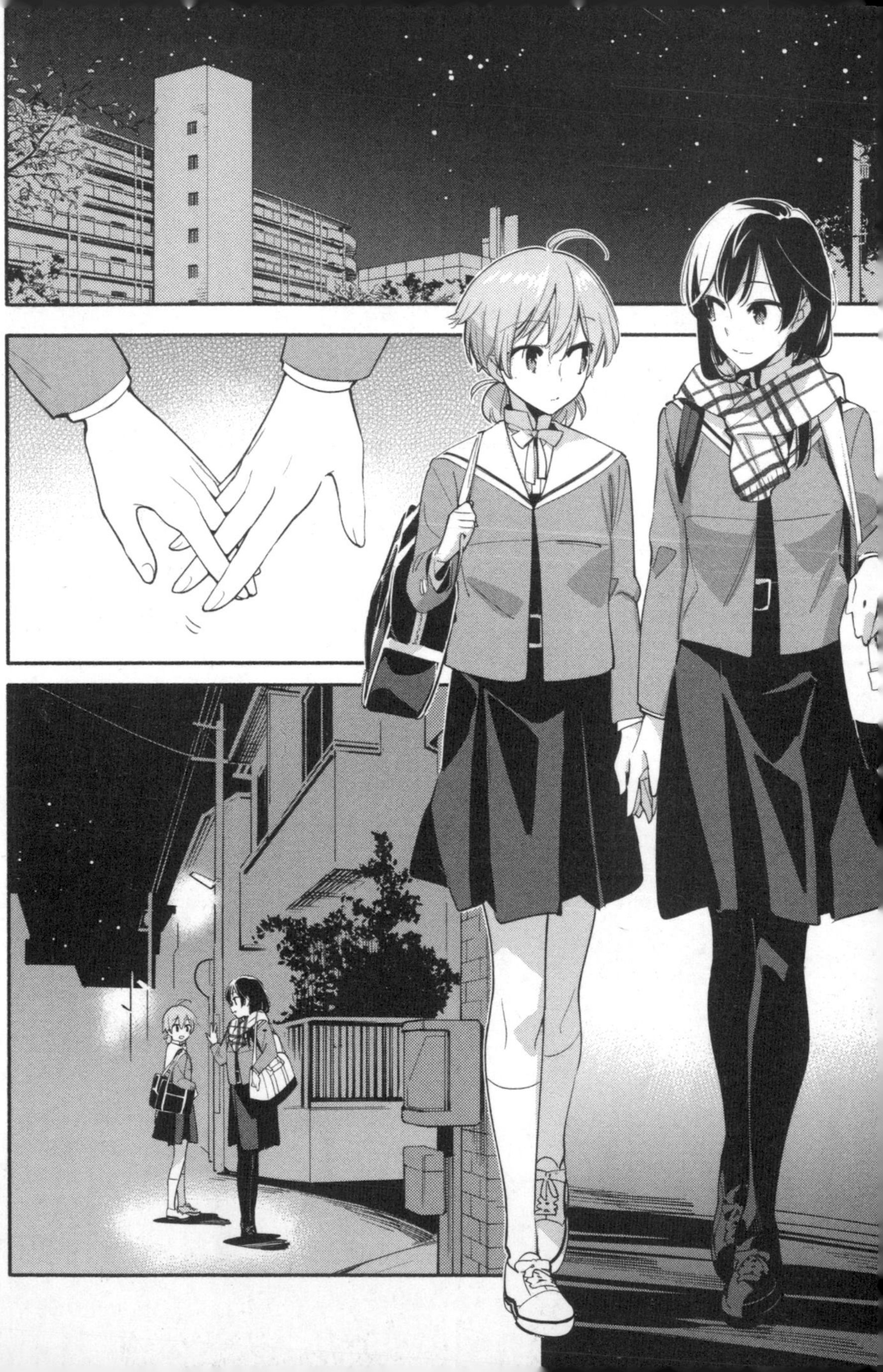

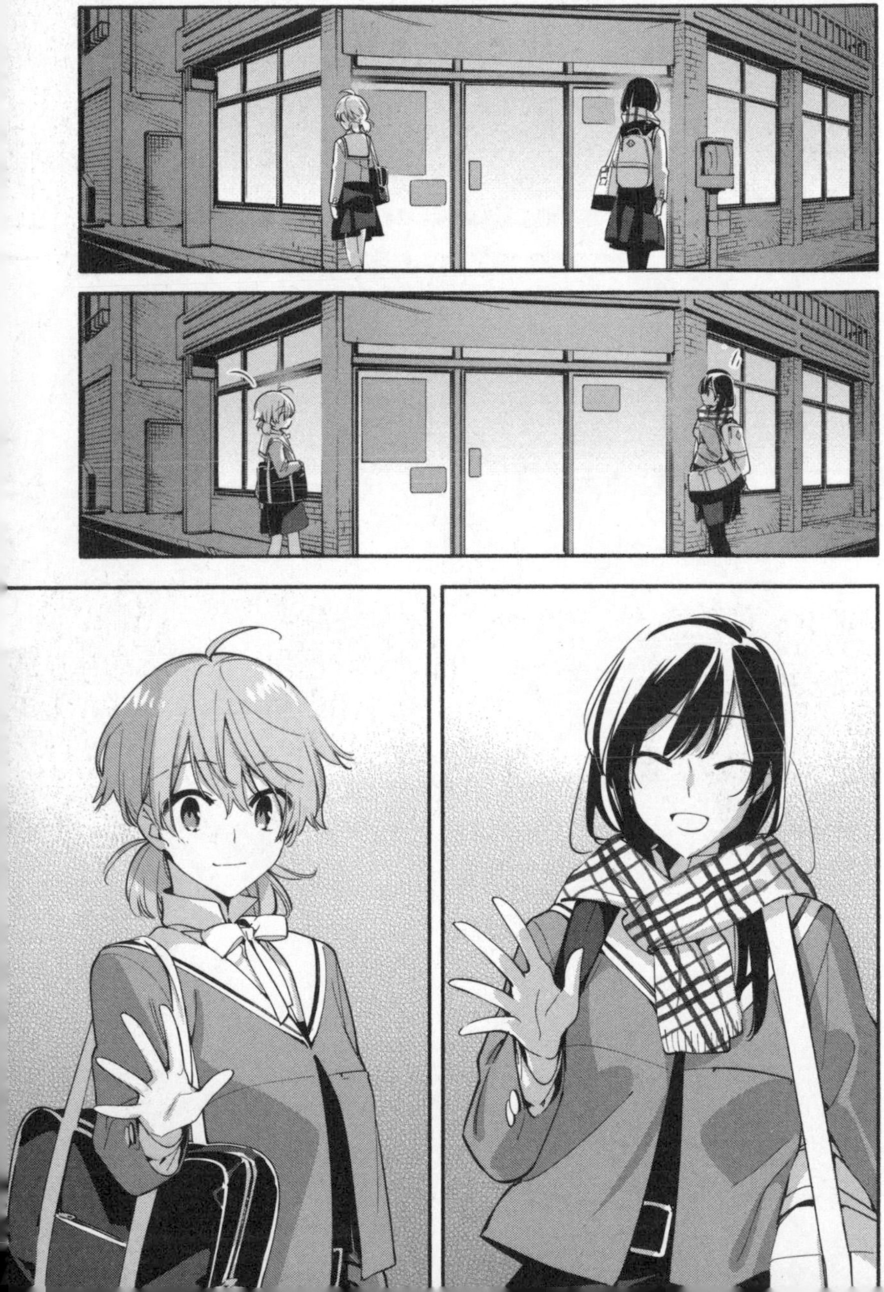

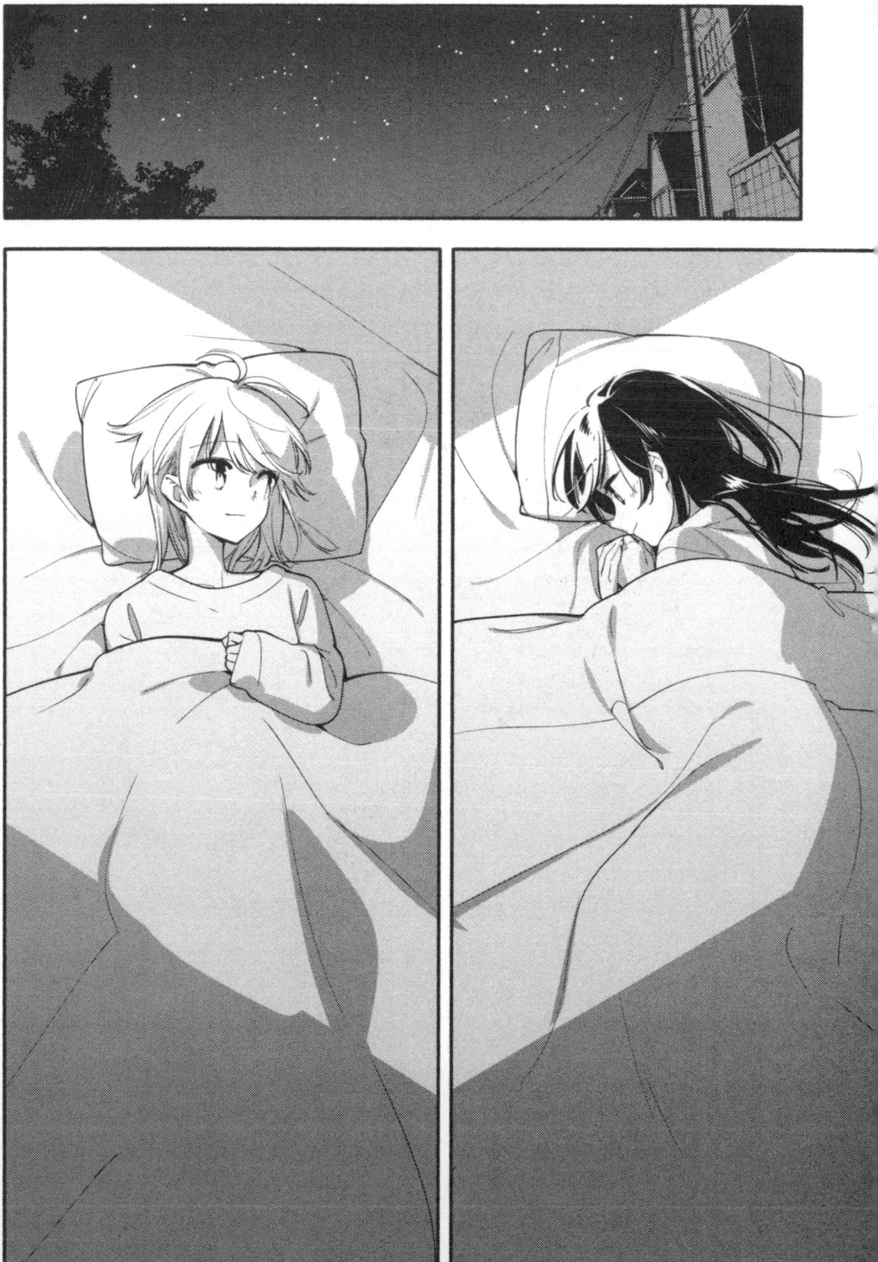

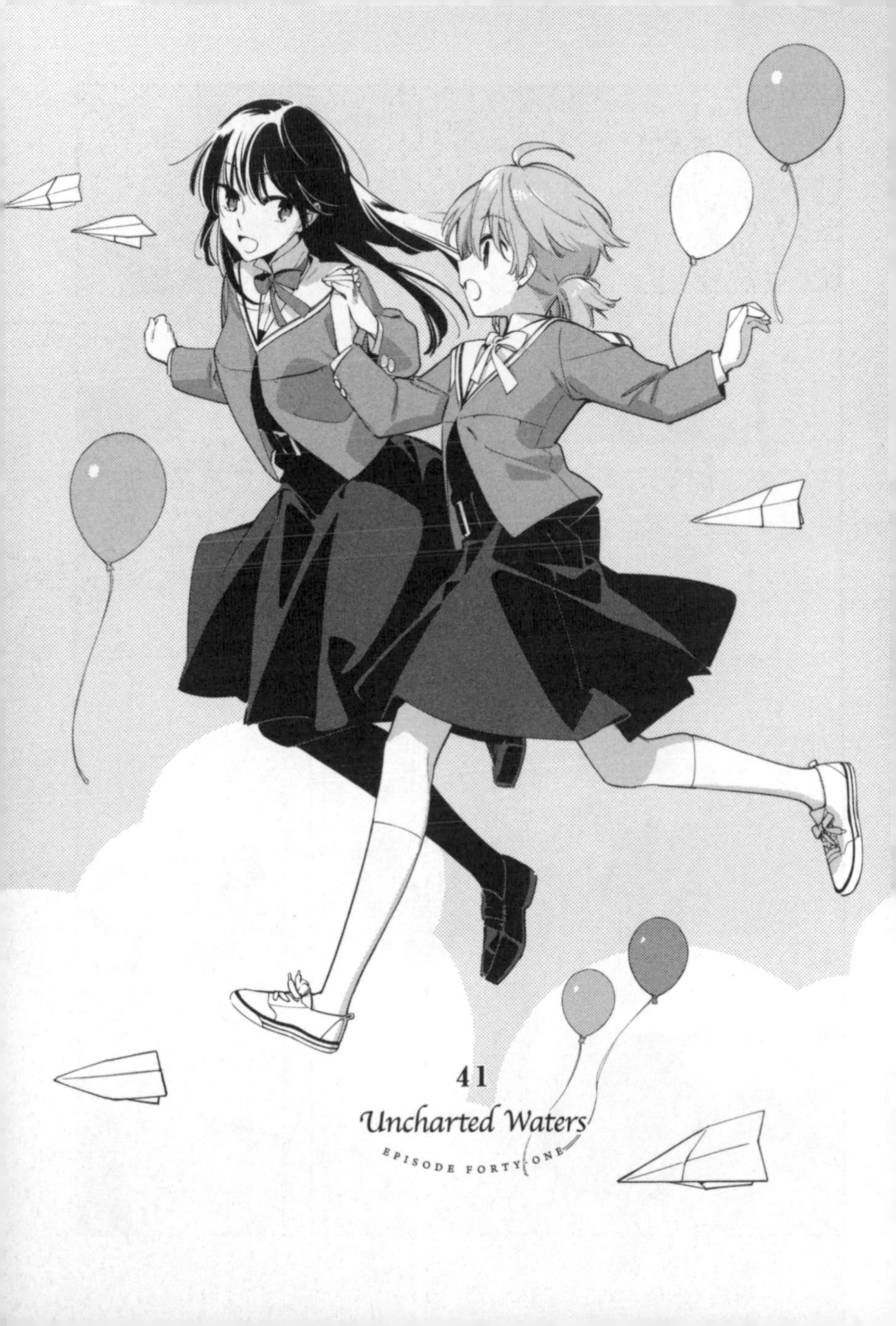

41

Uncharted Waters

EPISODE FORTY-ONE

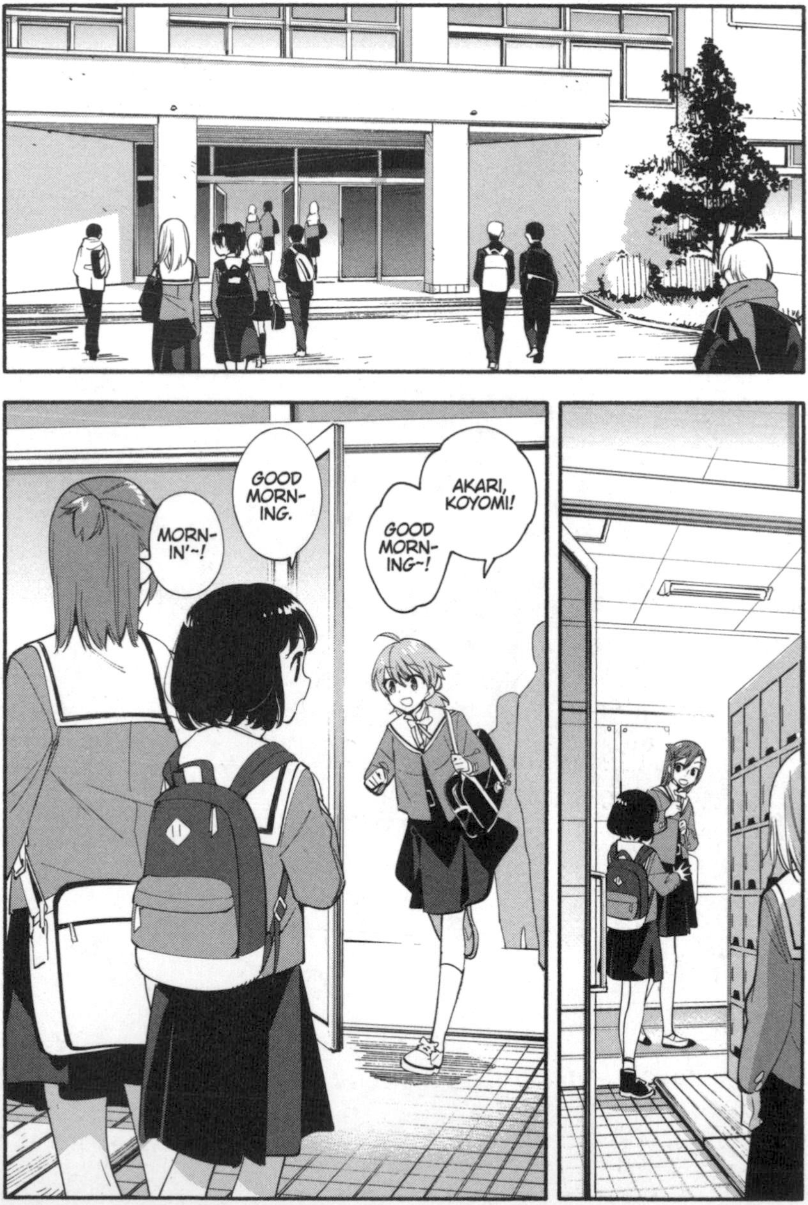
AKARI, KOYOMI!
GOOD MORN-ING~!
GOOD MORN-ING.
MORN-IN'~!

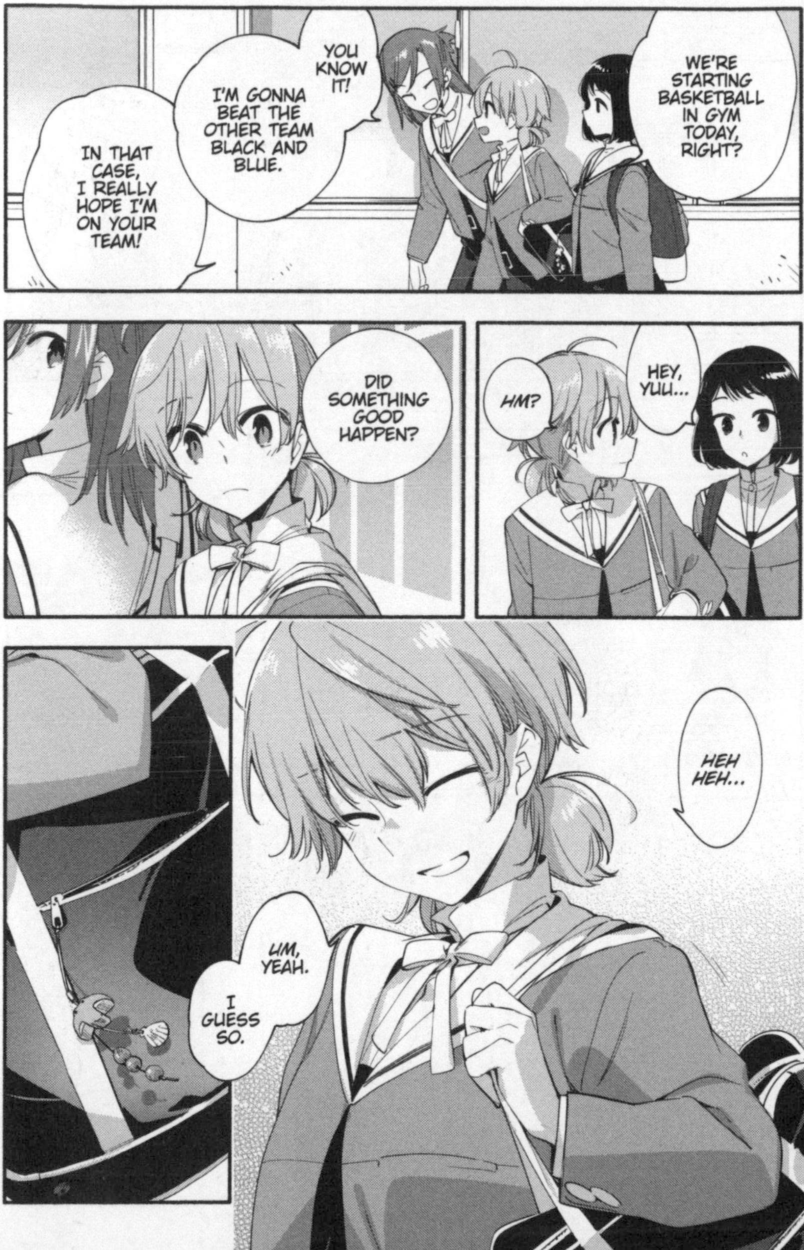
WE'RE STARTING BASKETBALL IN GYM TODAY, RIGHT?
YOU KNOW IT!
I'M GONNA BEAT THE OTHER TEAM BLACK AND BLUE.
IN THAT CASE, I REALLY HOPE I'M ON YOUR TEAM!
HEY, YUU...
HM?
DID SOMETHING GOOD HAPPEN?
HEH HEH...
UM, YEAH.
I GUESS SO.

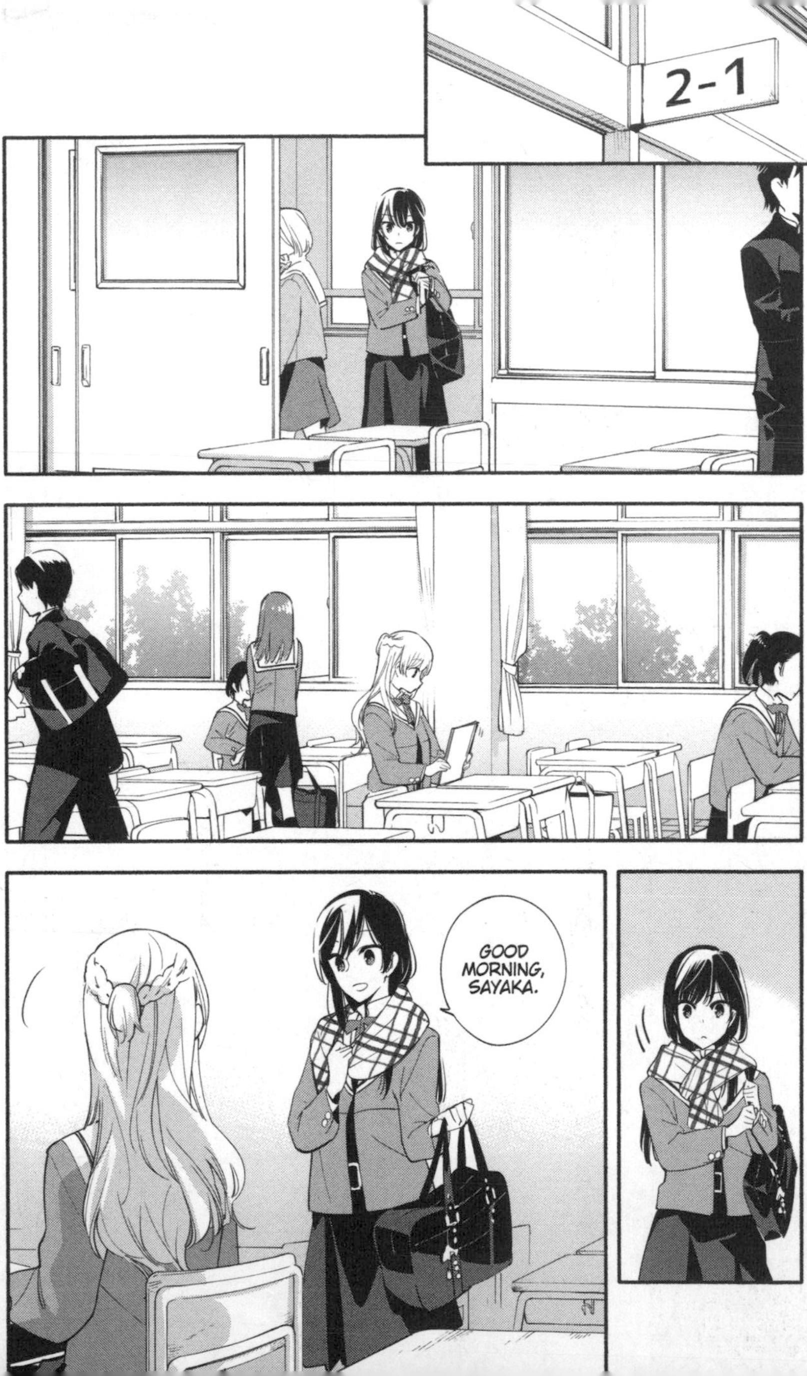
2-1
GOOD MORNING, SAYAKA.

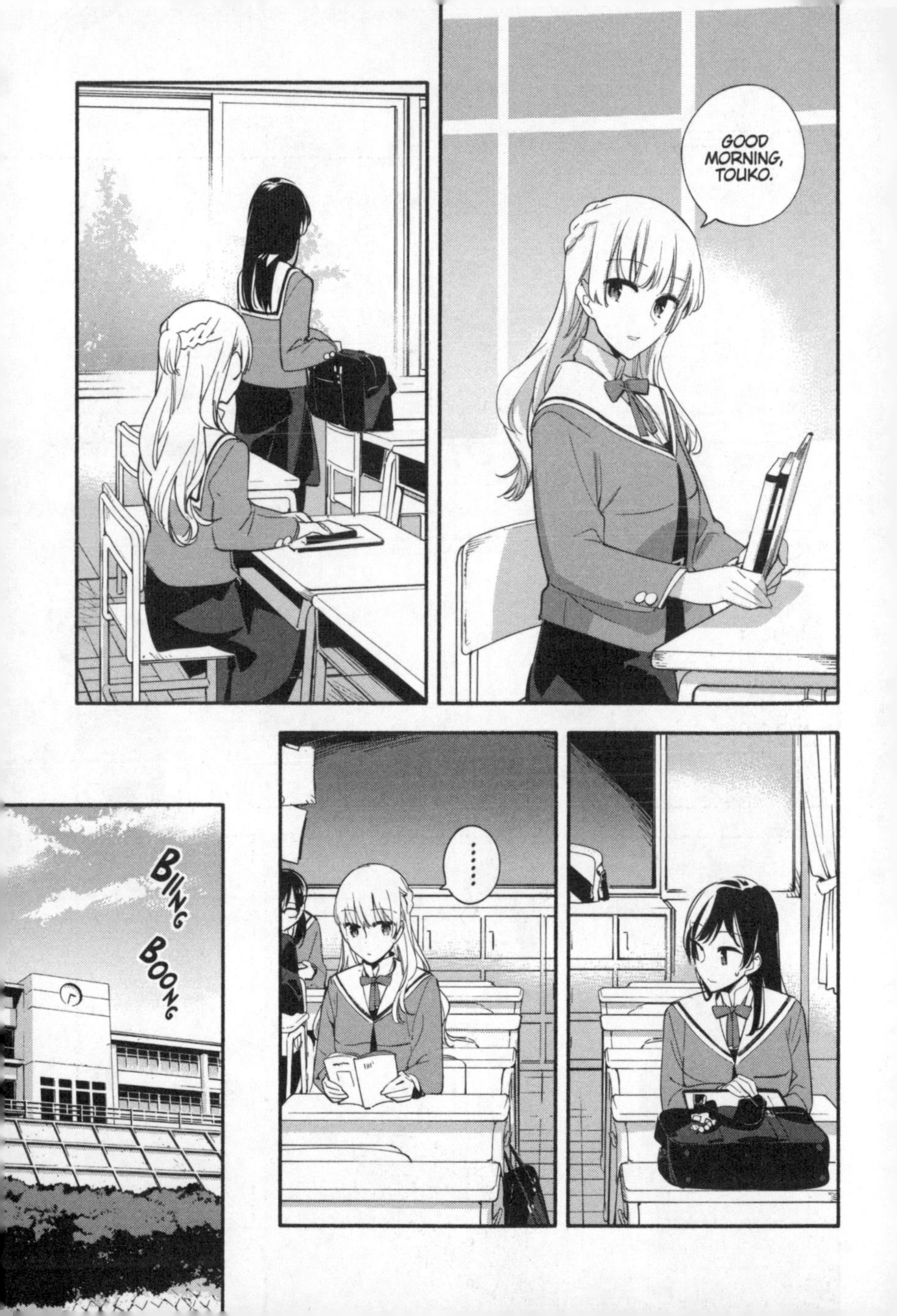
GOOD MORNING, TOUKO.
......
BIING BOONG

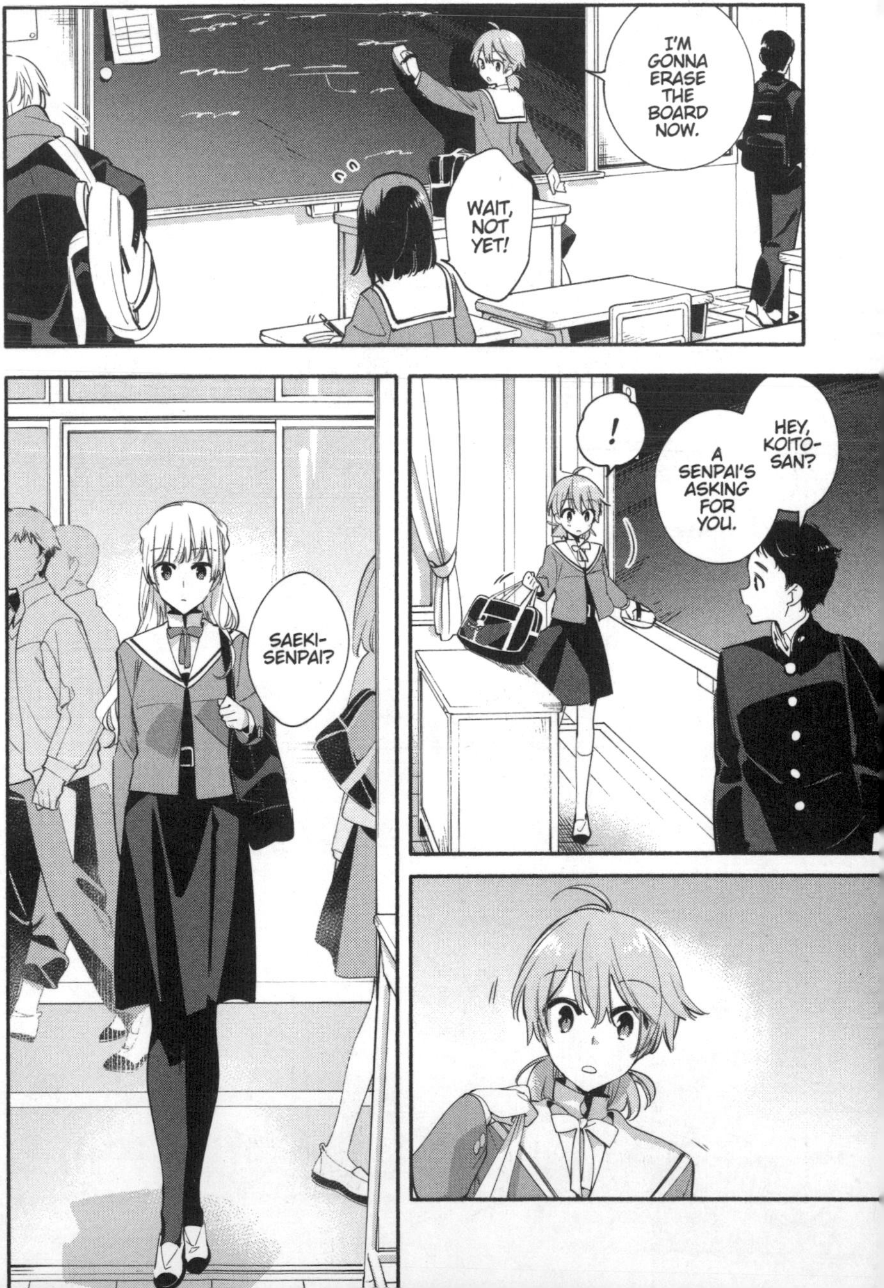
I'M GONNA ERASE THE BOARD NOW.
WAIT, NOT YET!
HEY, KOITO-SAN?
A SENPAI'S ASKING FOR YOU.
!
SAEKI-SENPAI?

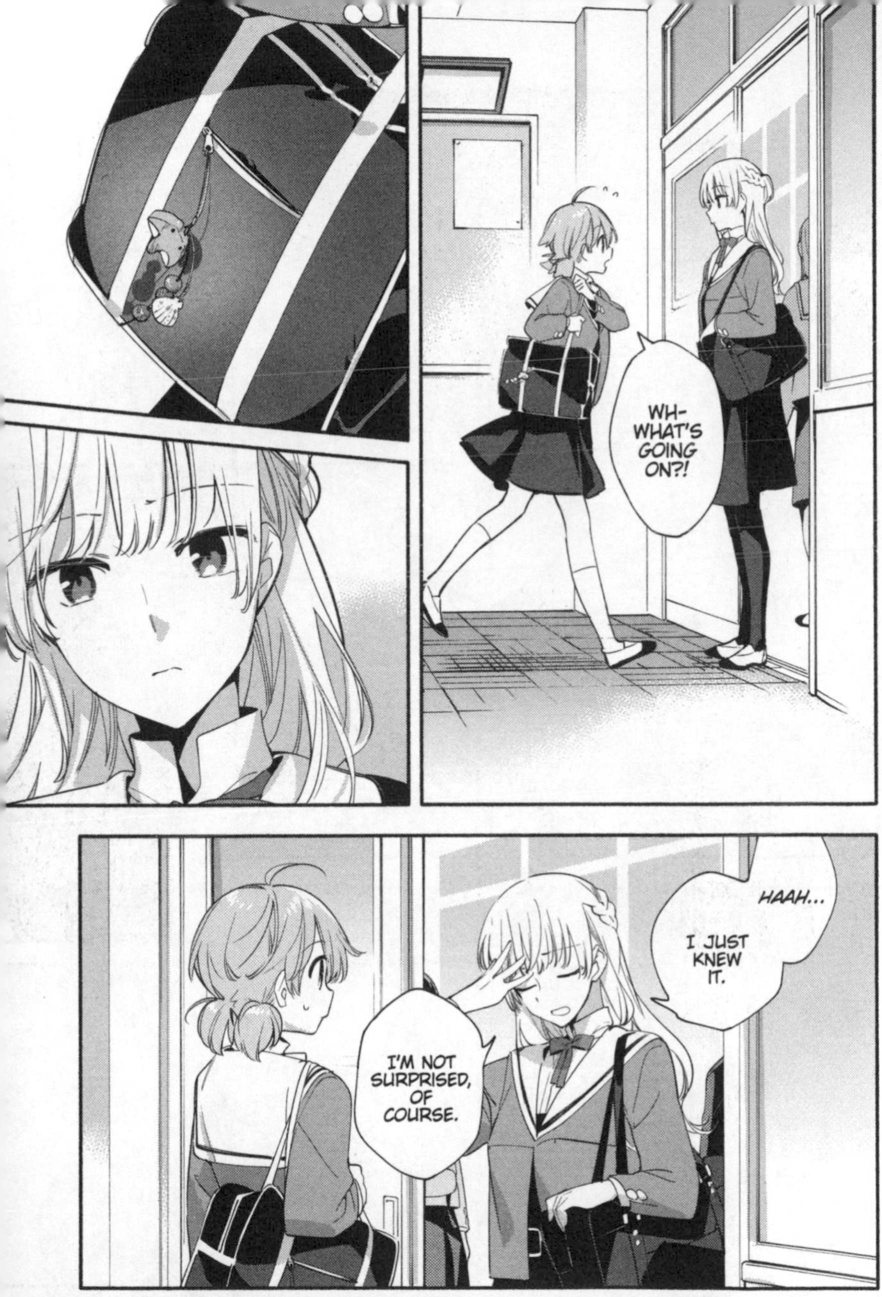
WH- WHAT'S GOING ON?!
HAAH... I JUST KNEW IT.
I'M NOT SURPRISED, OF COURSE.

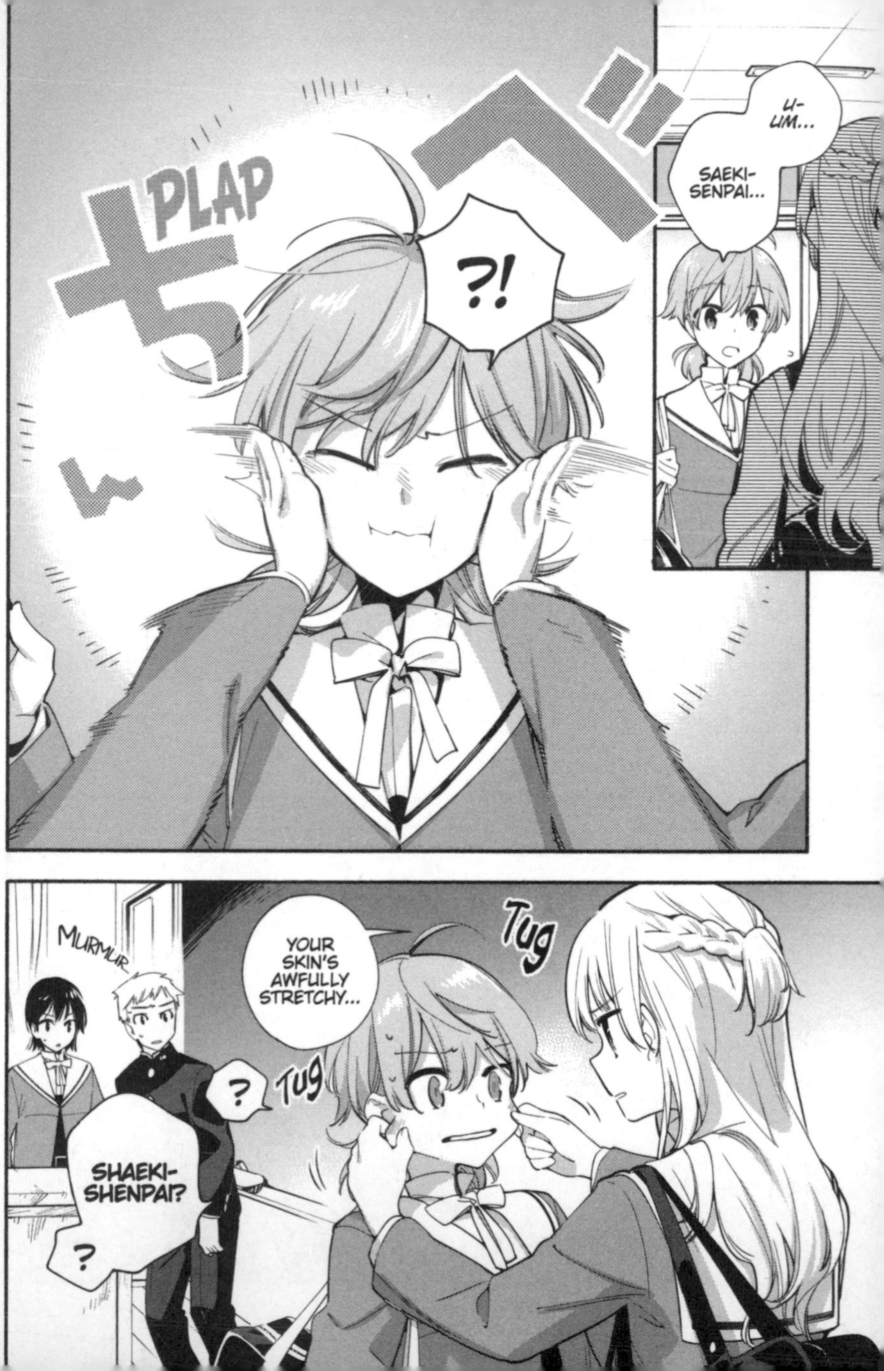
U-UM...
SAEKI-SENPAI...
PLAP
?!
Tug
YOUR SKIN'S AWFULLY STRETCHY...
MURMUR
?
Tug
SHAEKI-SHENPAI?
?

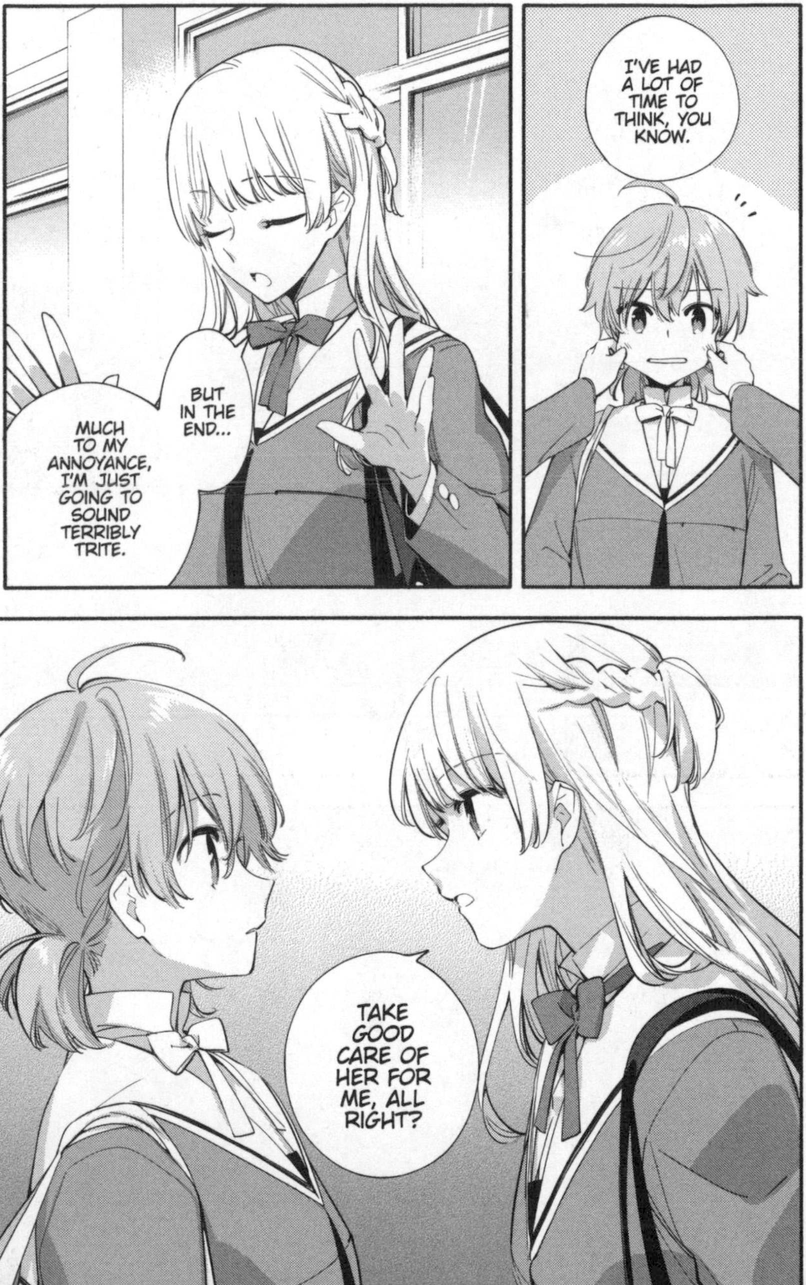
I'VE HAD A LOT OF TIME TO THINK, YOU KNOW.
BUT IN THE END...
MUCH TO MY ANNOYANCE, I'M JUST GOING TO SOUND TERRIBLY TRITE.
TAKE GOOD CARE OF HER FOR ME, ALL RIGHT?

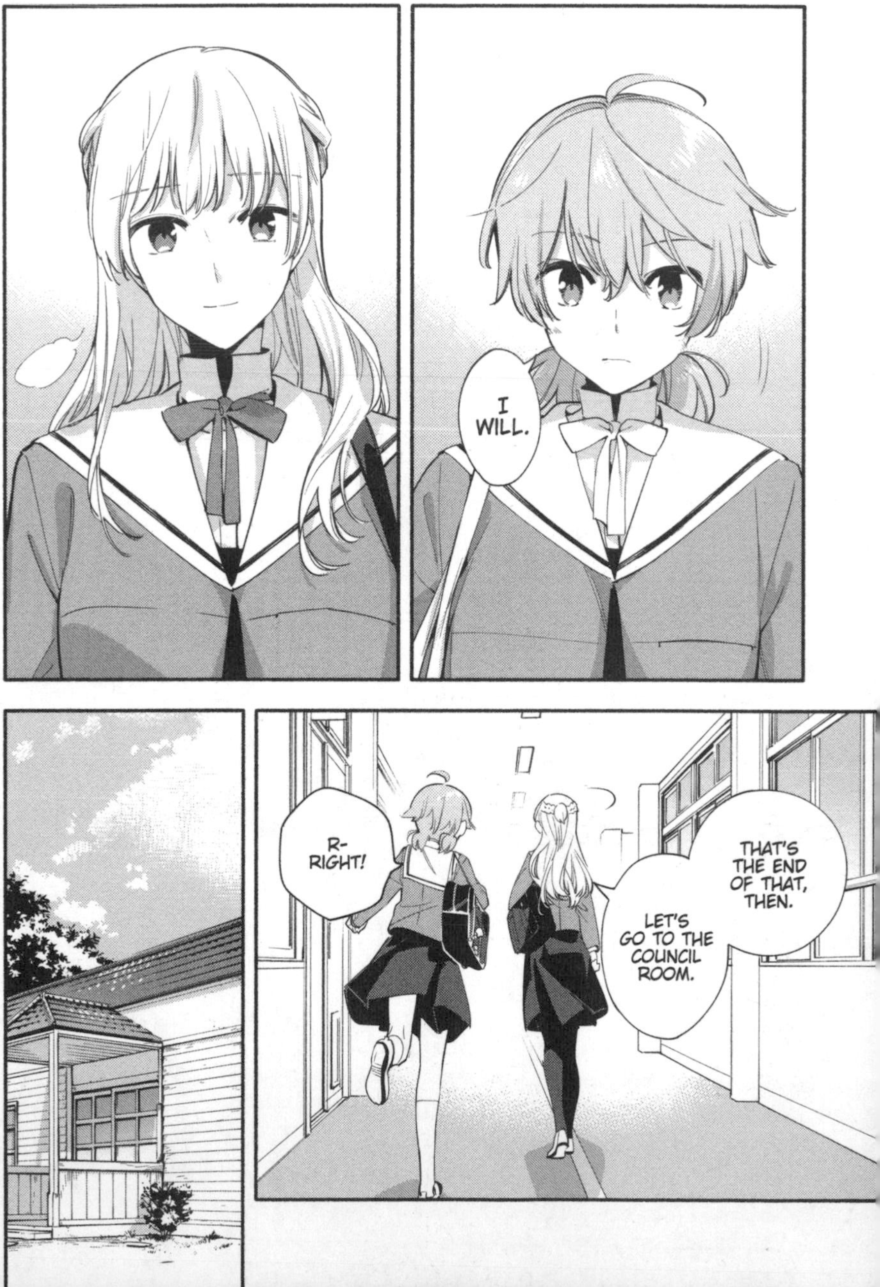
I WILL.
THAT'S THE END OF THAT, THEN.
LET'S GO TO THE COUNCIL ROOM.
R-RIGHT!

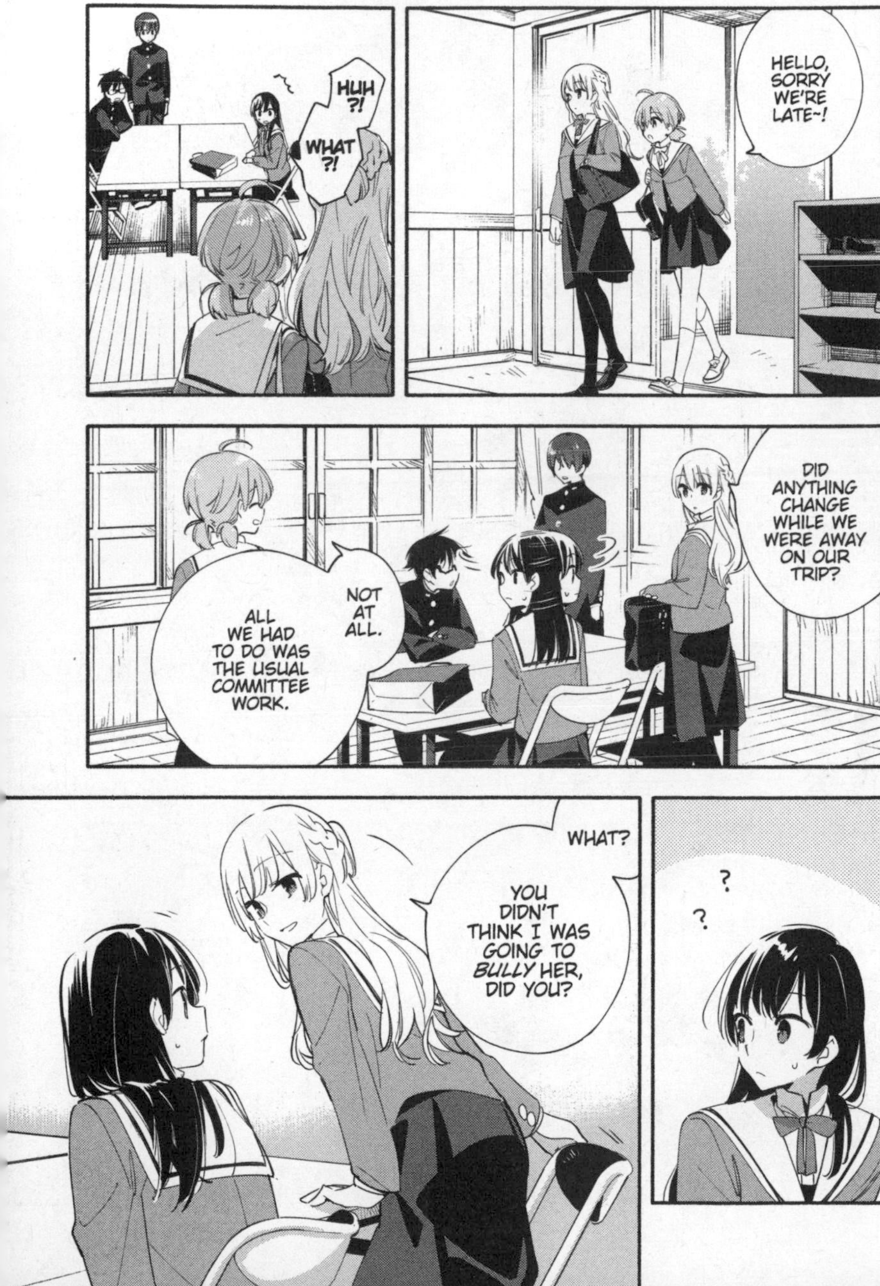
HELLO, SORRY WE'RE LATE~!
HUH?!
WHAT?!
DID ANYTHING CHANGE WHILE WE WERE AWAY ON OUR TRIP?
NOT AT ALL.
ALL WE HAD TO DO WAS THE USUAL COMMITTEE WORK.
?
?
WHAT?
YOU DIDN'T THINK I WAS GOING TO *BULLY* HER, DID YOU?

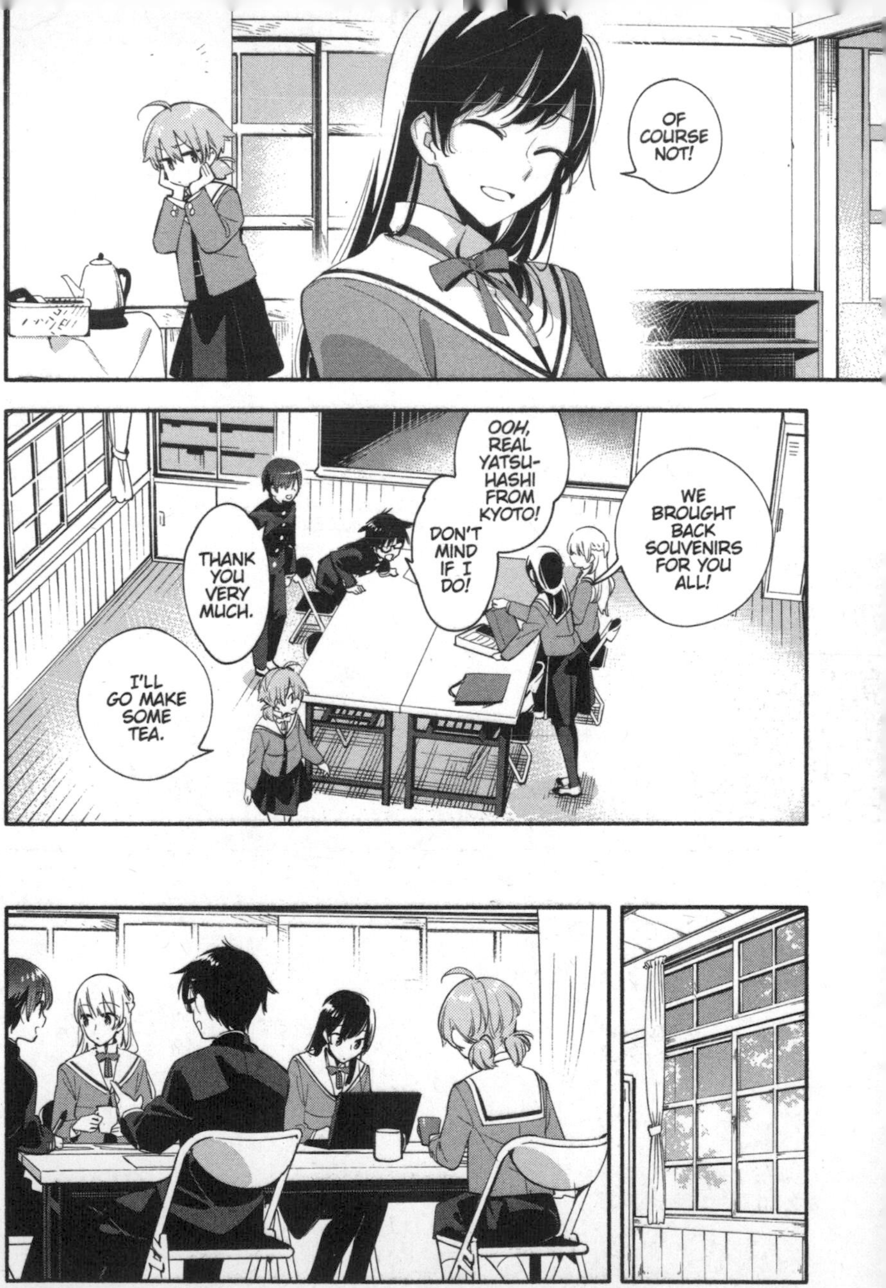
OF COURSE NOT!
WE BROUGHT BACK SOUVENIRS FOR YOU ALL!
OOH, REAL YATSU-HASHI FROM KYOTO!
DON'T MIND IF I DO!
THANK YOU VERY MUCH.
I'LL GO MAKE SOME TEA.

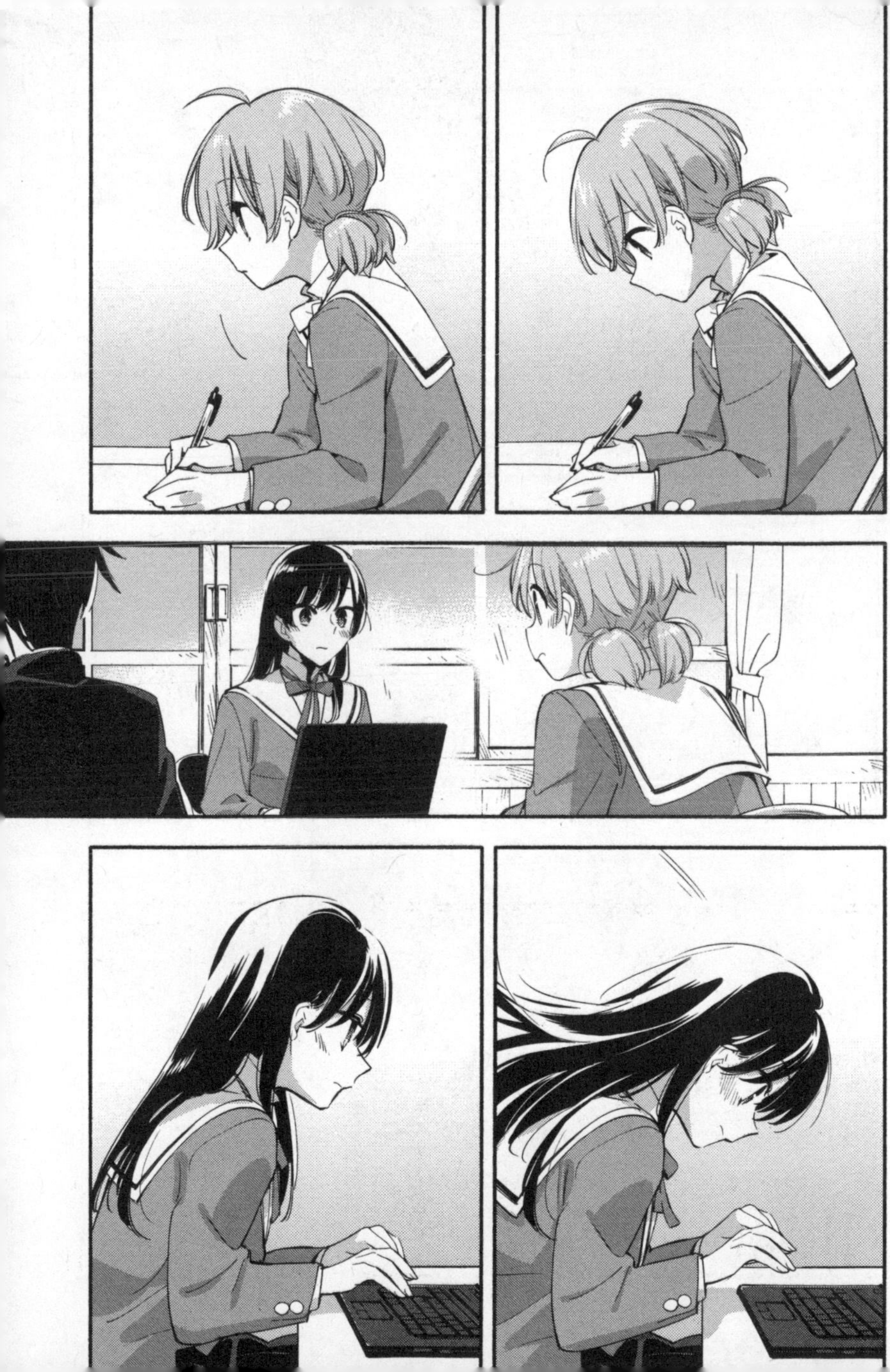

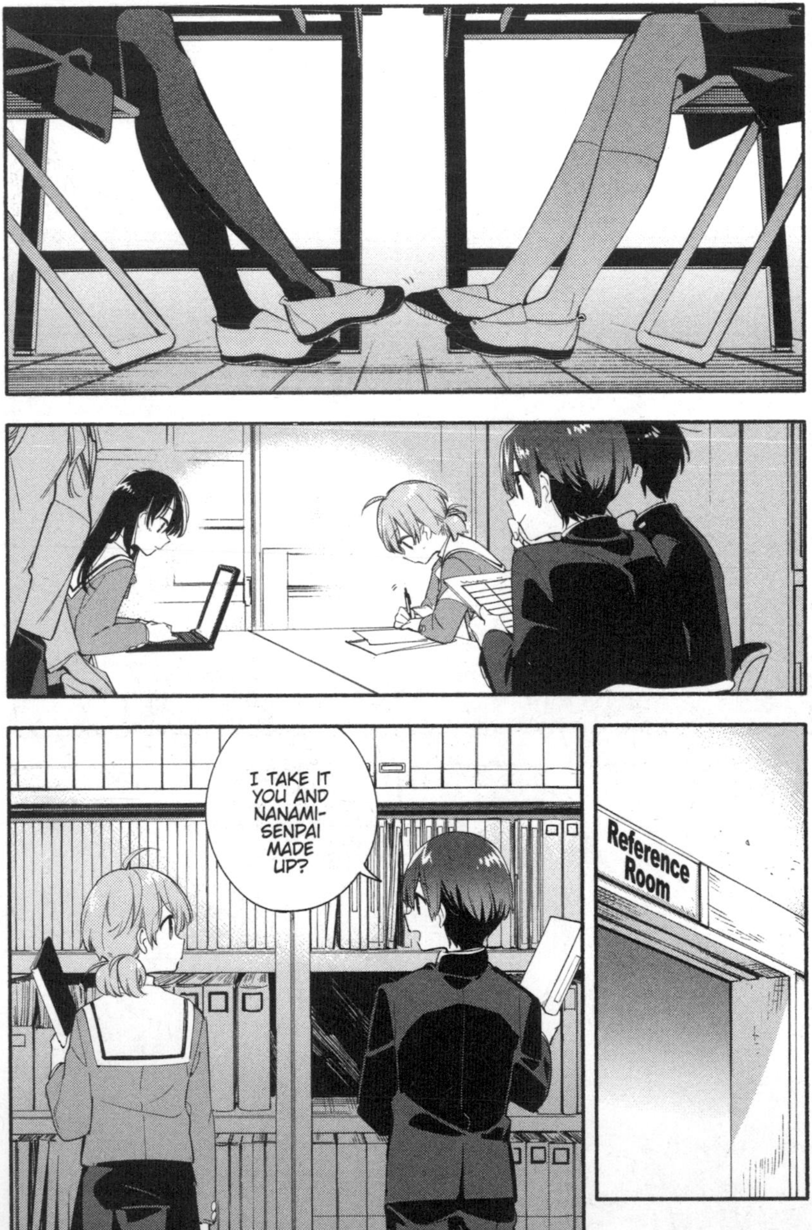
Reference Room
I TAKE IT YOU AND NANAMI-SENPAI MADE UP?

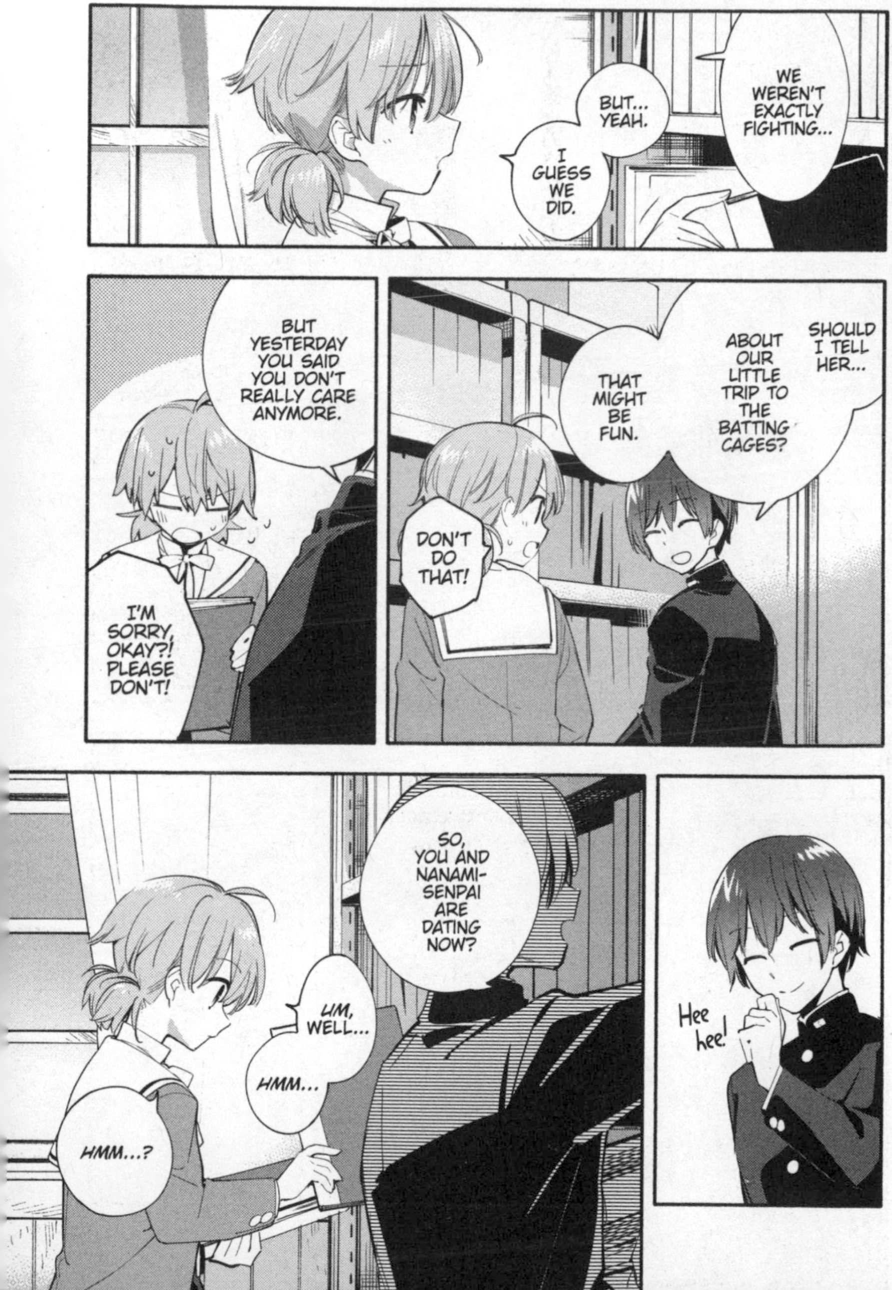
WE WEREN'T EXACTLY FIGHTING...
BUT... YEAH.
I GUESS WE DID.
SHOULD I TELL HER...
ABOUT OUR LITTLE TRIP TO THE BATTING CAGES?
THAT MIGHT BE FUN.
DON'T DO THAT!
BUT YESTERDAY YOU SAID YOU DON'T REALLY CARE ANYMORE.
I'M SORRY, OKAY?! PLEASE DON'T!
Hee hee!
SO, YOU AND NANAMI-SENPAI ARE DATING NOW?
UM, WELL...
HMM...
HMM...?

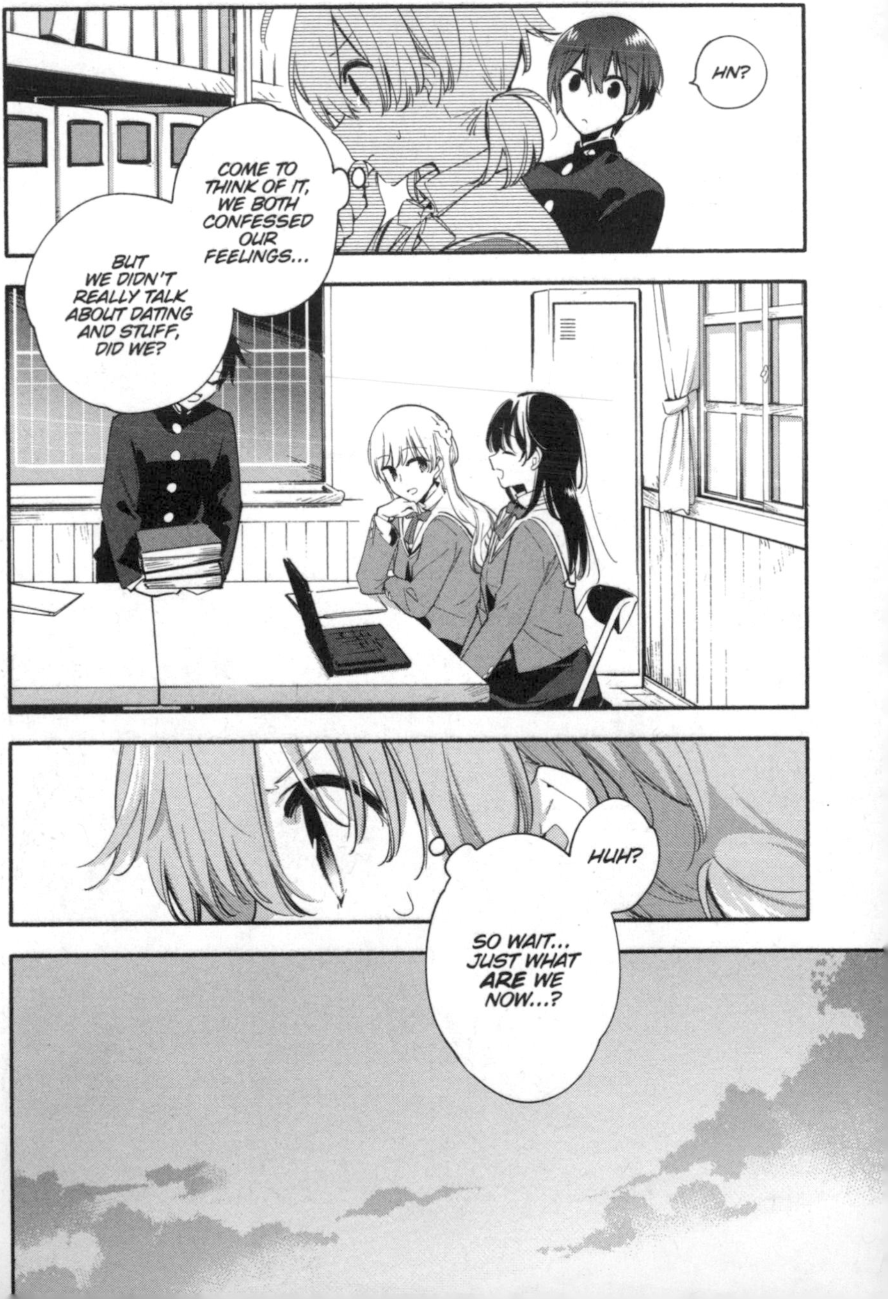
HN?
COME TO THINK OF IT, WE BOTH CONFESSED OUR FEELINGS...
BUT WE DIDN'T REALLY TALK ABOUT DATING AND STUFF, DID WE?
HUH?
SO WAIT... JUST WHAT ARE WE NOW...?

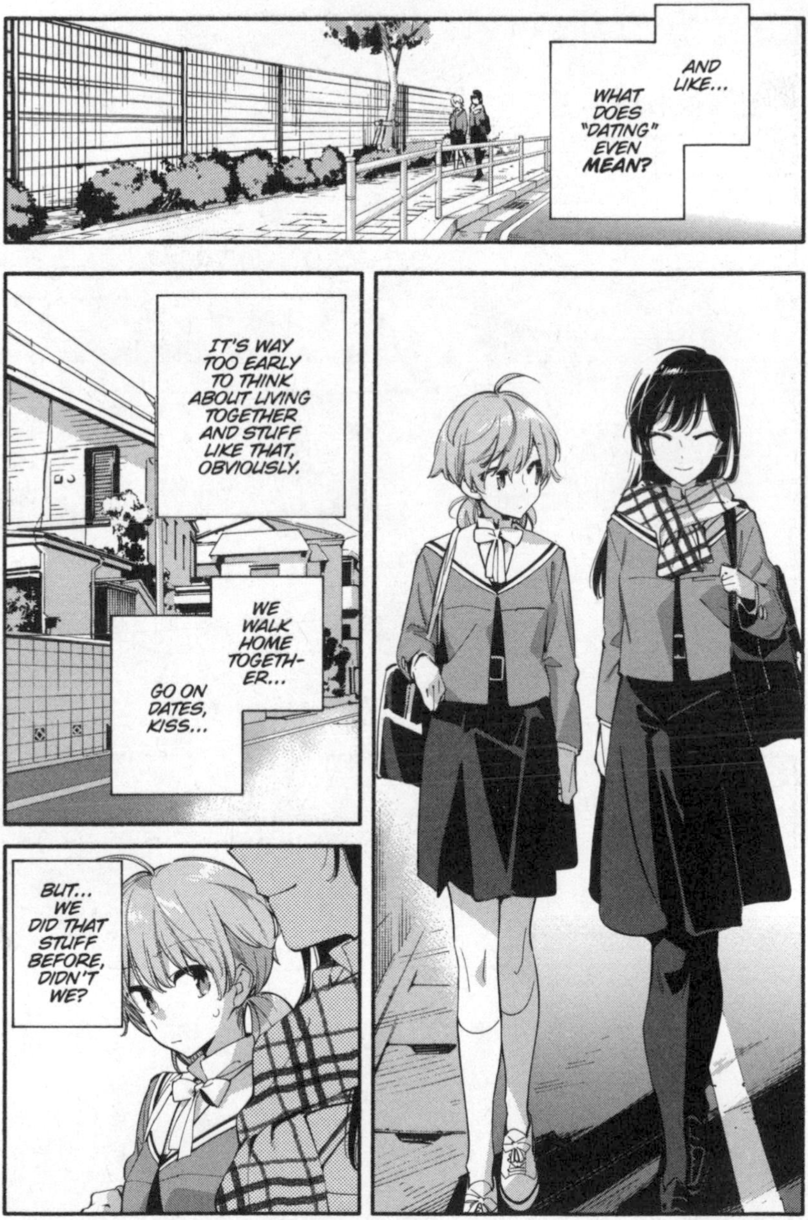
AND LIKE...
WHAT DOES "DATING" EVEN MEAN?
IT'S WAY TOO EARLY TO THINK ABOUT LIVING TOGETHER AND STUFF LIKE THAT, OBVIOUSLY.
WE WALK HOME TOGETHER...
GO ON DATES, KISS...
BUT... WE DID THAT STUFF BEFORE, DIDN'T WE?

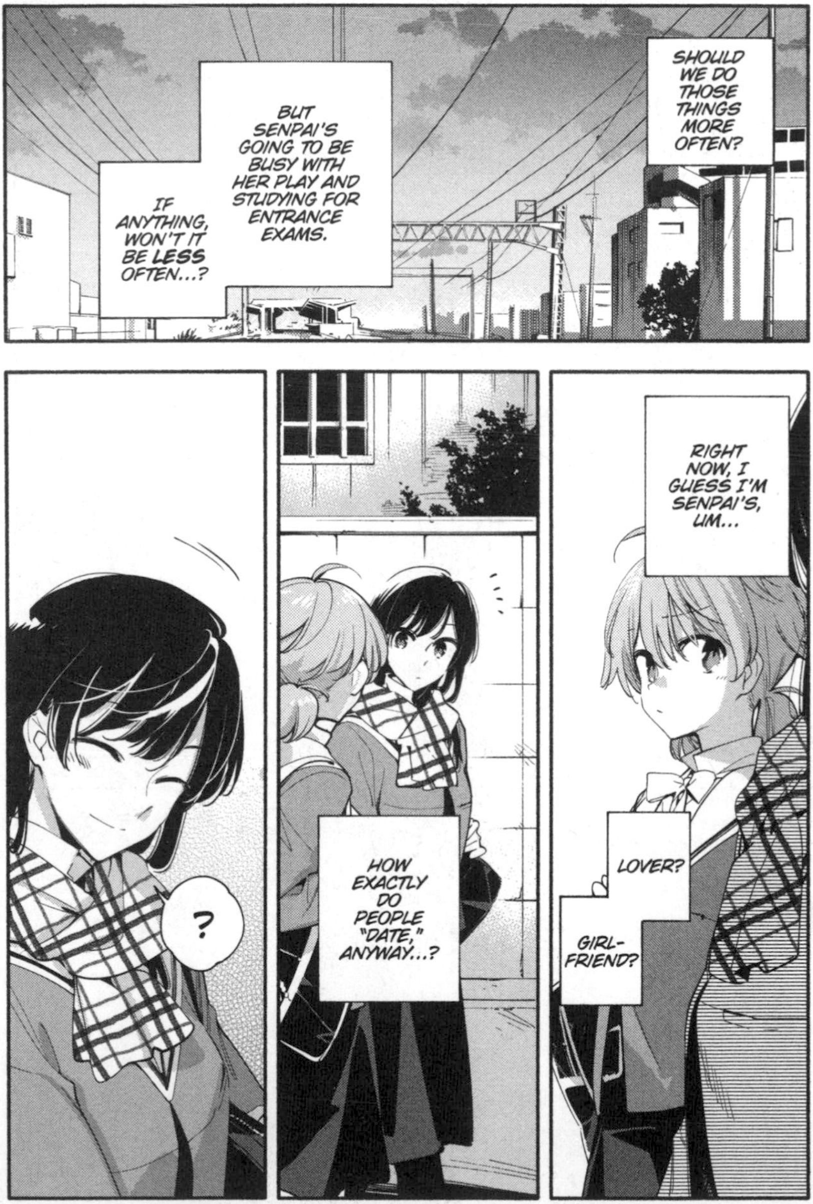
SHOULD WE DO THOSE THINGS MORE OFTEN?
BUT SENPAI'S GOING TO BE BUSY WITH HER PLAY AND STUDYING FOR ENTRANCE EXAMS.
IF ANYTHING, WON'T IT BE **LESS** OFTEN...?
RIGHT NOW, I GUESS I'M SENPAI'S, UM...
LOVER?
GIRL-FRIEND?
HOW EXACTLY DO PEOPLE "DATE," ANYWAY...?
?

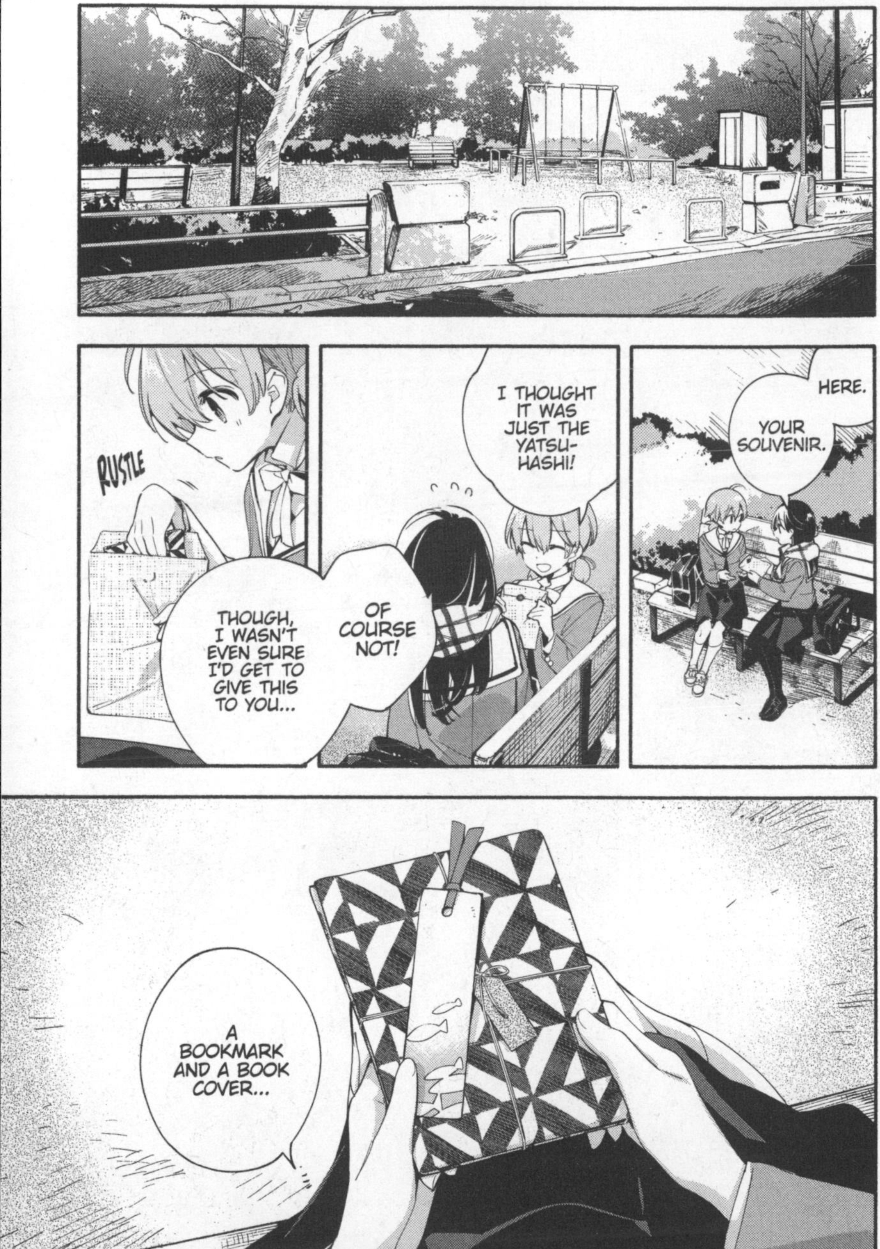
HERE.
YOUR SOUVENIR.
I THOUGHT IT WAS JUST THE YATSU-HASHI!
OF COURSE NOT!
RUSTLE
THOUGH, I WASN'T EVEN SURE I'D GET TO GIVE THIS TO YOU...
A BOOKMARK AND A BOOK COVER...

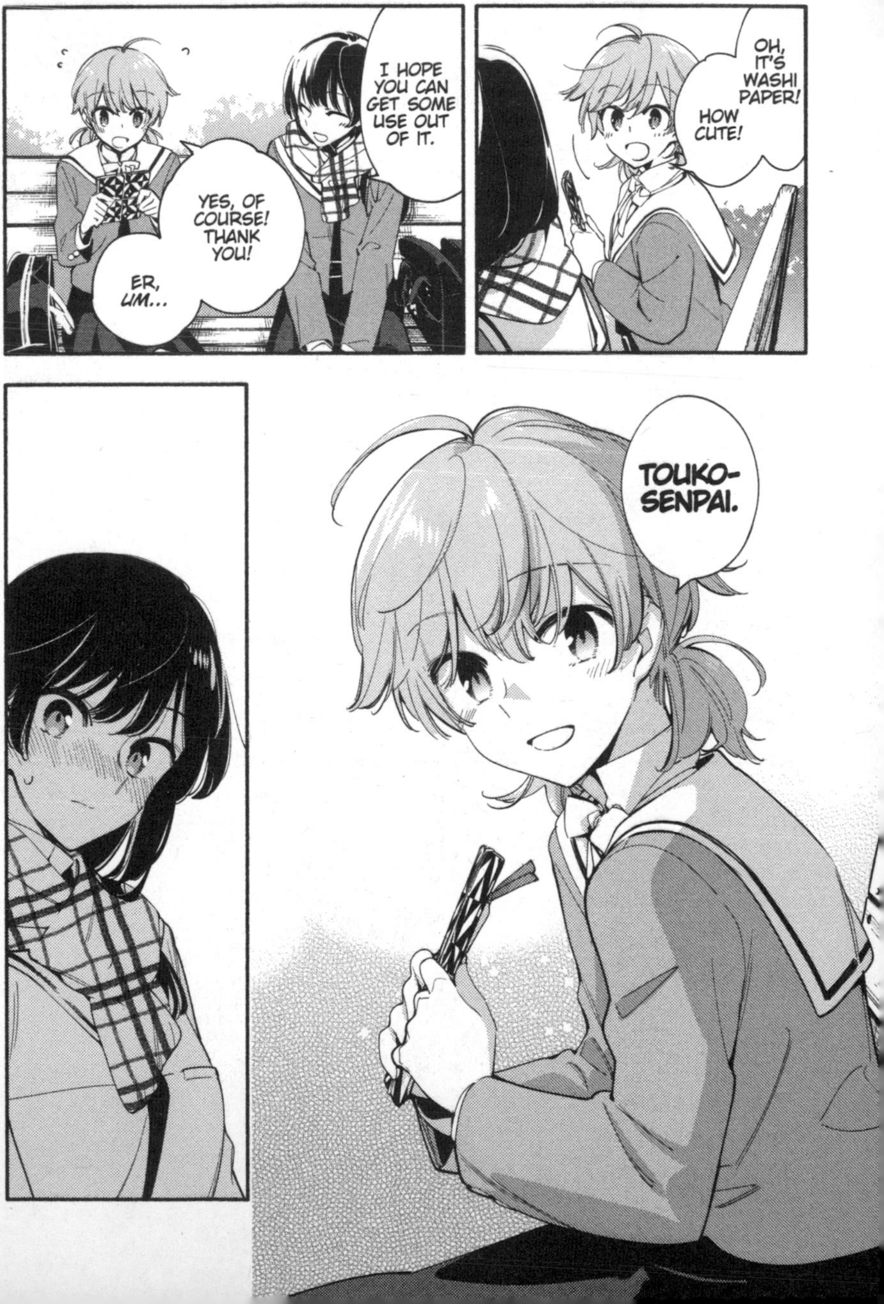
OH, IT'S WASHI PAPER!
HOW CUTE!
I HOPE YOU CAN GET SOME USE OUT OF IT.
YES, OF COURSE! THANK YOU!
ER, UM...
TOUKO-SENPAI.

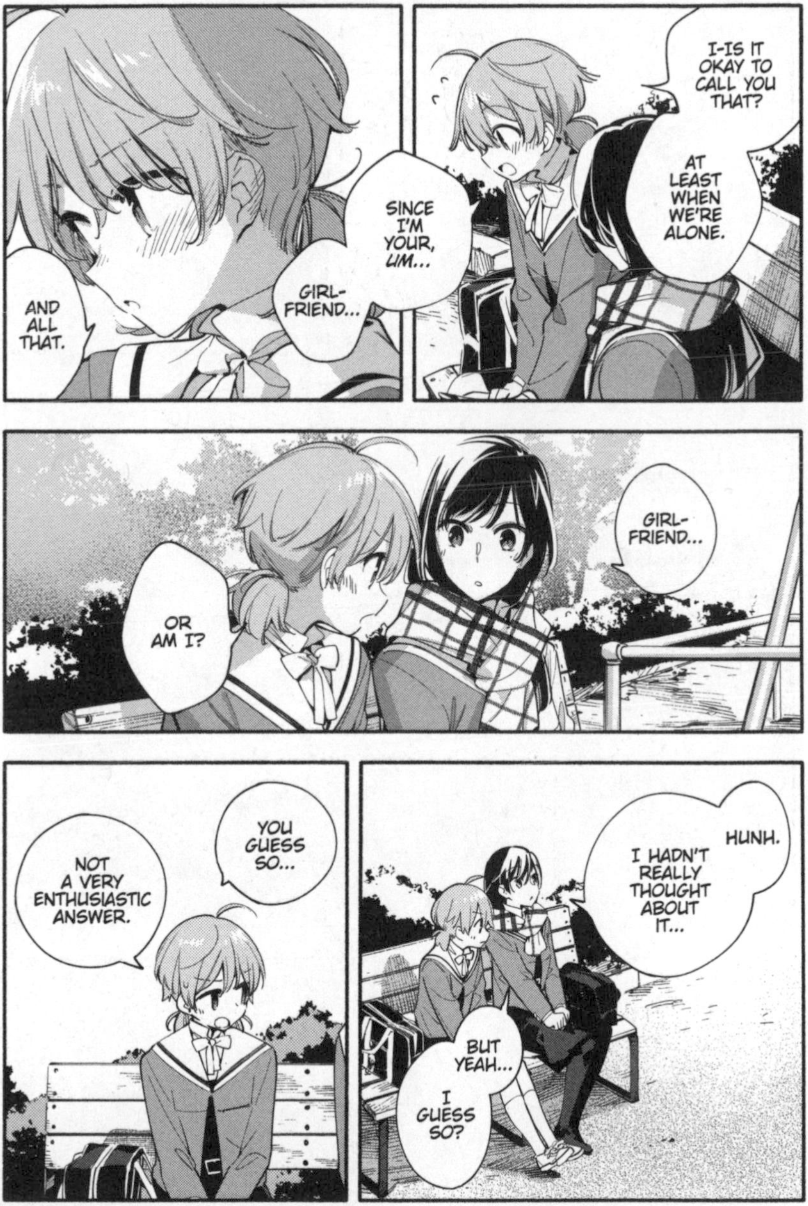
I-IS IT OKAY TO CALL YOU THAT?
AT LEAST WHEN WE'RE ALONE.
SINCE I'M YOUR, UM...
GIRL-FRIEND...
AND ALL THAT.
GIRL-FRIEND...
OR AM I?
HUNH.
I HADN'T REALLY THOUGHT ABOUT IT...
BUT YEAH...
I GUESS SO?
YOU GUESS SO...
NOT A VERY ENTHUSIASTIC ANSWER.

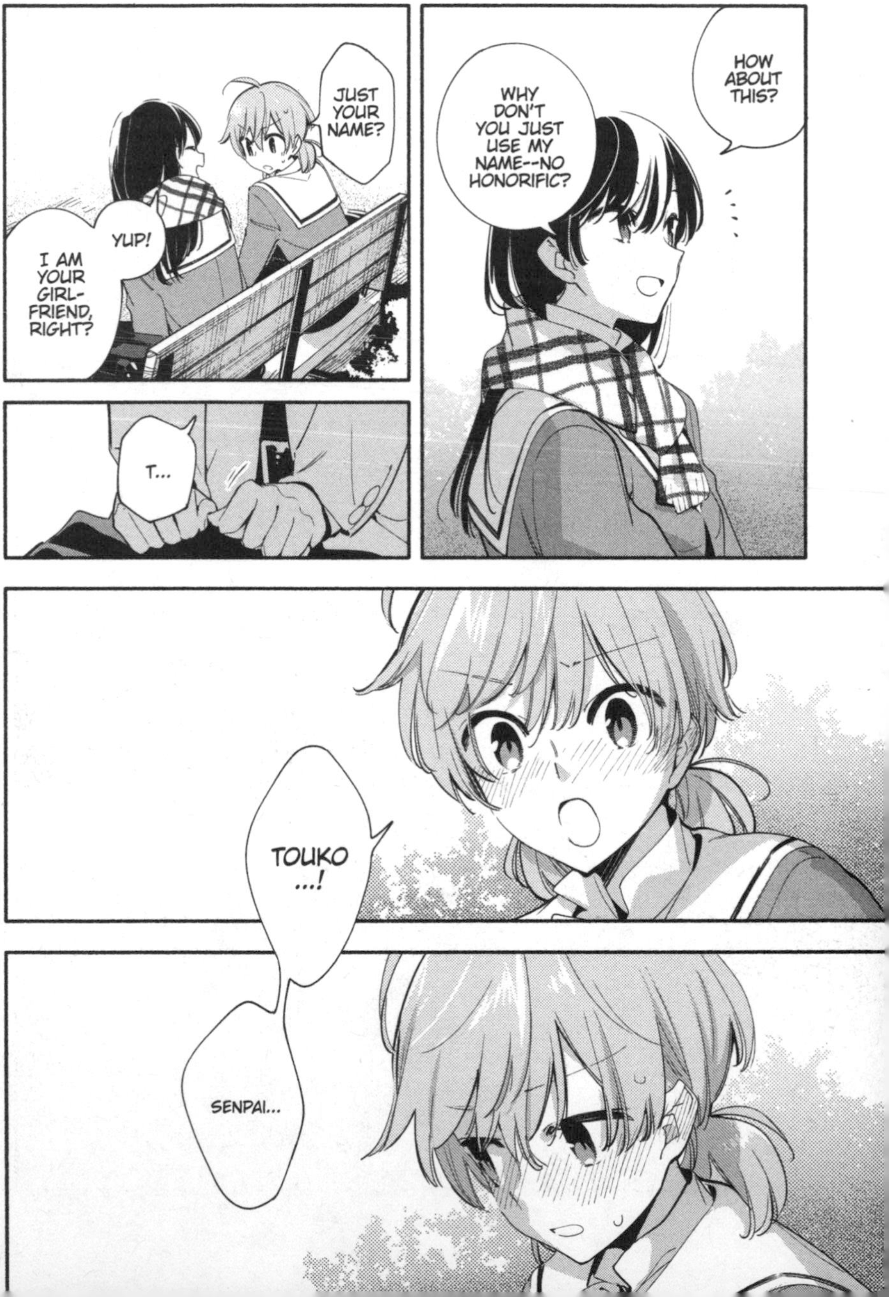
HOW ABOUT THIS?
WHY DON'T YOU JUST USE MY NAME--NO HONORIFIC?
JUST YOUR NAME?
YUP! I AM YOUR GIRL-FRIEND, RIGHT?
T...
TOUKO ...!
SENPAI...

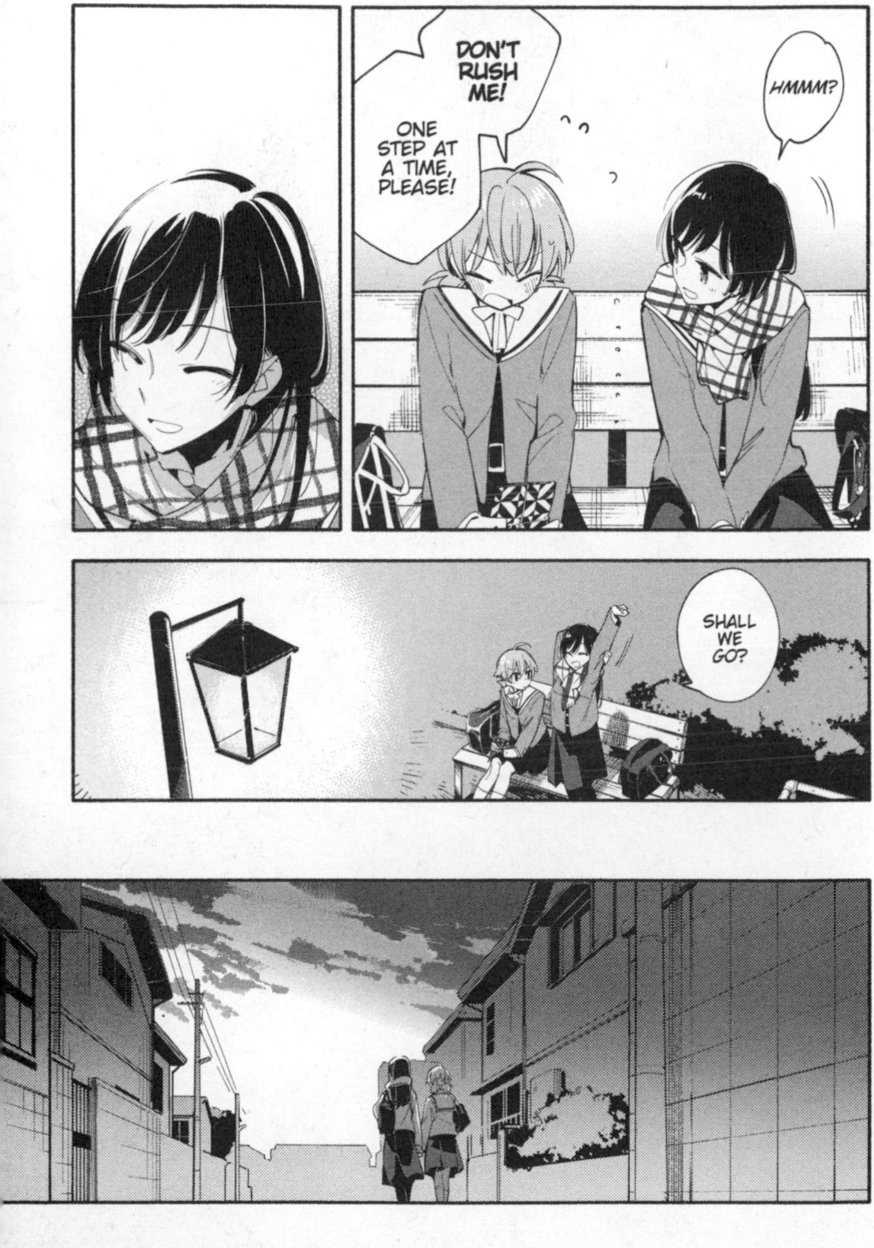
HMMM?
DON'T RUSH ME!
ONE STEP AT A TIME, PLEASE!
SHALL WE GO?

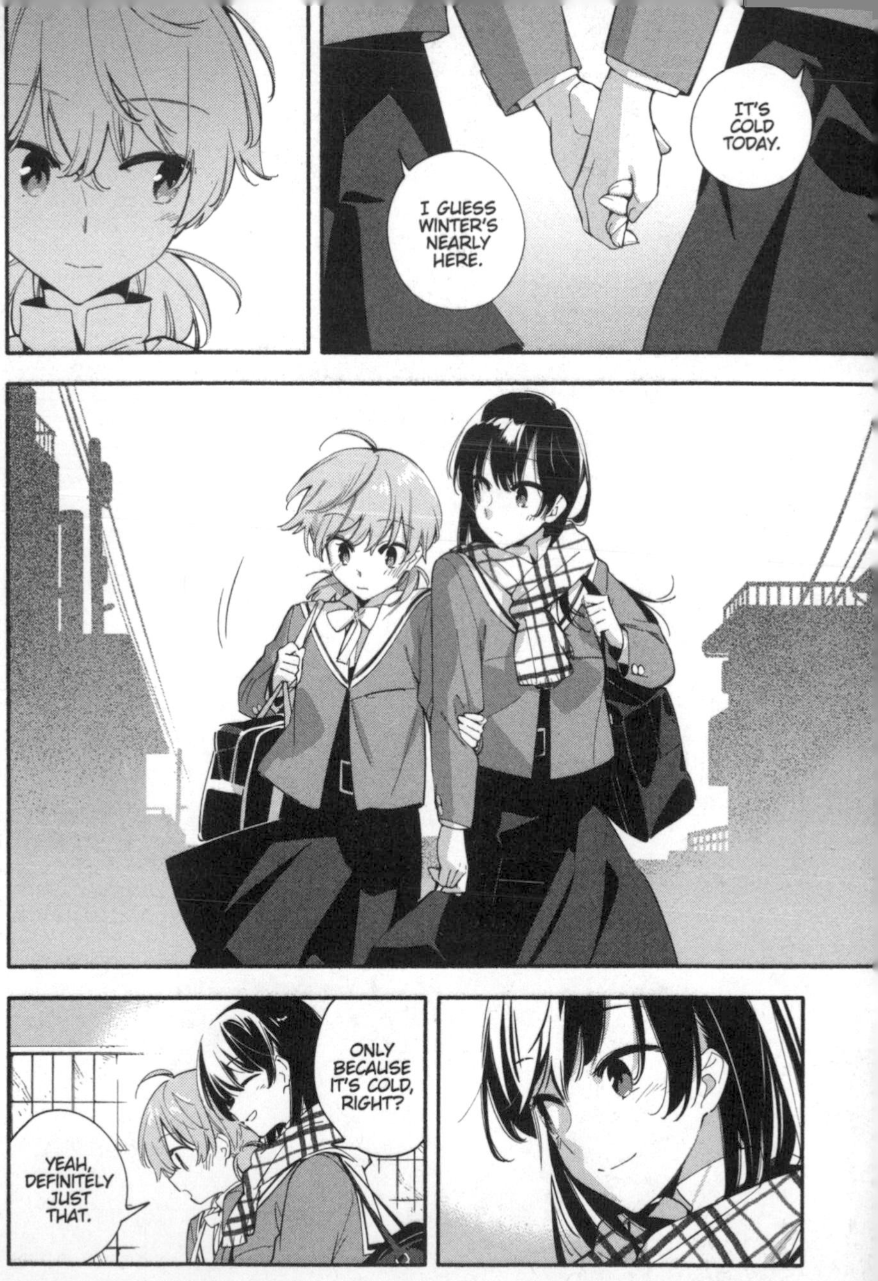
IT'S COLD TODAY.
I GUESS WINTER'S NEARLY HERE.
ONLY BECAUSE IT'S COLD, RIGHT?
YEAH, DEFINITELY JUST THAT.

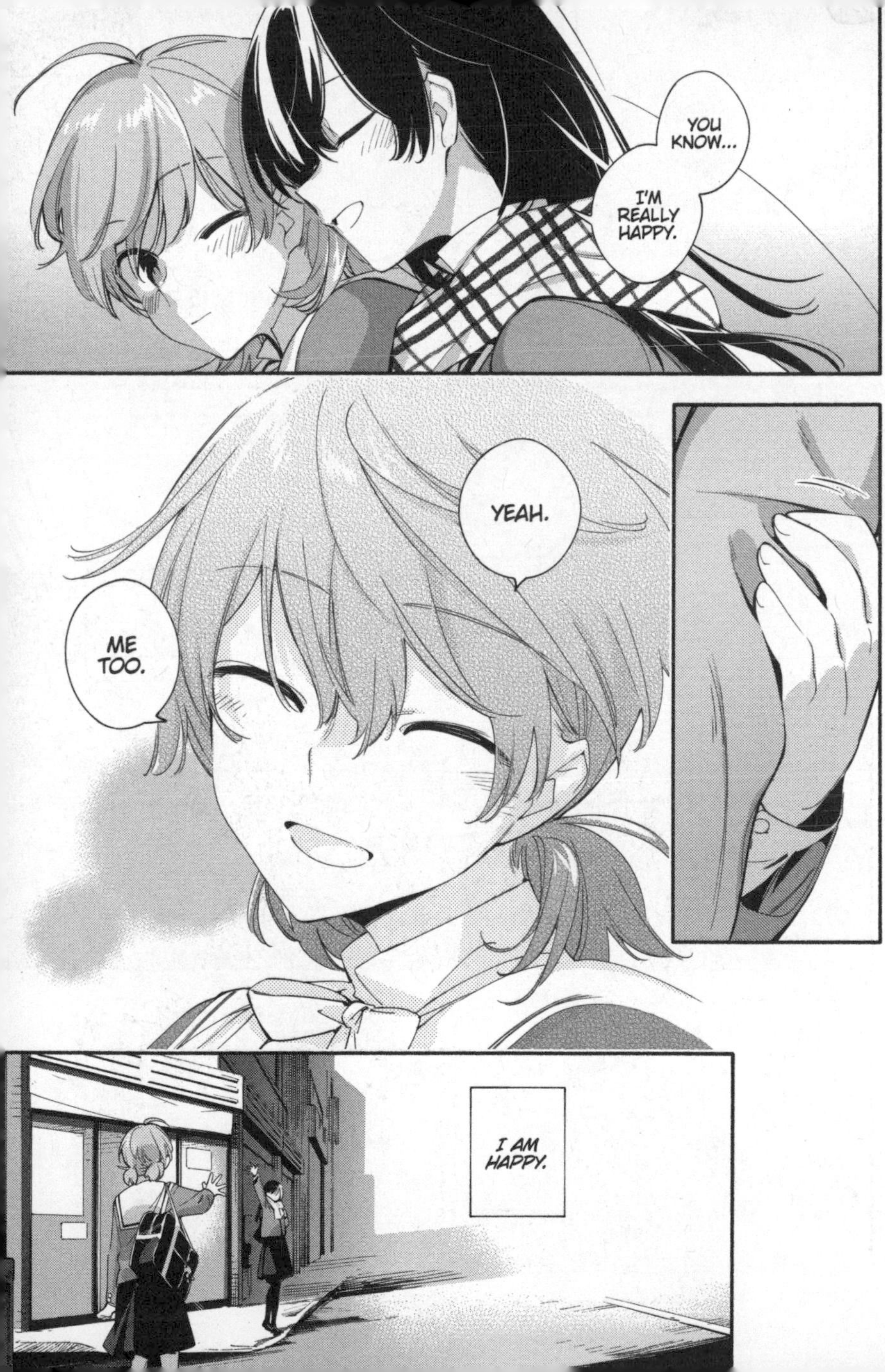
YOU KNOW...
I'M REALLY HAPPY.
YEAH.
ME TOO.
I AM HAPPY.

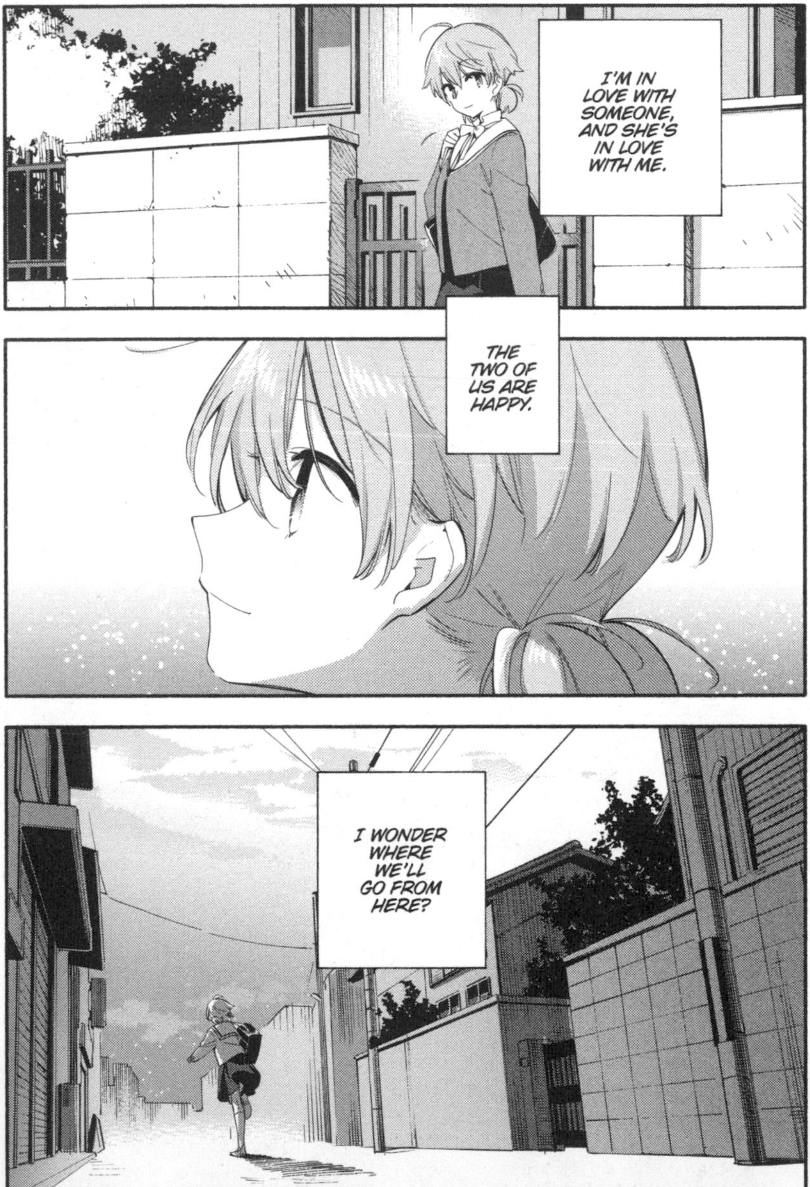
I'M IN LOVE WITH SOMEONE, AND SHE'S IN LOVE WITH ME.
THE TWO OF US ARE HAPPY.
I WONDER WHERE WE'LL GO FROM HERE?

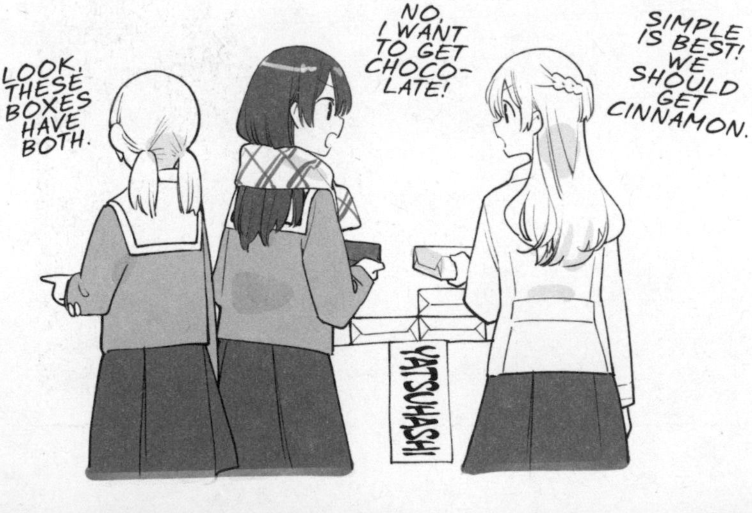
SIMPLE IS BEST! WE SHOULD GET CINNAMON.
NO, I WANT TO GET CHOCO-LATE!
LOOK, THESE BOXES HAVE BOTH.
YATSUHASHI

(Bloom Into You)

42

Essay Question

EPISODE FORTY-TWO

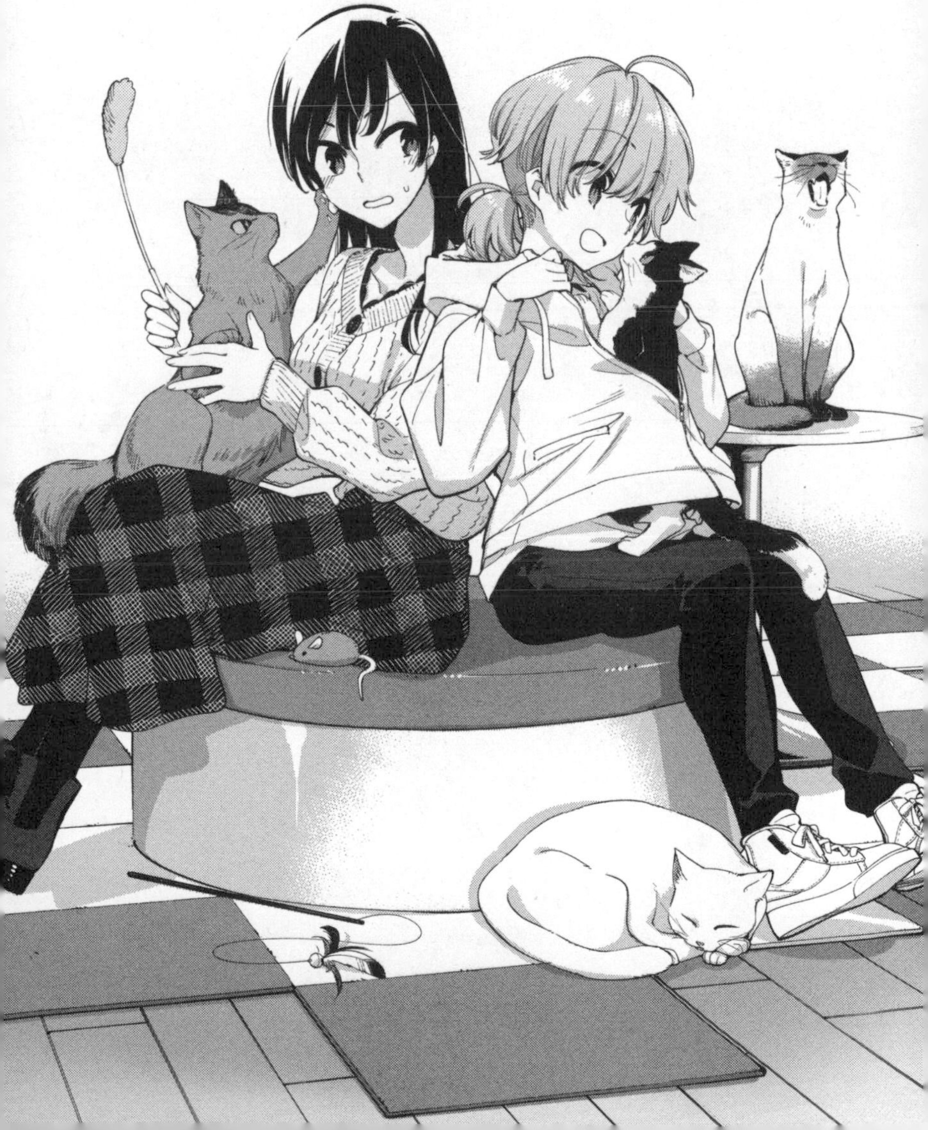

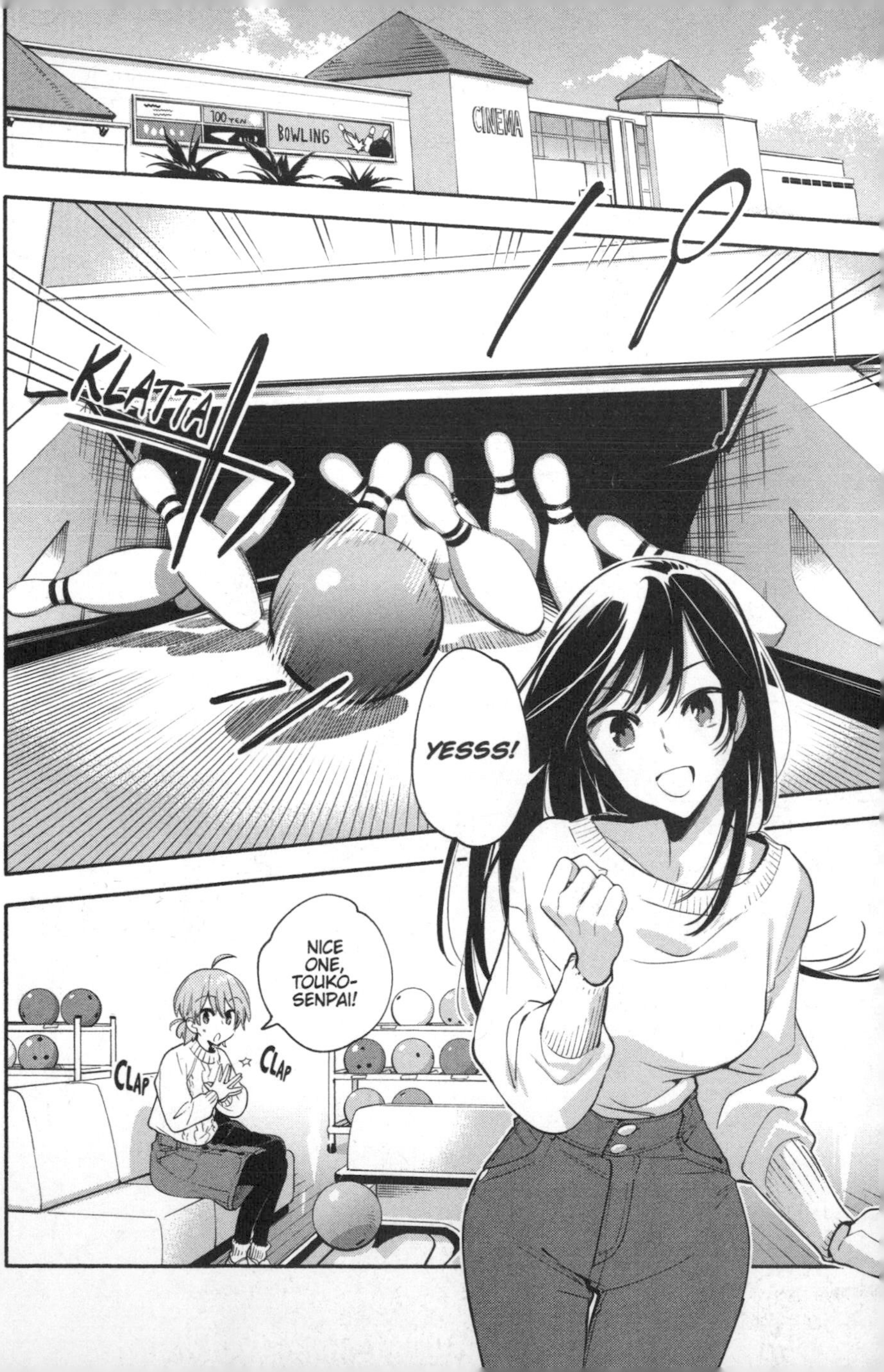
CINEMA
100 YEN
BOWLING
KLATTA
YESSS!
NICE ONE, TOUKO-SENPAI!
CLAP
CLAP

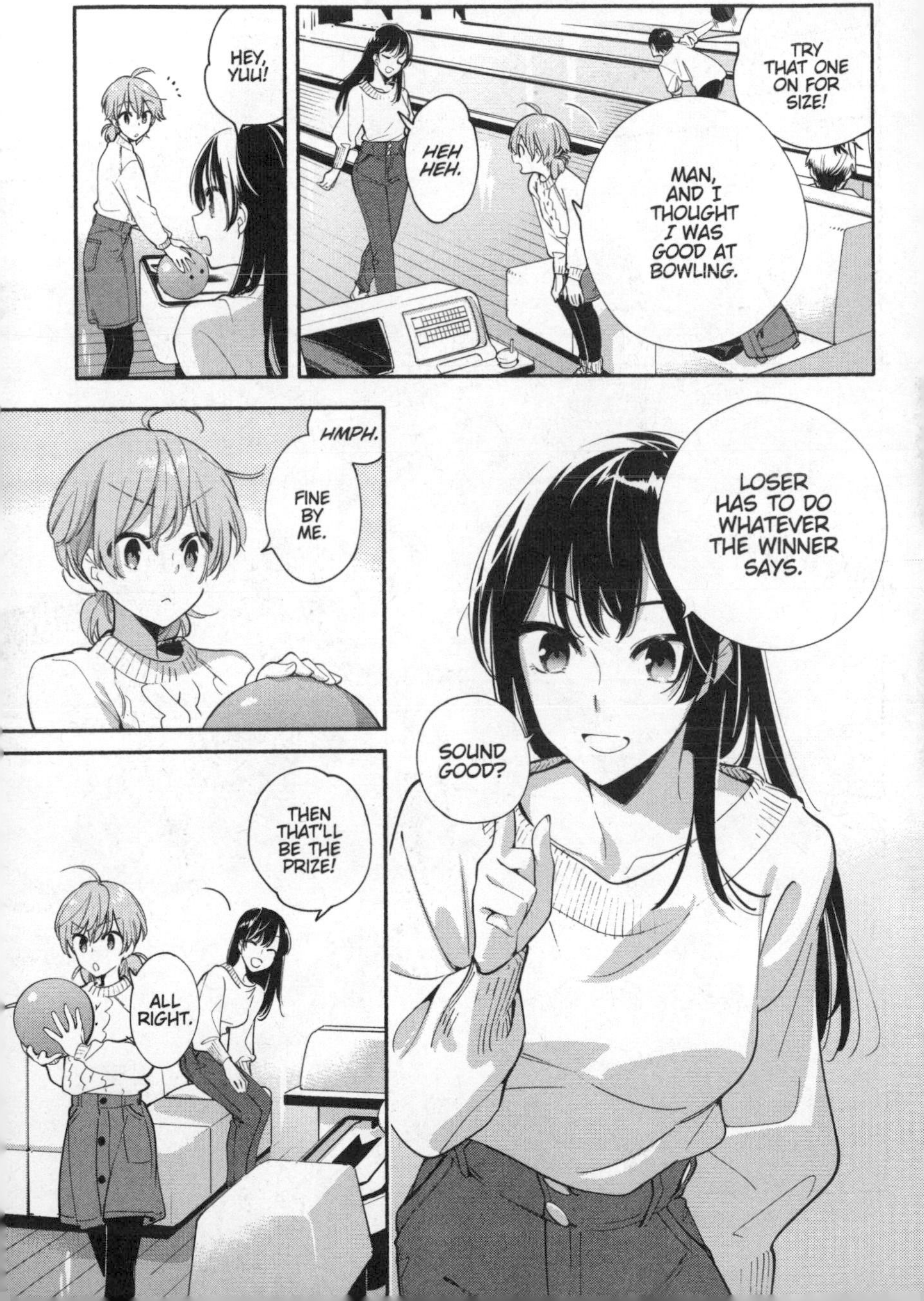
TRY THAT ONE ON FOR SIZE!
HEH HEH.
MAN, AND I THOUGHT I WAS GOOD AT BOWLING.
HEY, YUU!
LOSER HAS TO DO WHATEVER THE WINNER SAYS.
SOUND GOOD?
HMPH.
FINE BY ME.
THEN THAT'LL BE THE PRIZE!
ALL RIGHT.

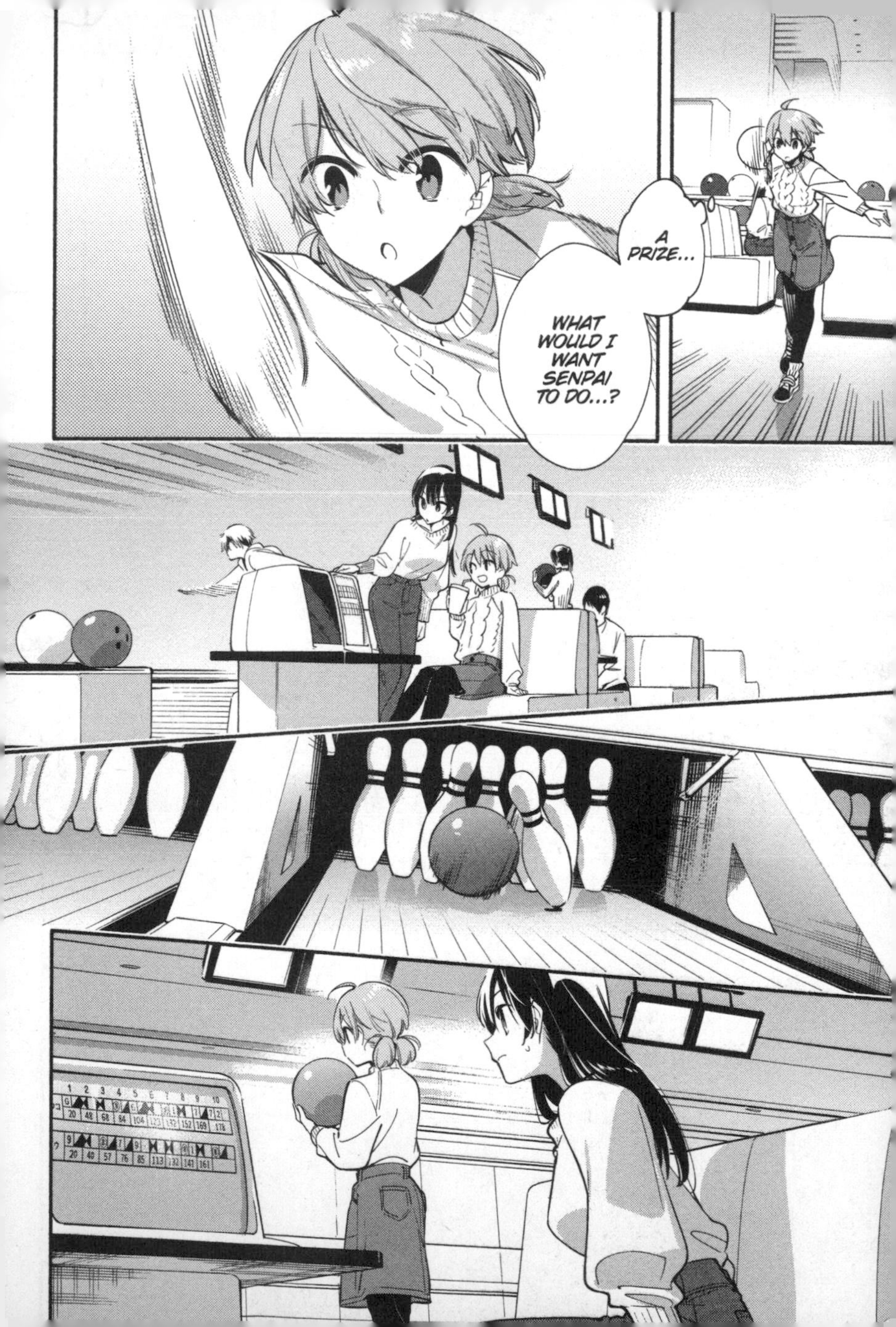
A PRIZE...
WHAT WOULD I WANT SENPAI TO DO...?

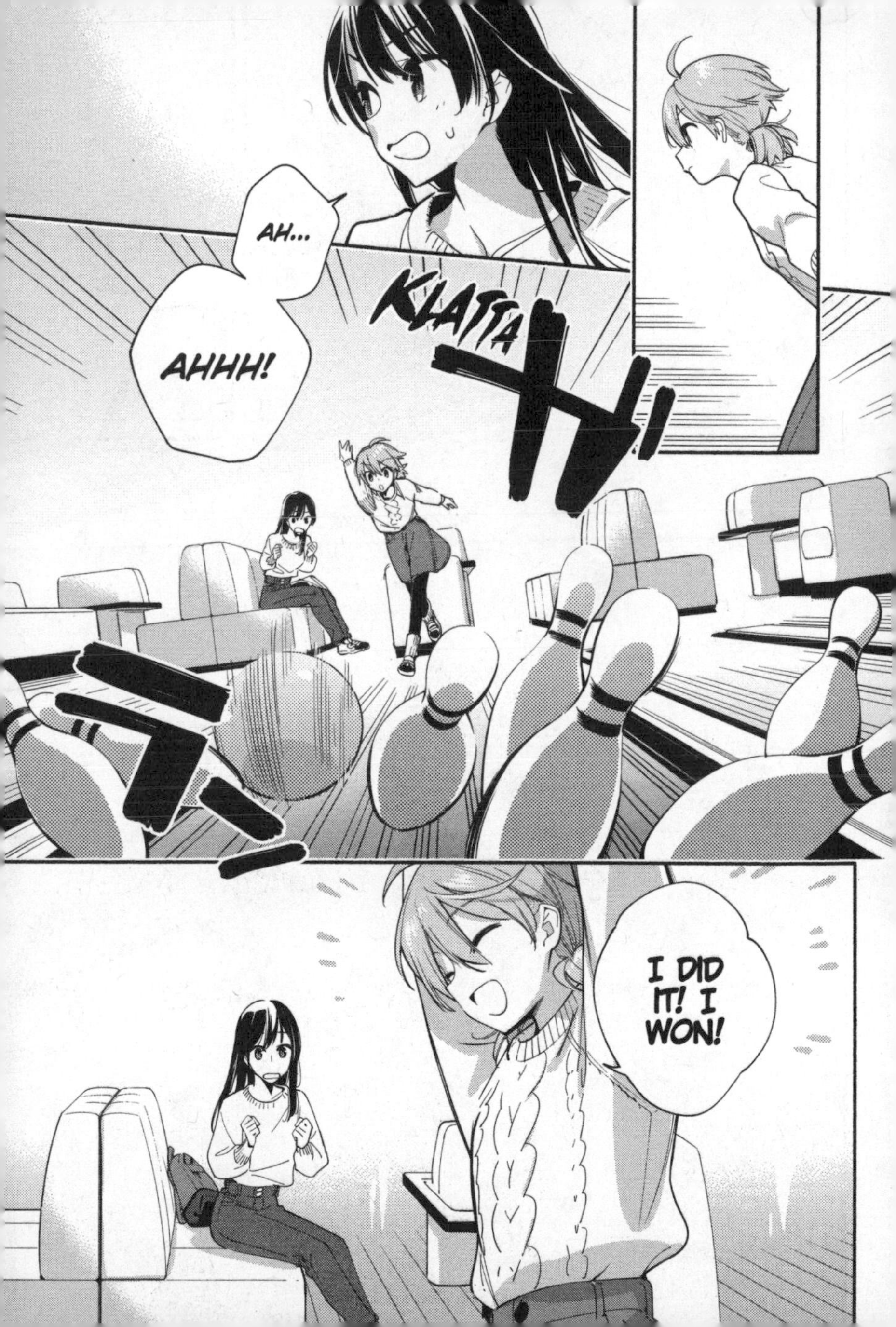
AH...
AHHH!
KLATTA
I DID IT! I WON!

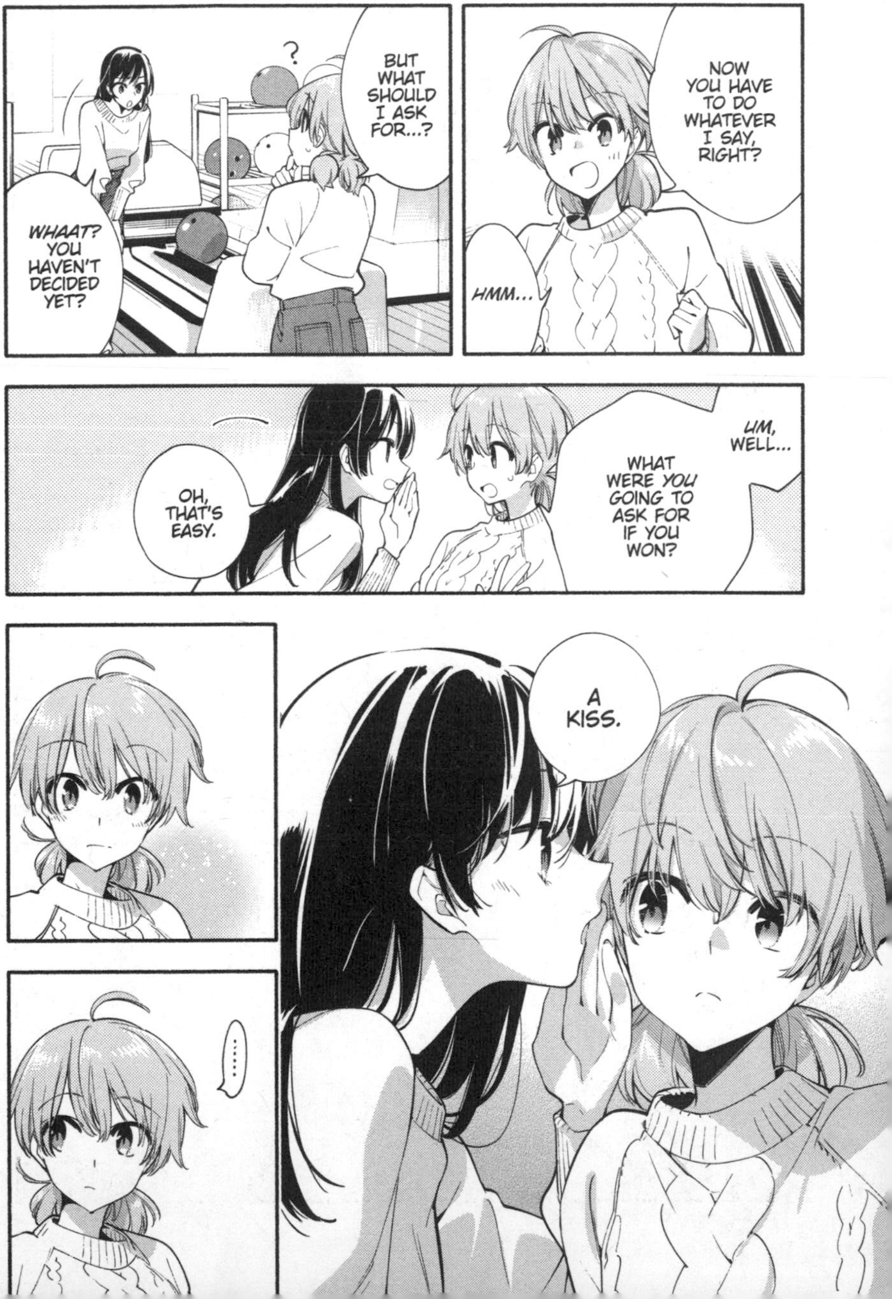
NOW YOU HAVE TO DO WHATEVER I SAY, RIGHT?
HMM...
BUT WHAT SHOULD I ASK FOR...?
?
WHAAT? YOU HAVEN'T DECIDED YET?
UM, WELL...
WHAT WERE *YOU* GOING TO ASK FOR IF YOU WON?
OH, THAT'S EASY.
A KISS.
......

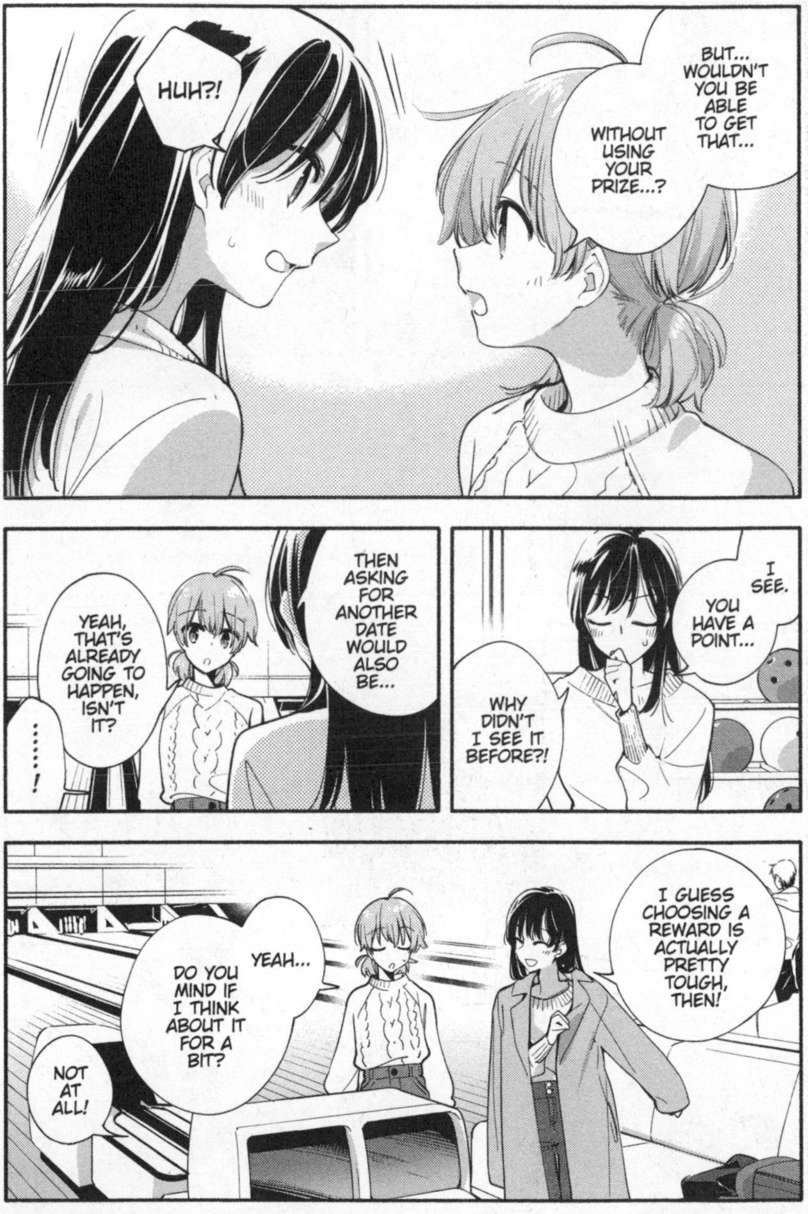
BUT... WOULDN'T YOU BE ABLE TO GET THAT...
WITHOUT USING YOUR PRIZE...?
HUH?!
I SEE. YOU HAVE A POINT...
WHY DIDN'T I SEE IT BEFORE?!
THEN ASKING FOR ANOTHER DATE WOULD ALSO BE...
YEAH, THAT'S ALREADY GOING TO HAPPEN, ISN'T IT?
......!
I GUESS CHOOSING A REWARD IS ACTUALLY PRETTY TOUGH, THEN!
YEAH...
DO YOU MIND IF I THINK ABOUT IT FOR A BIT?
NOT AT ALL!

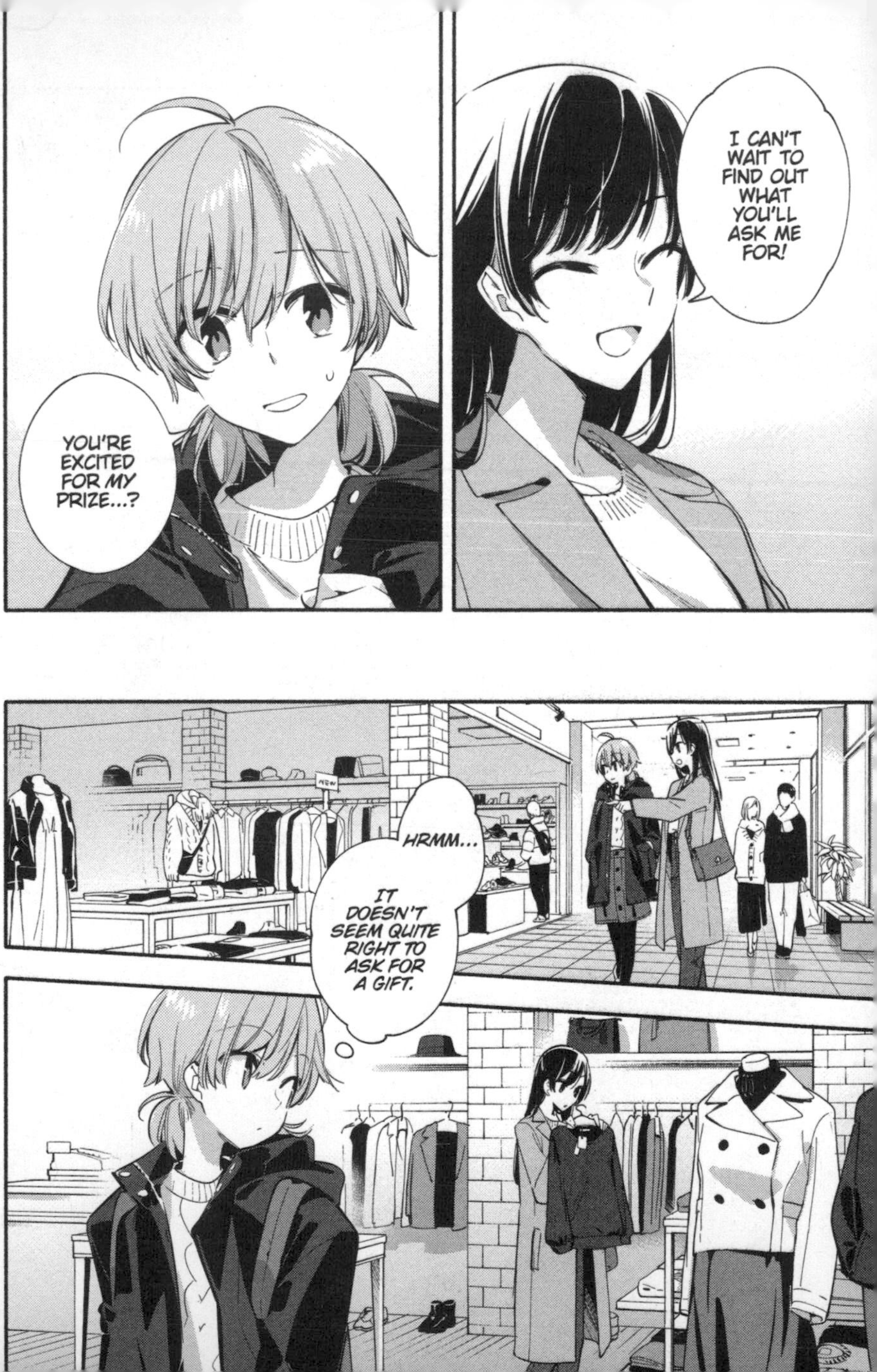
I CAN'T WAIT TO FIND OUT WHAT YOU'LL ASK ME FOR!
YOU'RE EXCITED FOR MY PRIZE...?
HRMM...
IT DOESN'T SEEM QUITE RIGHT TO ASK FOR A GIFT.

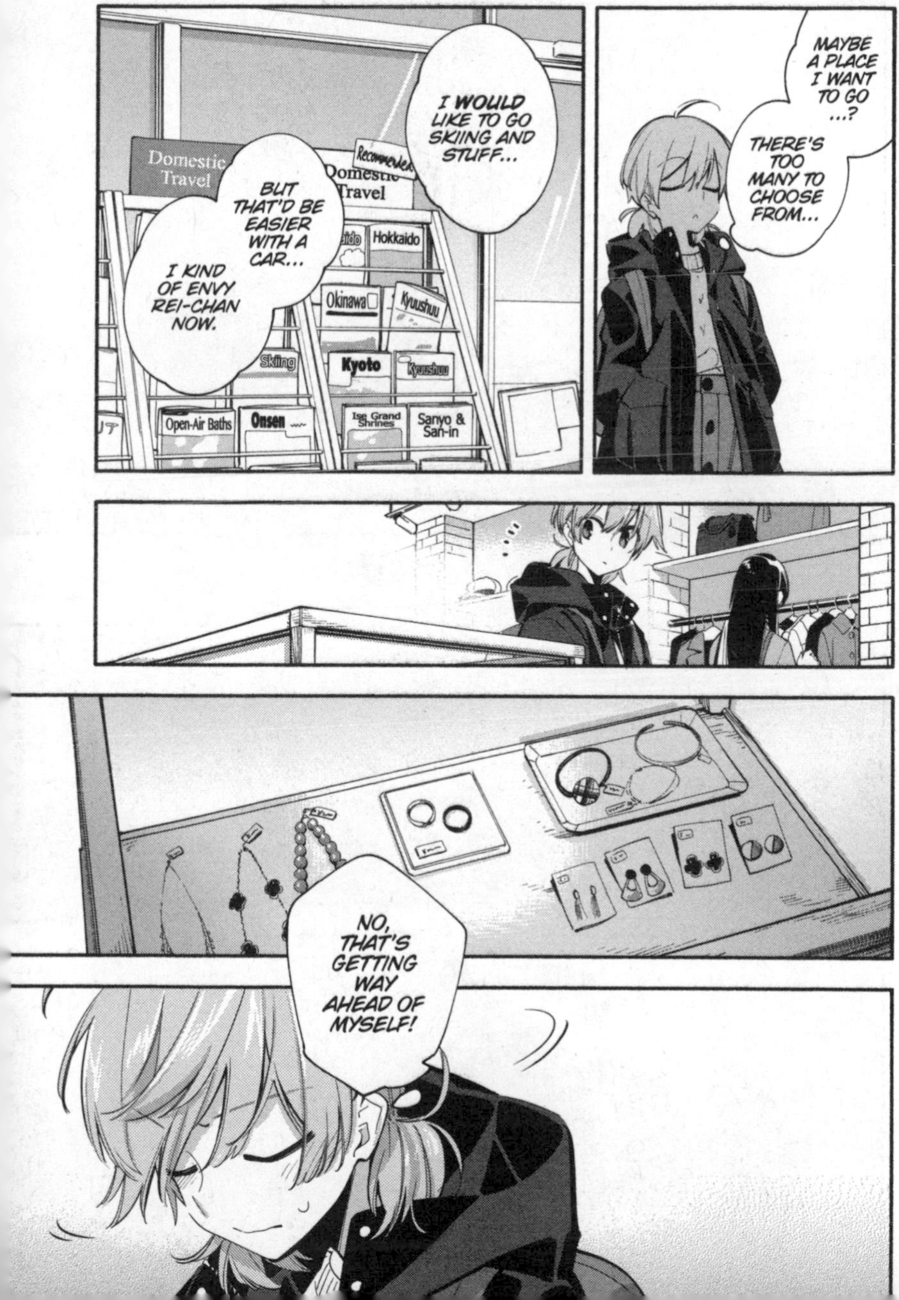
MAYBE A PLACE I WANT TO GO ...?
THERE'S TOO MANY TO CHOOSE FROM...
I WOULD LIKE TO GO SKIING AND STUFF...
BUT THAT'D BE EASIER WITH A CAR...
I KIND OF ENVY REI-CHAN NOW.
Recommended
Domestic Travel
Domestic Travel
Hokkaido
Okinawa
Kyuushuu
Skiing
Kyoto
Kyuushuu
Open-Air Baths
Onsen
Ise Grand Shrines
Sanyo & San-in
NO, THAT'S GETTING WAY AHEAD OF MYSELF!

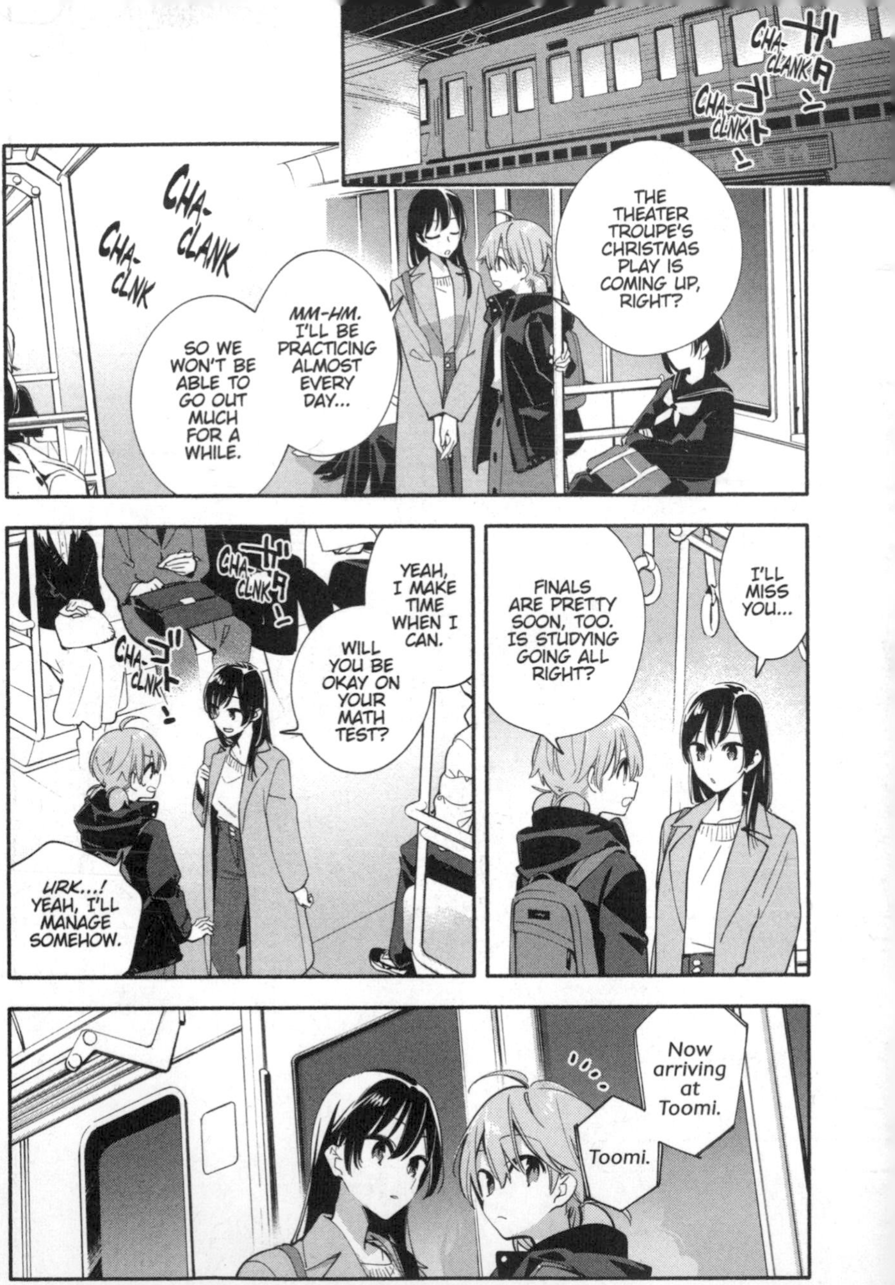
CHA-CLANK
ガタン
CHA-CLNK
ゴトン
THE THEATER TROUPE'S CHRISTMAS PLAY IS COMING UP, RIGHT?
MM-HM. I'LL BE PRACTICING ALMOST EVERY DAY...
SO WE WON'T BE ABLE TO GO OUT MUCH FOR A WHILE.
CHA-CLANK
CHA-CLNK
I'LL MISS YOU...
FINALS ARE PRETTY SOON, TOO. IS STUDYING GOING ALL RIGHT?
YEAH, I MAKE TIME WHEN I CAN.
CHA-CLNK
ガタン
WILL YOU BE OKAY ON YOUR MATH TEST?
CHA-CLNK
ゴトン
URK...! YEAH, I'LL MANAGE SOMEHOW.
Now arriving at Toomi.
Toomi.

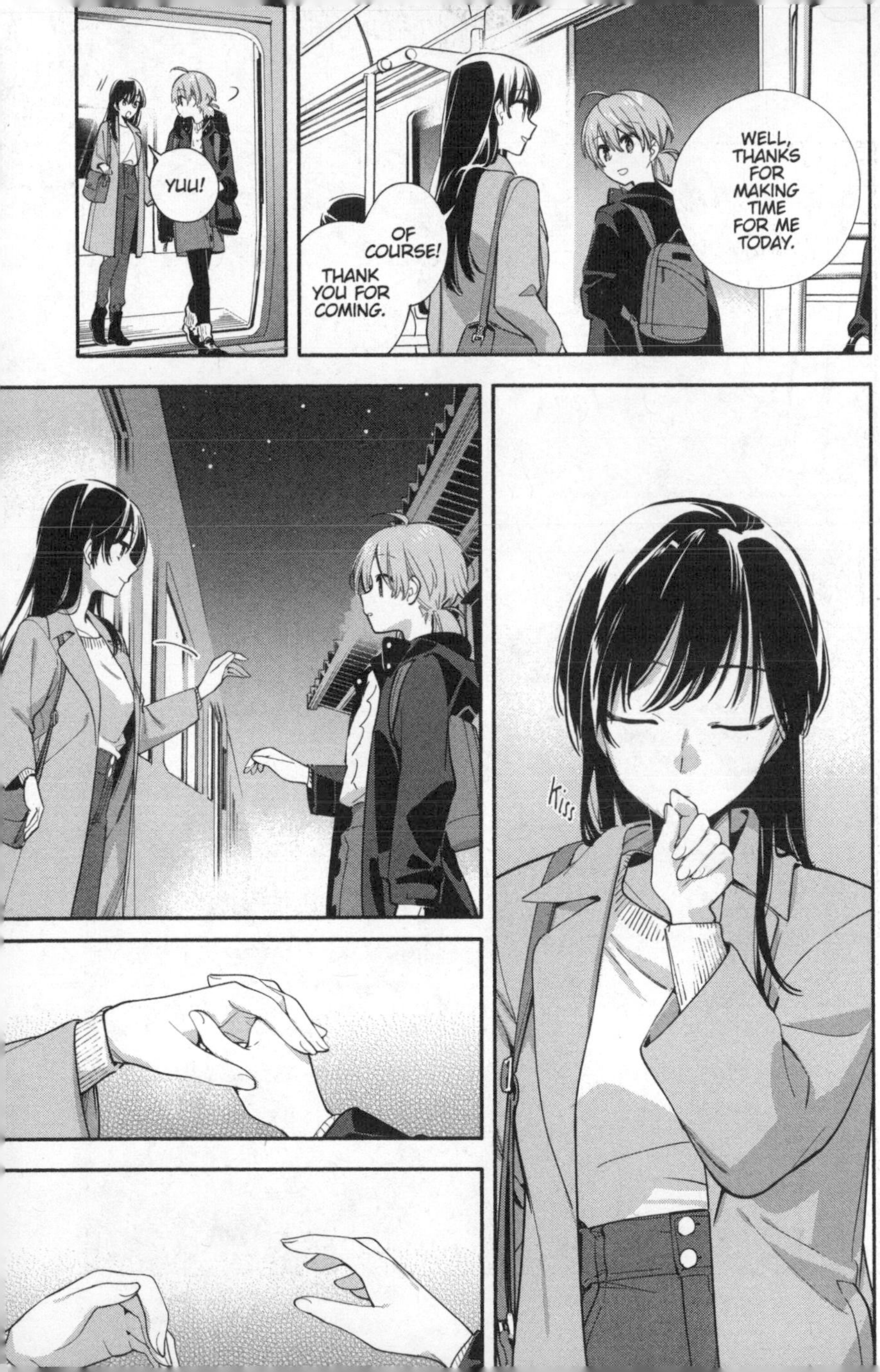
WELL, THANKS FOR MAKING TIME FOR ME TODAY.
OF COURSE!
THANK YOU FOR COMING.
YUU!
Kiss

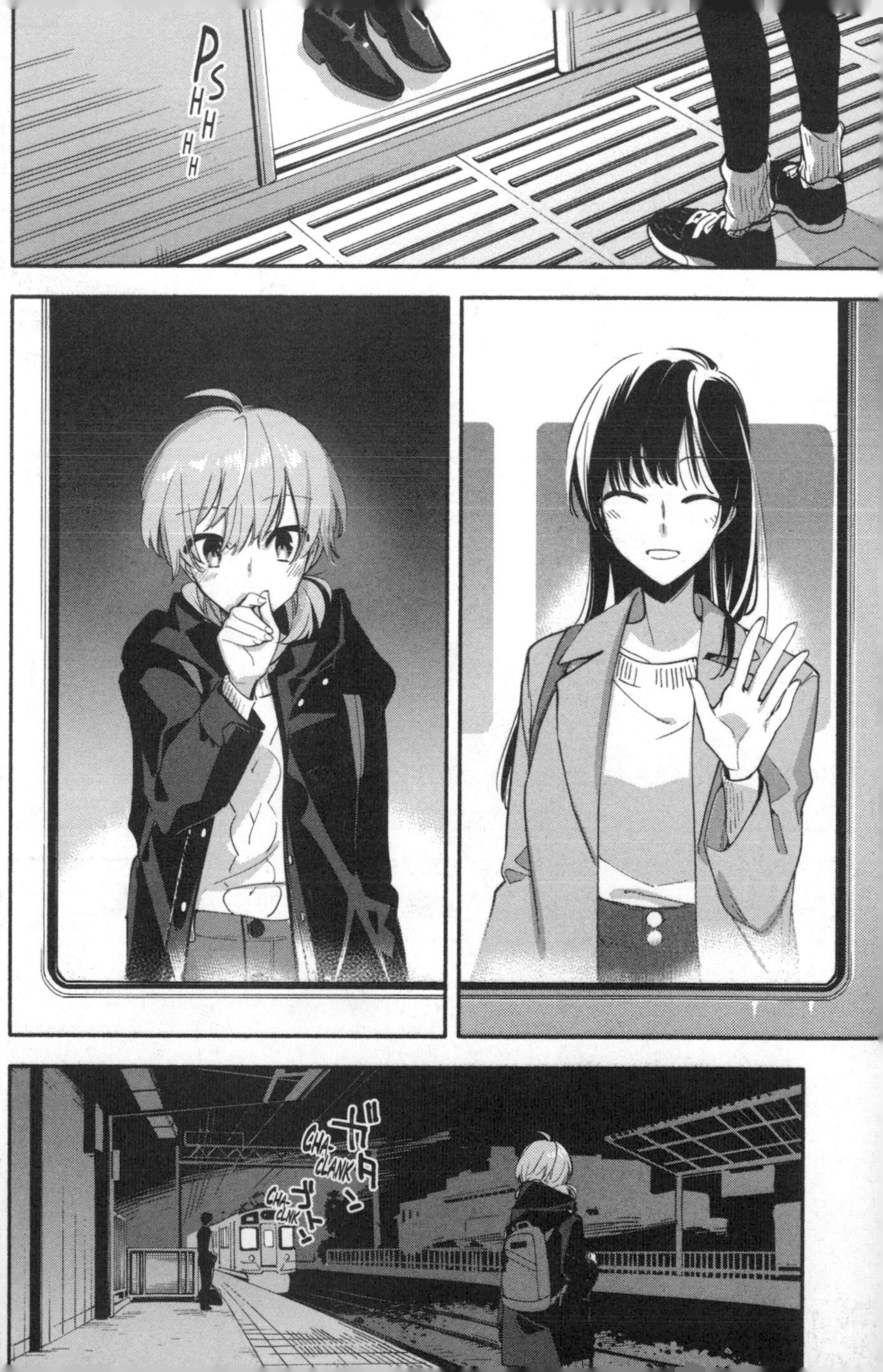
PSHHHH
CHA-CLANK
CHA-CLNK

CHATTER
CHATTER
CHATTER

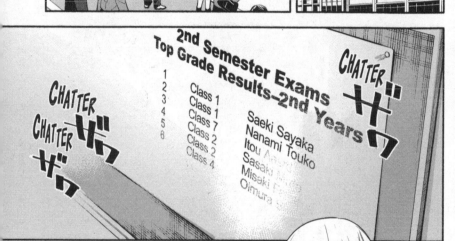

CHATTER

2nd Semester Exams
Top Grade Results–2nd Years

1	Class 1	
2	Class 1	Saeki Sayaka
3	Class 7	Nanami Touko
4	Class 2	Itou Akari
5	Class 2	Sasaki Mio
6	Class 4	Misaki Fen
		Oimura

CHATTER

CHATTER

CHATTER "ズ

......!

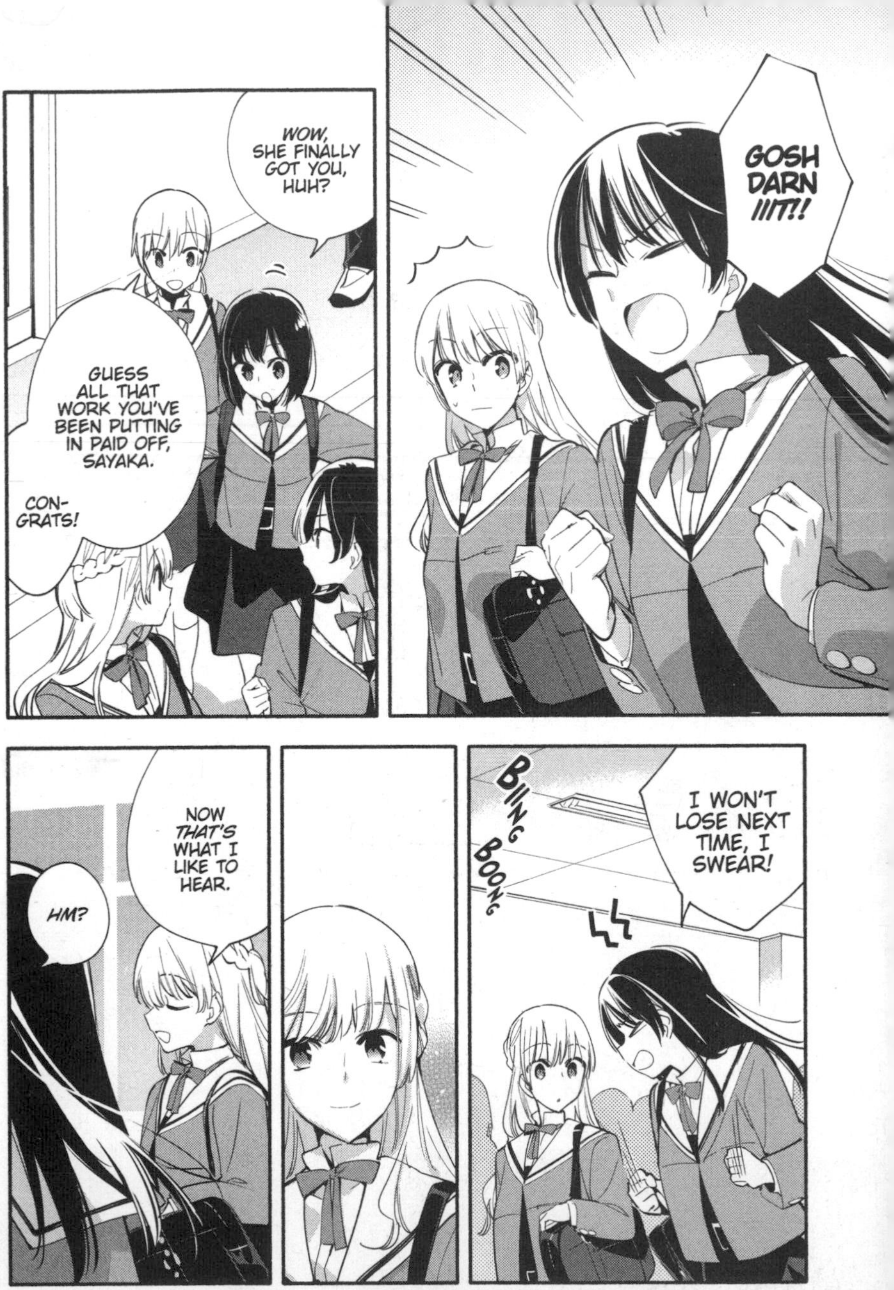
GOSH DARN IIIT!!
WOW, SHE FINALLY GOT YOU, HUH?
GUESS ALL THAT WORK YOU'VE BEEN PUTTING IN PAID OFF, SAYAKA.
CON-GRATS!
BIING BOONG
I WON'T LOSE NEXT TIME, I SWEAR!
NOW THAT'S WHAT I LIKE TO HEAR.
HM?

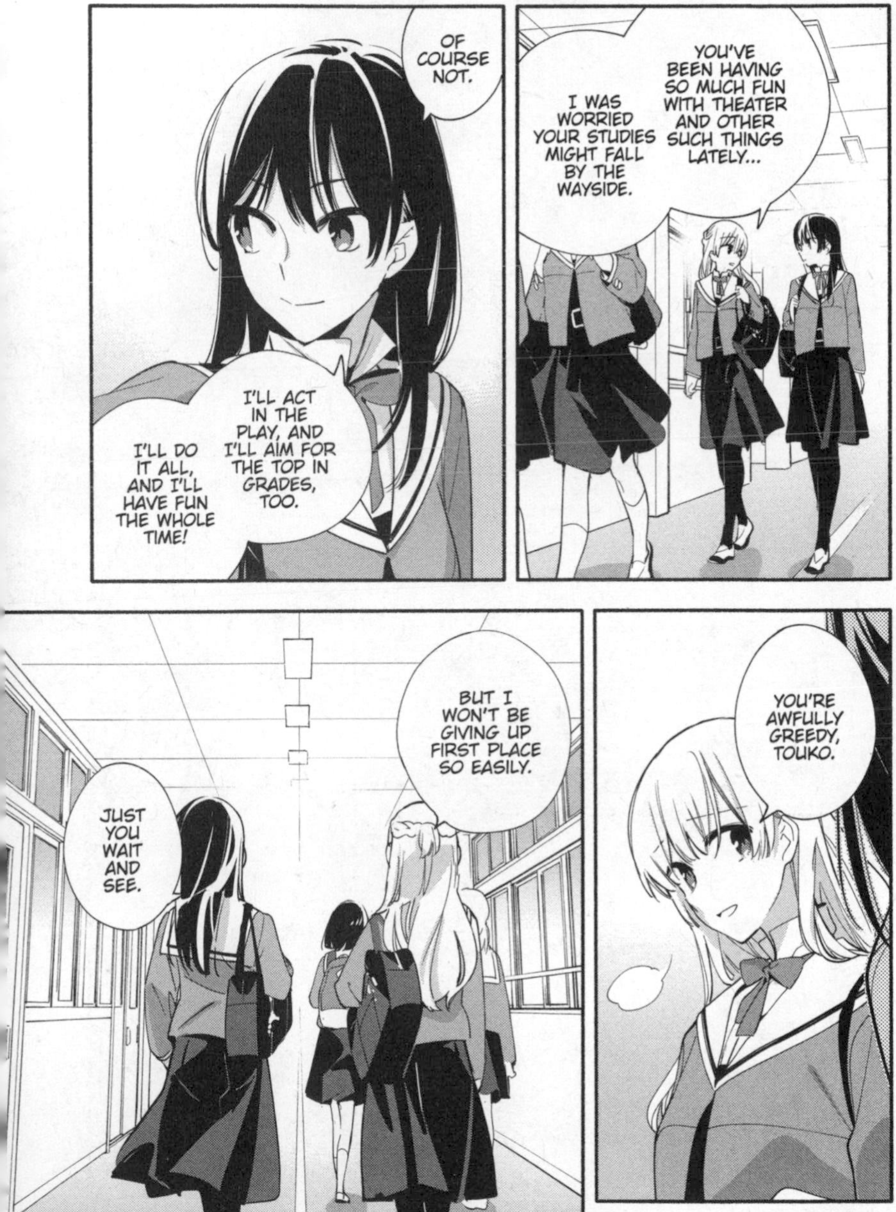
YOU'VE BEEN HAVING SO MUCH FUN WITH THEATER AND OTHER SUCH THINGS LATELY...
I WAS WORRIED YOUR STUDIES MIGHT FALL BY THE WAYSIDE.
OF COURSE NOT.
I'LL ACT IN THE PLAY, AND I'LL AIM FOR THE TOP IN GRADES, TOO.
I'LL DO IT ALL, AND I'LL HAVE FUN THE WHOLE TIME!
YOU'RE AWFULLY GREEDY, TOUKO.
BUT I WON'T BE GIVING UP FIRST PLACE SO EASILY.
JUST YOU WAIT AND SEE.

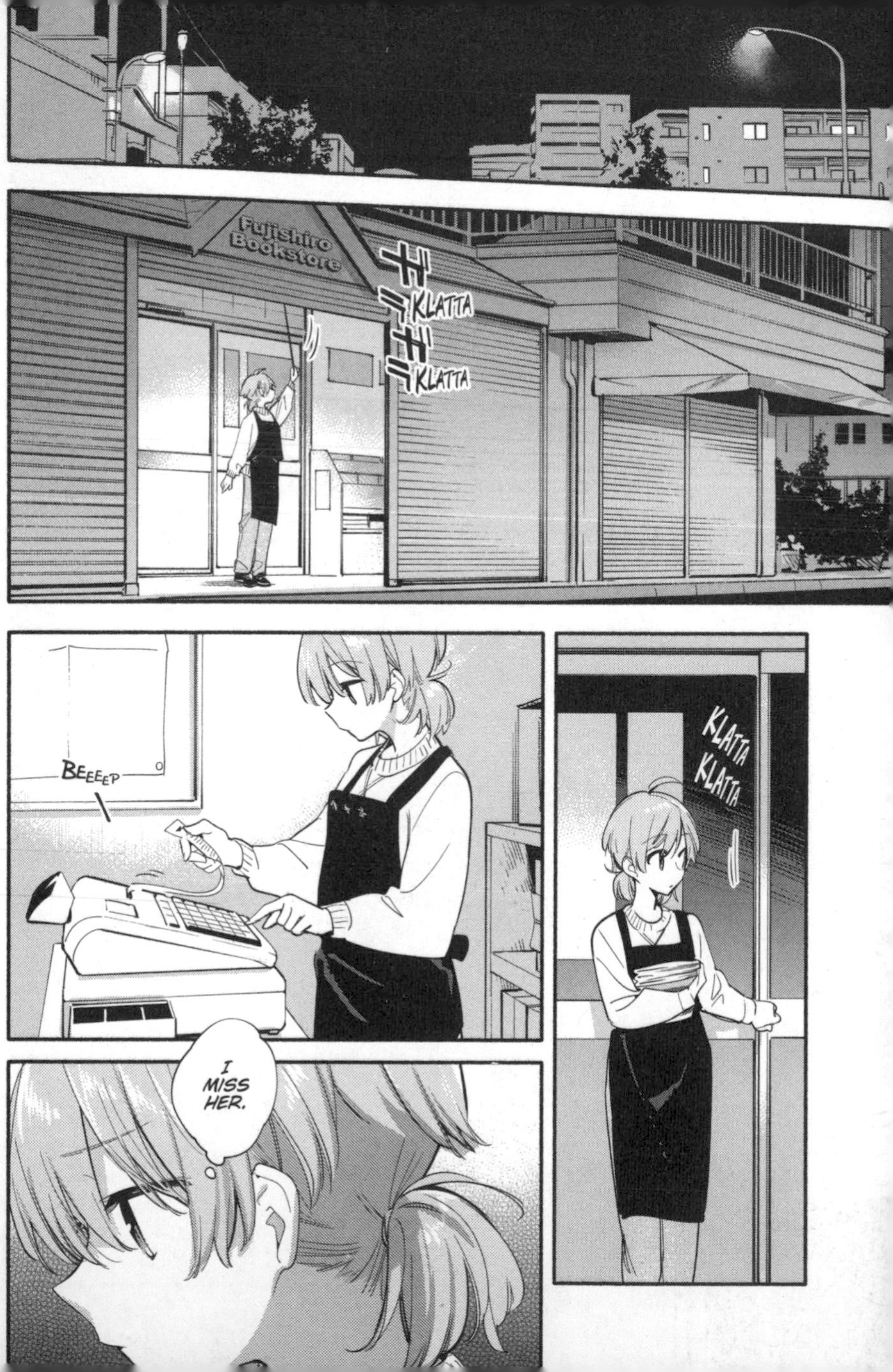
Fujishiro Bookstore
KLATTA
KLATTA
KLATTA KLATTA
BEEEEP
I MISS HER.

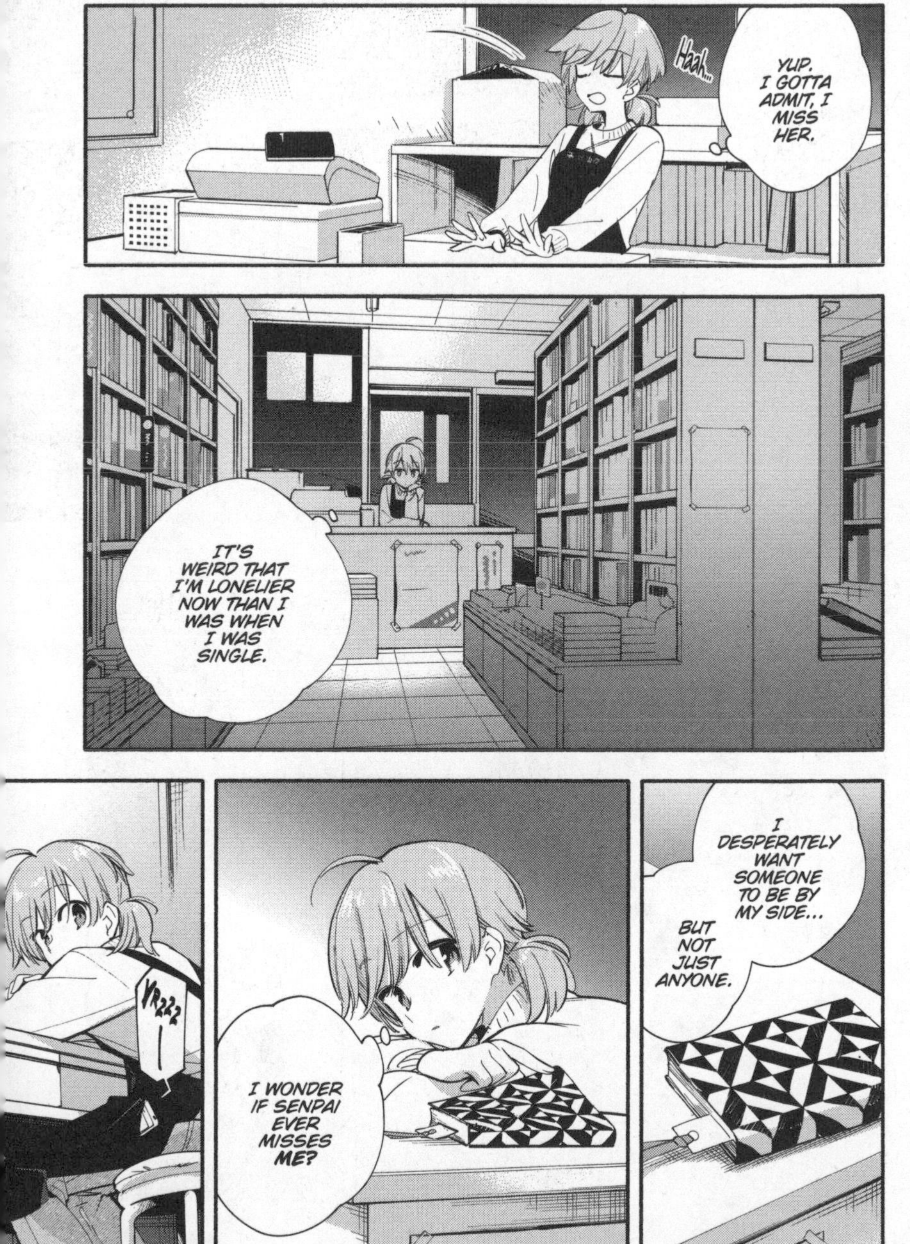
YUP. I GOTTA ADMIT, I MISS HER.
Haah...
IT'S WEIRD THAT I'M LONELIER NOW THAN I WAS WHEN I WAS SINGLE.
I DESPERATELY WANT SOMEONE TO BE BY MY SIDE...
BUT NOT JUST ANYONE.
I WONDER IF SENPAI EVER MISSES ME?
VRzzz

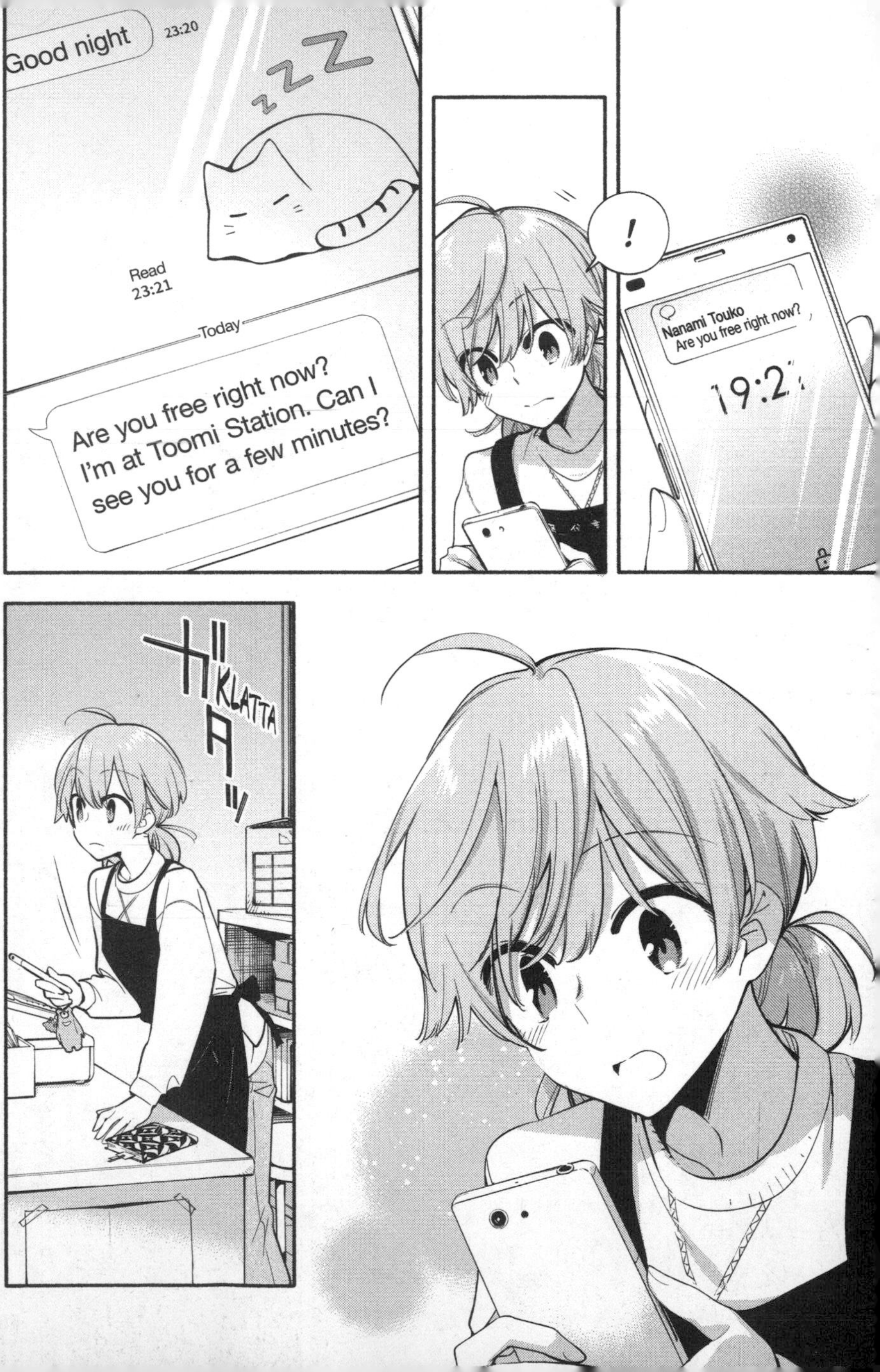

Nanami Touko
Are you free right now?
19:2
!
Good night
23:20
Read
23:21
Today
Are you free right now? I'm at Toomi Station. Can I see you for a few minutes?
KLATTA

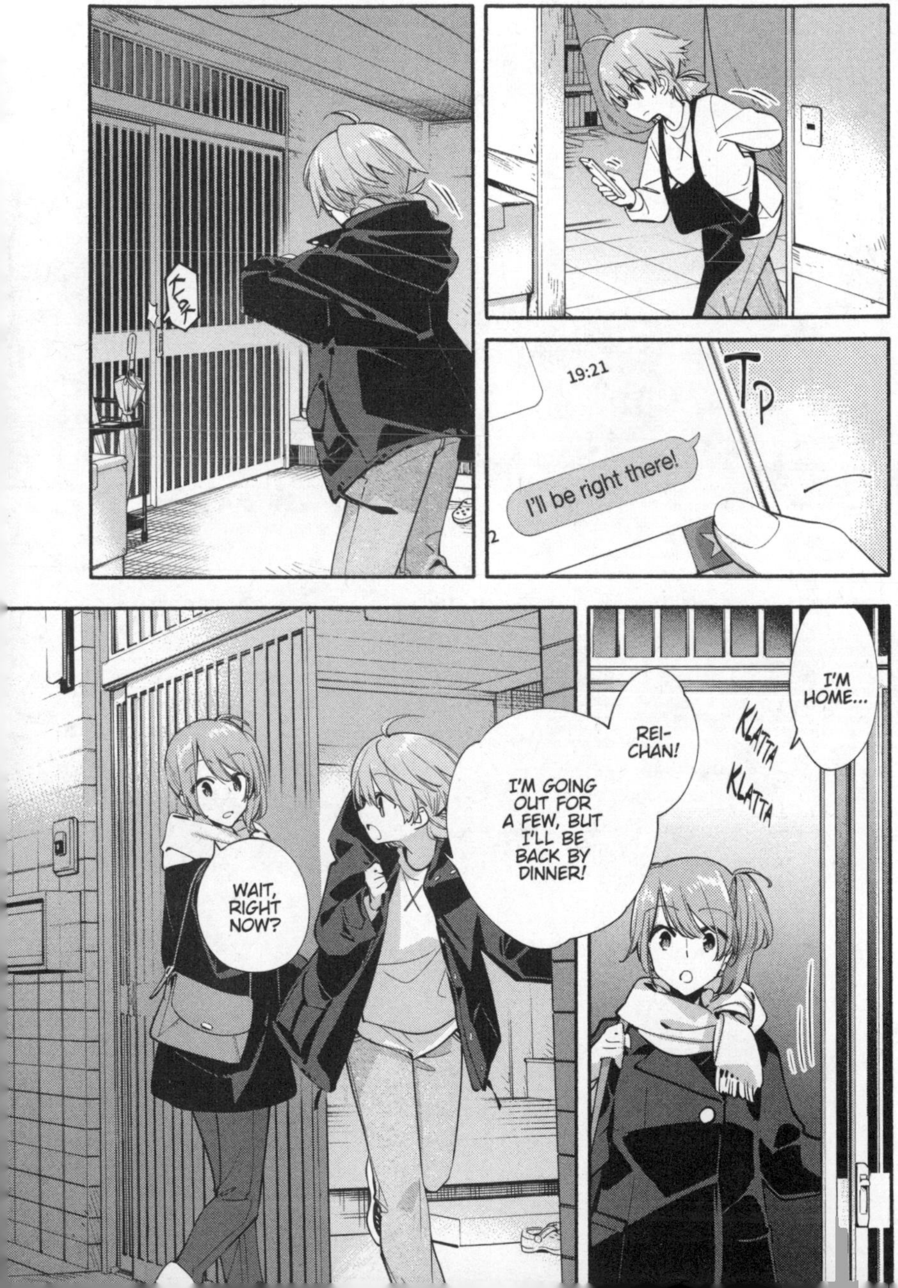
19:21
TP
I'll be right there!
KLAK
I'M HOME...
KLATTA KLATTA
REI-CHAN!
I'M GOING OUT FOR A FEW, BUT I'LL BE BACK BY DINNER!
WAIT, RIGHT NOW?

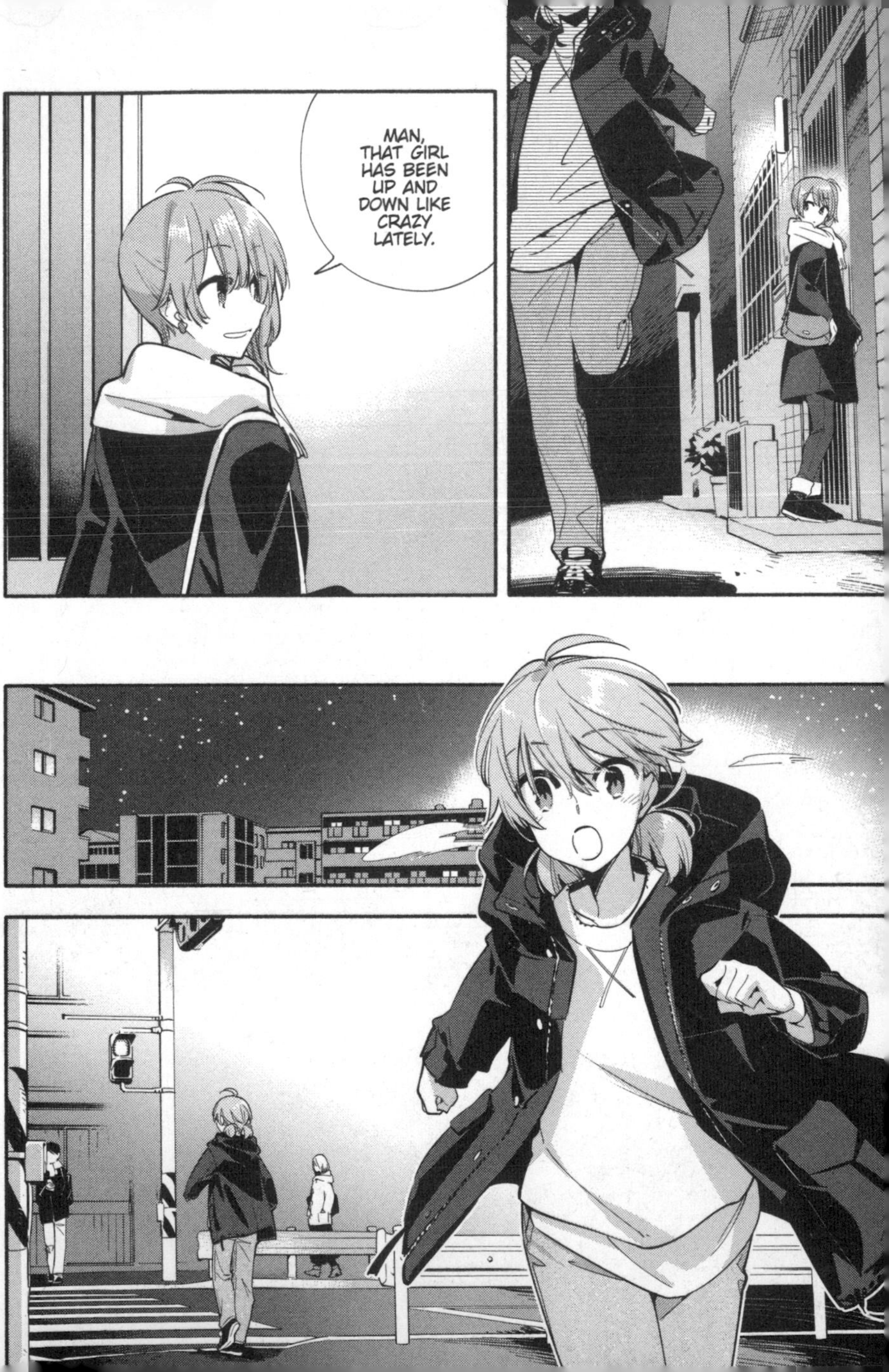
MAN, THAT GIRL HAS BEEN UP AND DOWN LIKE CRAZY LATELY.

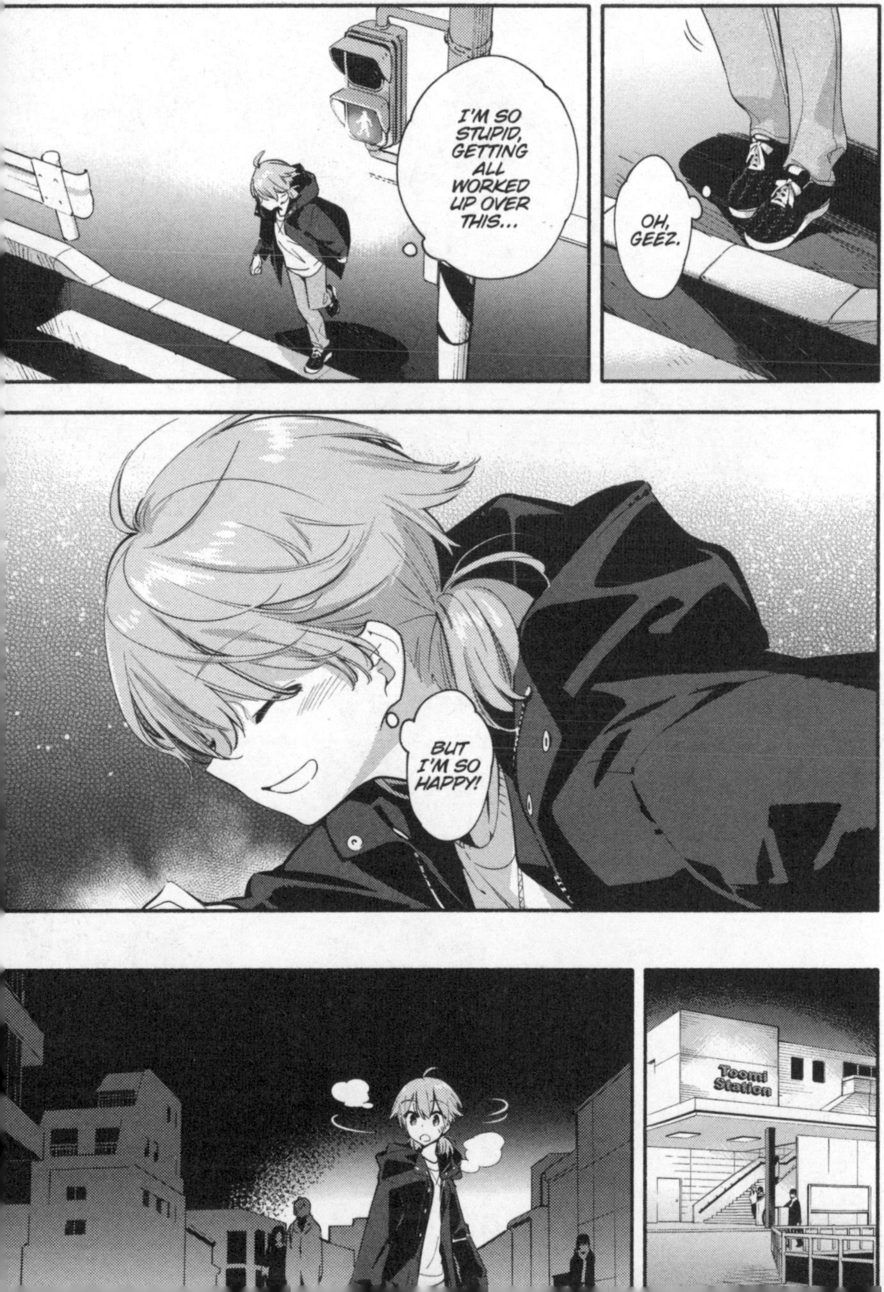
OH, GEEZ.
I'M SO STUPID, GETTING ALL WORKED UP OVER THIS...
BUT I'M SO HAPPY!
Toomi Station

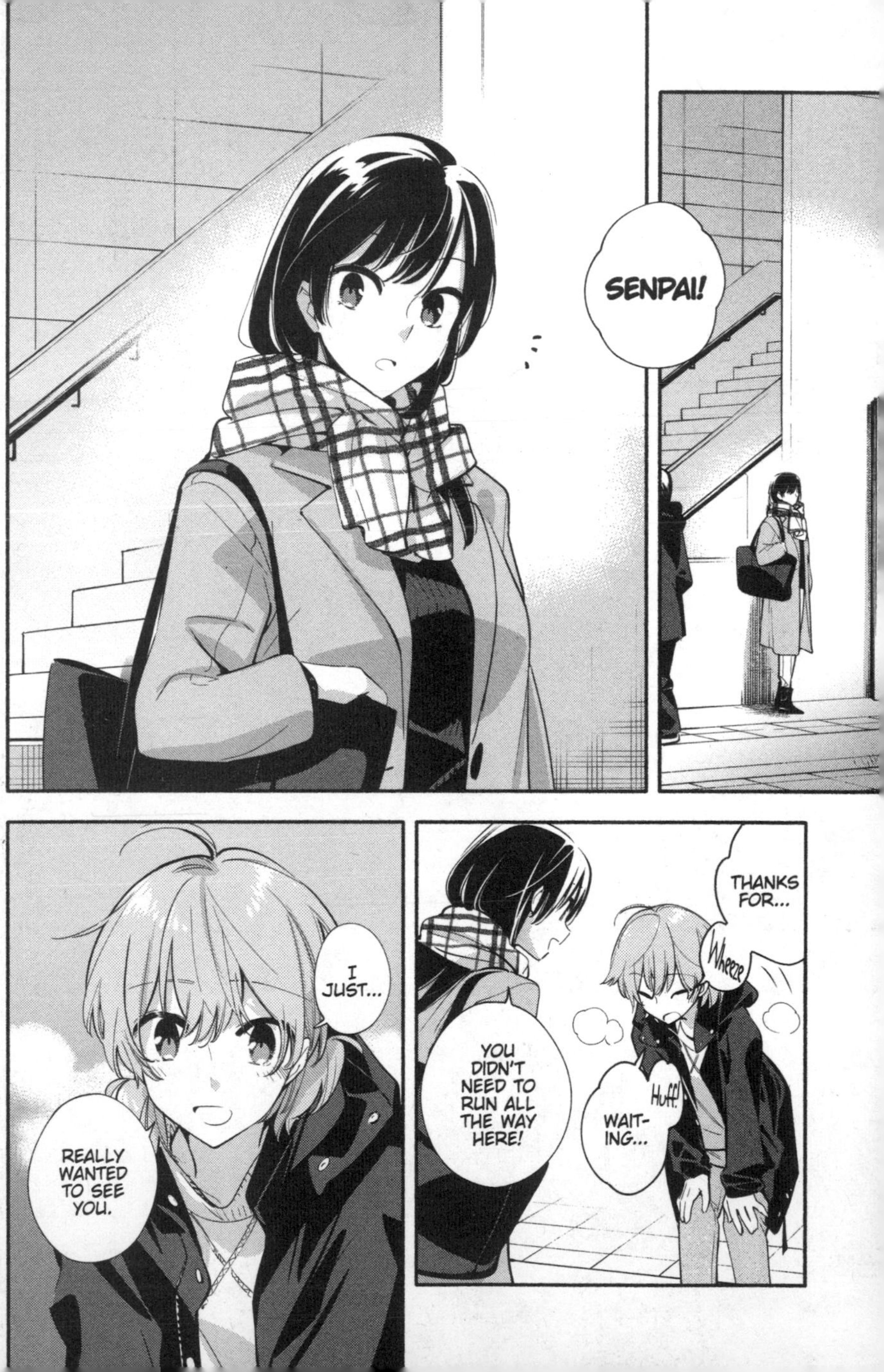
SENPAI!
THANKS FOR...
Wheeze
Huff!
WAIT-ING...
YOU DIDN'T NEED TO RUN ALL THE WAY HERE!
I JUST...
REALLY WANTED TO SEE YOU.

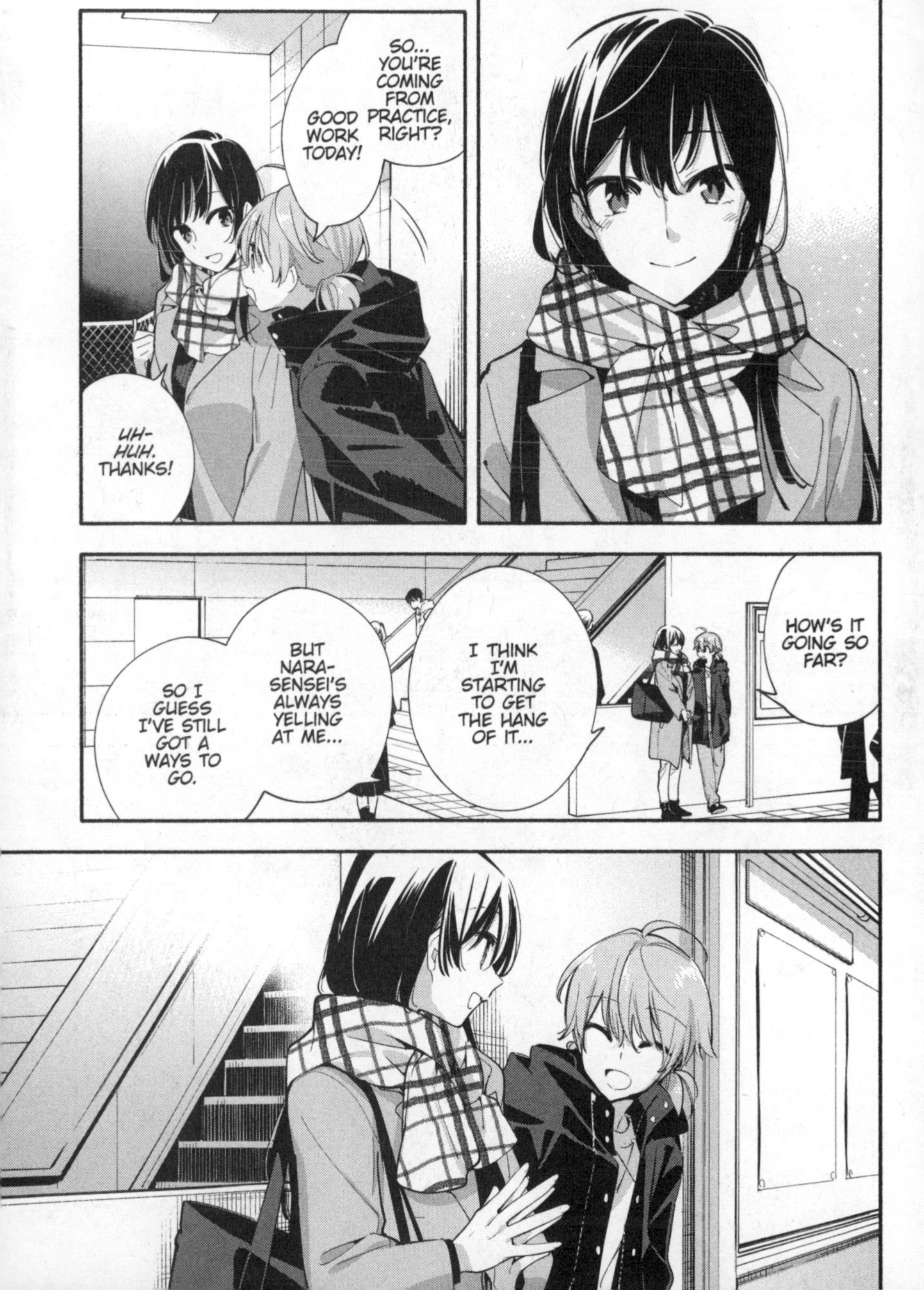
SO... YOU'RE COMING FROM PRACTICE, RIGHT?
GOOD WORK TODAY!
UH-HUH. THANKS!
HOW'S IT GOING SO FAR?
I THINK I'M STARTING TO GET THE HANG OF IT...
BUT NARA-SENSEI'S ALWAYS YELLING AT ME...
SO I GUESS I'VE STILL GOT A WAYS TO GO.

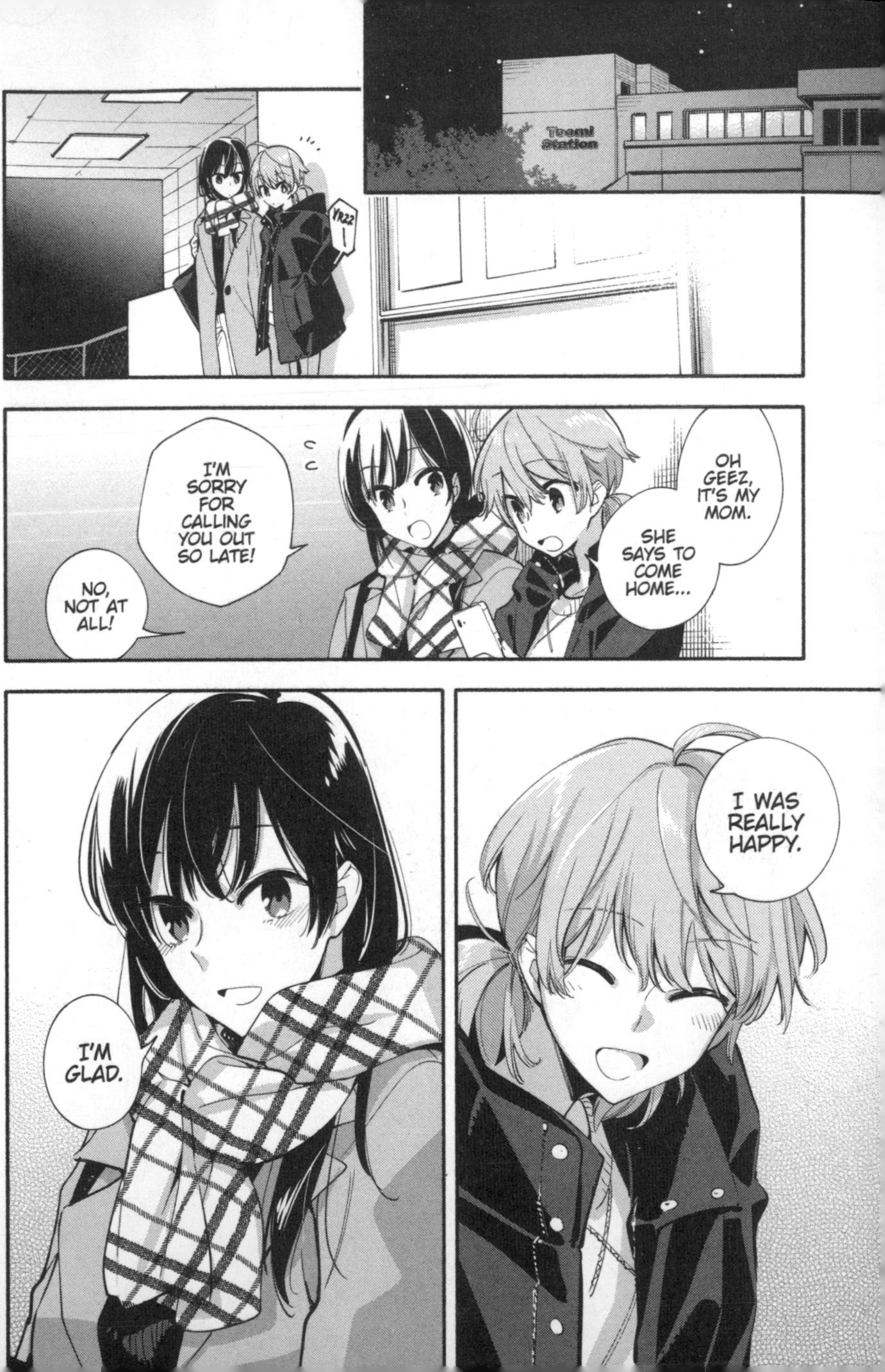
Toomi Station
YRZZ
OH GEEZ, IT'S MY MOM.
SHE SAYS TO COME HOME...
I'M SORRY FOR CALLING YOU OUT SO LATE!
NO, NOT AT ALL!
I WAS REALLY HAPPY.
I'M GLAD.

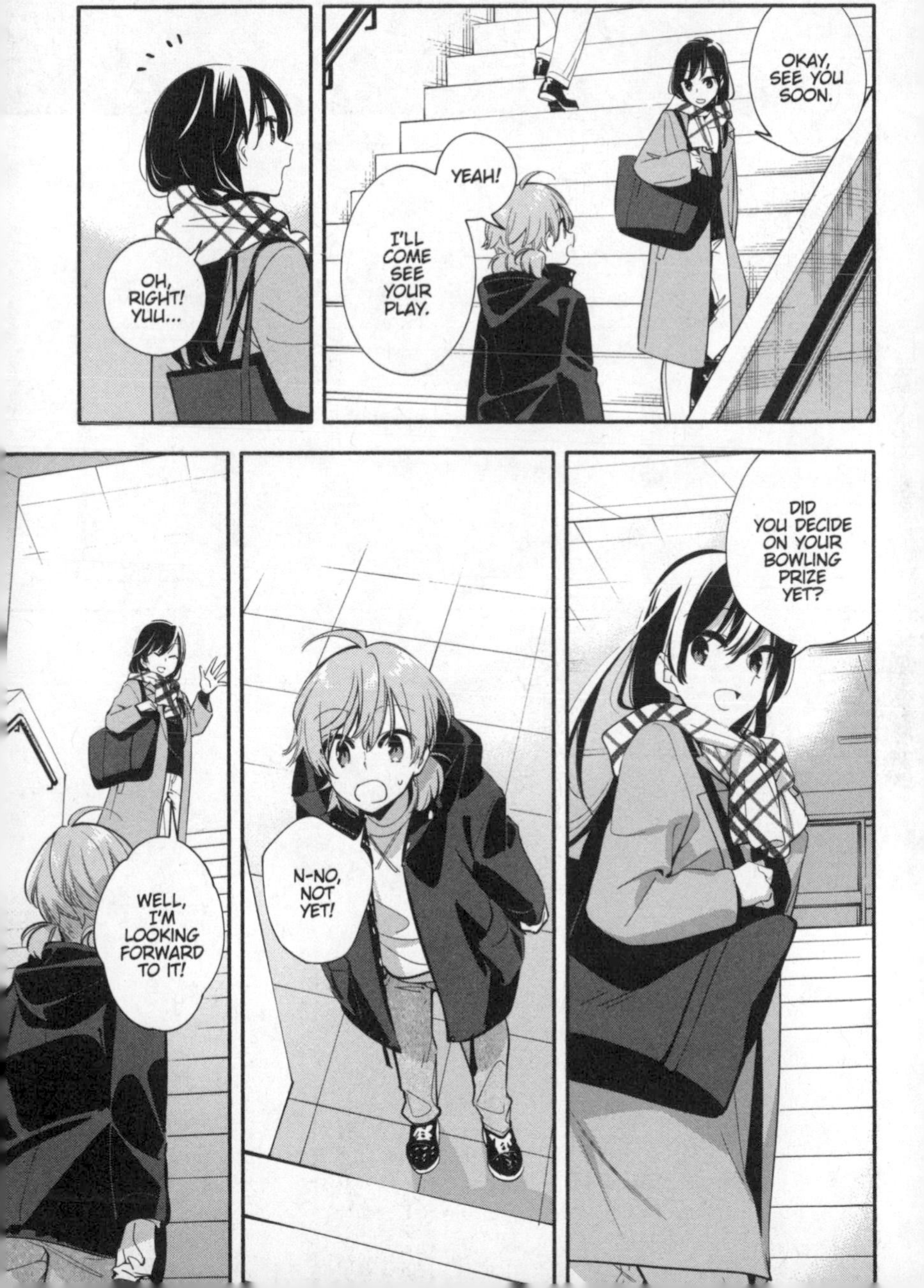
OKAY, SEE YOU SOON.
YEAH!
I'LL COME SEE YOUR PLAY.
OH, RIGHT! YUU...
DID YOU DECIDE ON YOUR BOWLING PRIZE YET?
N-NO, NOT YET!
WELL, I'M LOOKING FORWARD TO IT!

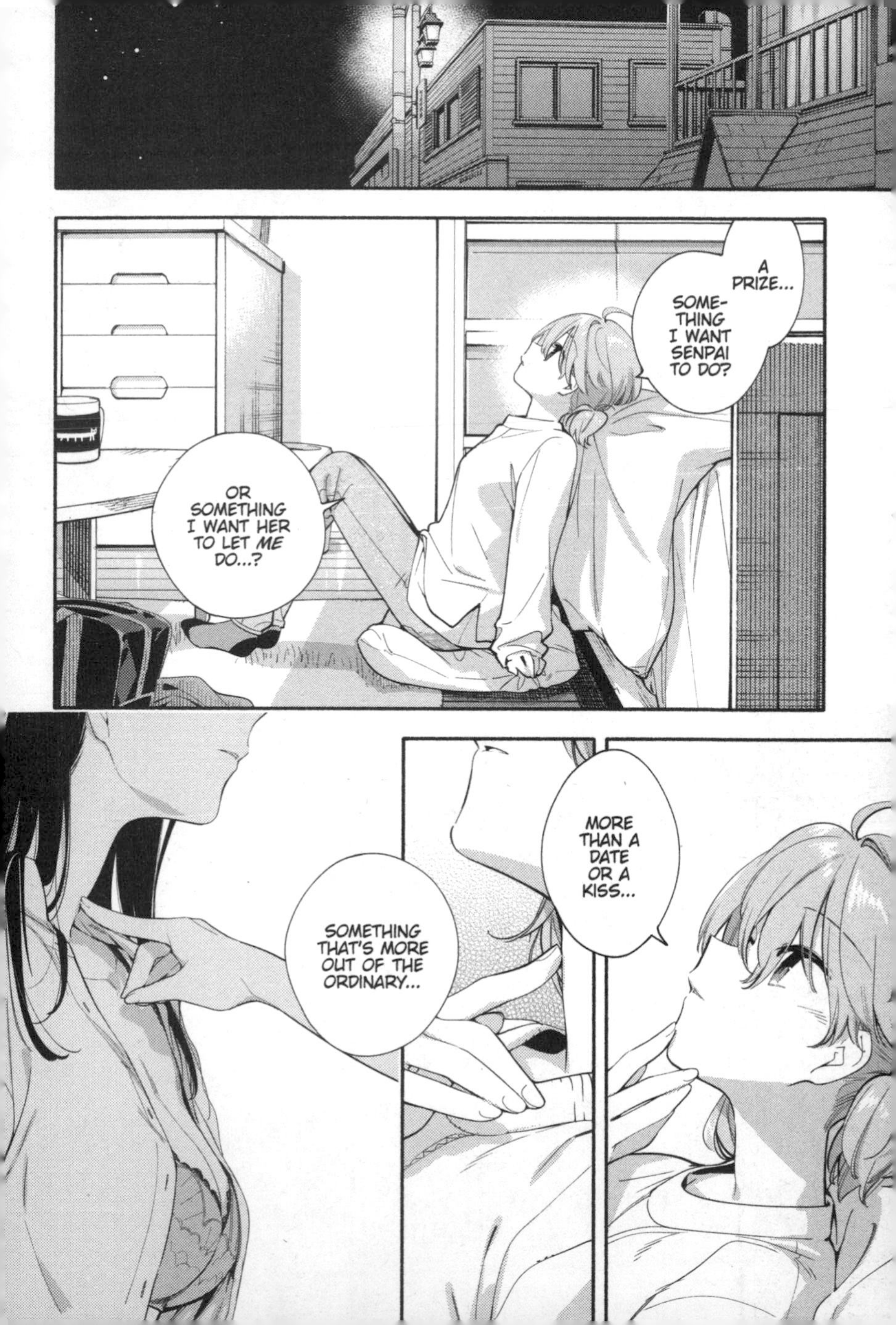
A PRIZE... SOMETHING I WANT SENPAI TO DO?
OR SOMETHING I WANT HER TO LET *ME* DO...?
MORE THAN A DATE OR A KISS...
SOMETHING THAT'S MORE OUT OF THE ORDINARY...

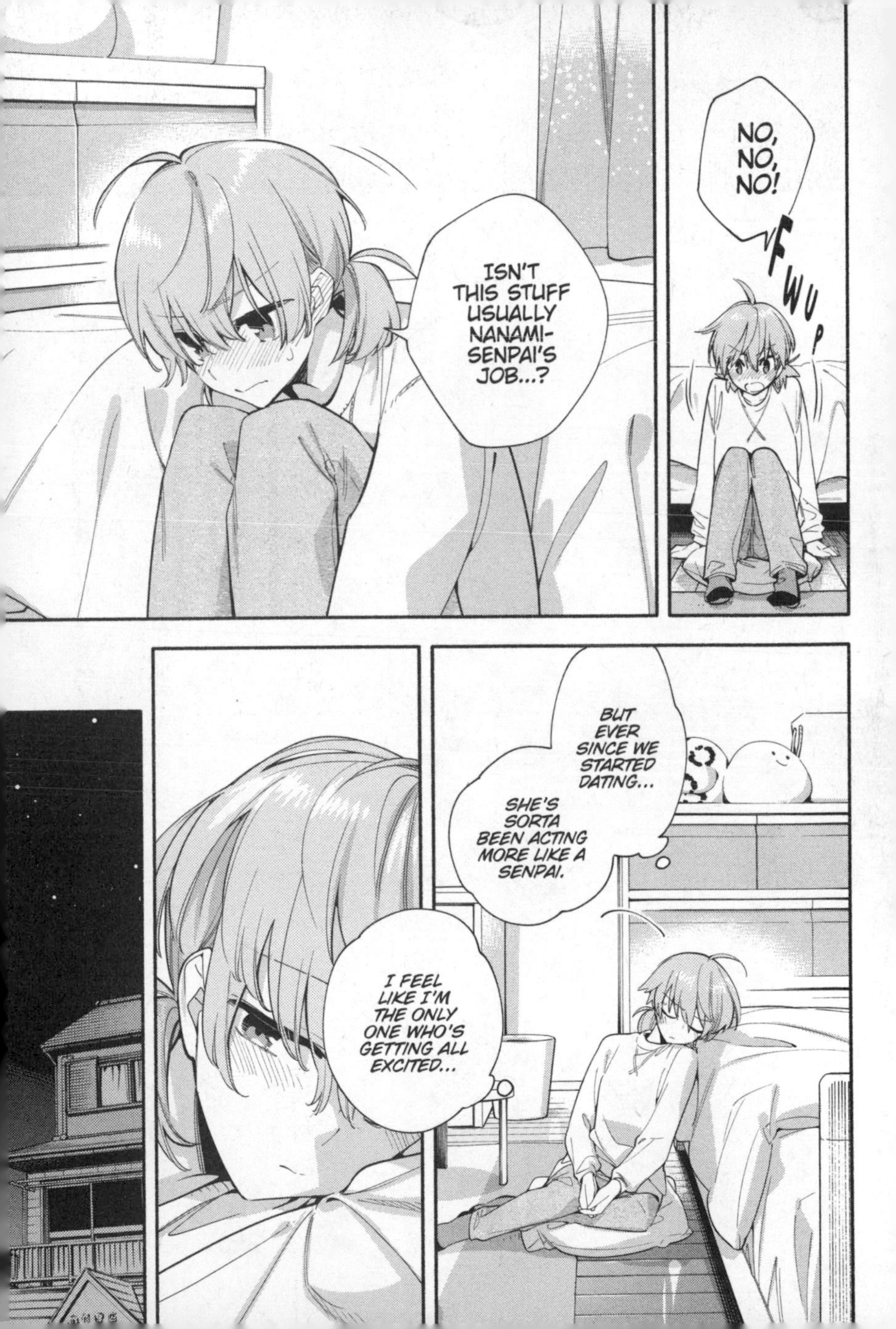
NO, NO, NO!
FWUP
ISN'T THIS STUFF USUALLY NANAMI-SENPAI'S JOB...?
BUT EVER SINCE WE STARTED DATING...
SHE'S SORTA BEEN ACTING MORE LIKE A SENPAI.
I FEEL LIKE I'M THE ONLY ONE WHO'S GETTING ALL EXCITED...

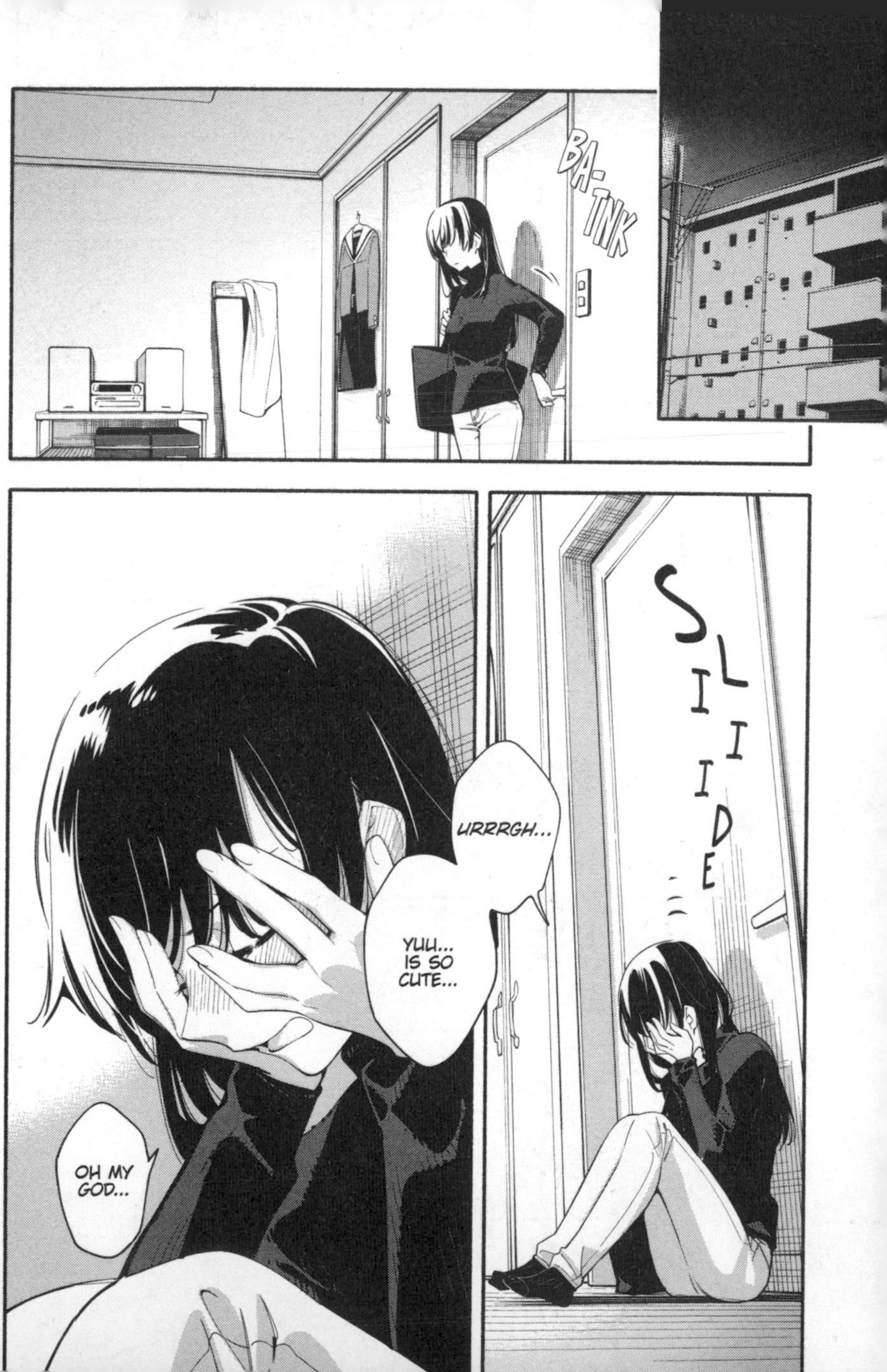
BA-TNK
SLIIIDE
URRRGH...
YUU... IS SO CUTE...
OH MY GOD...

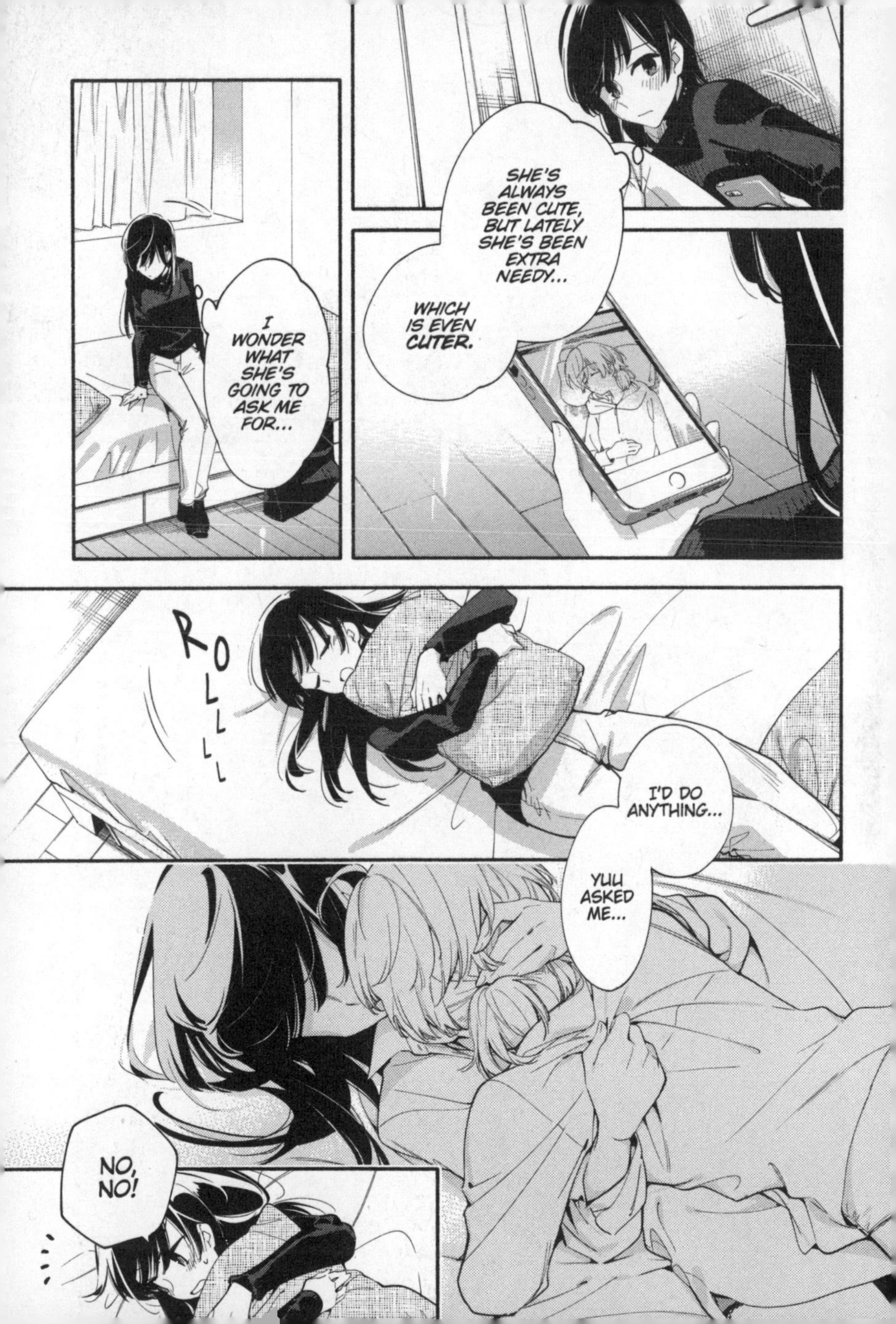
SHE'S ALWAYS BEEN CUTE, BUT LATELY SHE'S BEEN EXTRA NEEDY...
WHICH IS EVEN CUTER.
I WONDER WHAT SHE'S GOING TO ASK ME FOR...
ROLLLL
I'D DO ANYTHING...
YUU ASKED ME...
NO, NO!

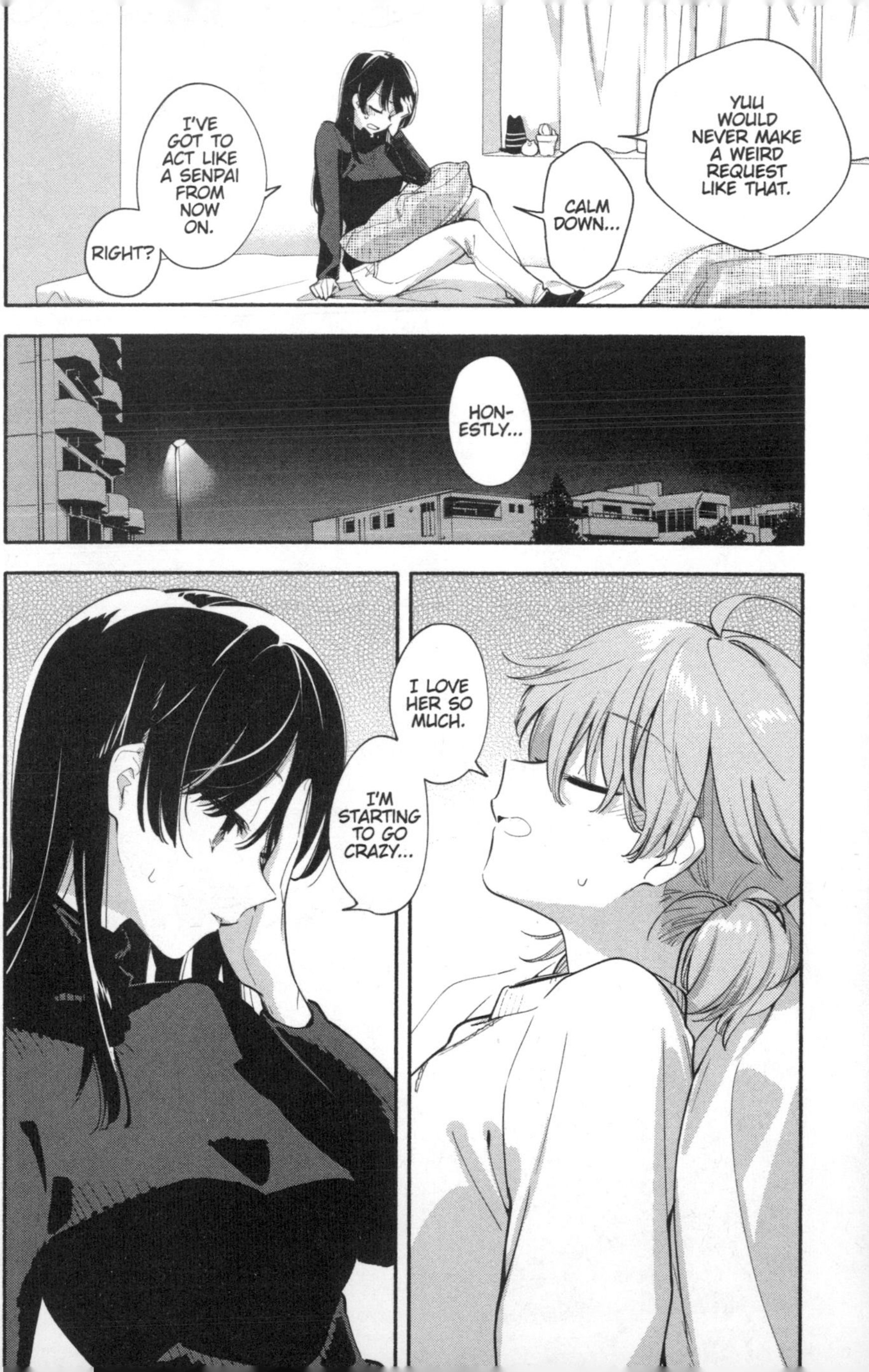
YUU WOULD NEVER MAKE A WEIRD REQUEST LIKE THAT.
CALM DOWN...
I'VE GOT TO ACT LIKE A SENPAI FROM NOW ON.
RIGHT?
HON-ESTLY...
I LOVE HER SO MUCH.
I'M STARTING TO GO CRAZY...

WE'RE ALWAYS WATCHING...

(Bloom Into You)

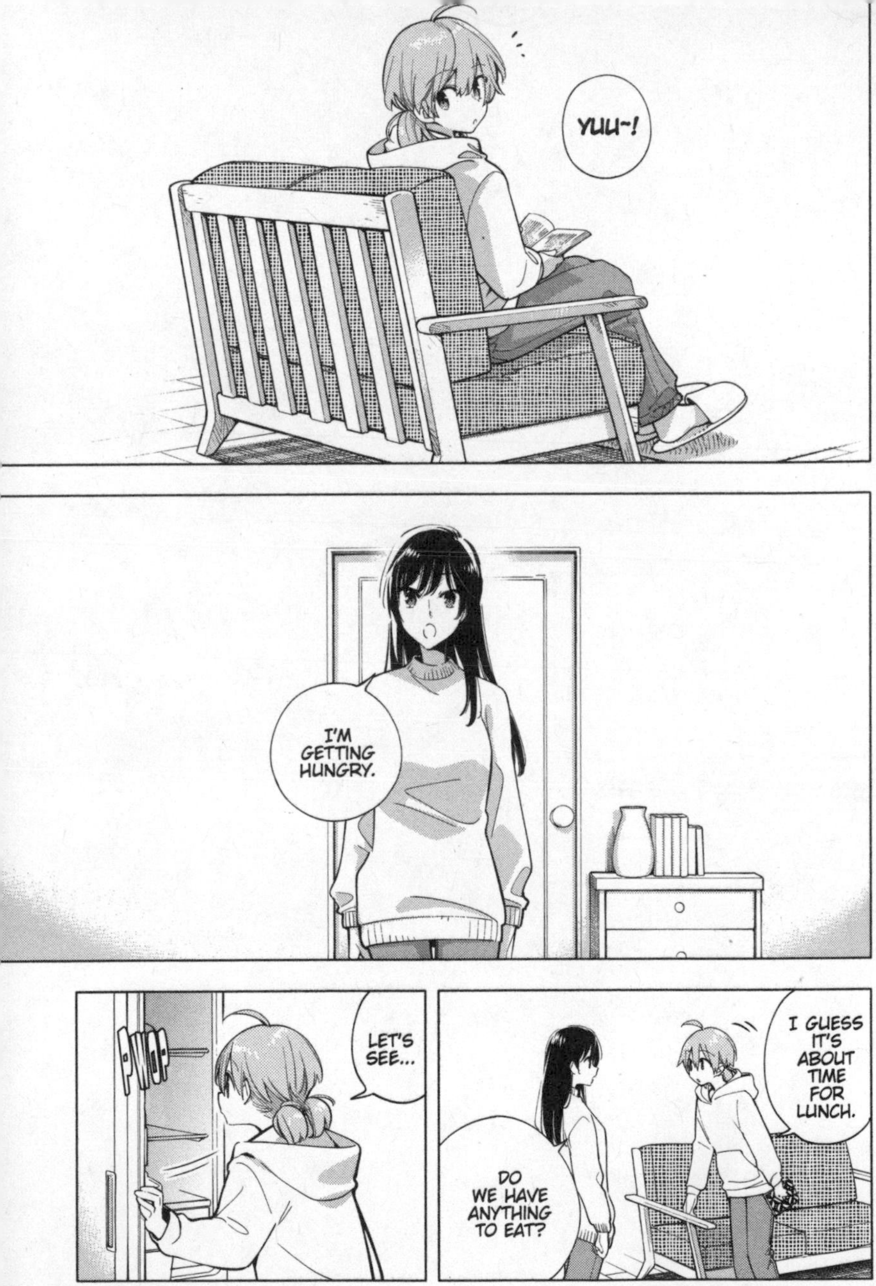
YUU~!
I'M GETTING HUNGRY.
I GUESS IT'S ABOUT TIME FOR LUNCH.
DO WE HAVE ANYTHING TO EAT?
PWOP
LET'S SEE...

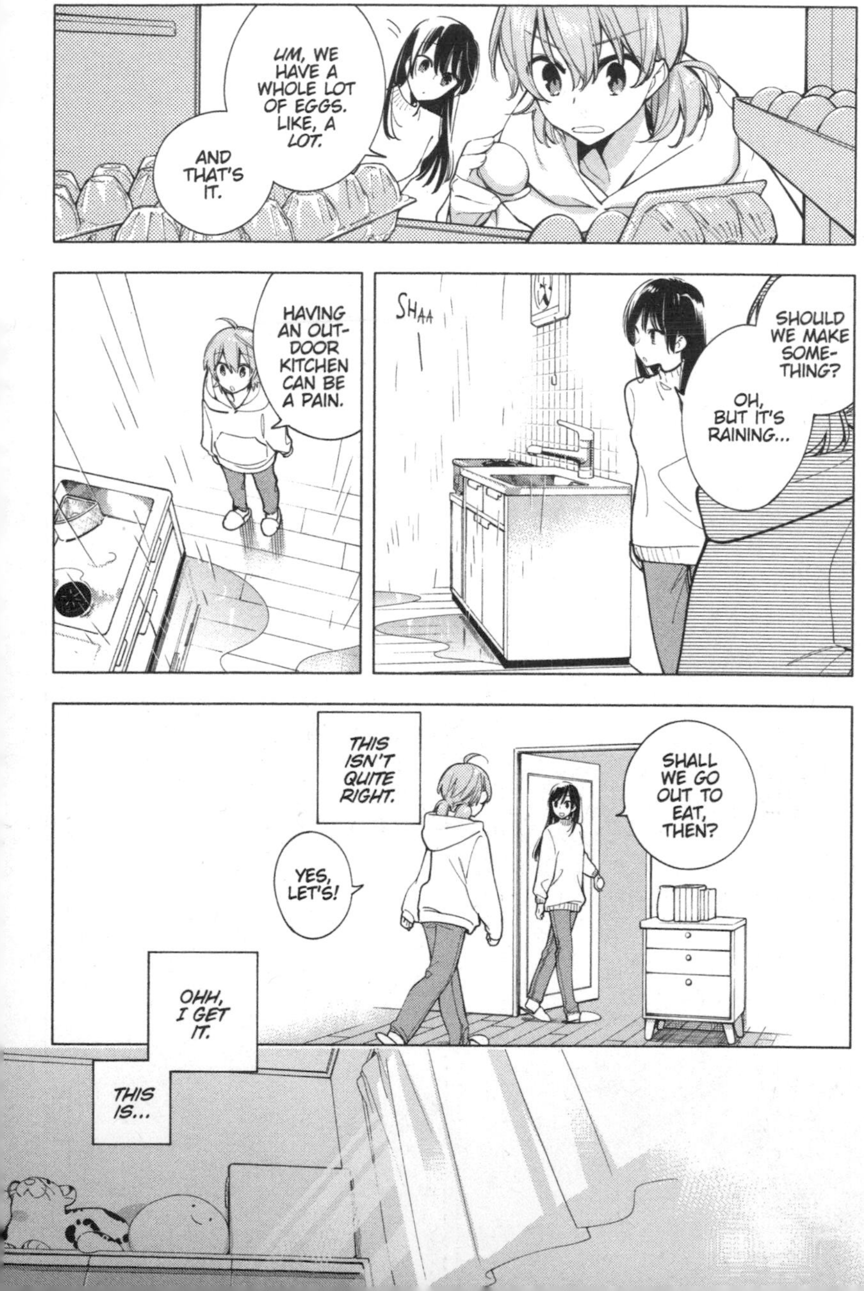
UM, WE HAVE A WHOLE LOT OF EGGS. LIKE, A LOT.
AND THAT'S IT.
SHAA
SHOULD WE MAKE SOMETHING?
OH, BUT IT'S RAINING...
HAVING AN OUT-DOOR KITCHEN CAN BE A PAIN.
SHALL WE GO OUT TO EAT, THEN?
THIS ISN'T QUITE RIGHT.
YES, LET'S!
OHH, I GET IT.
THIS IS...

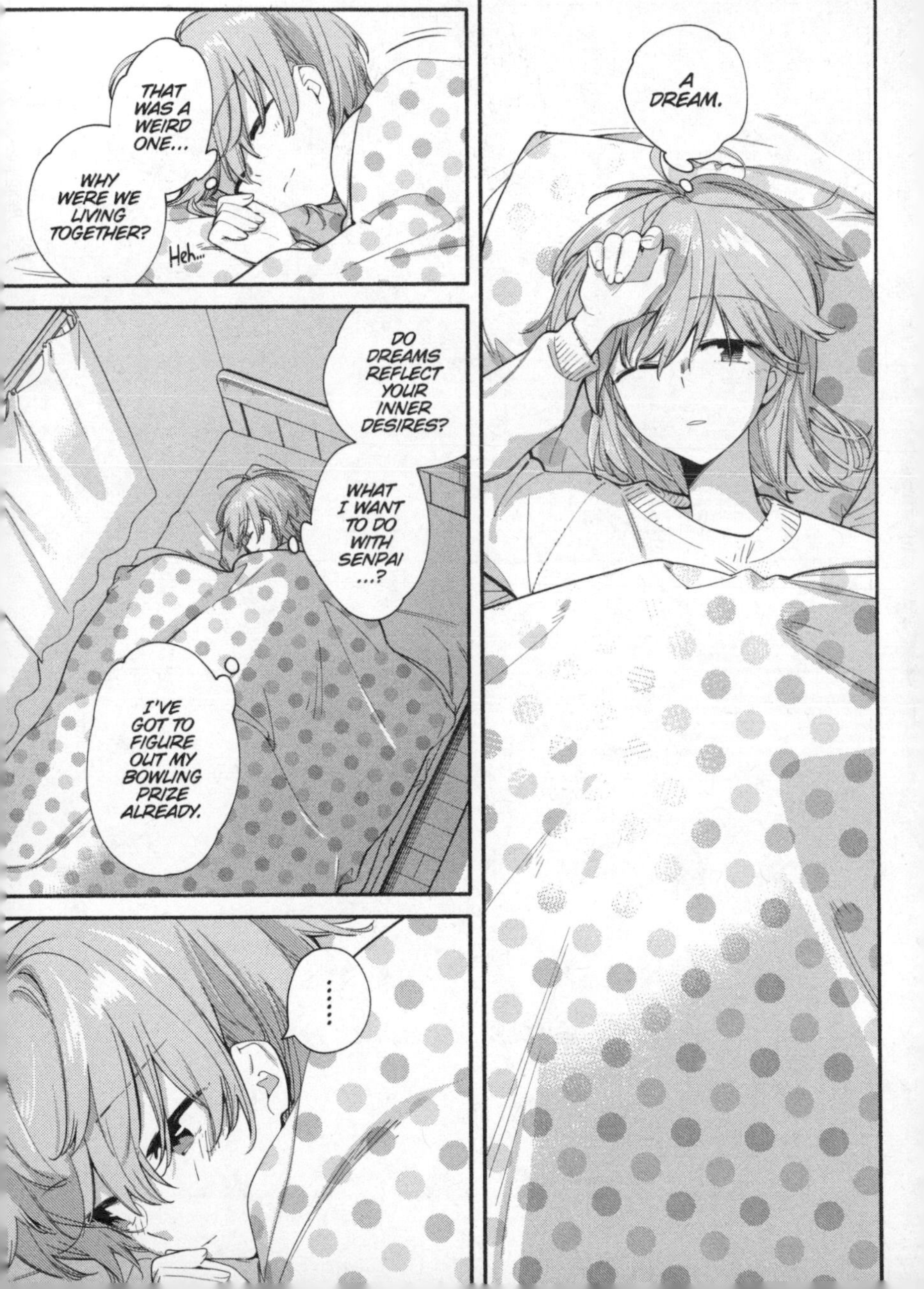
A DREAM.
THAT WAS A WEIRD ONE...
WHY WERE WE LIVING TOGETHER?
Heh...
DO DREAMS REFLECT YOUR INNER DESIRES?
WHAT I WANT TO DO WITH SENPAI ...?
I'VE GOT TO FIGURE OUT MY BOWLING PRIZE ALREADY.
......

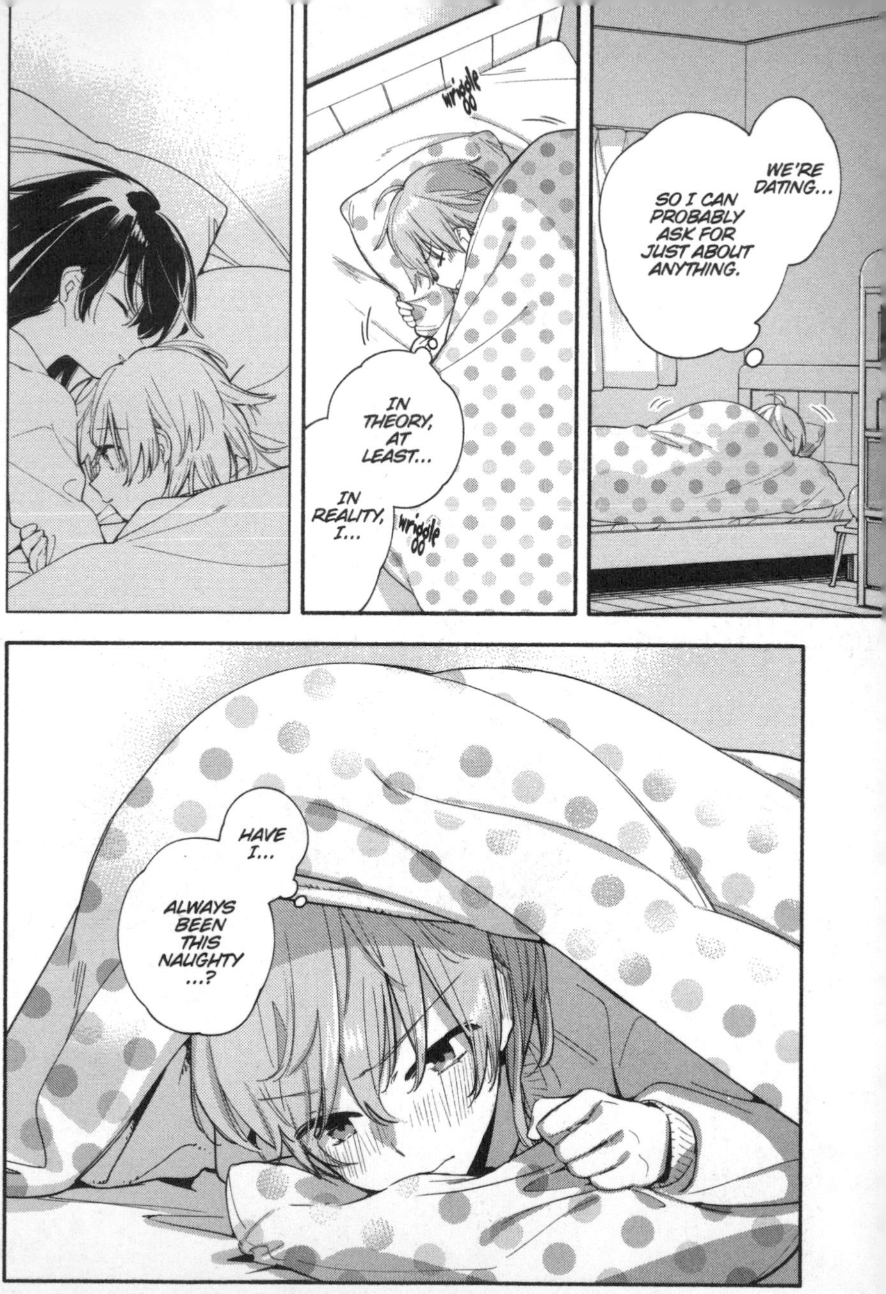
WE'RE DATING...
SO I CAN PROBABLY ASK FOR JUST ABOUT ANYTHING.
wriggle
IN THEORY, AT LEAST...
IN REALITY, I...
wriggle
HAVE I...
ALWAYS BEEN THIS NAUGHTY ...?

43

Essay Question, Continued

EPISODE FORTY-THREE

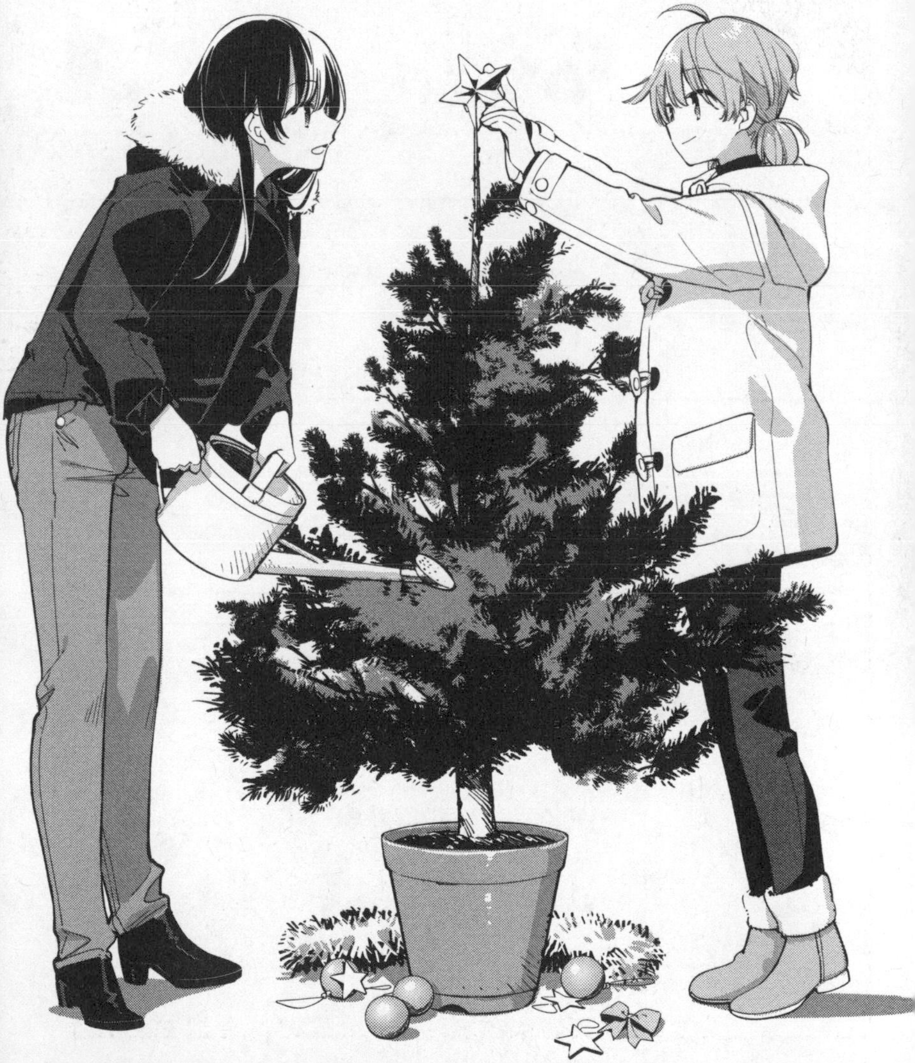

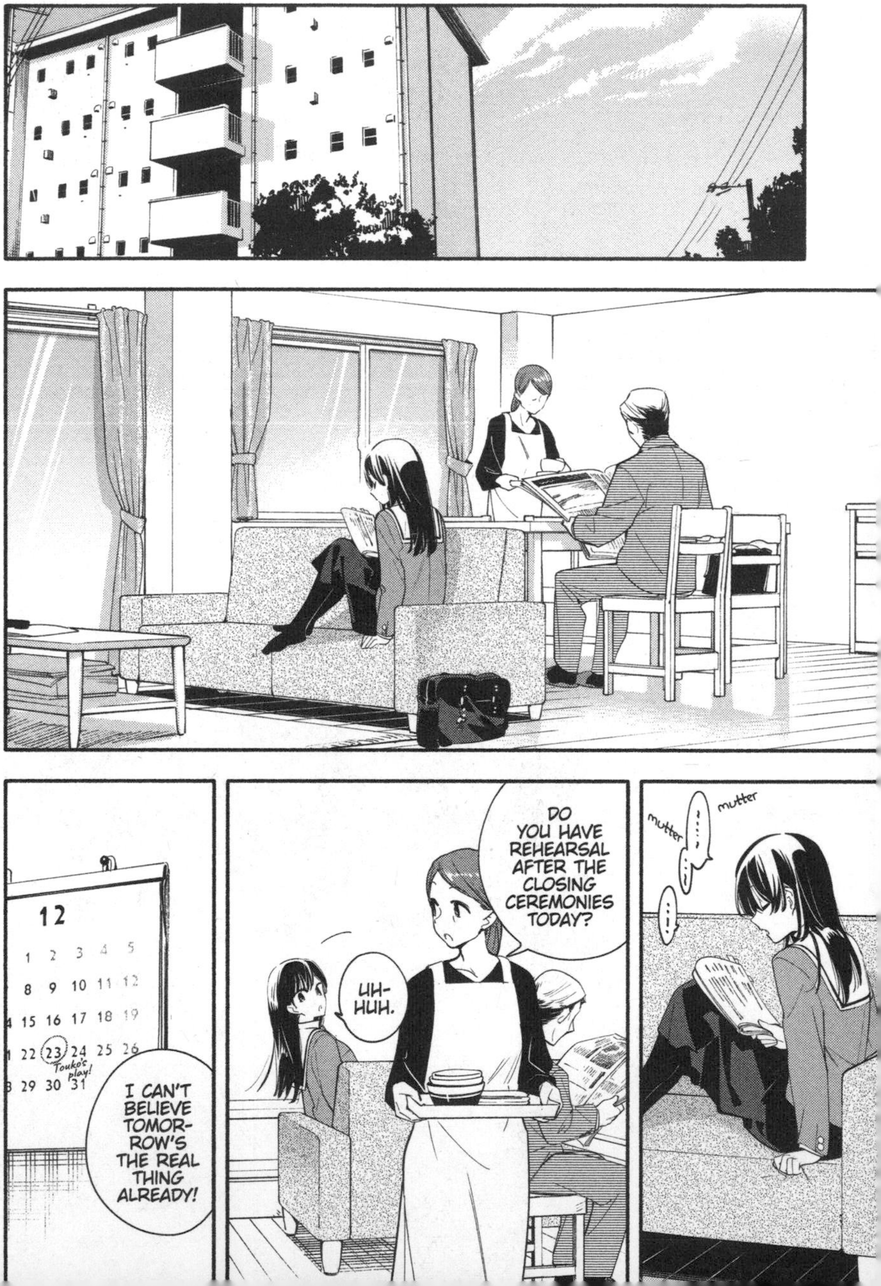
mutter
mutter
DO YOU HAVE REHEARSAL AFTER THE CLOSING CEREMONIES TODAY?
UH-HUH.
12
Touko's play!
I CAN'T BELIEVE TOMORROW'S THE REAL THING ALREADY!

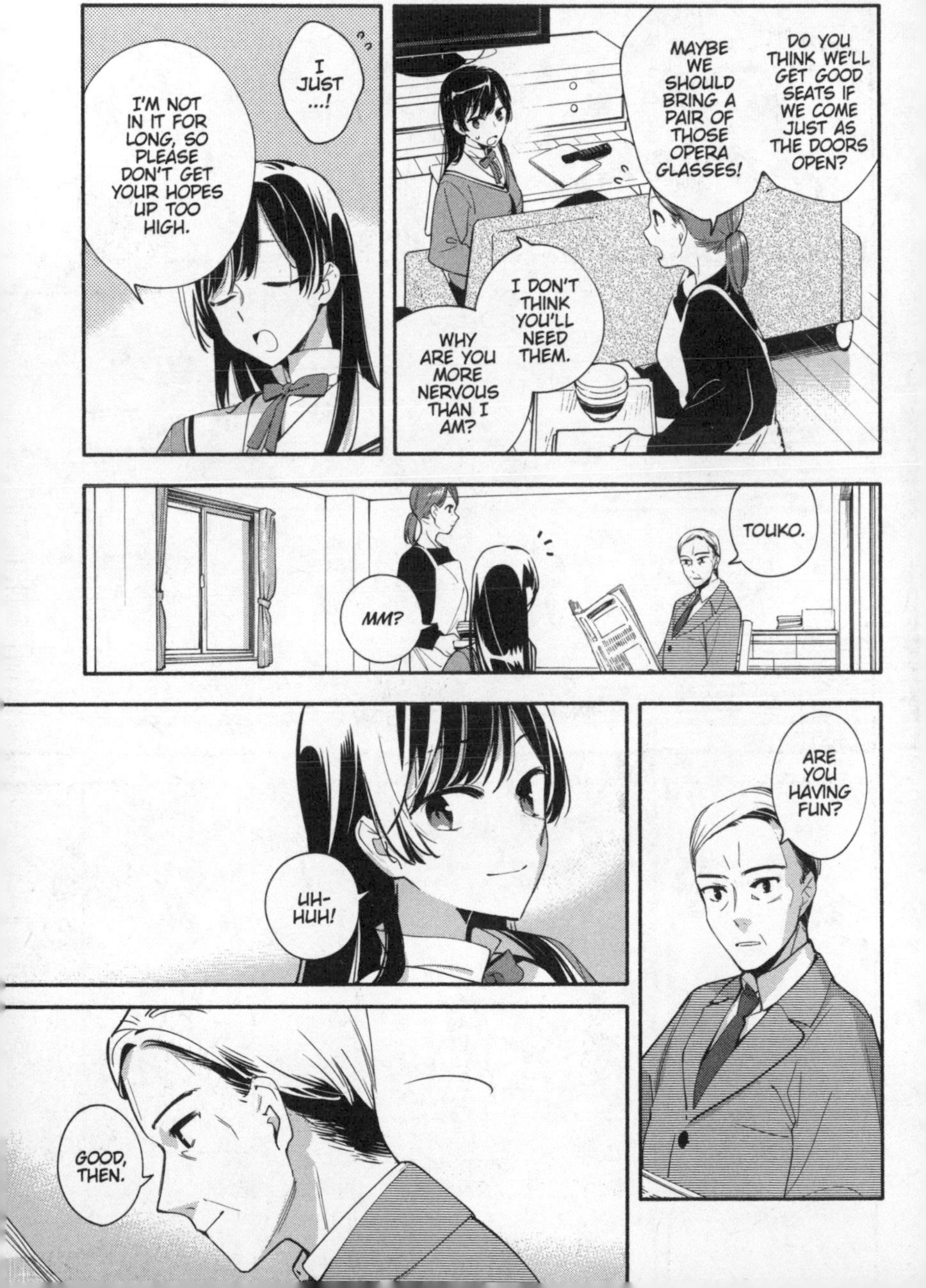
DO YOU THINK WE'LL GET GOOD SEATS IF WE COME JUST AS THE DOORS OPEN?
MAYBE WE SHOULD BRING A PAIR OF THOSE OPERA GLASSES!
I DON'T THINK YOU'LL NEED THEM.
WHY ARE YOU MORE NERVOUS THAN I AM?
I JUST ...!
I'M NOT IN IT FOR LONG, SO PLEASE DON'T GET YOUR HOPES UP TOO HIGH.
TOUKO.
MM?
ARE YOU HAVING FUN?
UH-HUH!
GOOD, THEN.

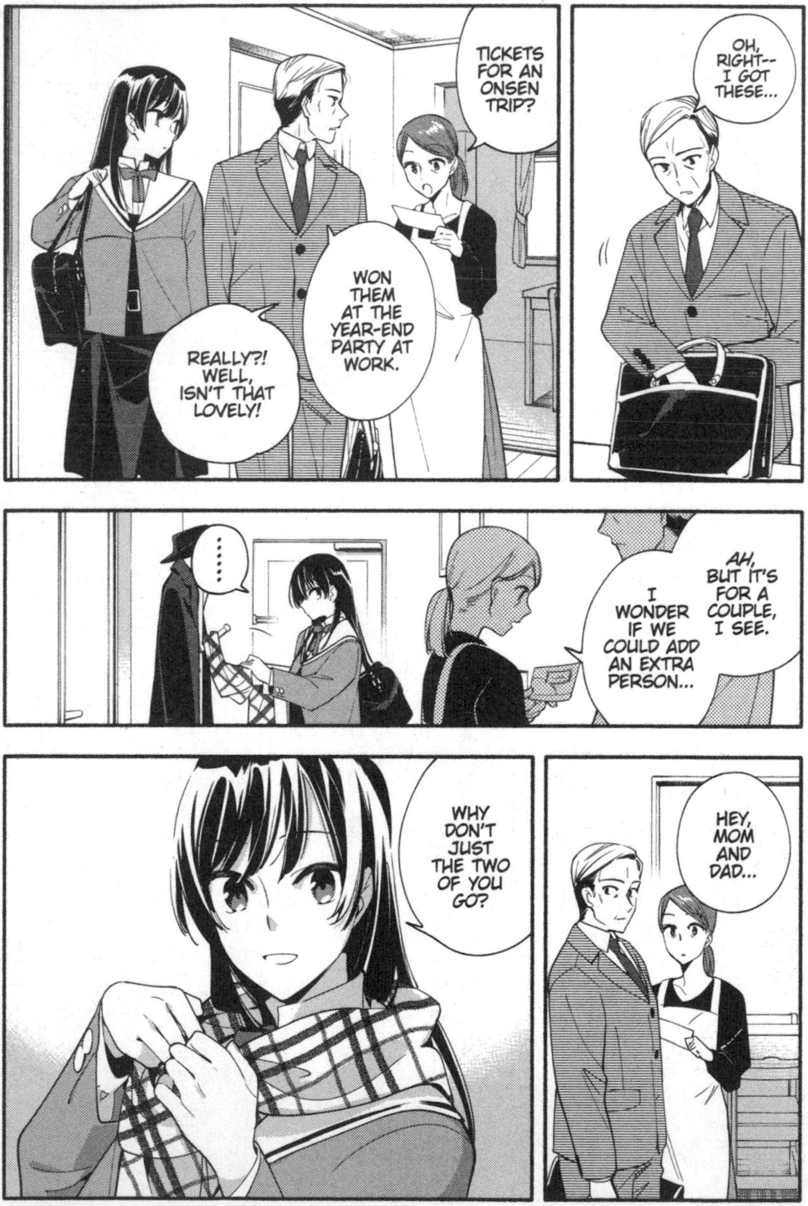
OH, RIGHT-- I GOT THESE...
TICKETS FOR AN ONSEN TRIP?
WON THEM AT THE YEAR-END PARTY AT WORK.
REALLY?! WELL, ISN'T THAT LOVELY!
AH, BUT IT'S FOR A COUPLE, I SEE.
I WONDER IF WE COULD ADD AN EXTRA PERSON...
......
HEY, MOM AND DAD...
WHY DON'T JUST THE TWO OF YOU GO?

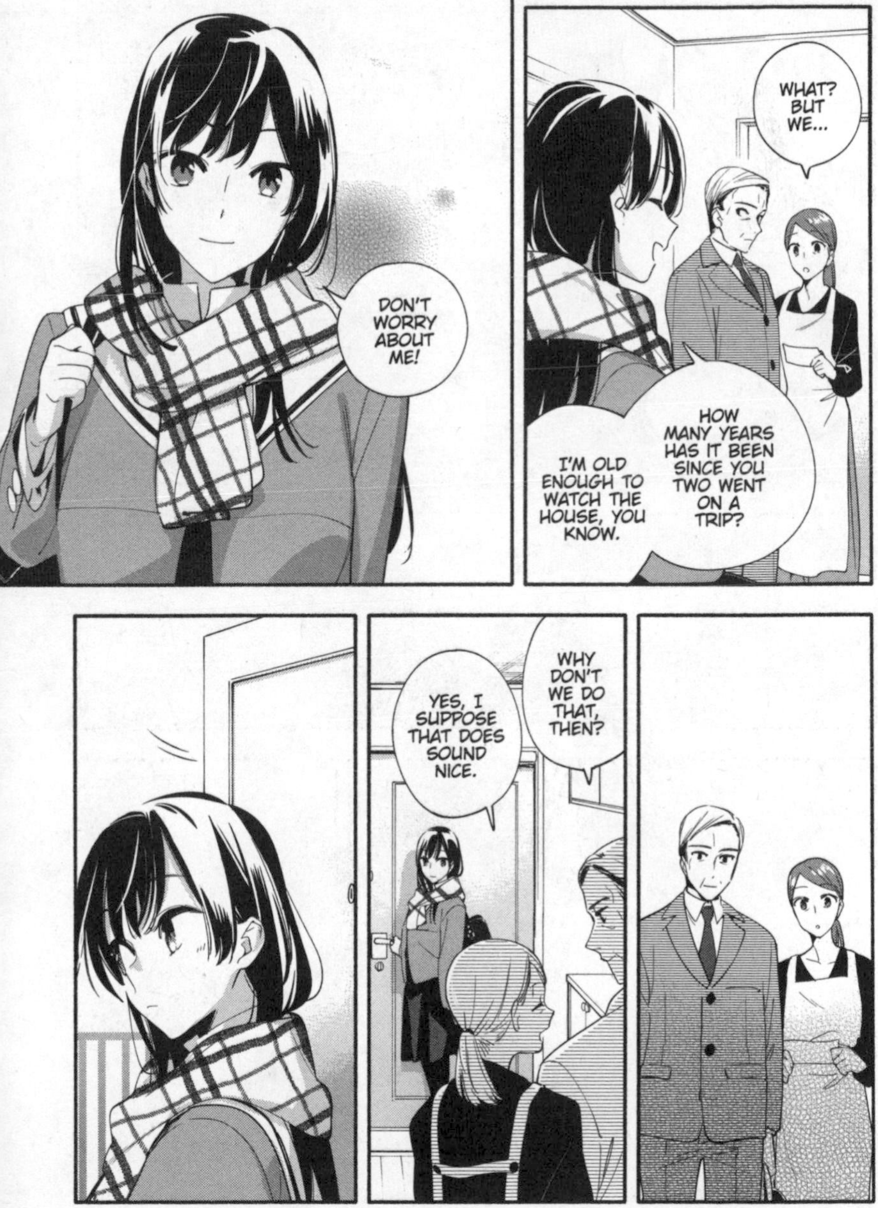
WHAT? BUT WE...
HOW MANY YEARS HAS IT BEEN SINCE YOU TWO WENT ON A TRIP?
I'M OLD ENOUGH TO WATCH THE HOUSE, YOU KNOW.
DON'T WORRY ABOUT ME!
WHY DON'T WE DO THAT, THEN?
YES, I SUPPOSE THAT DOES SOUND NICE.

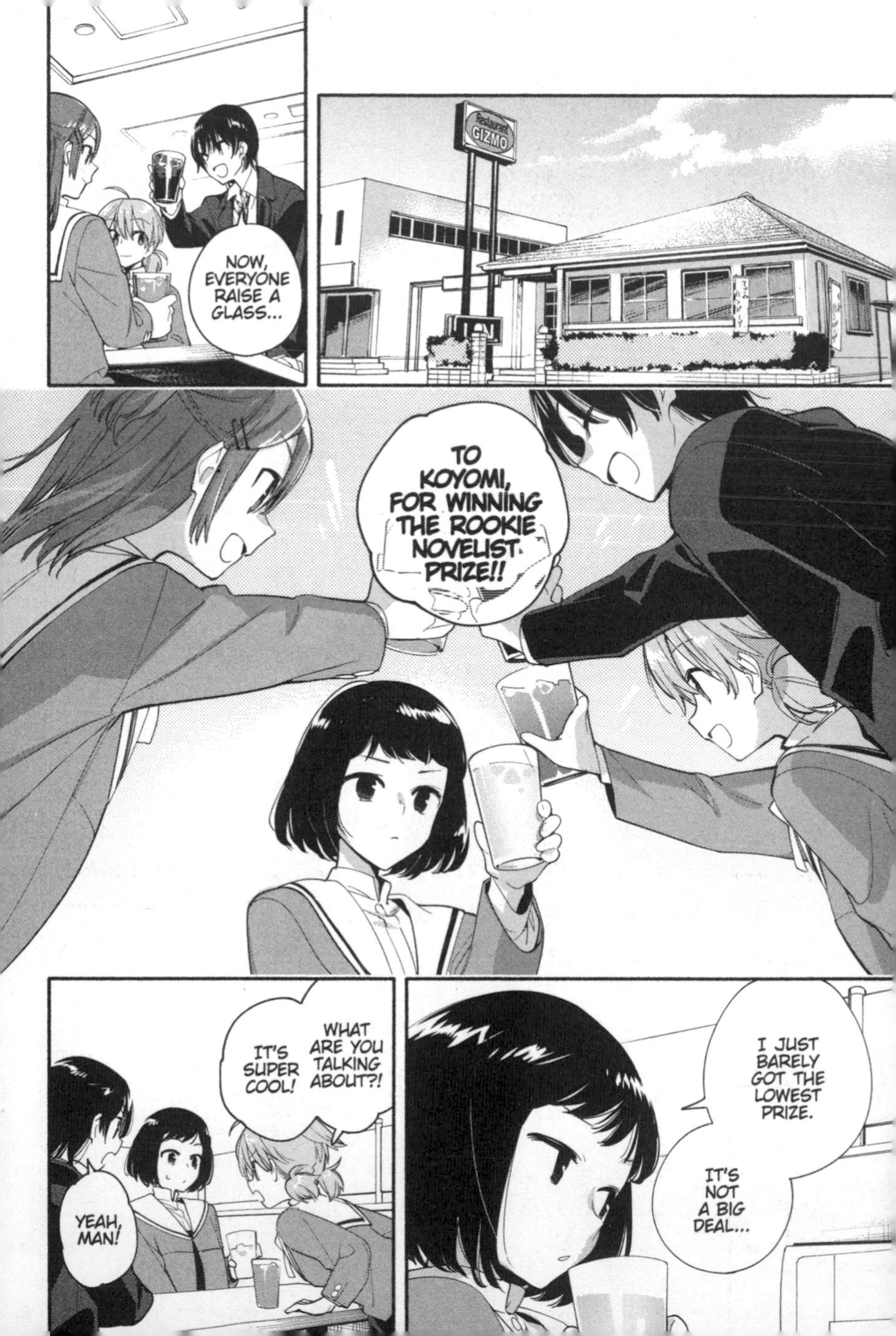
Restaurant GIZMO
NOW, EVERYONE RAISE A GLASS...
TO KOYOMI, FOR WINNING THE ROOKIE NOVELIST PRIZE!!
I JUST BARELY GOT THE LOWEST PRIZE.
IT'S NOT A BIG DEAL...
WHAT ARE YOU TALKING ABOUT?!
IT'S SUPER COOL!
YEAH, MAN!

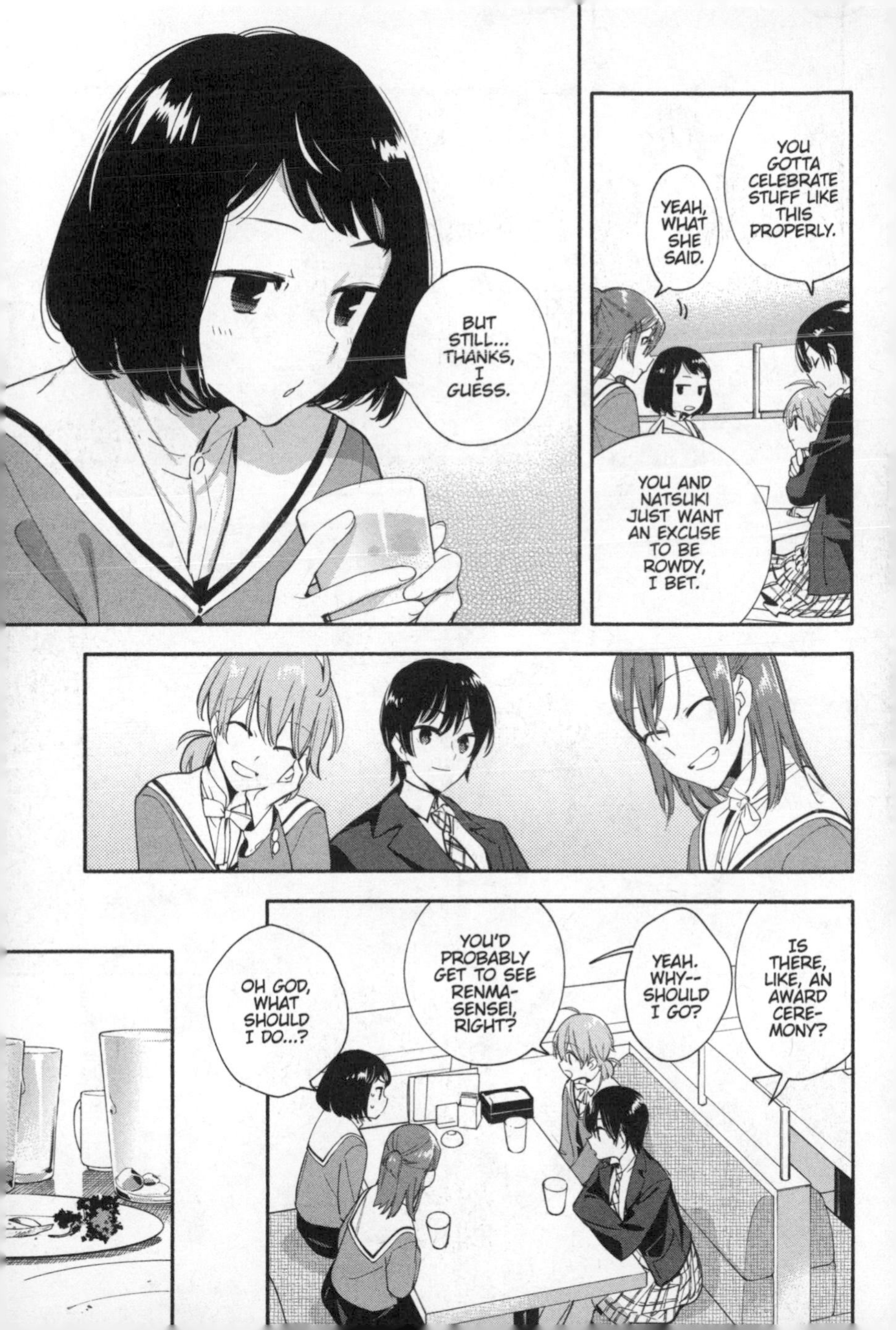
YOU GOTTA CELEBRATE STUFF LIKE THIS PROPERLY.
YEAH, WHAT SHE SAID.
YOU AND NATSUKI JUST WANT AN EXCUSE TO BE ROWDY, I BET.
BUT STILL... THANKS, I GUESS.
IS THERE, LIKE, AN AWARD CERE-MONY?
YEAH. WHY-- SHOULD I GO?
YOU'D PROBABLY GET TO SEE RENMA-SENSEI, RIGHT?
OH GOD, WHAT SHOULD I DO...?

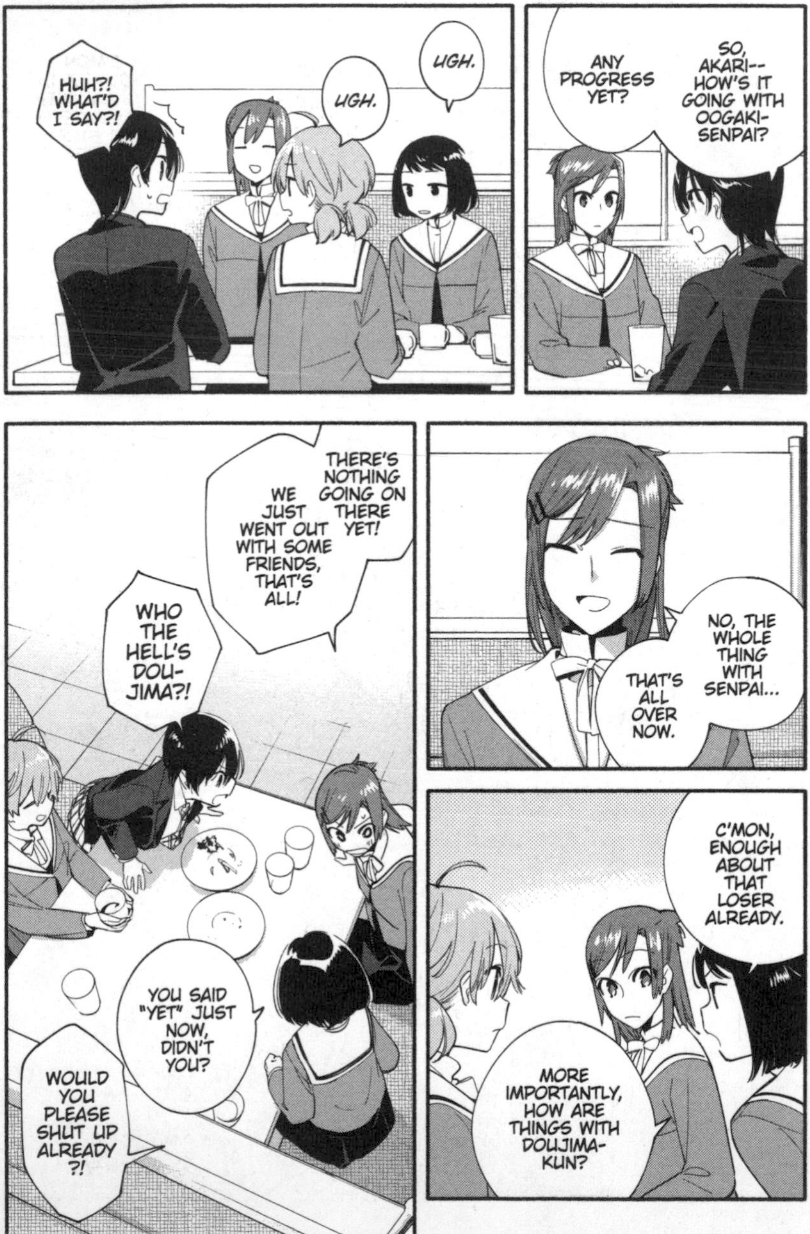
SO, AKARI-- HOW'S IT GOING WITH OOGAKI-SENPAI?
ANY PROGRESS YET?
UGH.
UGH.
HUH?! WHAT'D I SAY?!
NO, THE WHOLE THING WITH SENPAI...
THAT'S ALL OVER NOW.
C'MON, ENOUGH ABOUT THAT LOSER ALREADY.
MORE IMPORTANTLY, HOW ARE THINGS WITH DOUJIMA-KUN?
THERE'S NOTHING GOING ON THERE YET!
WE JUST WENT OUT WITH SOME FRIENDS, THAT'S ALL!
WHO THE HELL'S DOUJIMA?!
YOU SAID "YET" JUST NOW, DIDN'T YOU?
WOULD YOU PLEASE SHUT UP ALREADY?!

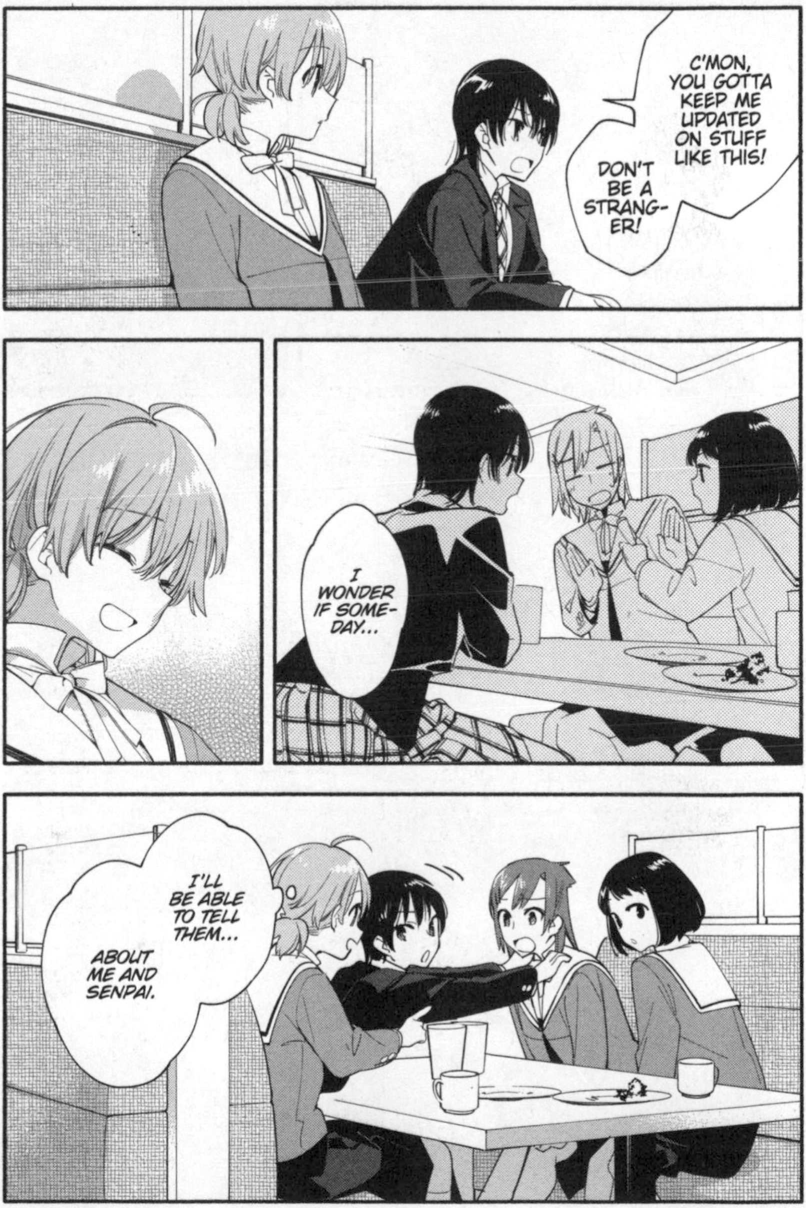
C'MON, YOU GOTTA KEEP ME UPDATED ON STUFF LIKE THIS!
DON'T BE A STRANGER!
I WONDER IF SOMEDAY...
I'LL BE ABLE TO TELL THEM...
ABOUT ME AND SENPAI.

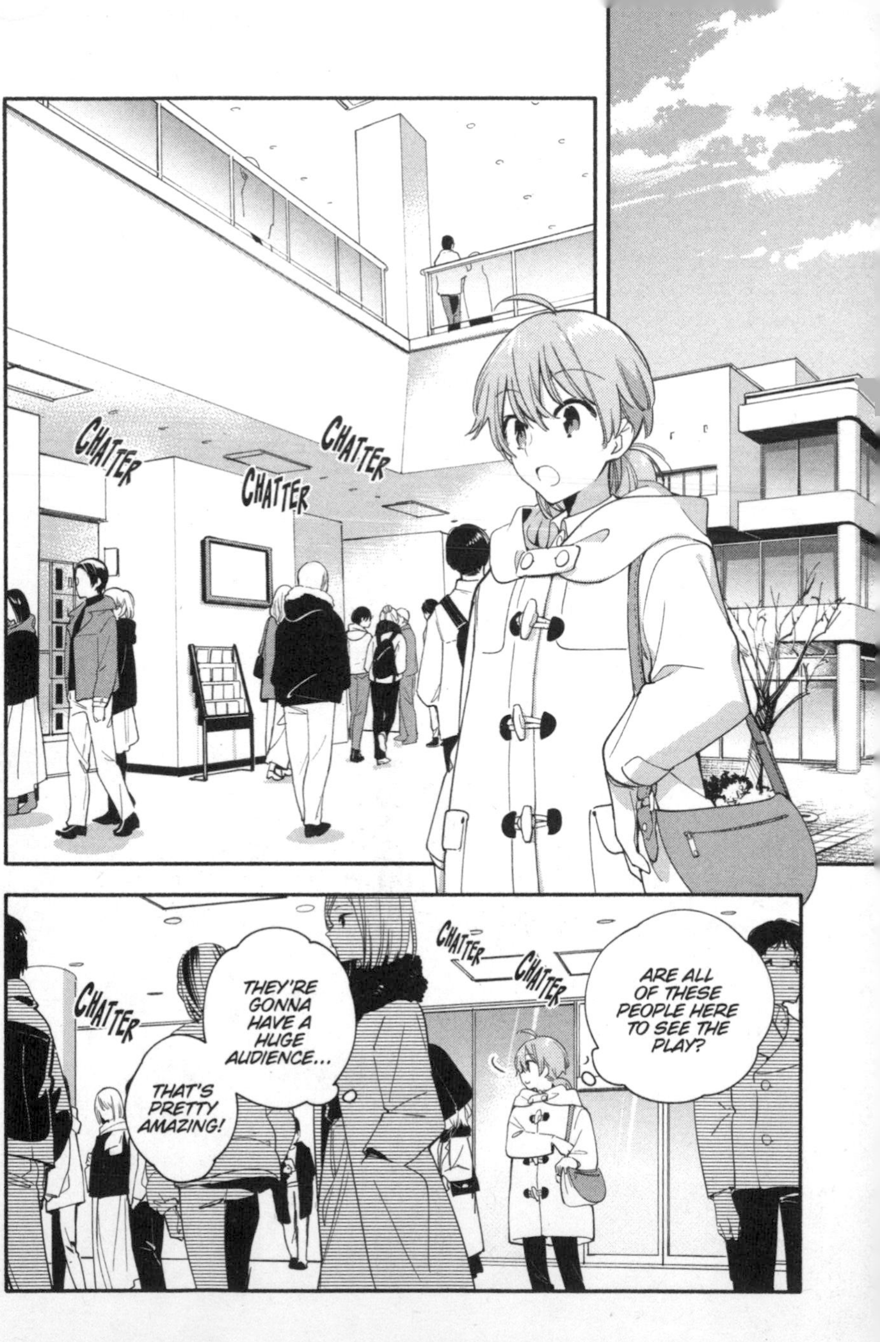
CHATTER
CHATTER
CHATTER
ARE ALL OF THESE PEOPLE HERE TO SEE THE PLAY?
CHATTER
CHATTER
THEY'RE GONNA HAVE A HUGE AUDIENCE...
THAT'S PRETTY AMAZING!
CHATTER

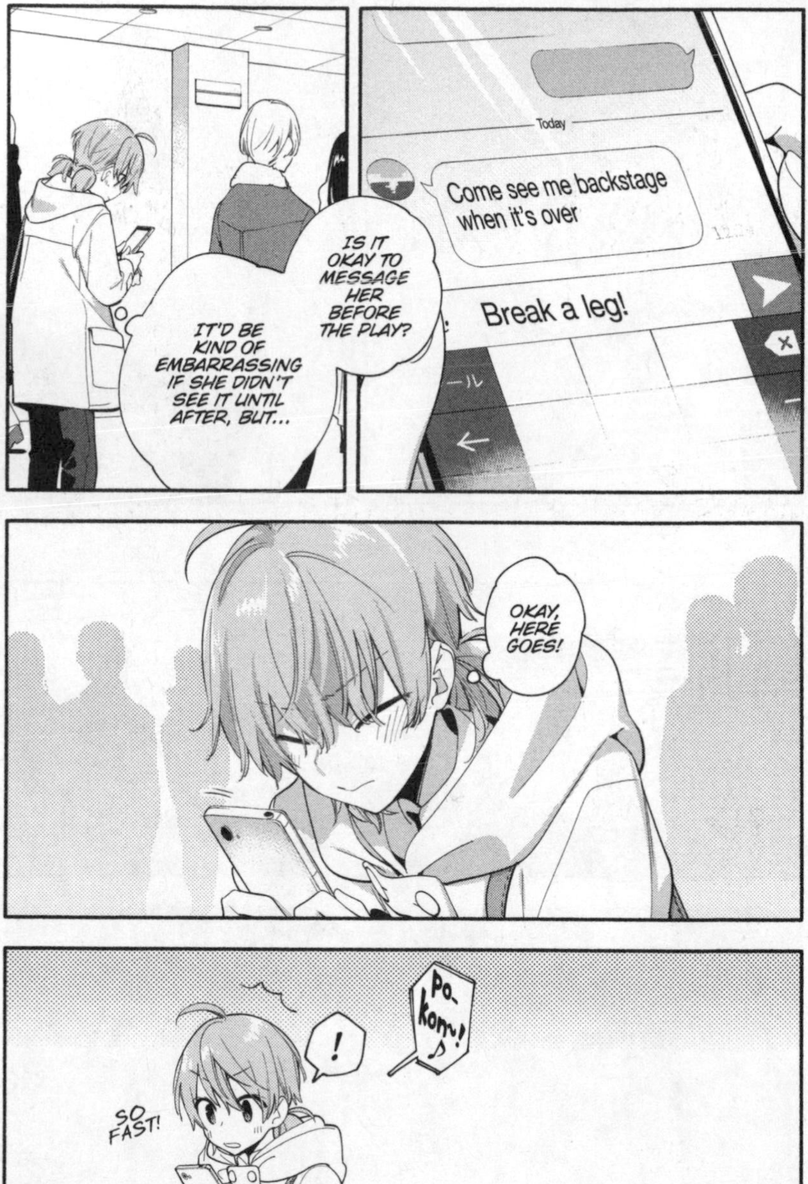
Today
Come see me backstage when it's over
Break a leg!
IS IT OKAY TO MESSAGE HER BEFORE THE PLAY?
IT'D BE KIND OF EMBARRASSING IF SHE DIDN'T SEE IT UNTIL AFTER, BUT...
OKAY, HERE GOES!
Po-kon~! ♪
!
SO FAST!

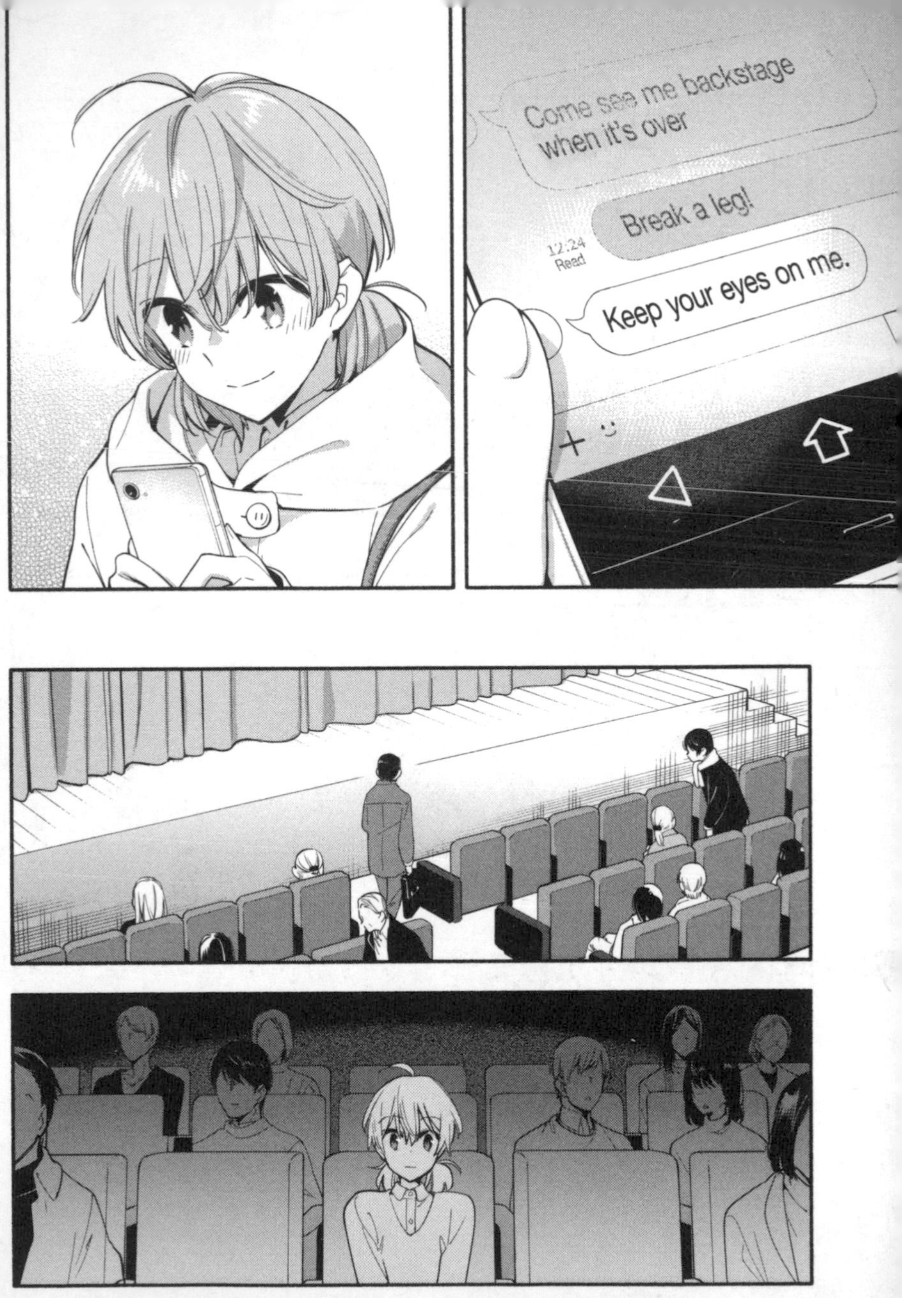
Come see me backstage when it's over
Break a leg!
12:24
Read
Keep your eyes on me.

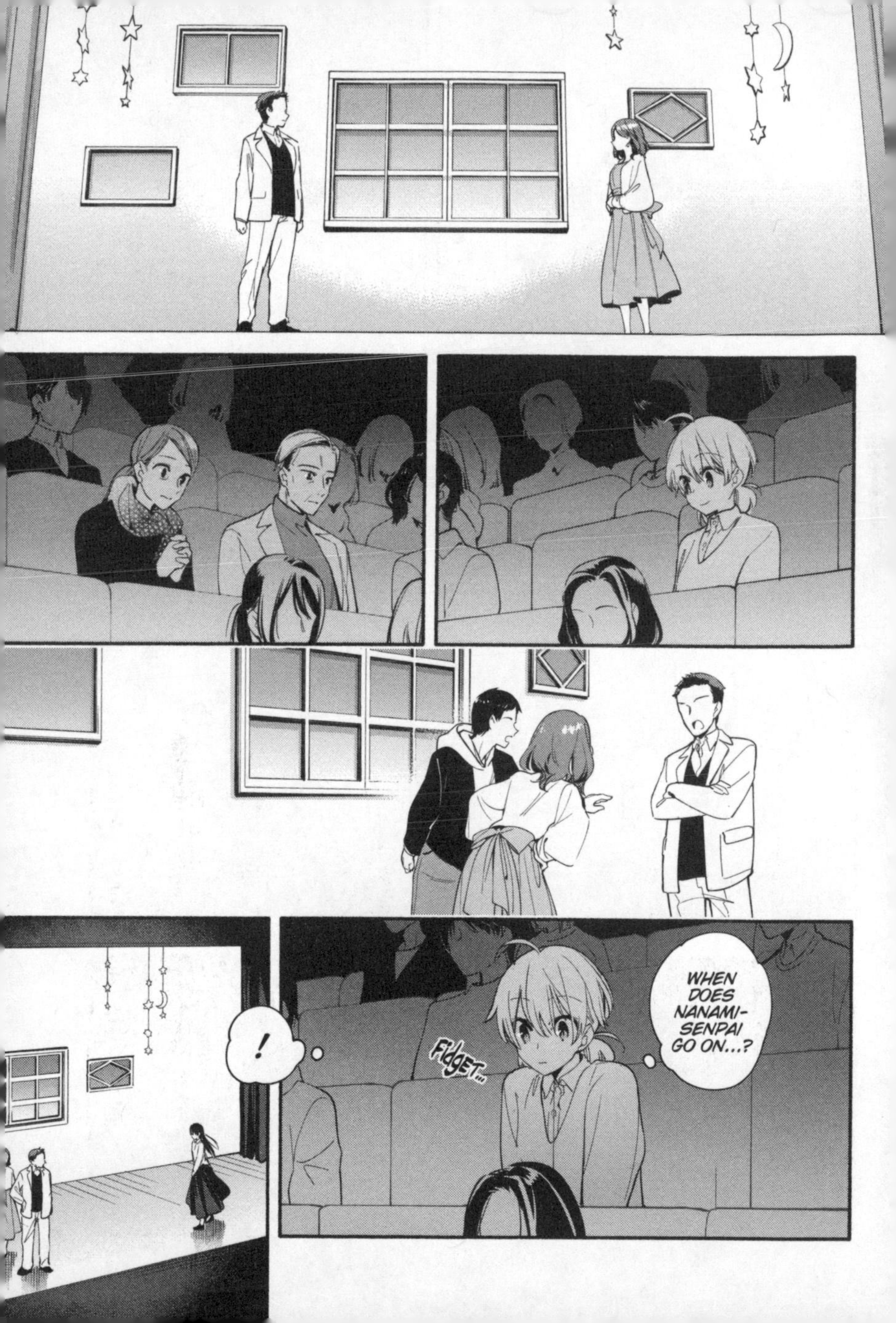
WHEN DOES NANAMI-SENPAI GO ON...?
Fidget...
!

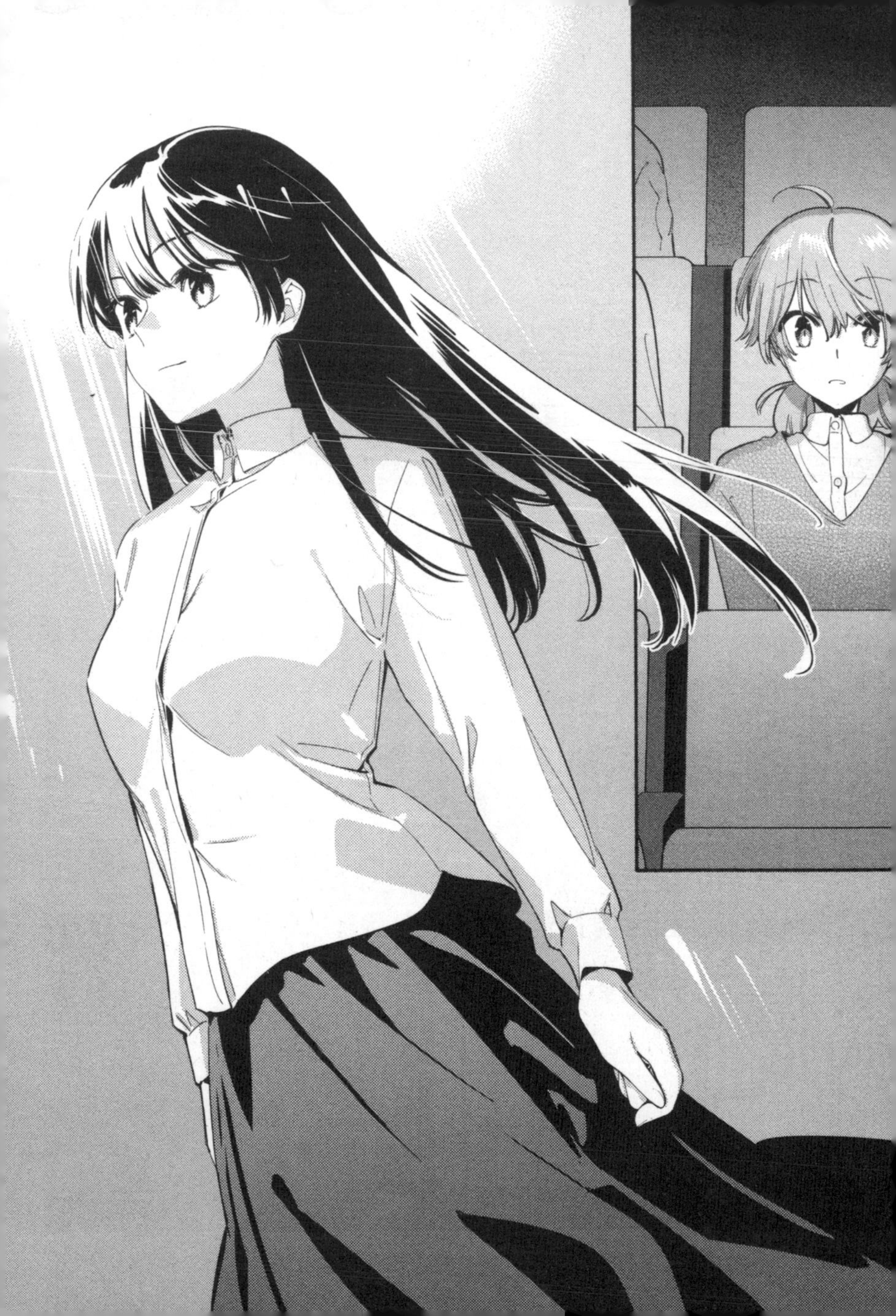

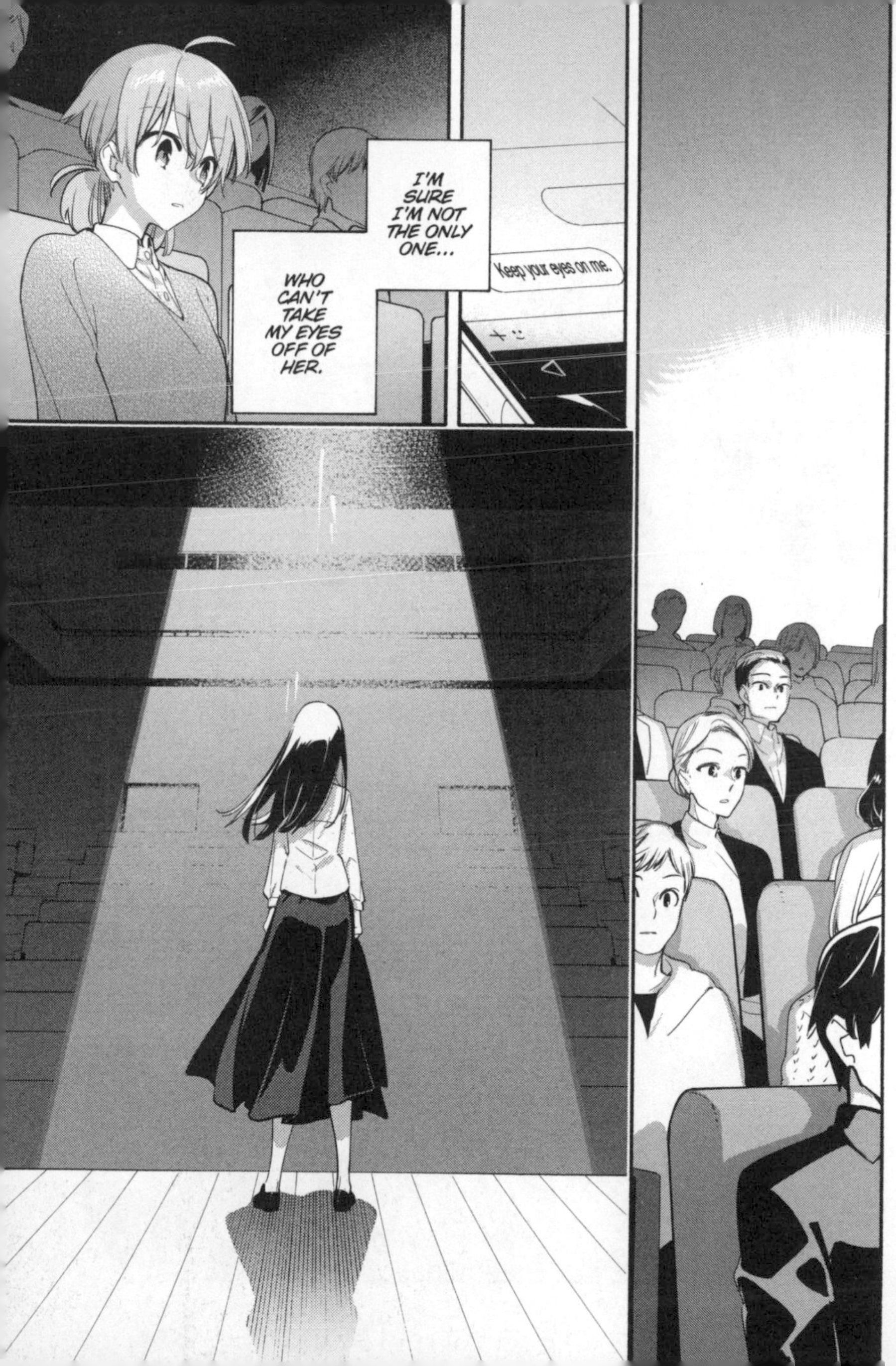
I'M SURE I'M NOT THE ONLY ONE...
WHO CAN'T TAKE MY EYES OFF OF HER.
Keep your eyes on me.

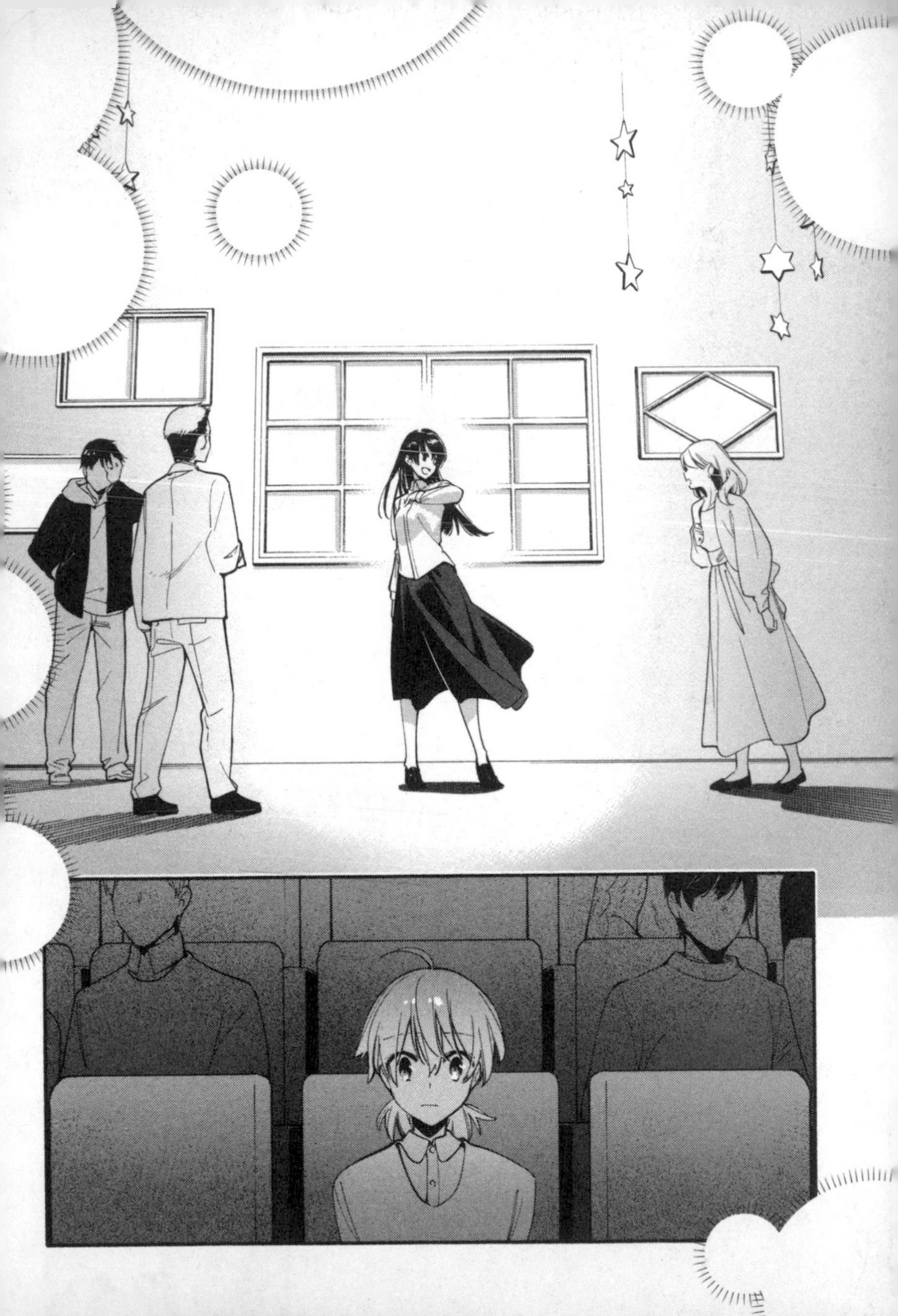

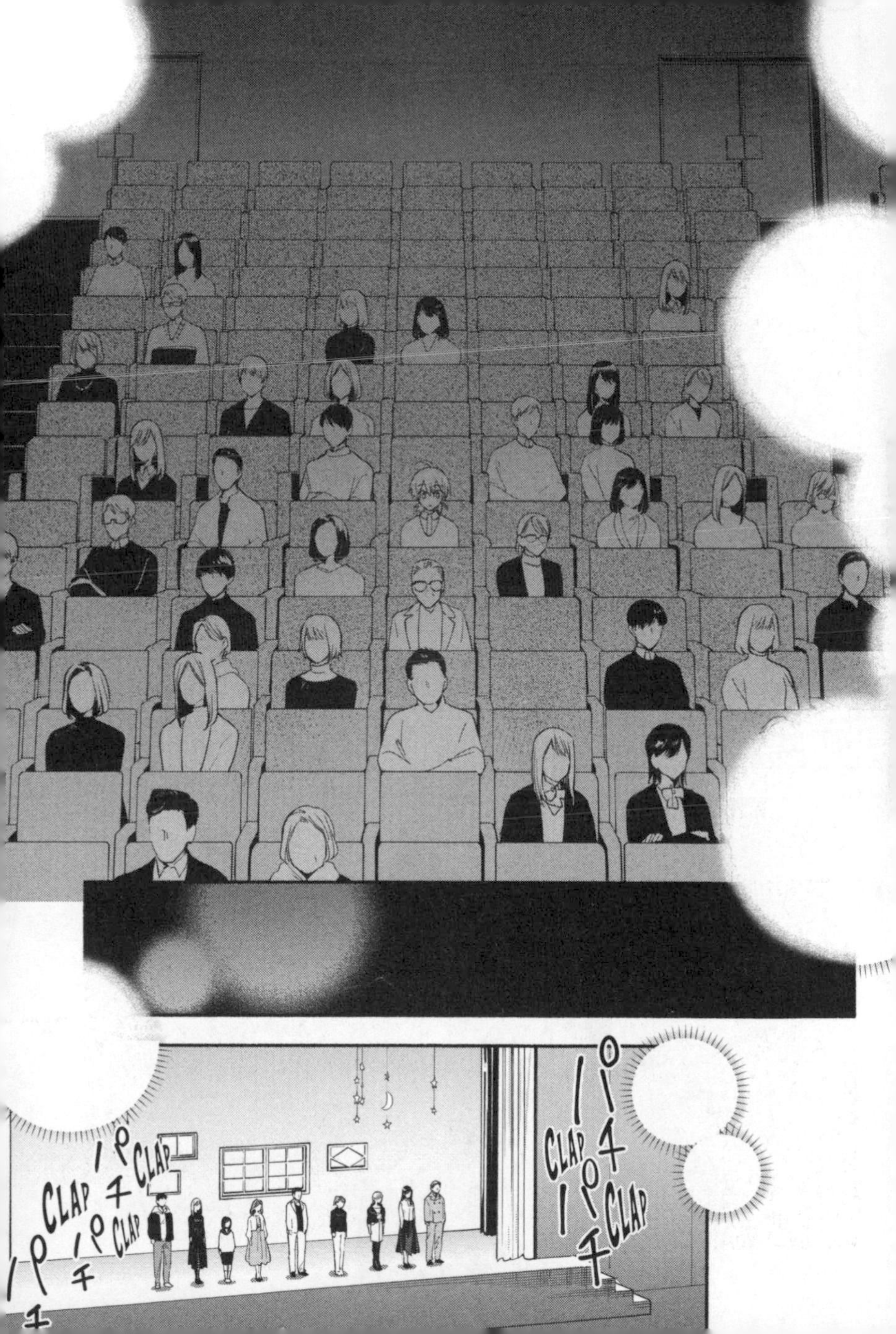
パチ
CLAP
パチ
CLAP
パチ
CLAP
パチ
CLAP
パチ
CLAP

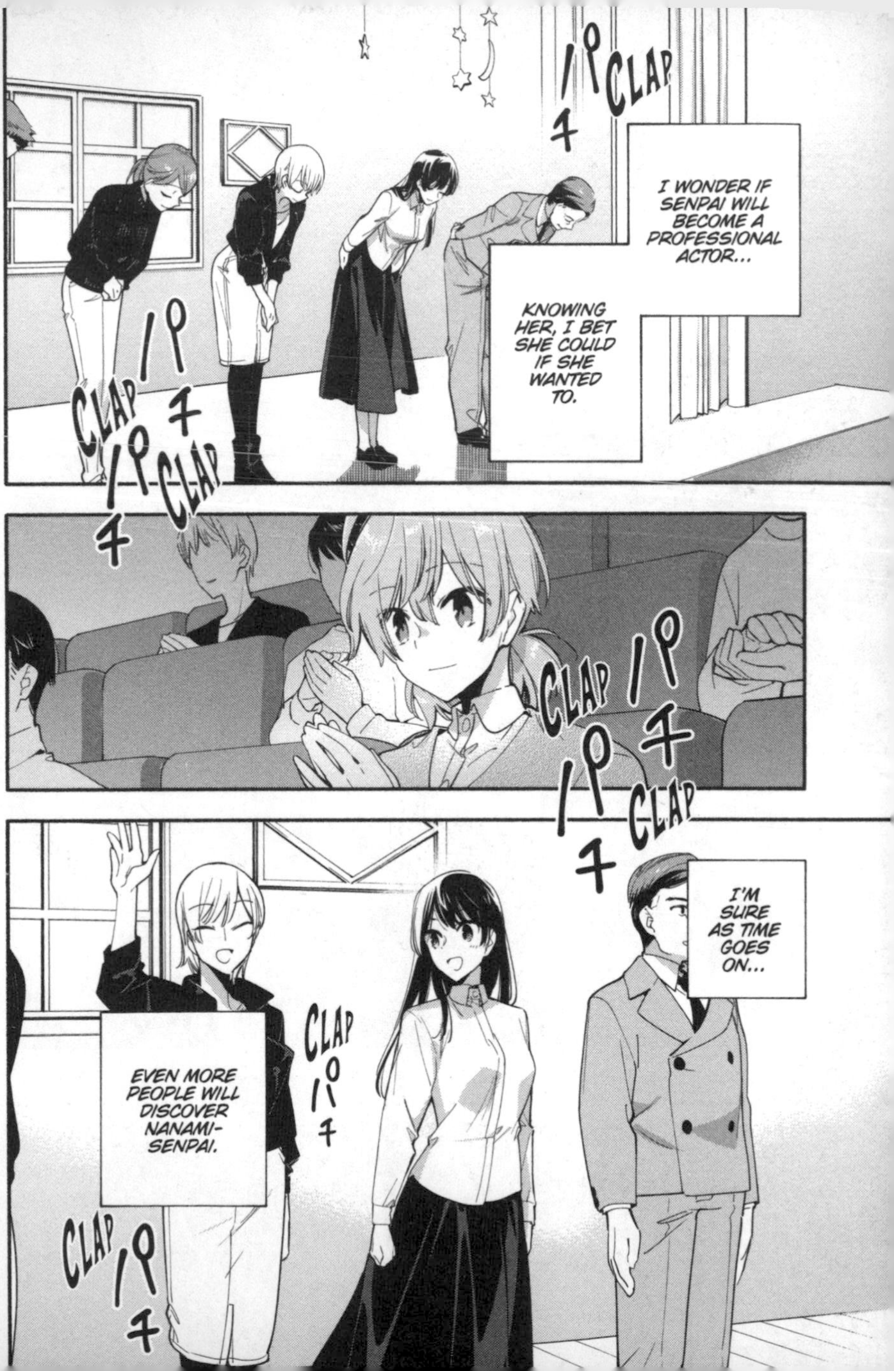
パチ CLAP
I WONDER IF SENPAI WILL BECOME A PROFESSIONAL ACTOR...
KNOWING HER, I BET SHE COULD IF SHE WANTED TO.
パチ CLAP
パチ CLAP
パチ CLAP
パチ CLAP
I'M SURE AS TIME GOES ON...
CLAP パチ
EVEN MORE PEOPLE WILL DISCOVER NANAMI-SENPAI.
CLAP パチ

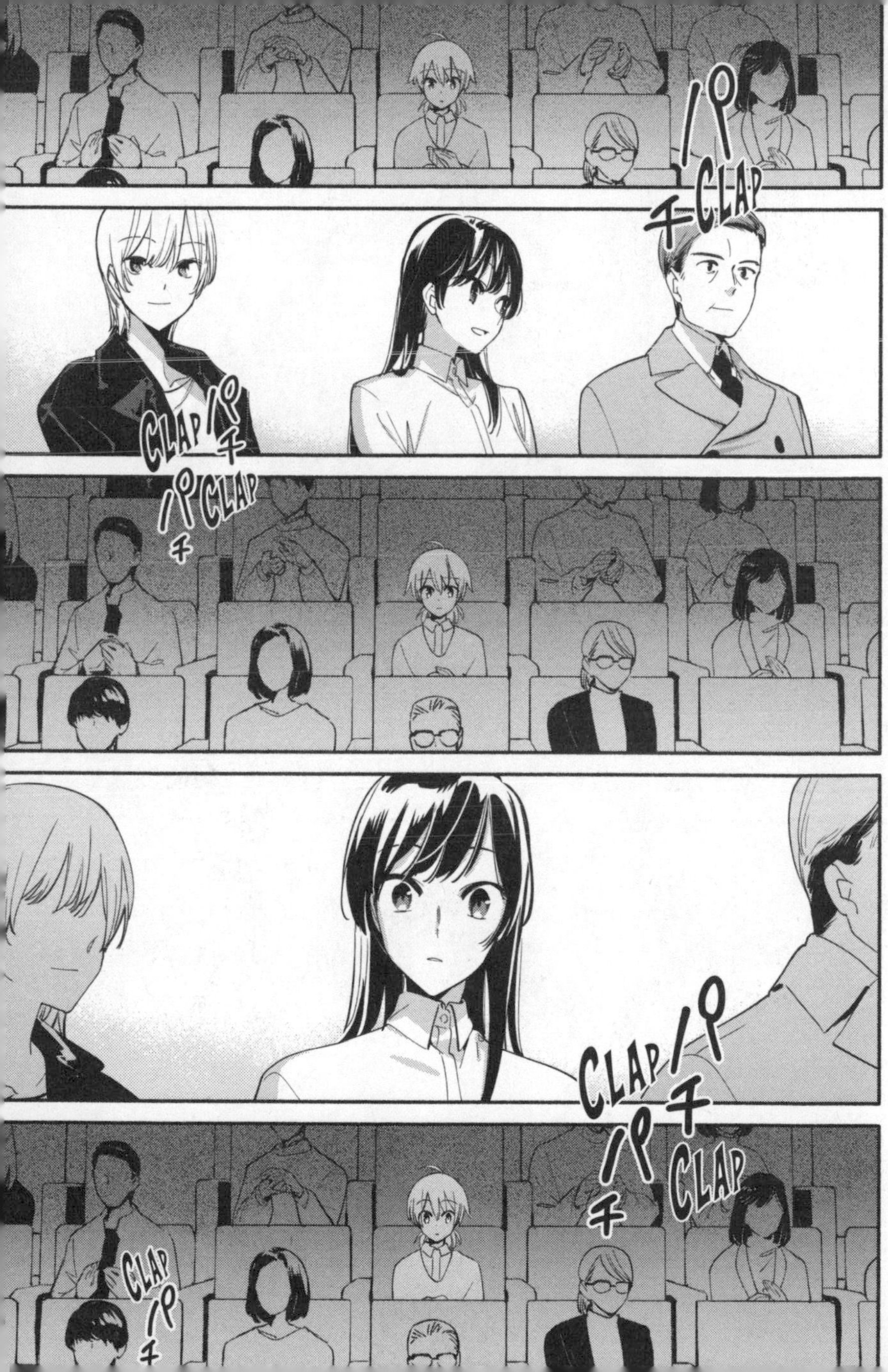
パチ
CLAP
パチ
CLAP
パチ
CLAP
パチ
CLAP
パチ
CLAP
パチ
CLAP
パチ
CLAP

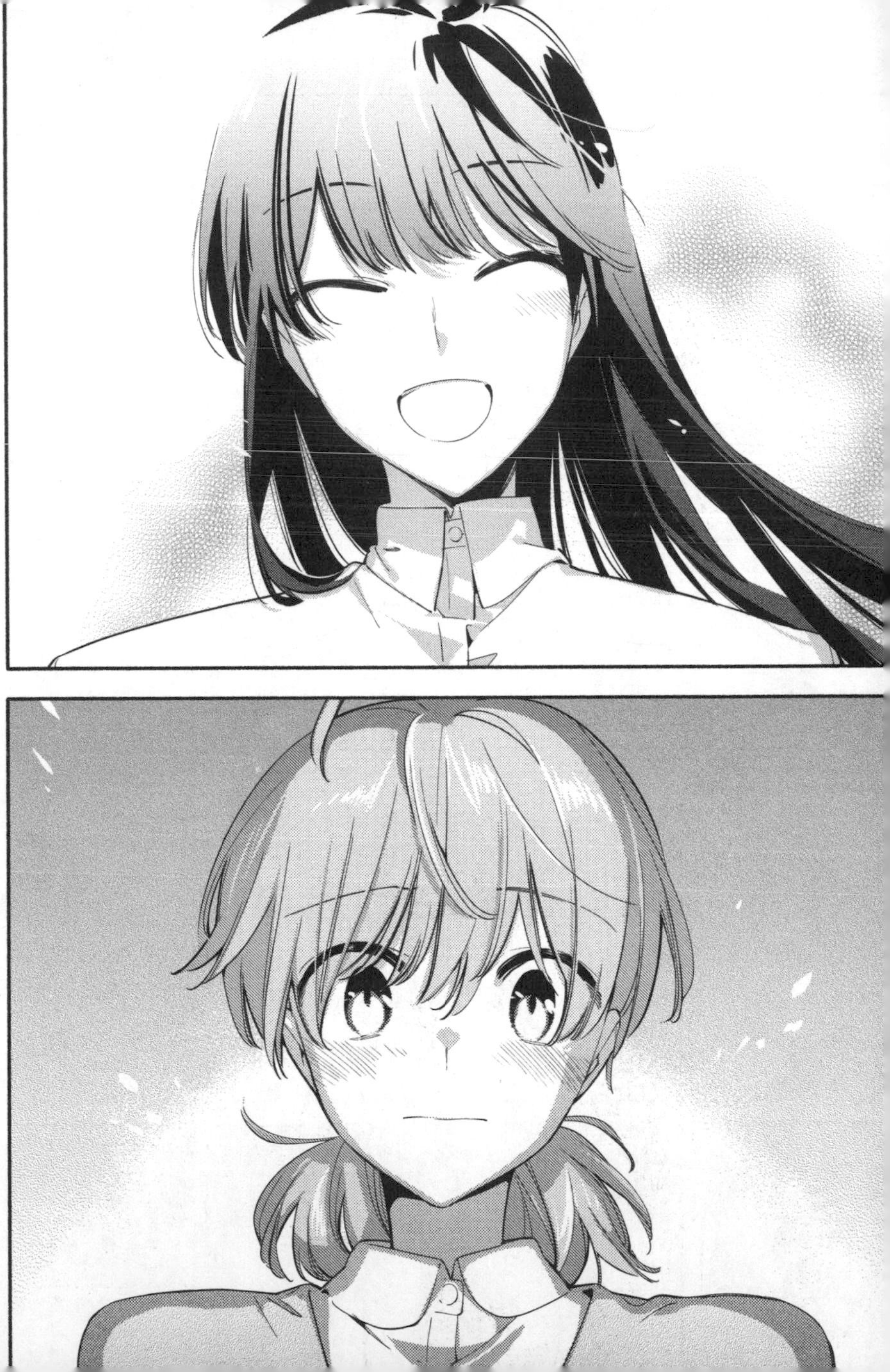

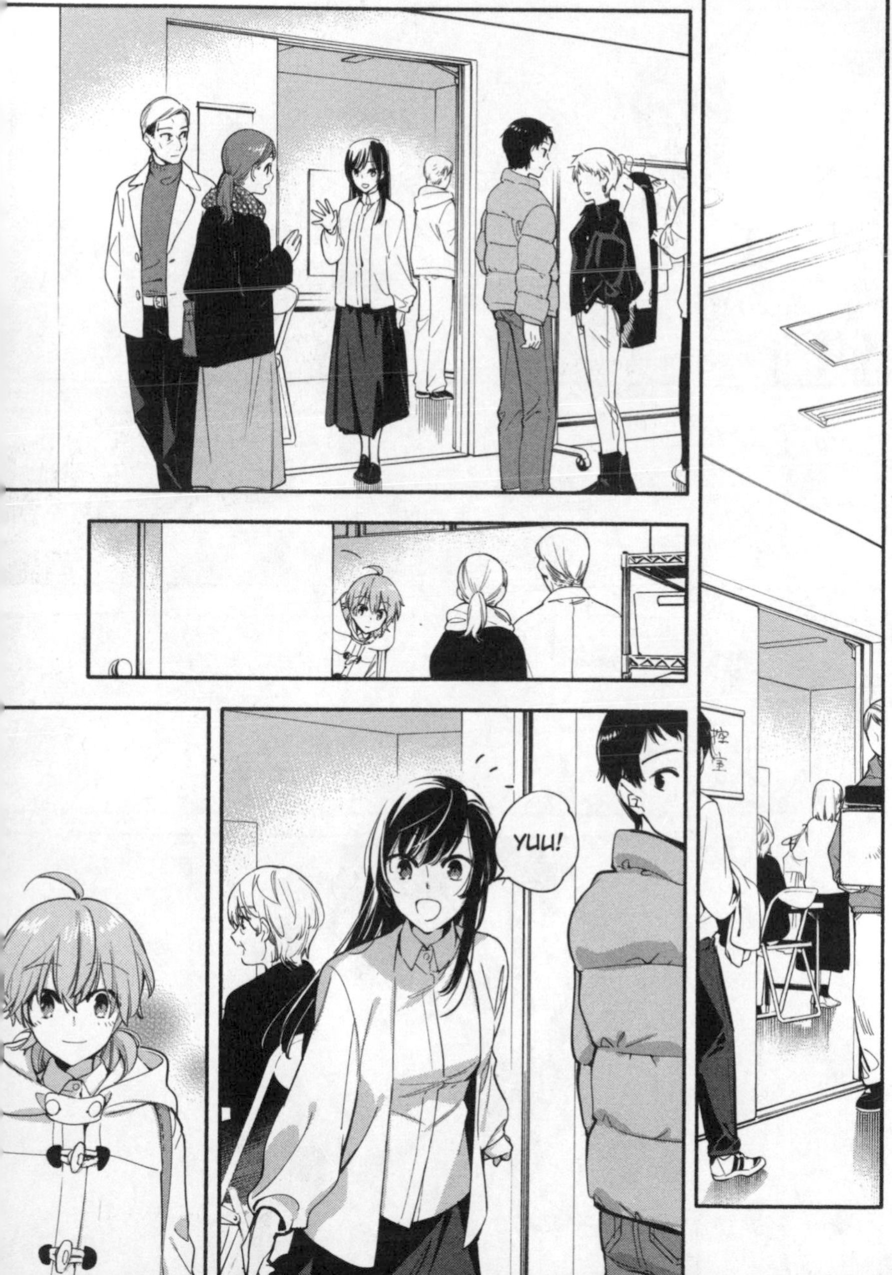
YUU!

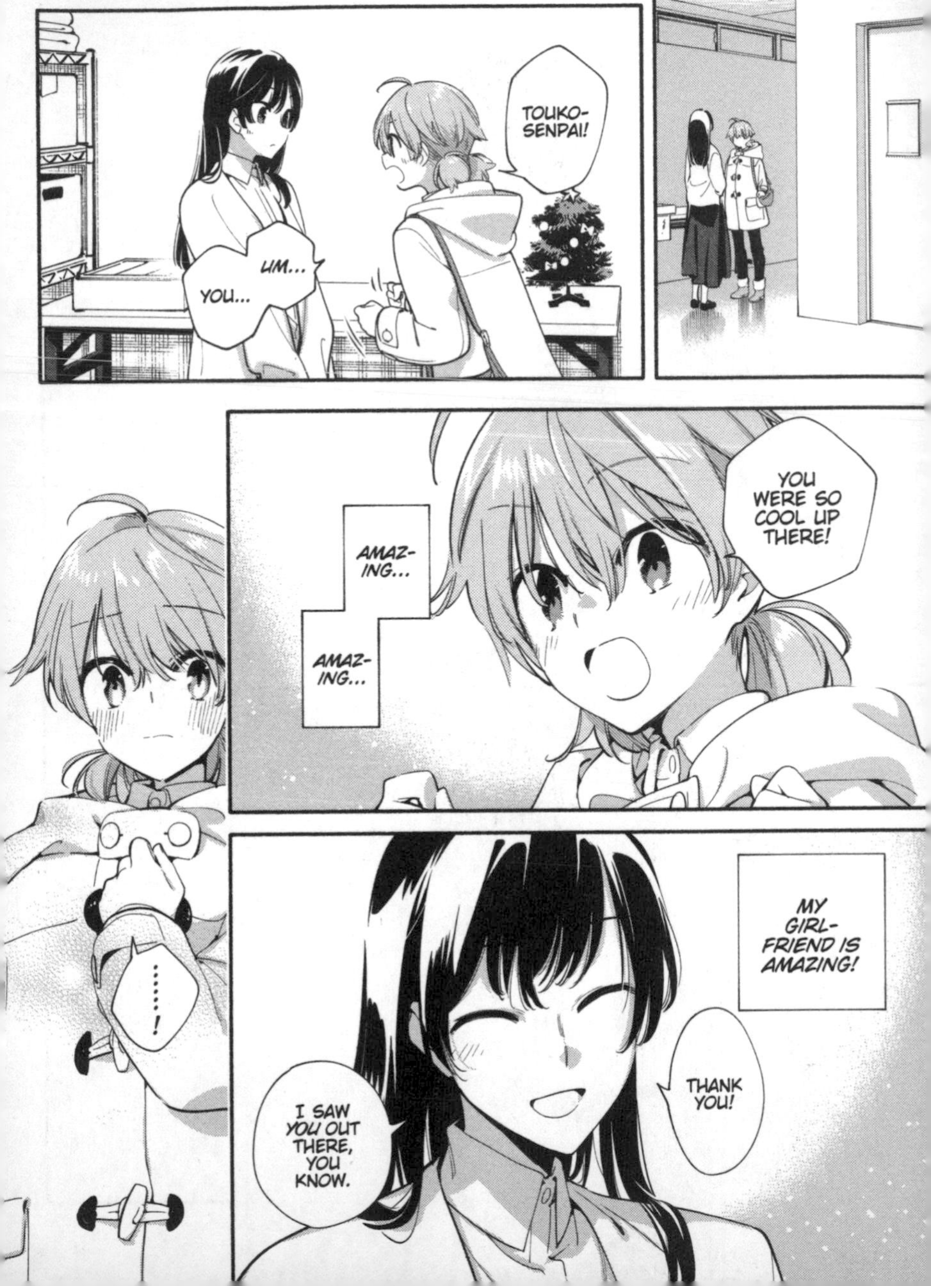
TOUKO-SENPAI!
UM... YOU...
YOU WERE SO COOL UP THERE!
AMAZ-ING...
AMAZ-ING...
MY GIRL-FRIEND IS AMAZING!
THANK YOU!
I SAW YOU OUT THERE, YOU KNOW.
......!

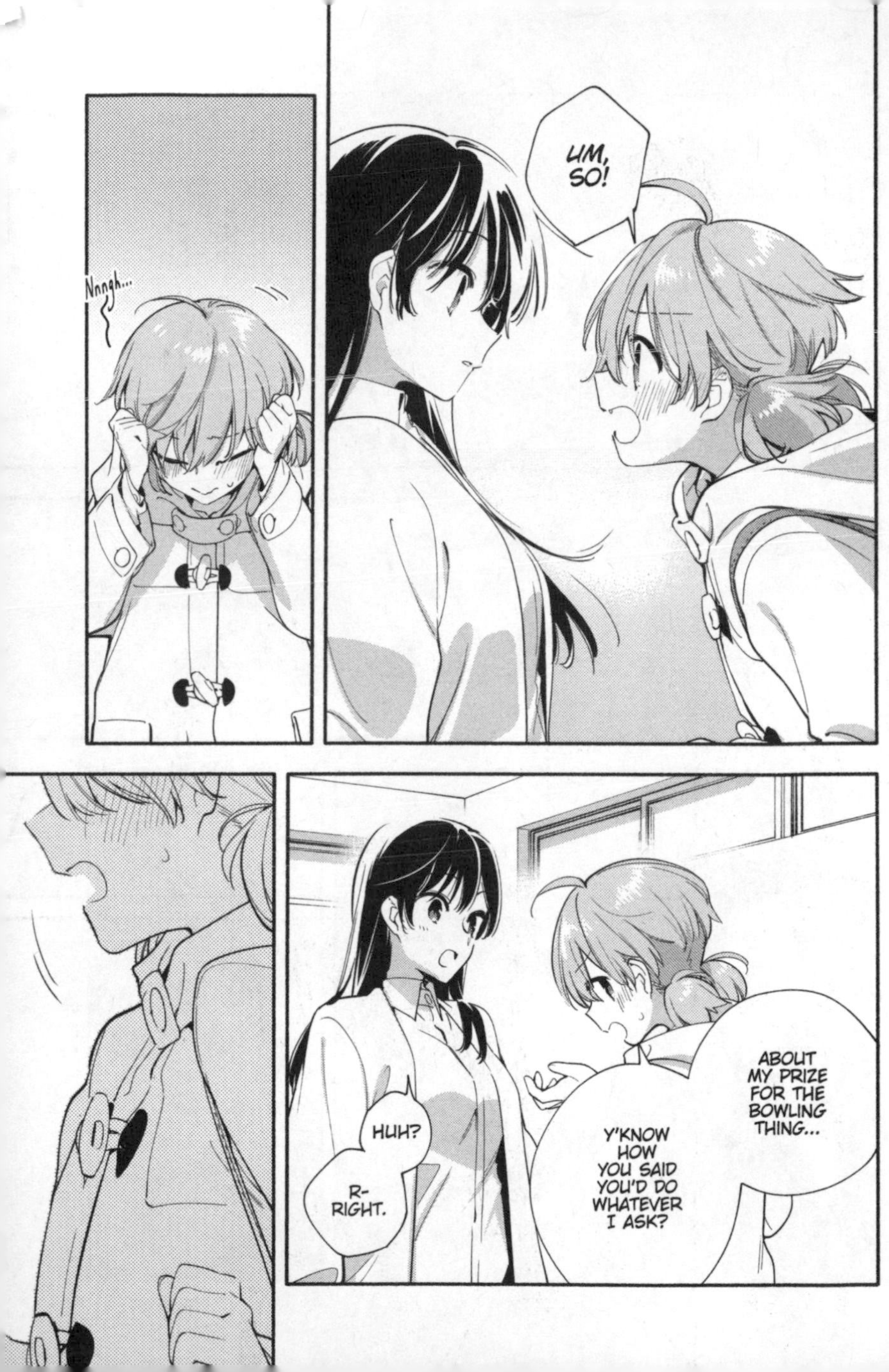
UM, SO!
Nnngh...
ABOUT MY PRIZE FOR THE BOWLING THING...
Y'KNOW HOW YOU SAID YOU'D DO WHATEVER I ASK?
HUH?
R-RIGHT.

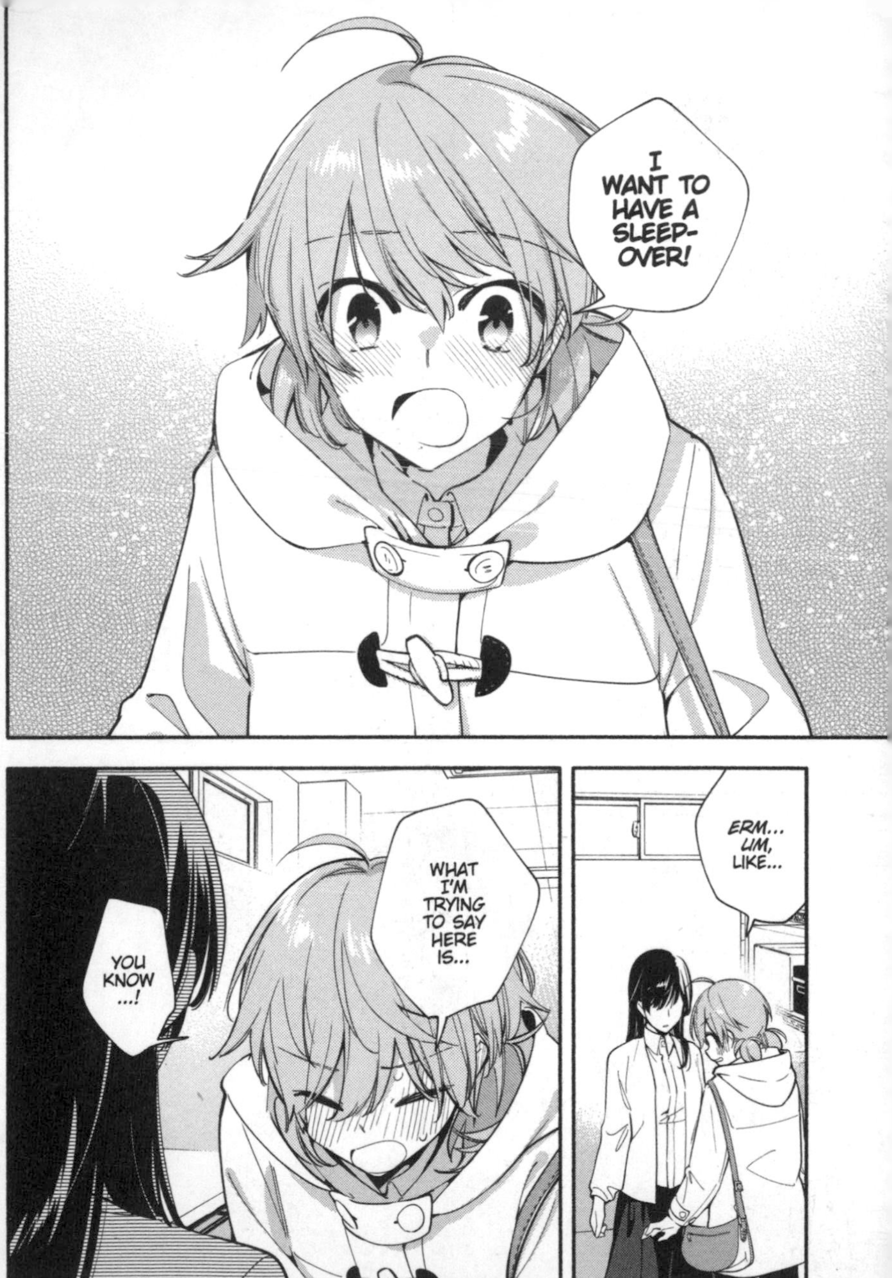
I WANT TO HAVE A SLEEP-OVER!
ERM... UM, LIKE...
WHAT I'M TRYING TO SAY HERE IS...
YOU KNOW ...!

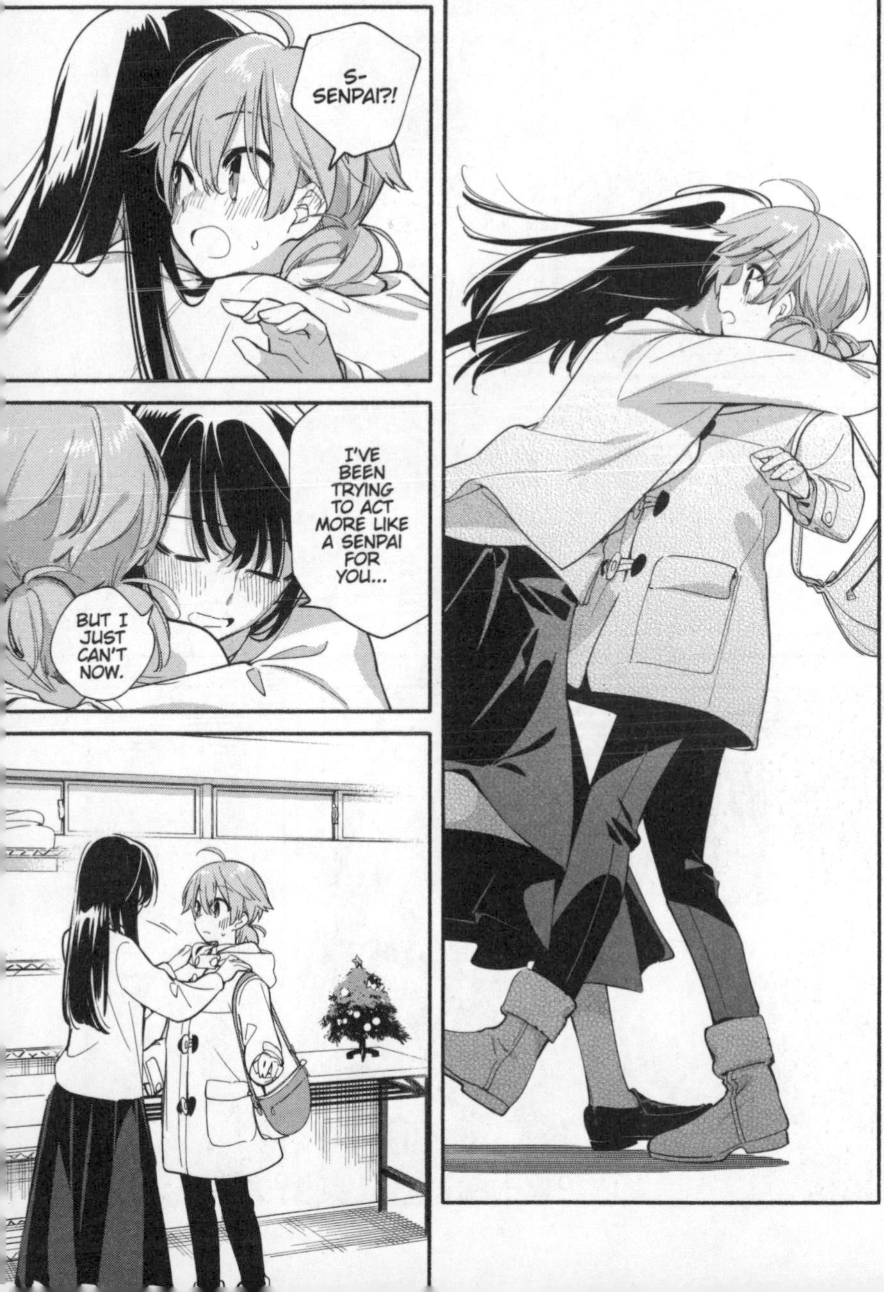
S-SENPAI?!
I'VE BEEN TRYING TO ACT MORE LIKE A SENPAI FOR YOU...
BUT I JUST CAN'T NOW.

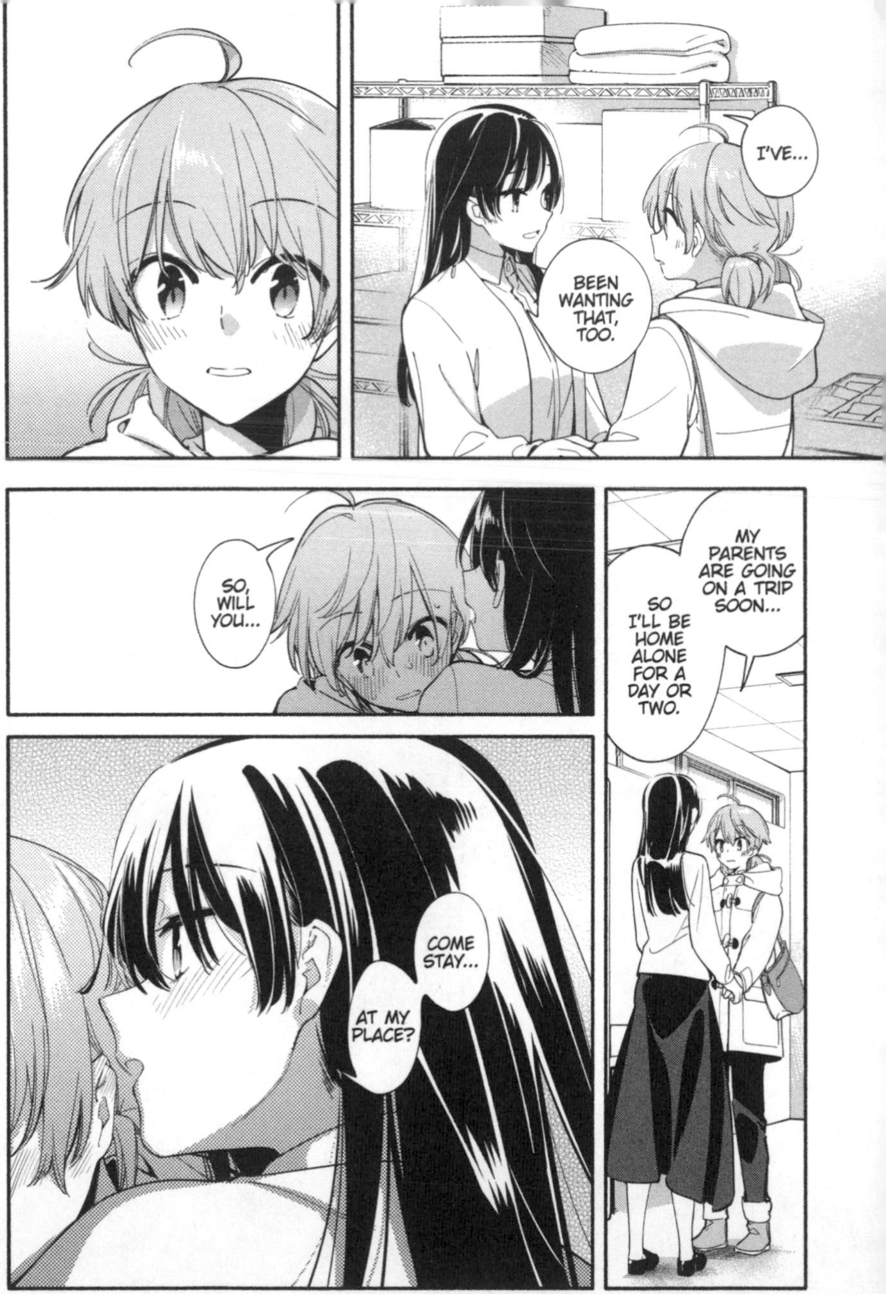
I'VE...
BEEN WANTING THAT, TOO.
MY PARENTS ARE GOING ON A TRIP SOON...
SO I'LL BE HOME ALONE FOR A DAY OR TWO.
SO, WILL YOU...
COME STAY...
AT MY PLACE?

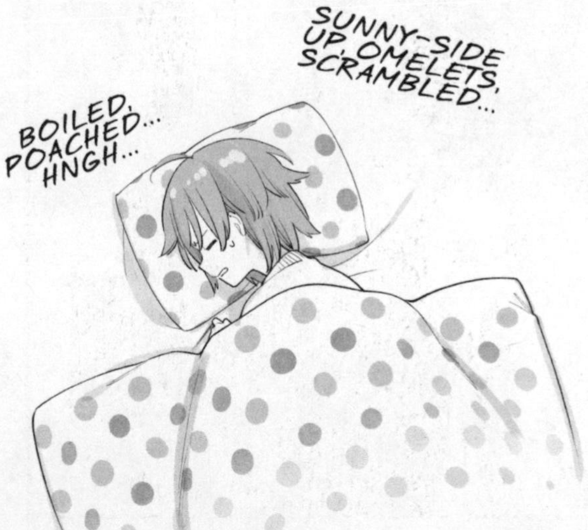
SUNNY-SIDE UP, OMELETS, SCRAMBLED...
BOILED, POACHED... HNGH...

(**Bloom Into You**)

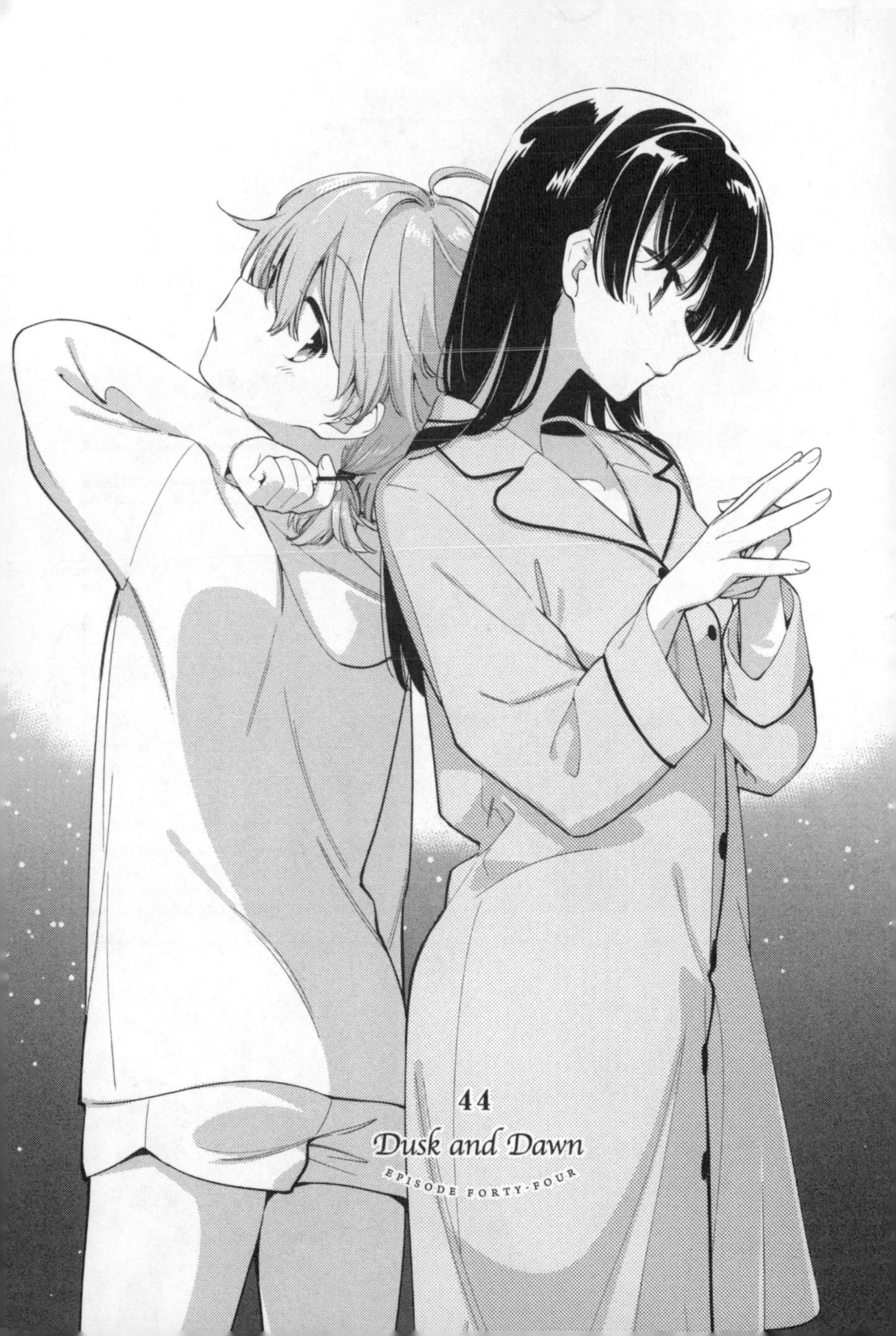

44

Dusk and Dawn

EPISODE FORTY-FOUR

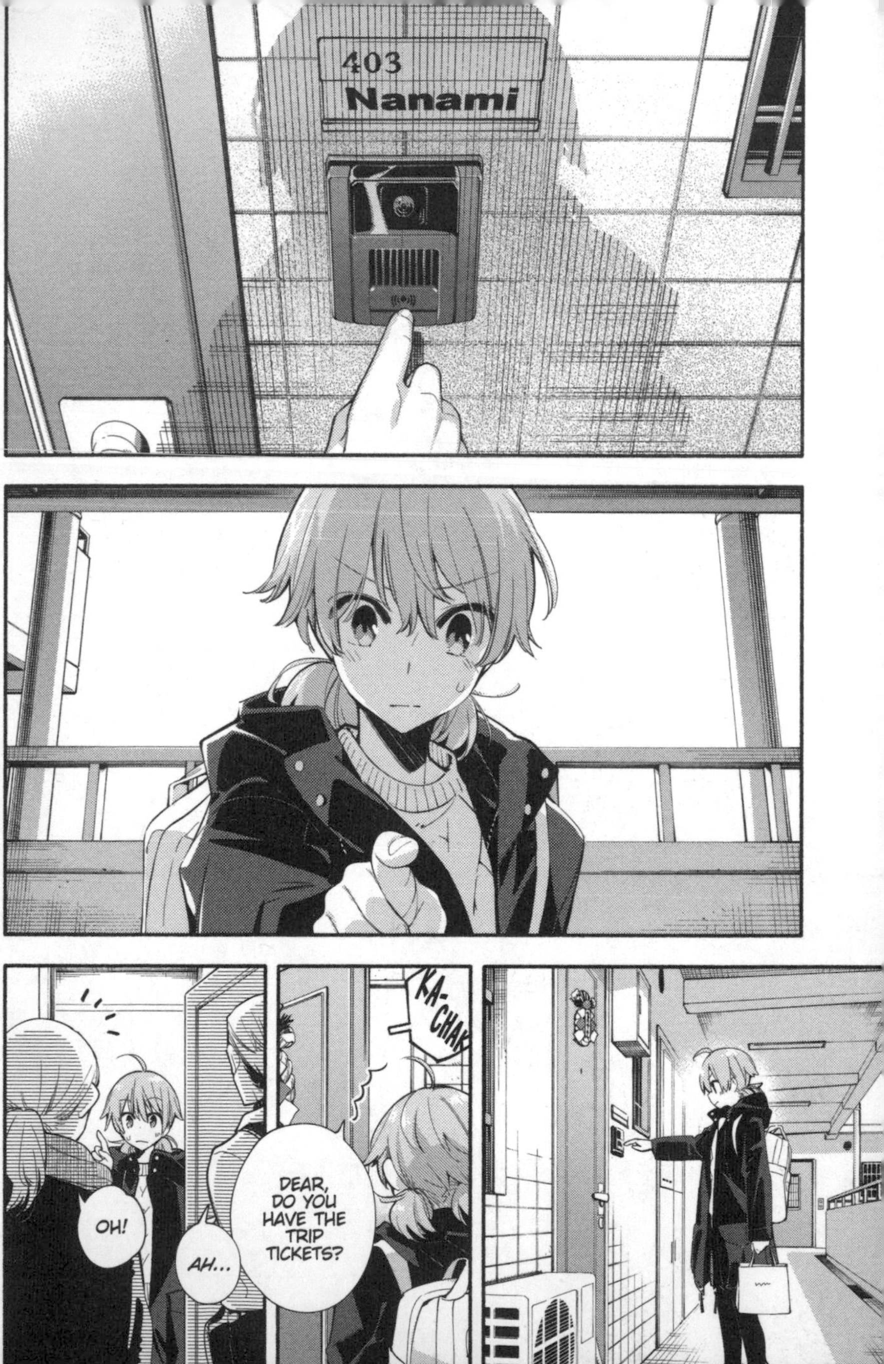
403
Nanami
KA-CHAK
DEAR, DO YOU HAVE THE TRIP TICKETS?
OH!
AH...

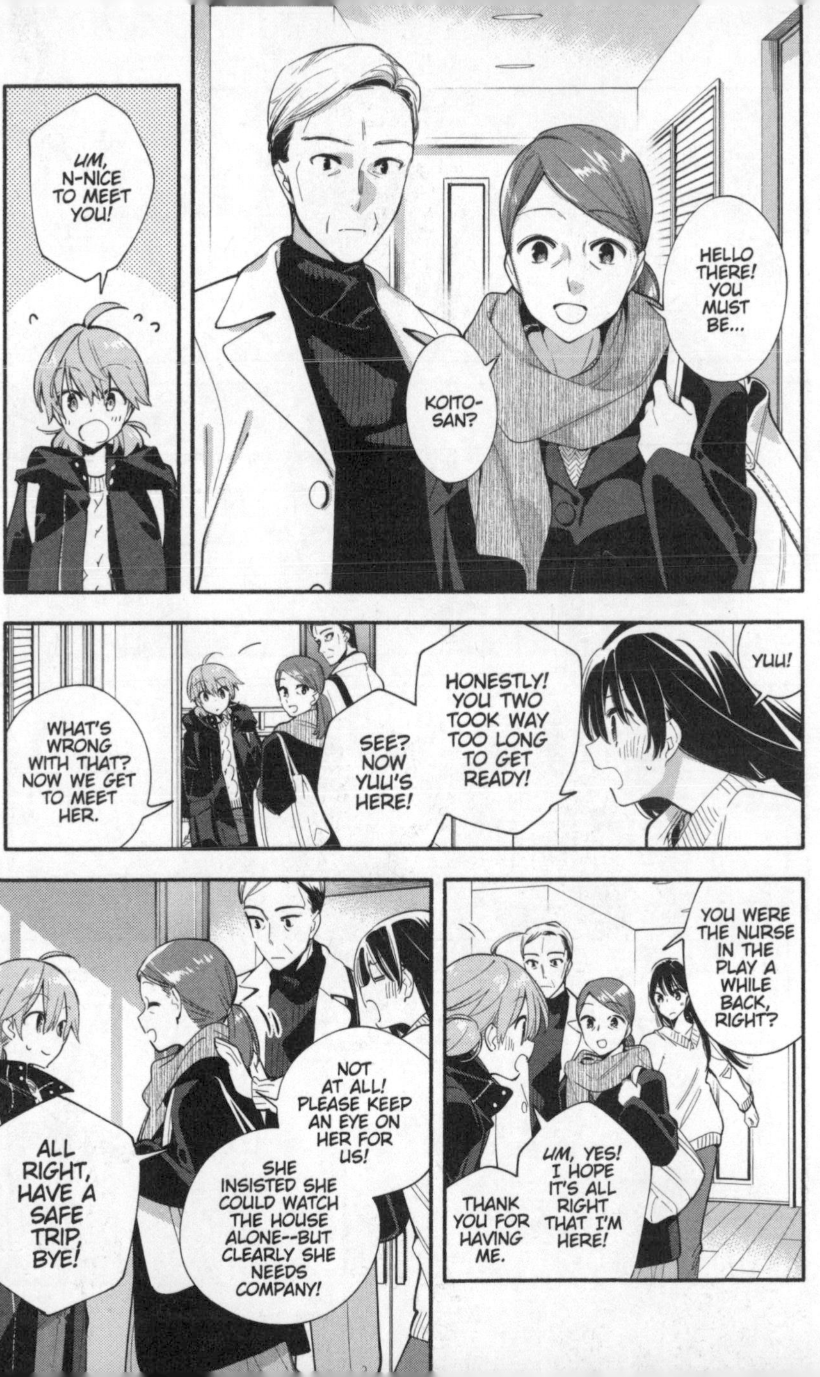
HELLO THERE! YOU MUST BE...
KOITO-SAN?
UM, N-NICE TO MEET YOU!
YUU!
HONESTLY! YOU TWO TOOK WAY TOO LONG TO GET READY!
SEE? NOW YUU'S HERE!
WHAT'S WRONG WITH THAT? NOW WE GET TO MEET HER.
YOU WERE THE NURSE IN THE PLAY A WHILE BACK, RIGHT?
UM, YES! I HOPE IT'S ALL RIGHT THAT I'M HERE!
THANK YOU FOR HAVING ME.
NOT AT ALL! PLEASE KEEP AN EYE ON HER FOR US!
SHE INSISTED SHE COULD WATCH THE HOUSE ALONE--BUT CLEARLY SHE NEEDS COMPANY!
ALL RIGHT, HAVE A SAFE TRIP, BYE!

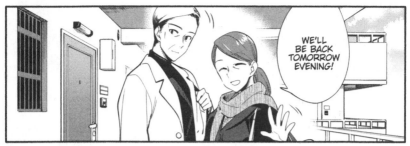

WE'LL BE BACK TOMORROW EVENING!
I KINDA FEEL LIKE WE'RE GETTING AWAY WITH SOME-THING...
WHY'S THAT?
I MEAN, I'M SPENDING THE NIGHT HERE.
IF I WERE A GUY...
I DOUBT THEY'D BE OKAY WITH THAT.
LUCKY US, THEN.
YOU'RE SHAME-LESS...

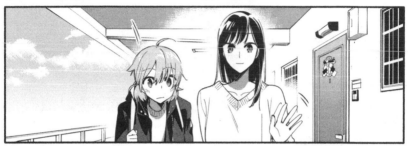

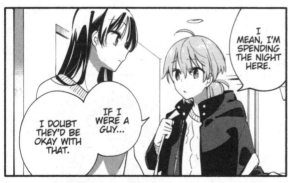

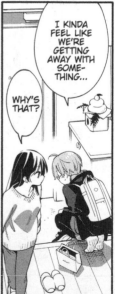

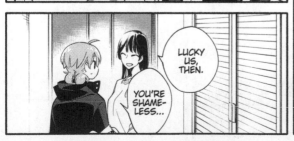

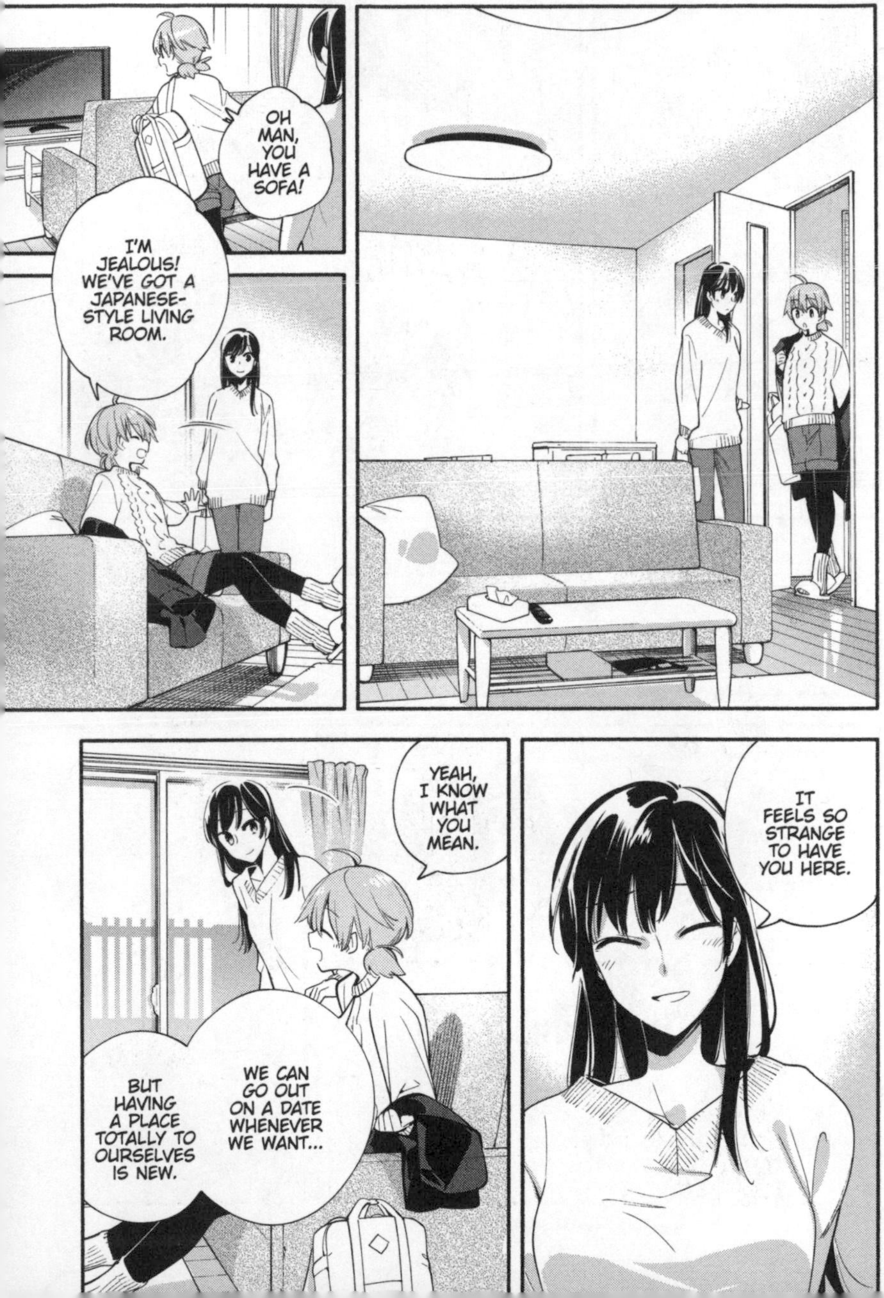
OH MAN, YOU HAVE A SOFA!
I'M JEALOUS! WE'VE GOT A JAPANESE-STYLE LIVING ROOM.
IT FEELS SO STRANGE TO HAVE YOU HERE.
YEAH, I KNOW WHAT YOU MEAN.
WE CAN GO OUT ON A DATE WHENEVER WE WANT...
BUT HAVING A PLACE TOTALLY TO OURSELVES IS NEW.

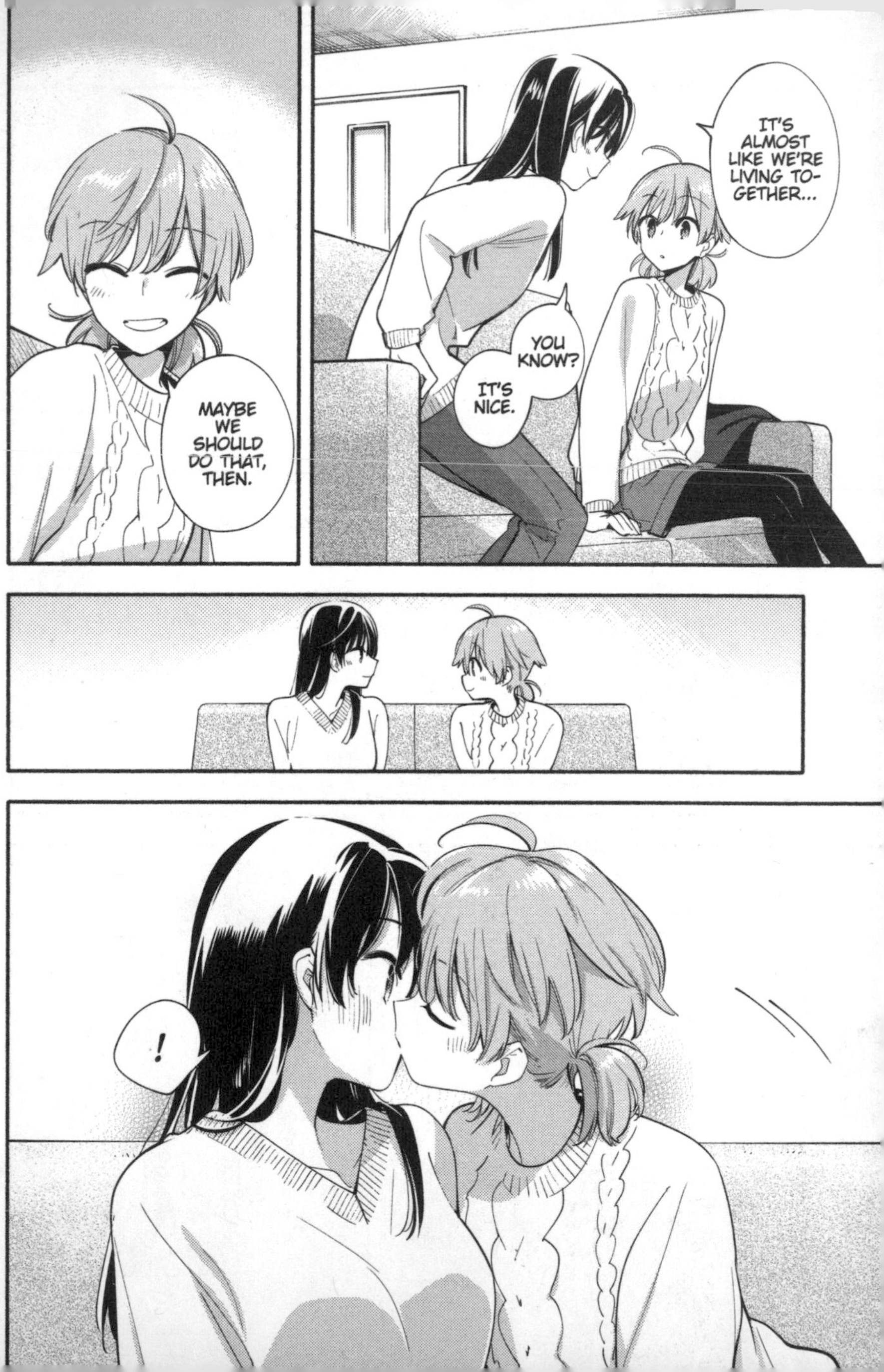
IT'S ALMOST LIKE WE'RE LIVING TO-GETHER...
YOU KNOW?
IT'S NICE.
MAYBE WE SHOULD DO THAT, THEN.
!

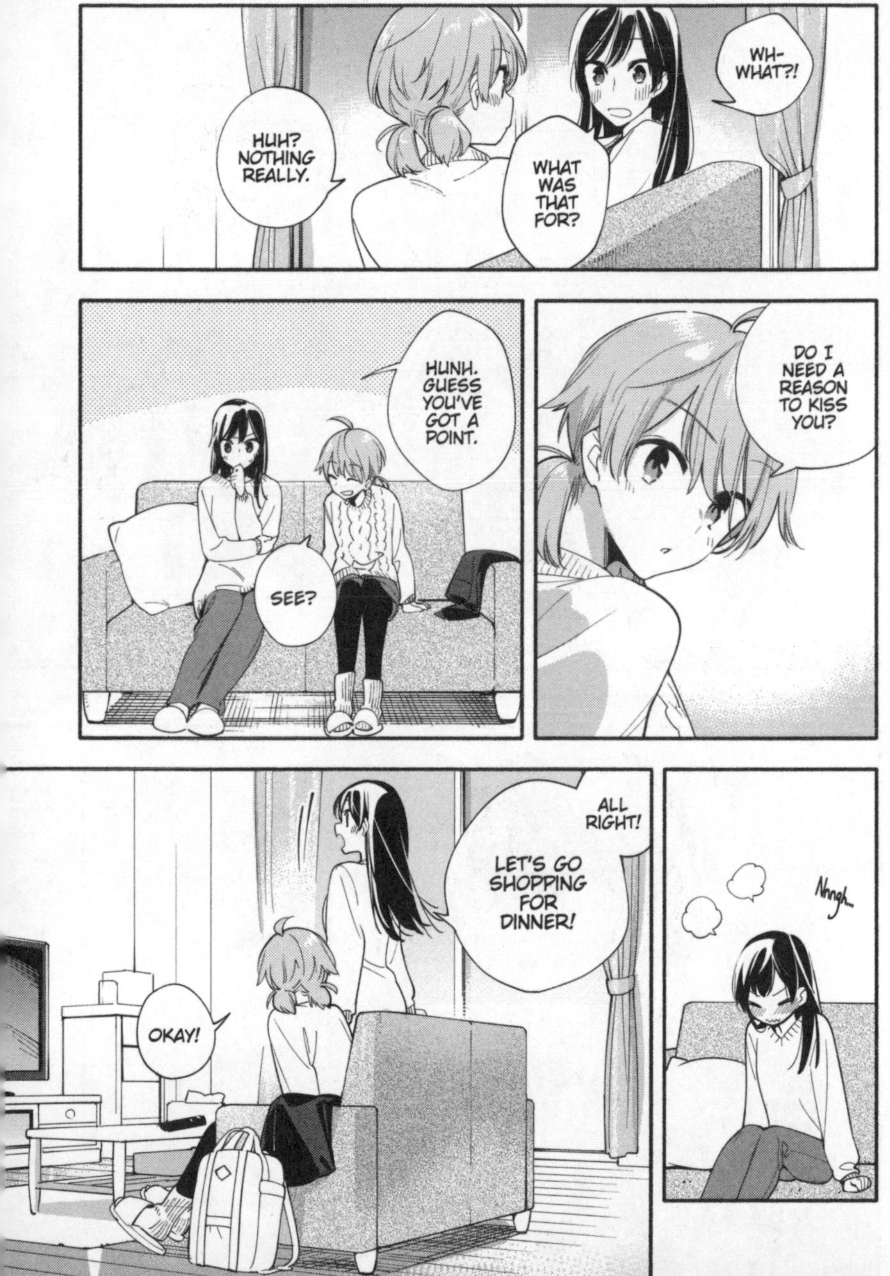
WH- WHAT?!
WHAT WAS THAT FOR?
HUH? NOTHING REALLY.
DO I NEED A REASON TO KISS YOU?
HUNH. GUESS YOU'VE GOT A POINT.
SEE?
Nnngh...
ALL RIGHT!
LET'S GO SHOPPING FOR DINNER!
OKAY!

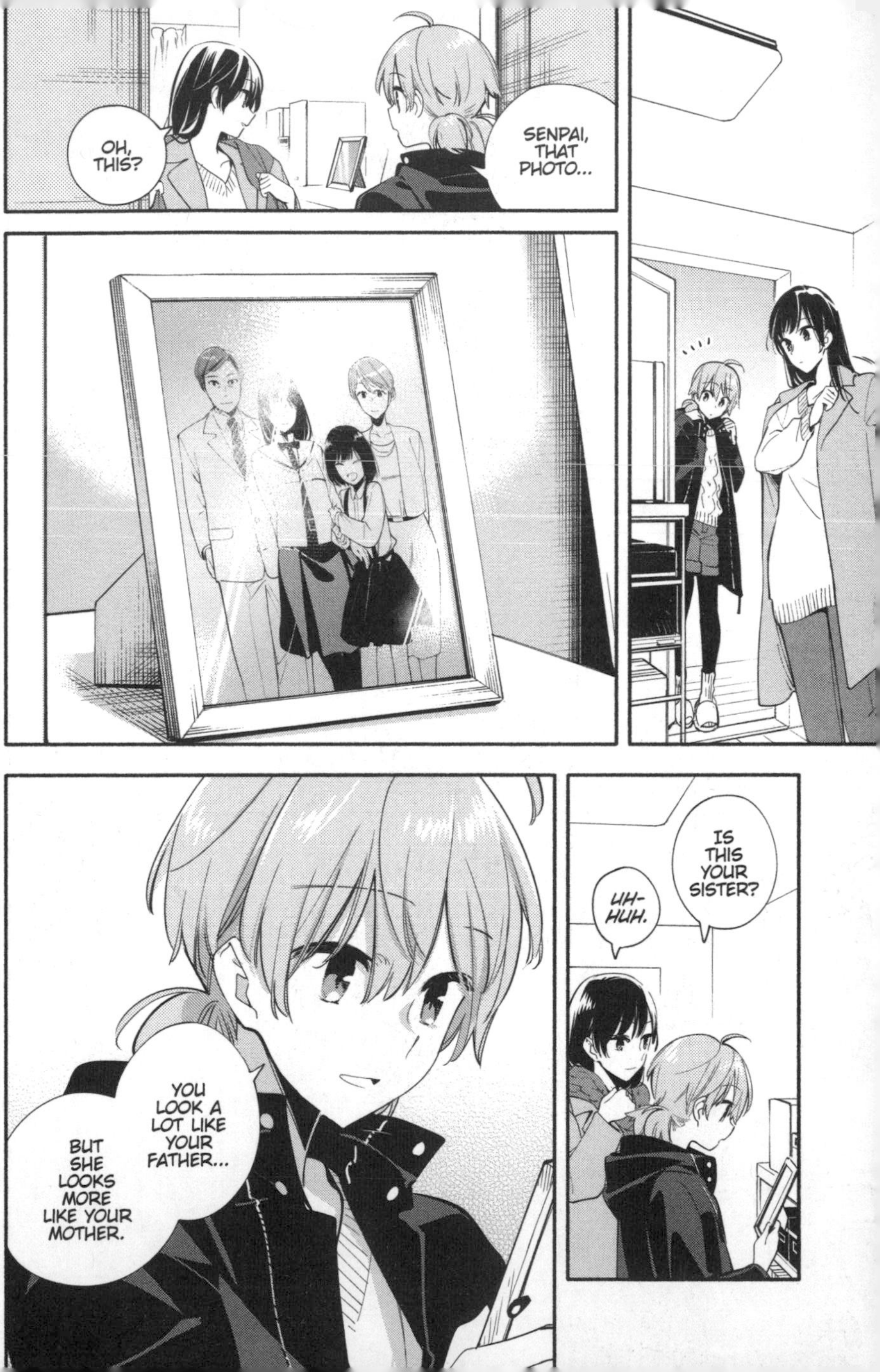
SENPAI, THAT PHOTO...
OH, THIS?
IS THIS YOUR SISTER?
UH-HUH.
YOU LOOK A LOT LIKE YOUR FATHER...
BUT SHE LOOKS MORE LIKE YOUR MOTHER.

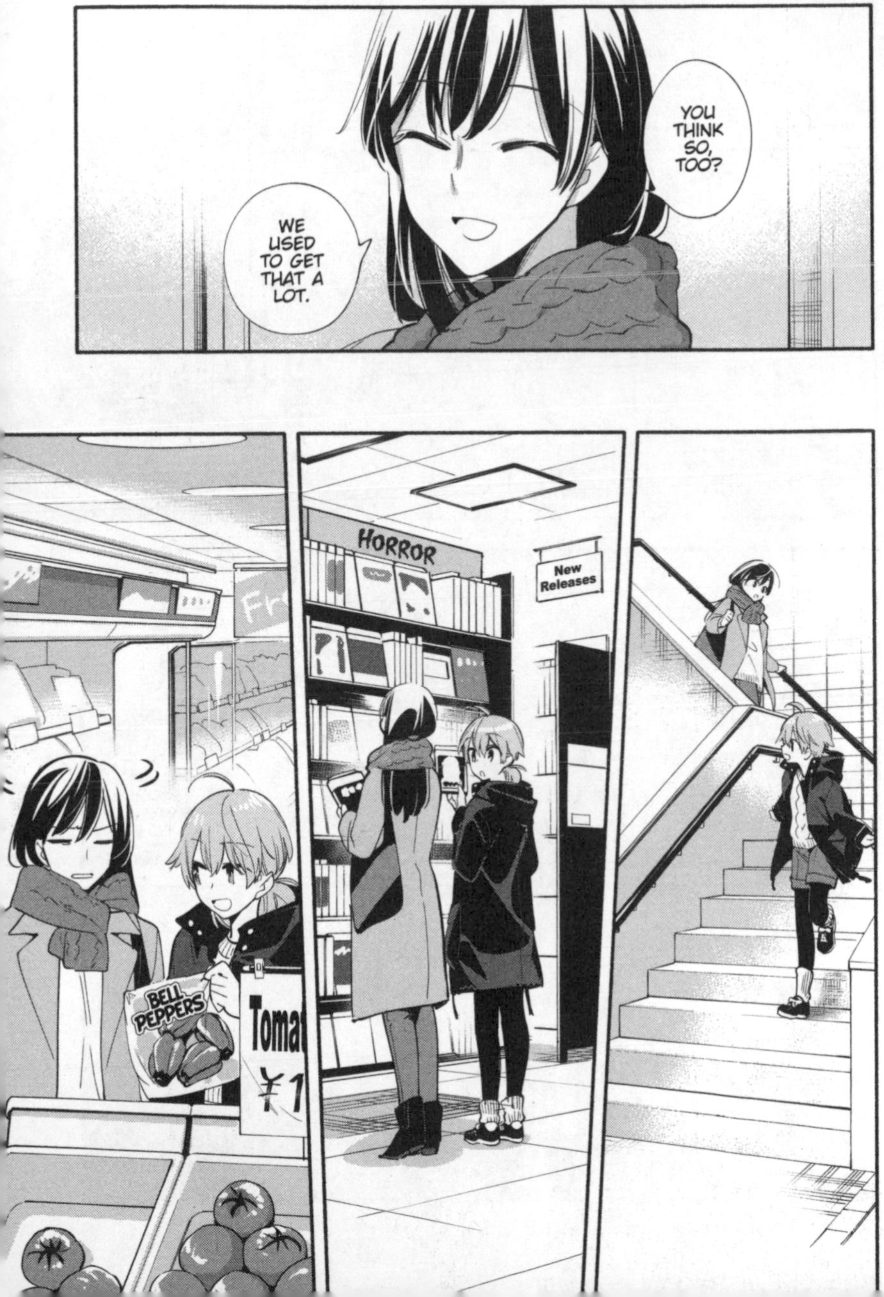
YOU THINK SO, TOO?
WE USED TO GET THAT A LOT.
HORROR
New Releases
BELL PEPPERS

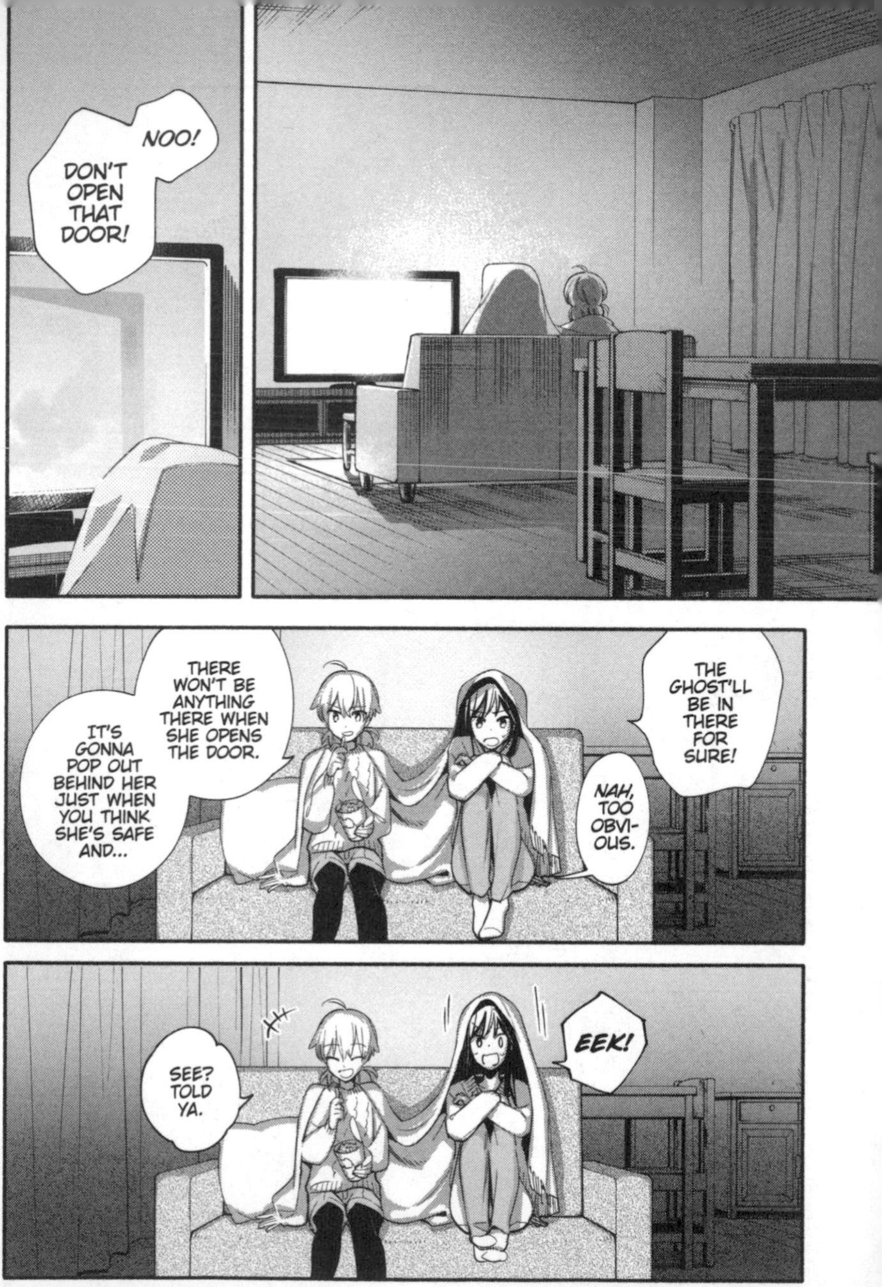
NOO! DON'T OPEN THAT DOOR!
THE GHOST'LL BE IN THERE FOR SURE!
NAH, TOO OBVI- OUS.
THERE WON'T BE ANYTHING THERE WHEN SHE OPENS THE DOOR.
IT'S GONNA POP OUT BEHIND HER JUST WHEN YOU THINK SHE'S SAFE AND...
EEK!
SEE? TOLD YA.

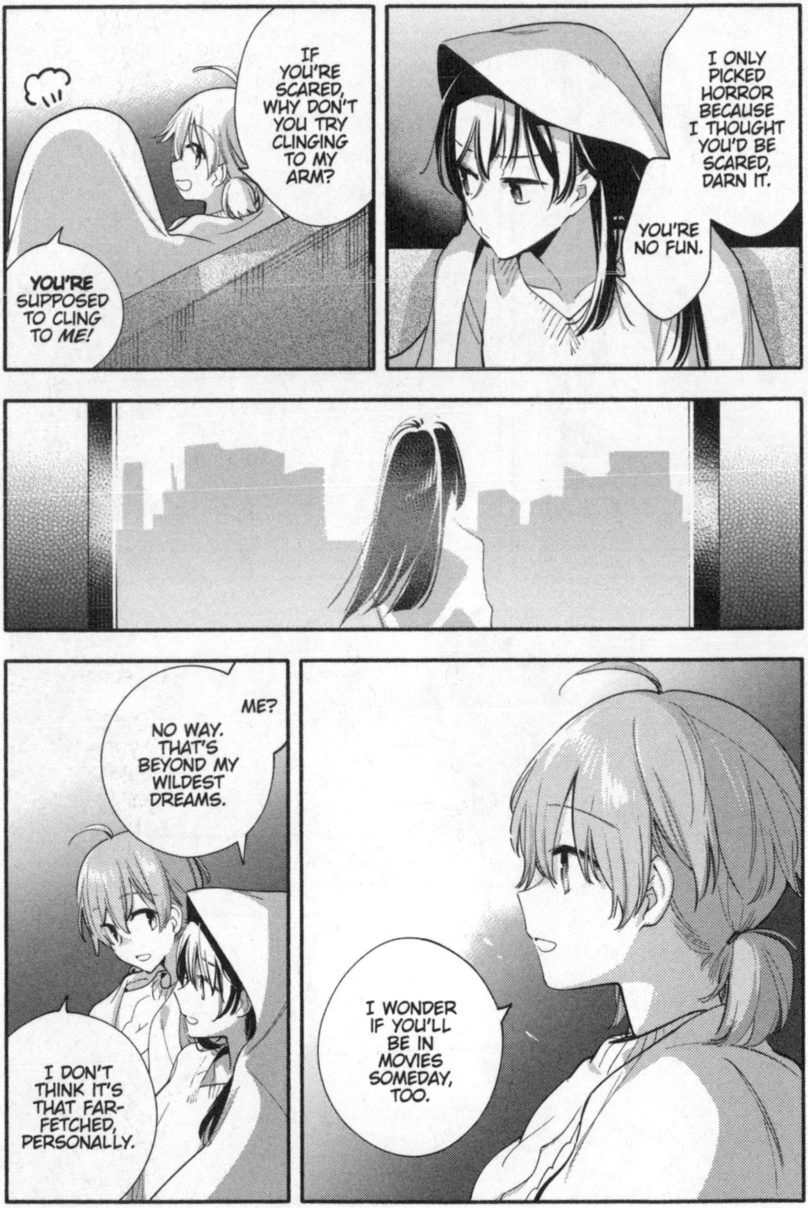
I ONLY PICKED HORROR BECAUSE I THOUGHT YOU'D BE SCARED, DARN IT.
YOU'RE NO FUN.
IF YOU'RE SCARED, WHY DON'T YOU TRY CLINGING TO MY ARM?
YOU'RE SUPPOSED TO CLING TO *ME*!
I WONDER IF YOU'LL BE IN MOVIES SOMEDAY, TOO.
ME?
NO WAY. THAT'S BEYOND MY WILDEST DREAMS.
I DON'T THINK IT'S THAT FAR-FETCHED, PERSONALLY.

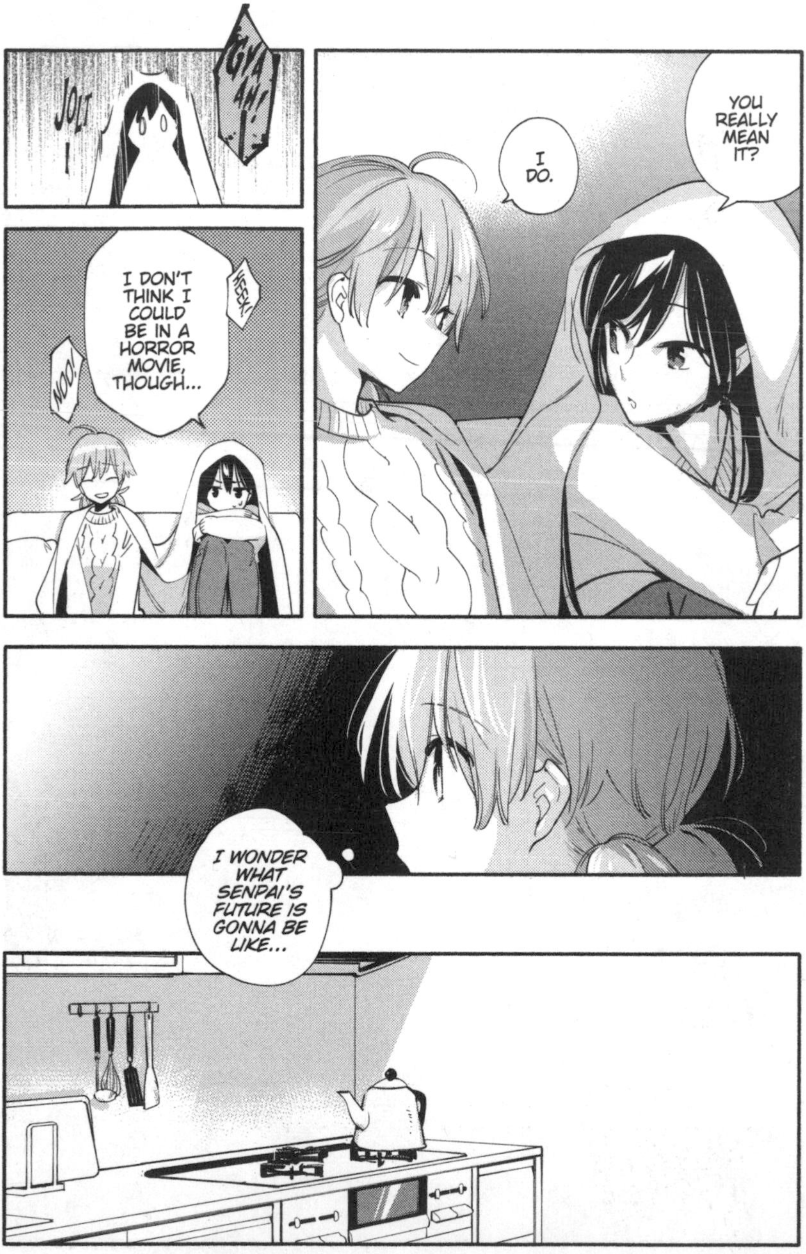
YOU REALLY MEAN IT?
I DO.
GYAAAH!!
JOLT
I DON'T THINK I COULD BE IN A HORROR MOVIE, THOUGH...
HEEK!
NOO!
I WONDER WHAT SENPAI'S FUTURE IS GONNA BE LIKE...

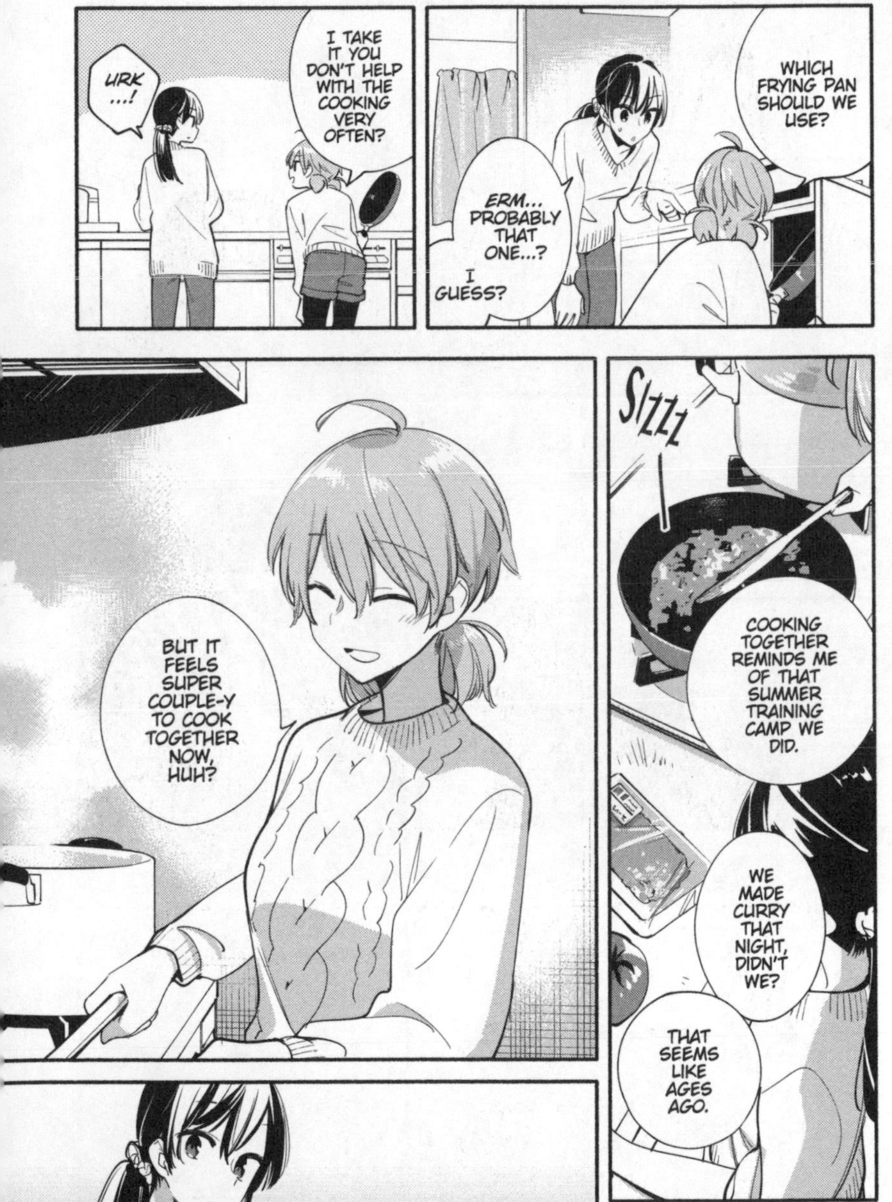
WHICH FRYING PAN SHOULD WE USE?
ERM... PROBABLY THAT ONE...?
I GUESS?
I TAKE IT YOU DON'T HELP WITH THE COOKING VERY OFTEN?
URK ...!
SIZZZ
COOKING TOGETHER REMINDS ME OF THAT SUMMER TRAINING CAMP WE DID.
WE MADE CURRY THAT NIGHT, DIDN'T WE?
THAT SEEMS LIKE AGES AGO.
BUT IT FEELS SUPER COUPLE-Y TO COOK TOGETHER NOW, HUH?

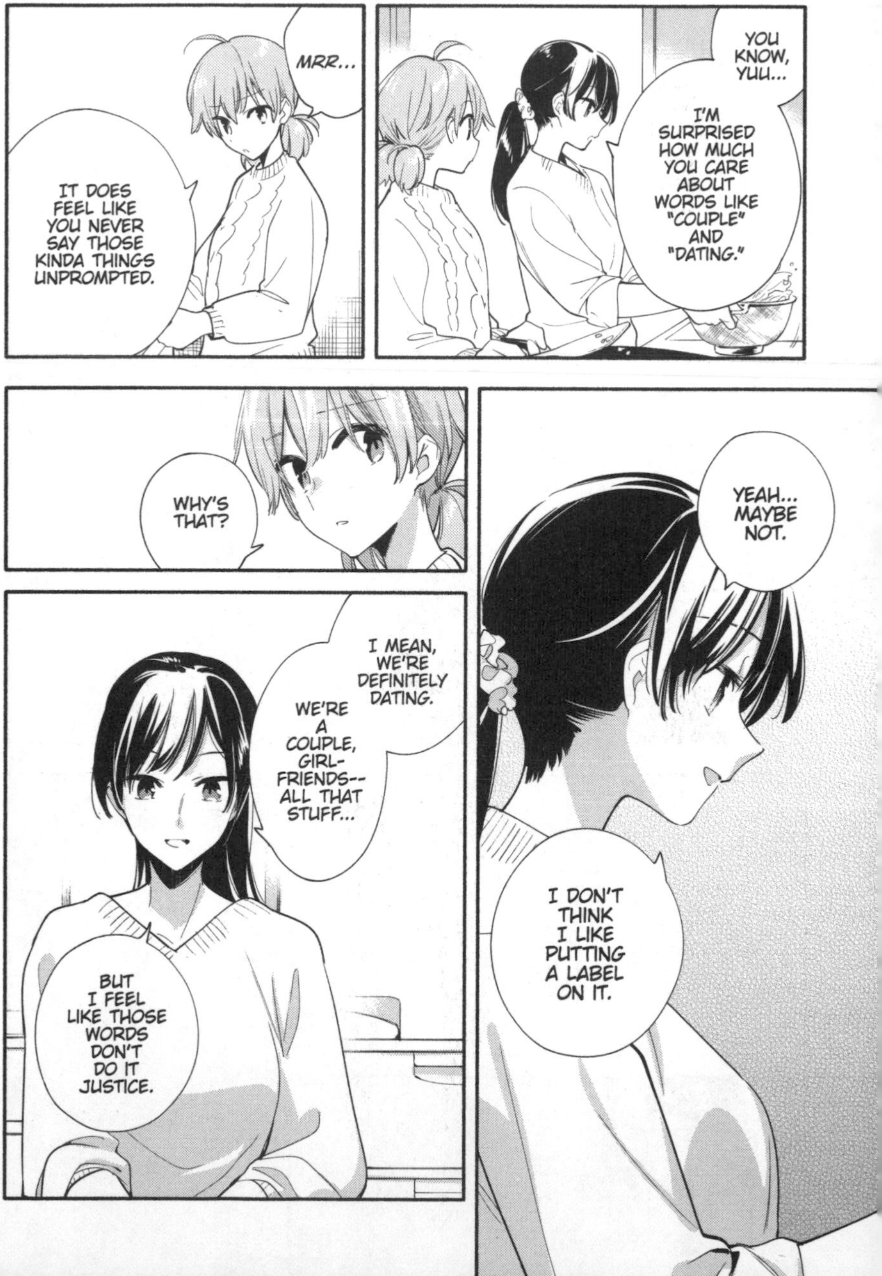
YOU KNOW, YUU...
I'M SURPRISED HOW MUCH YOU CARE ABOUT WORDS LIKE "COUPLE" AND "DATING."
MRR...
IT DOES FEEL LIKE YOU NEVER SAY THOSE KINDA THINGS UNPROMPTED.
YEAH... MAYBE NOT.
I DON'T THINK I LIKE PUTTING A LABEL ON IT.
WHY'S THAT?
I MEAN, WE'RE DEFINITELY DATING.
WE'RE A COUPLE, GIRL-FRIENDS--ALL THAT STUFF...
BUT I FEEL LIKE THOSE WORDS DON'T DO IT JUSTICE.

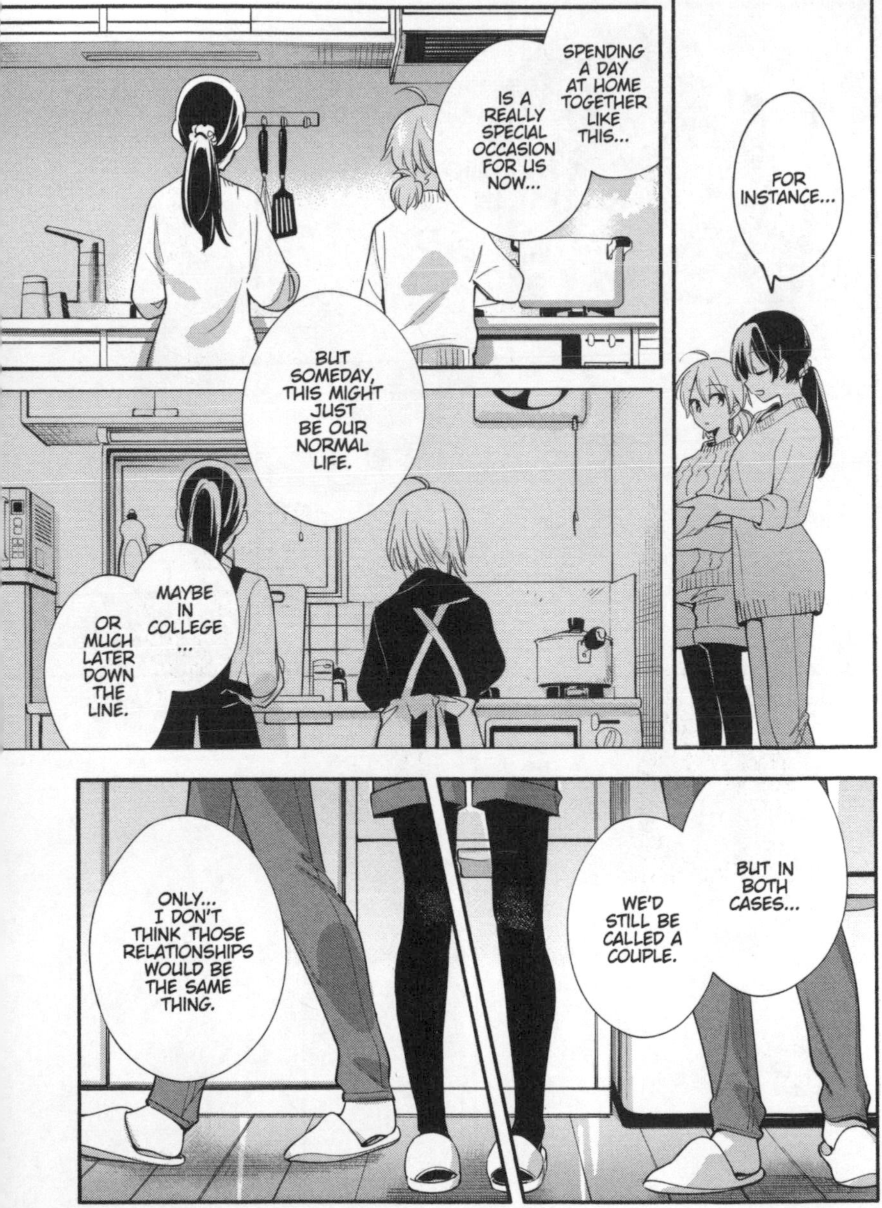
FOR INSTANCE...
SPENDING A DAY AT HOME TOGETHER LIKE THIS...
IS A REALLY SPECIAL OCCASION FOR US NOW...
BUT SOMEDAY, THIS MIGHT JUST BE OUR NORMAL LIFE.
MAYBE IN COLLEGE ...
OR MUCH LATER DOWN THE LINE.
BUT IN BOTH CASES...
WE'D STILL BE CALLED A COUPLE.
ONLY... I DON'T THINK THOSE RELATIONSHIPS WOULD BE THE SAME THING.

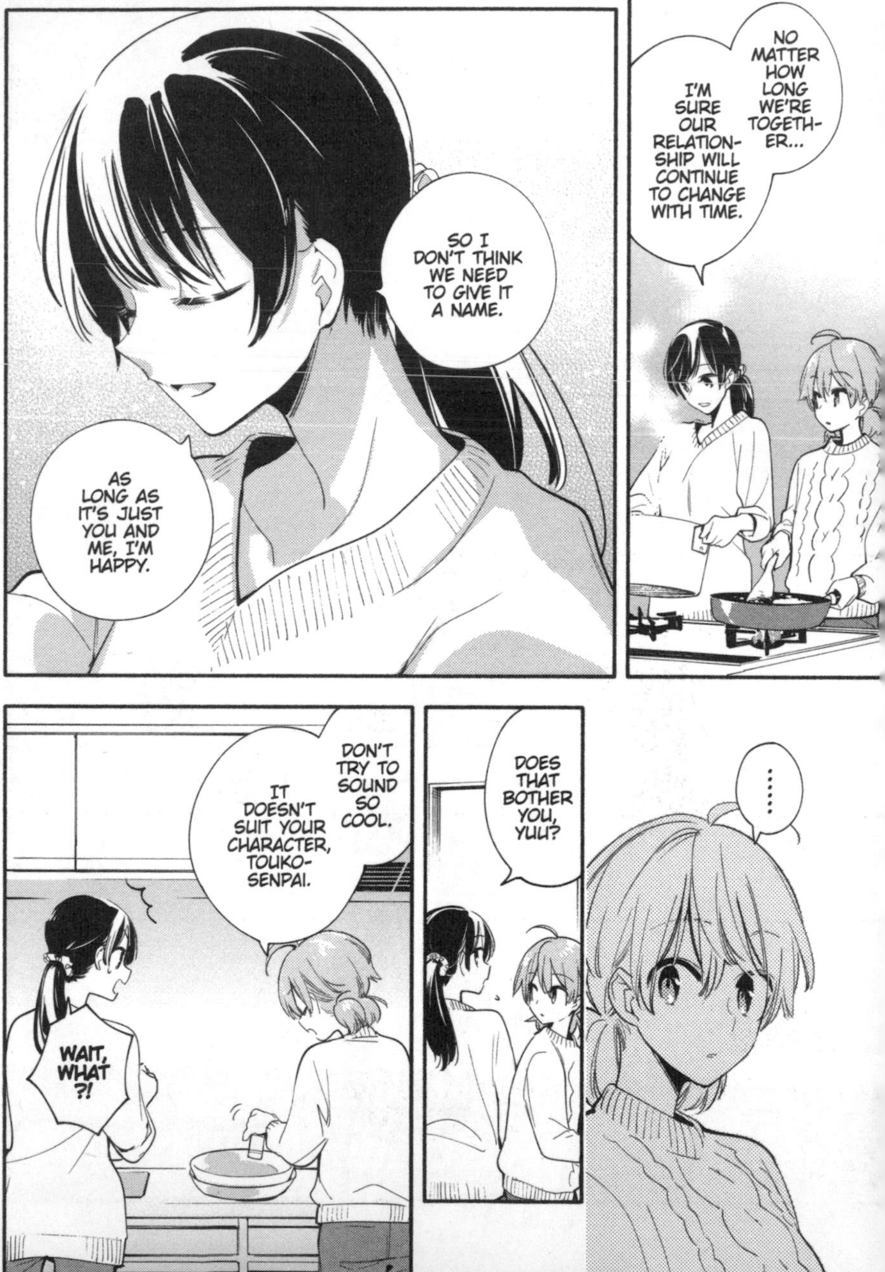
NO MATTER HOW LONG WE'RE TOGETHER...
I'M SURE OUR RELATIONSHIP WILL CONTINUE TO CHANGE WITH TIME.
SO I DON'T THINK WE NEED TO GIVE IT A NAME.
AS LONG AS IT'S JUST YOU AND ME, I'M HAPPY.
......
DOES THAT BOTHER YOU, YUU?
DON'T TRY TO SOUND SO COOL.
IT DOESN'T SUIT YOUR CHARACTER, TOUKO-SENPAI.
WAIT, WHAT?!

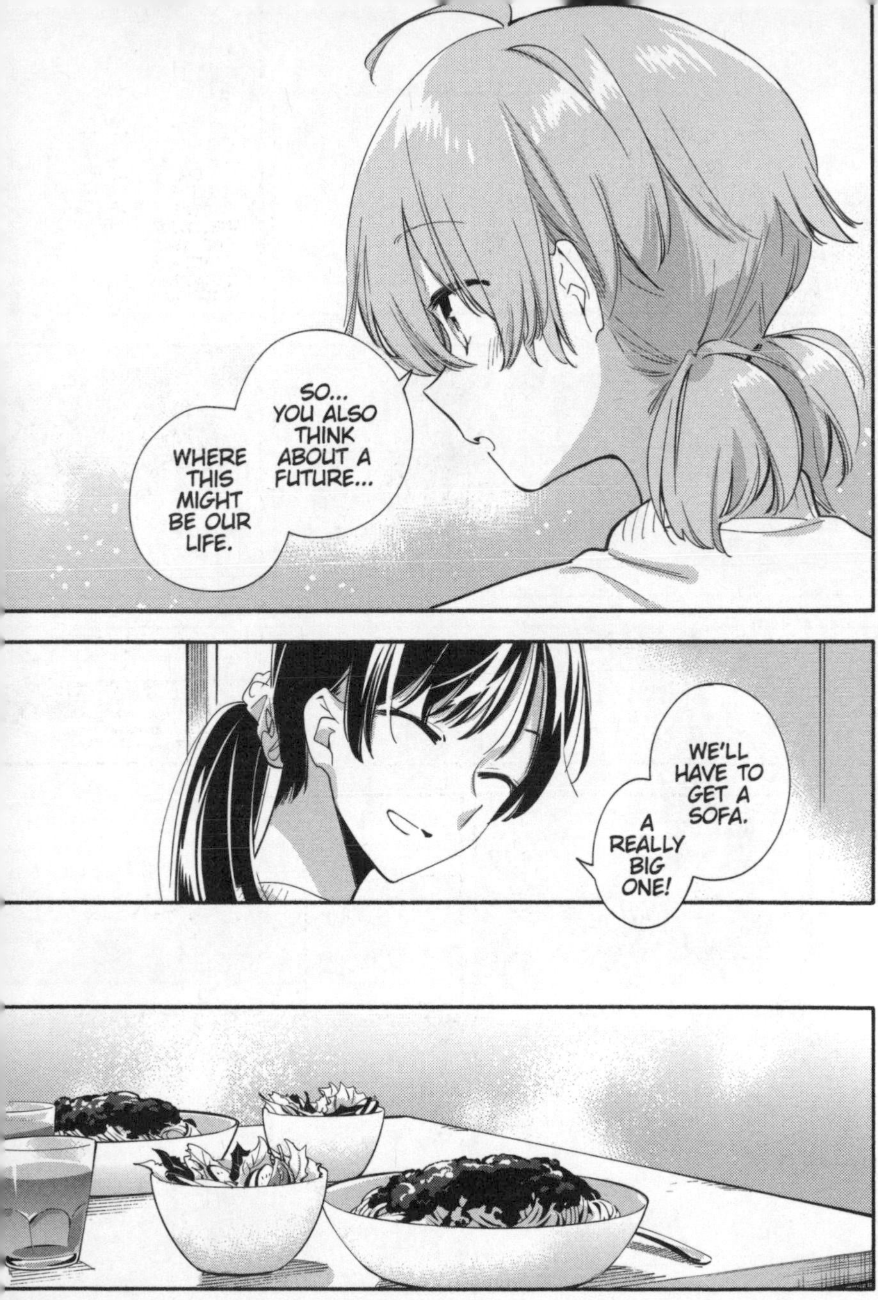
SO... YOU ALSO THINK ABOUT A FUTURE...
WHERE THIS MIGHT BE OUR LIFE.
WE'LL HAVE TO GET A SOFA.
A REALLY BIG ONE!

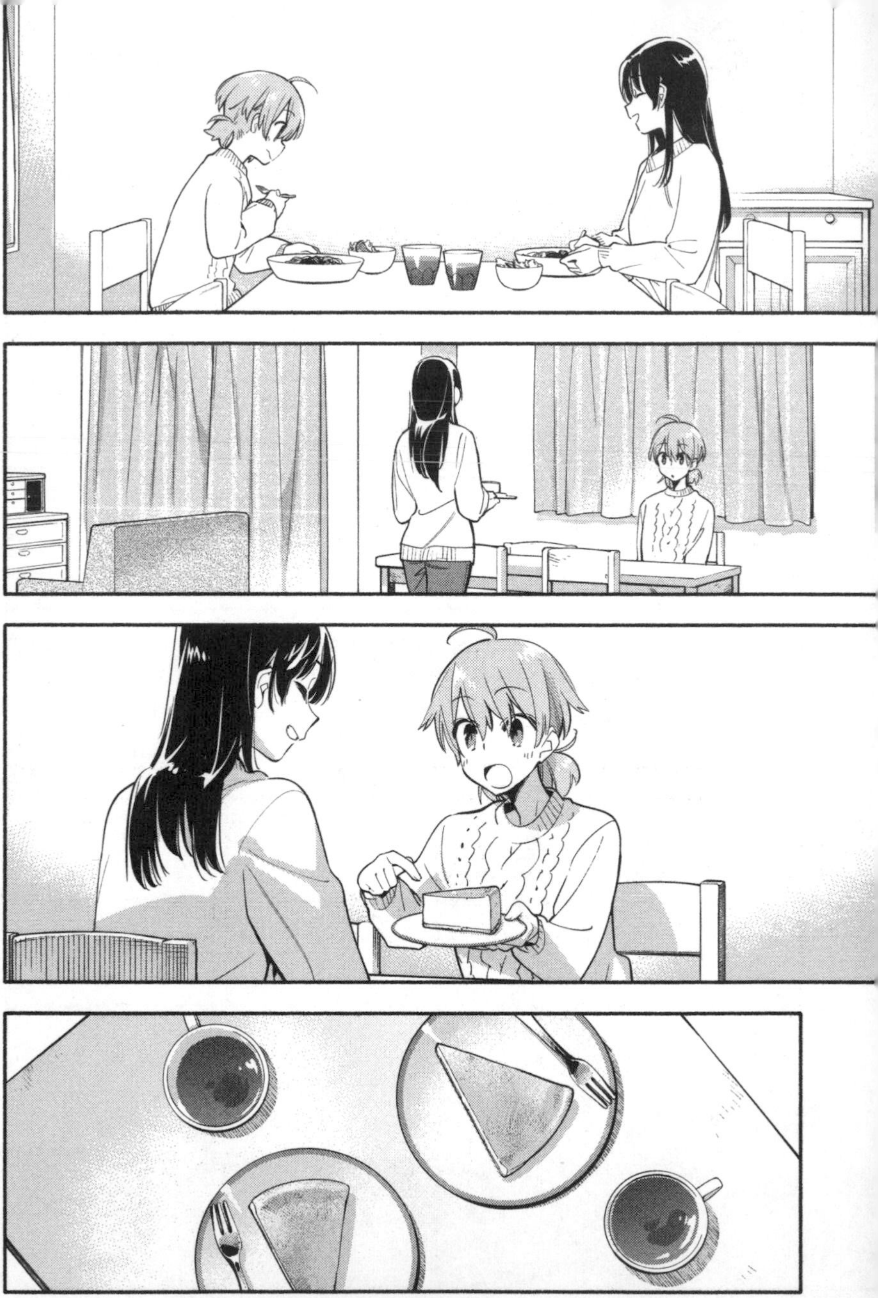

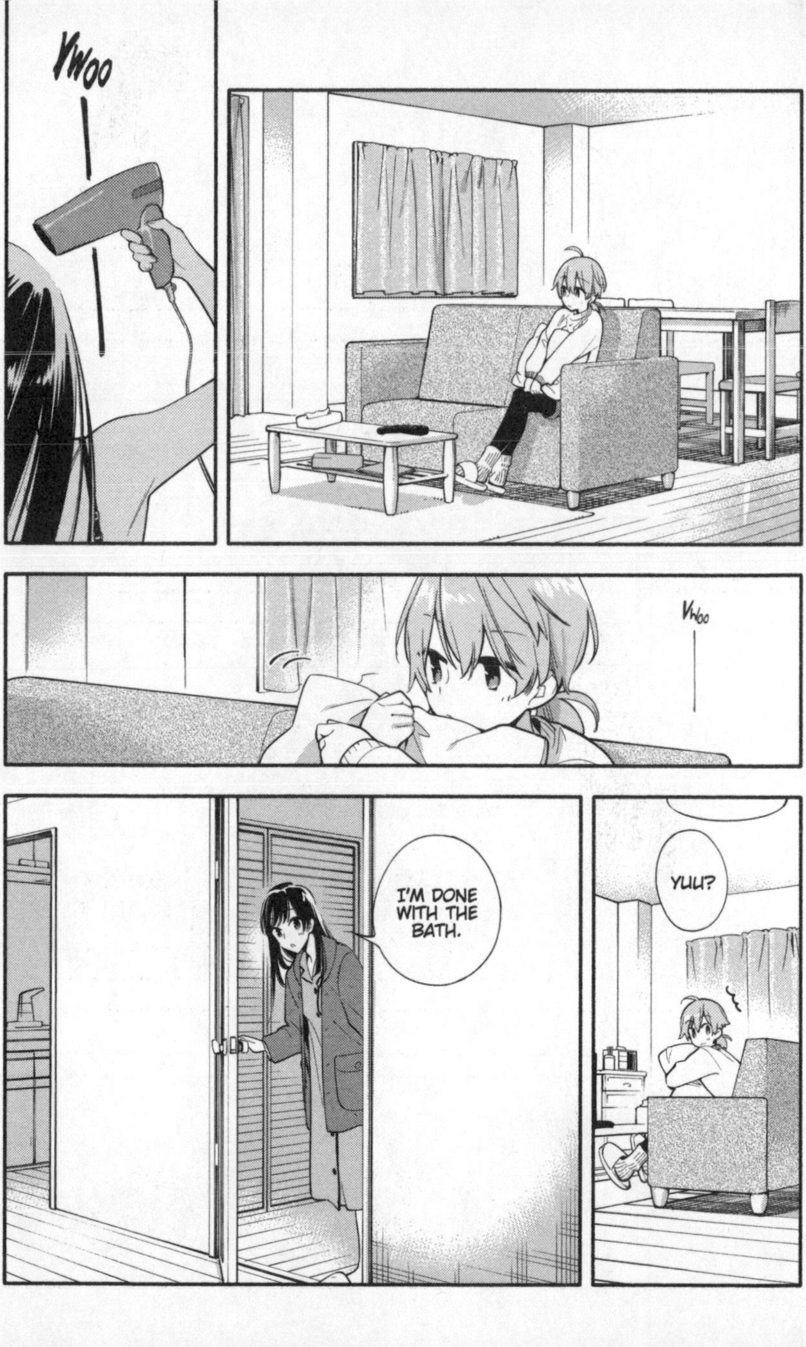
YWOO
VWOO
YUU?
I'M DONE WITH THE BATH.

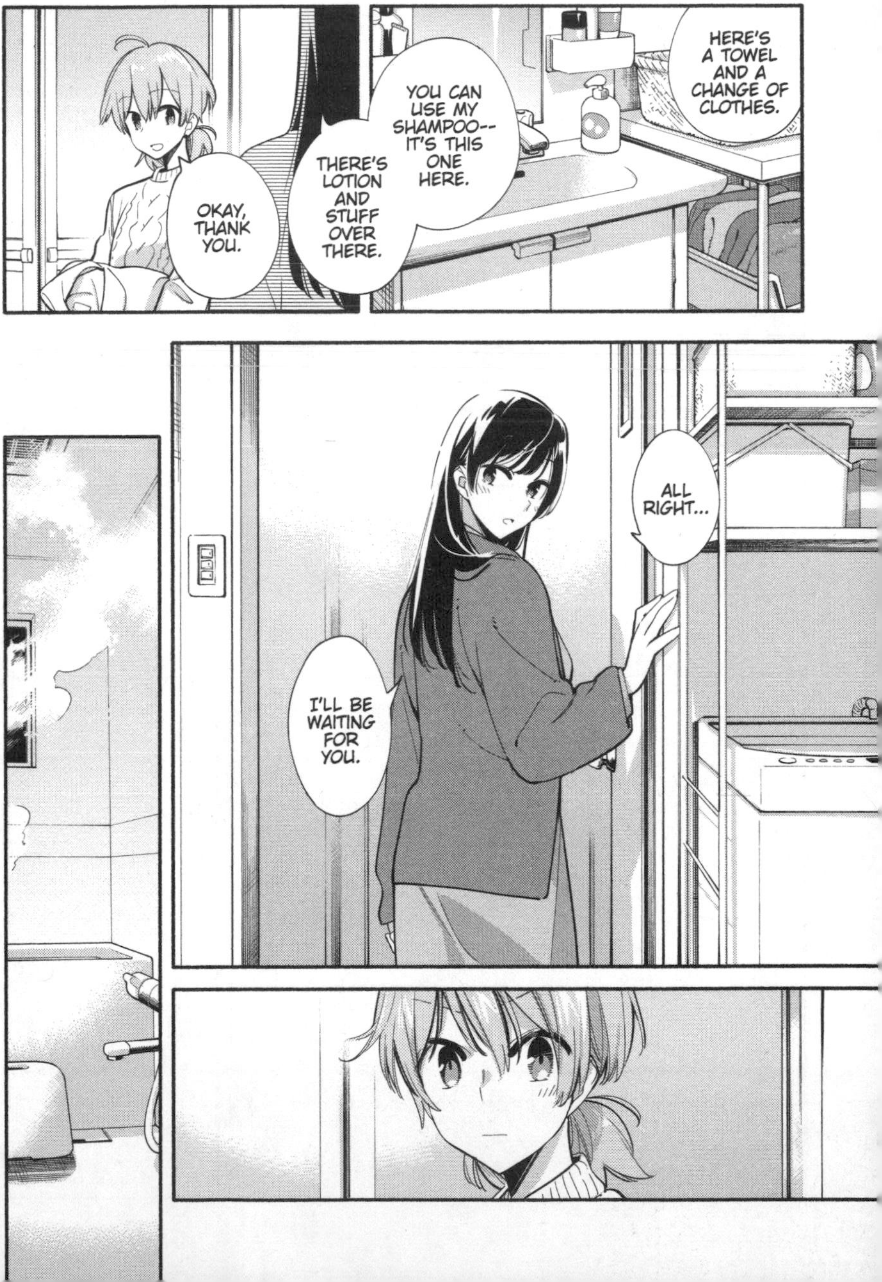
HERE'S A TOWEL AND A CHANGE OF CLOTHES.
YOU CAN USE MY SHAMPOO-- IT'S THIS ONE HERE.
THERE'S LOTION AND STUFF OVER THERE.
OKAY, THANK YOU.
ALL RIGHT...
I'LL BE WAITING FOR YOU.

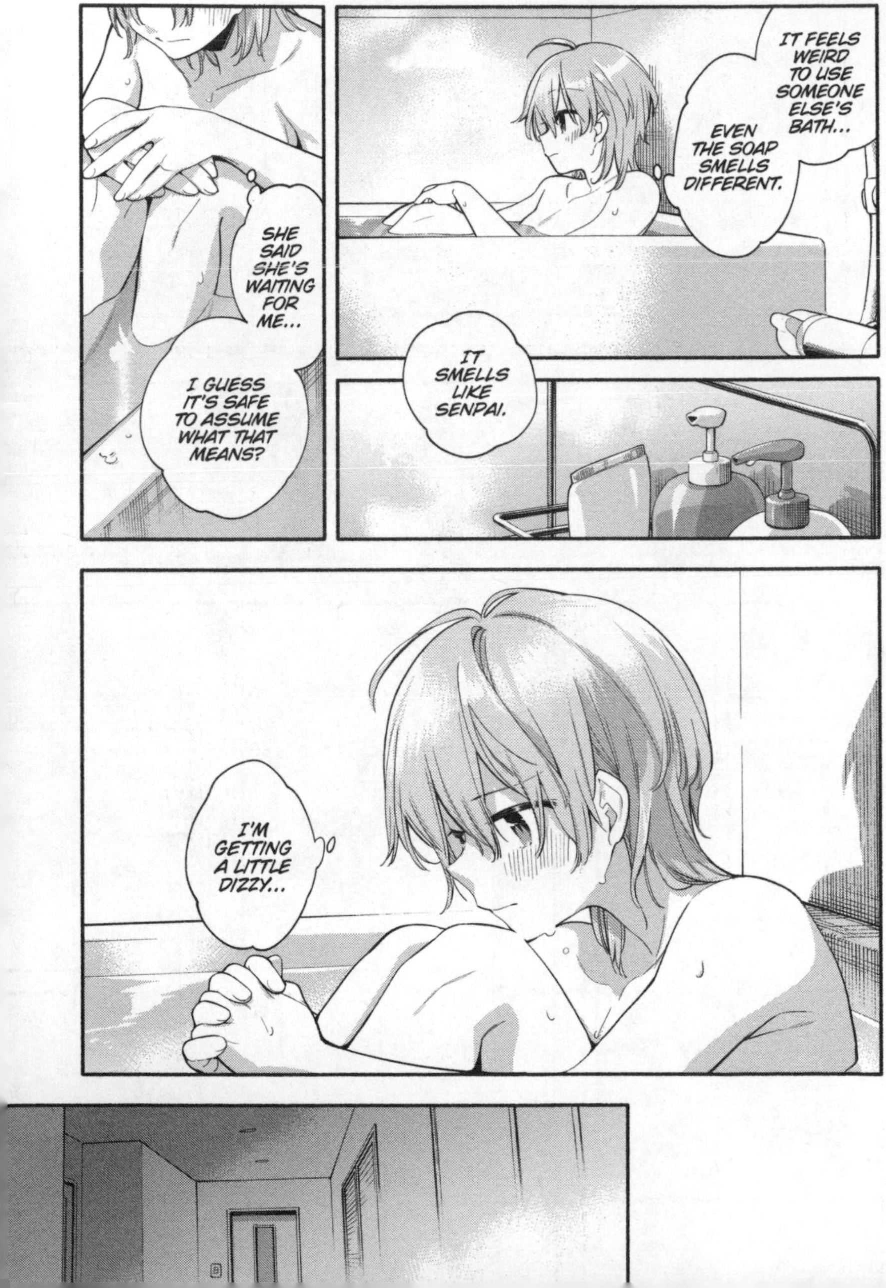
IT FEELS WEIRD TO USE SOMEONE ELSE'S BATH...
EVEN THE SOAP SMELLS DIFFERENT.
IT SMELLS LIKE SENPAI.
SHE SAID SHE'S WAITING FOR ME...
I GUESS IT'S SAFE TO ASSUME WHAT THAT MEANS?
I'M GETTING A LITTLE DIZZY...

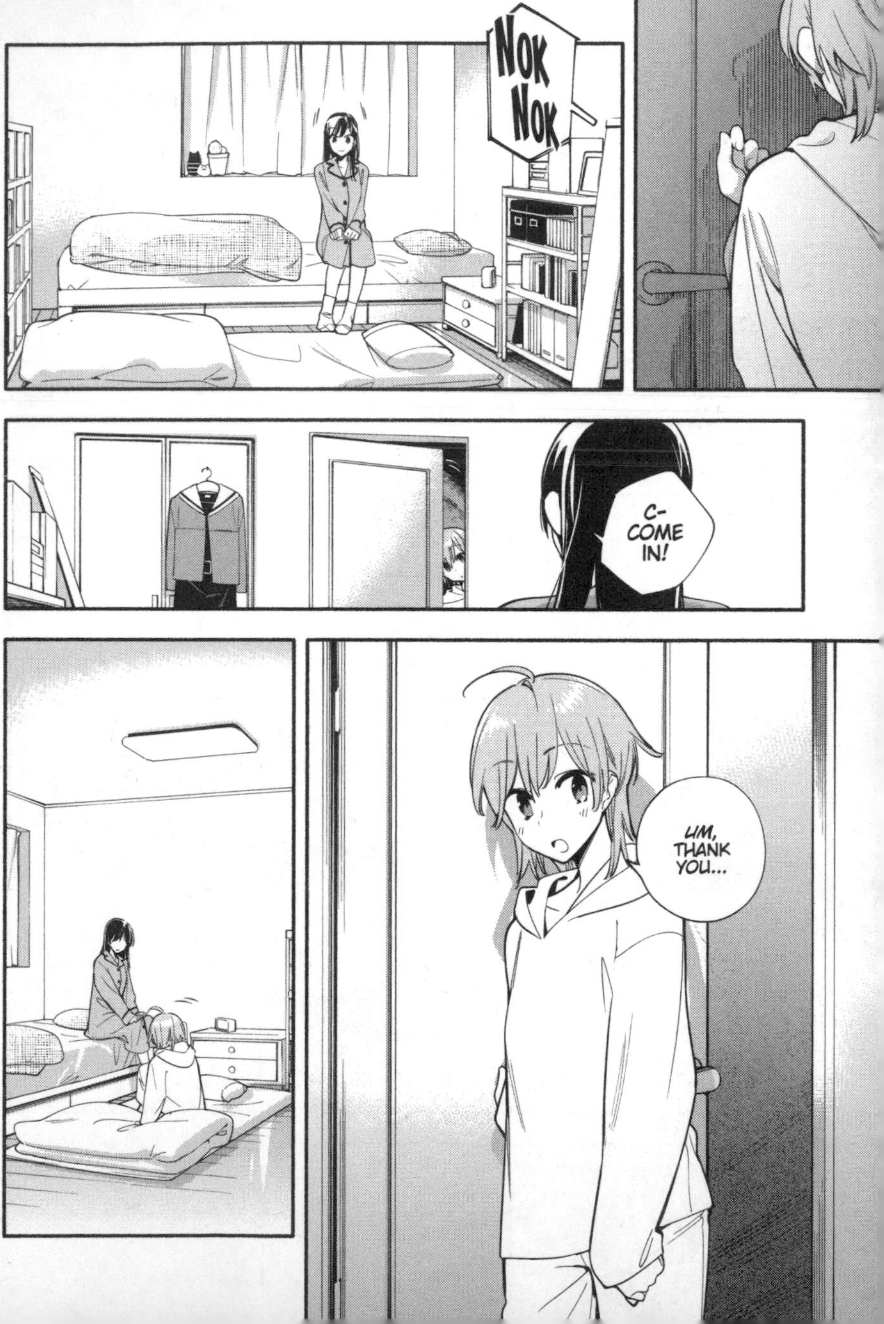
NOK NOK
C-COME IN!
UM, THANK YOU...

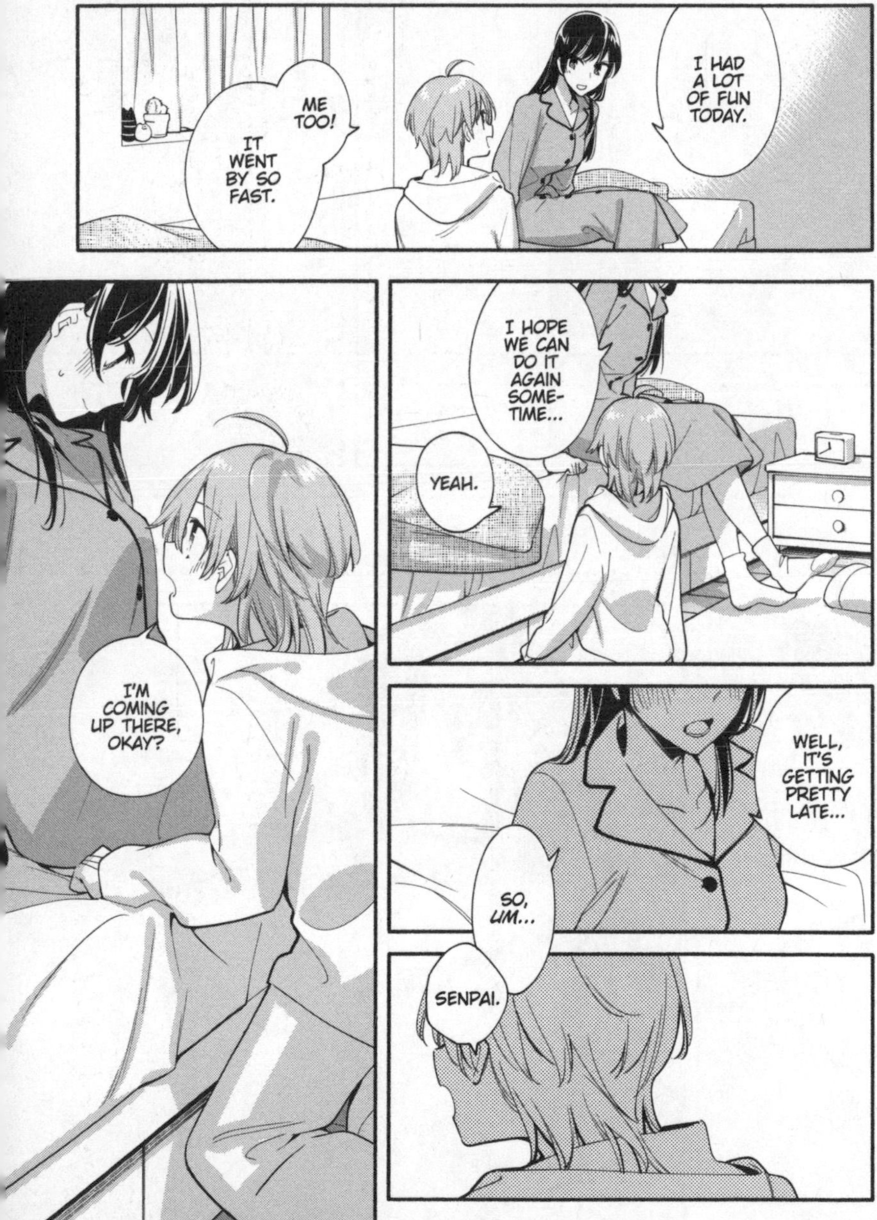
I HAD A LOT OF FUN TODAY.
ME TOO! IT WENT BY SO FAST.
I HOPE WE CAN DO IT AGAIN SOME-TIME...
YEAH.
WELL, IT'S GETTING PRETTY LATE...
SO, UM...
SENPAI.
I'M COMING UP THERE, OKAY?

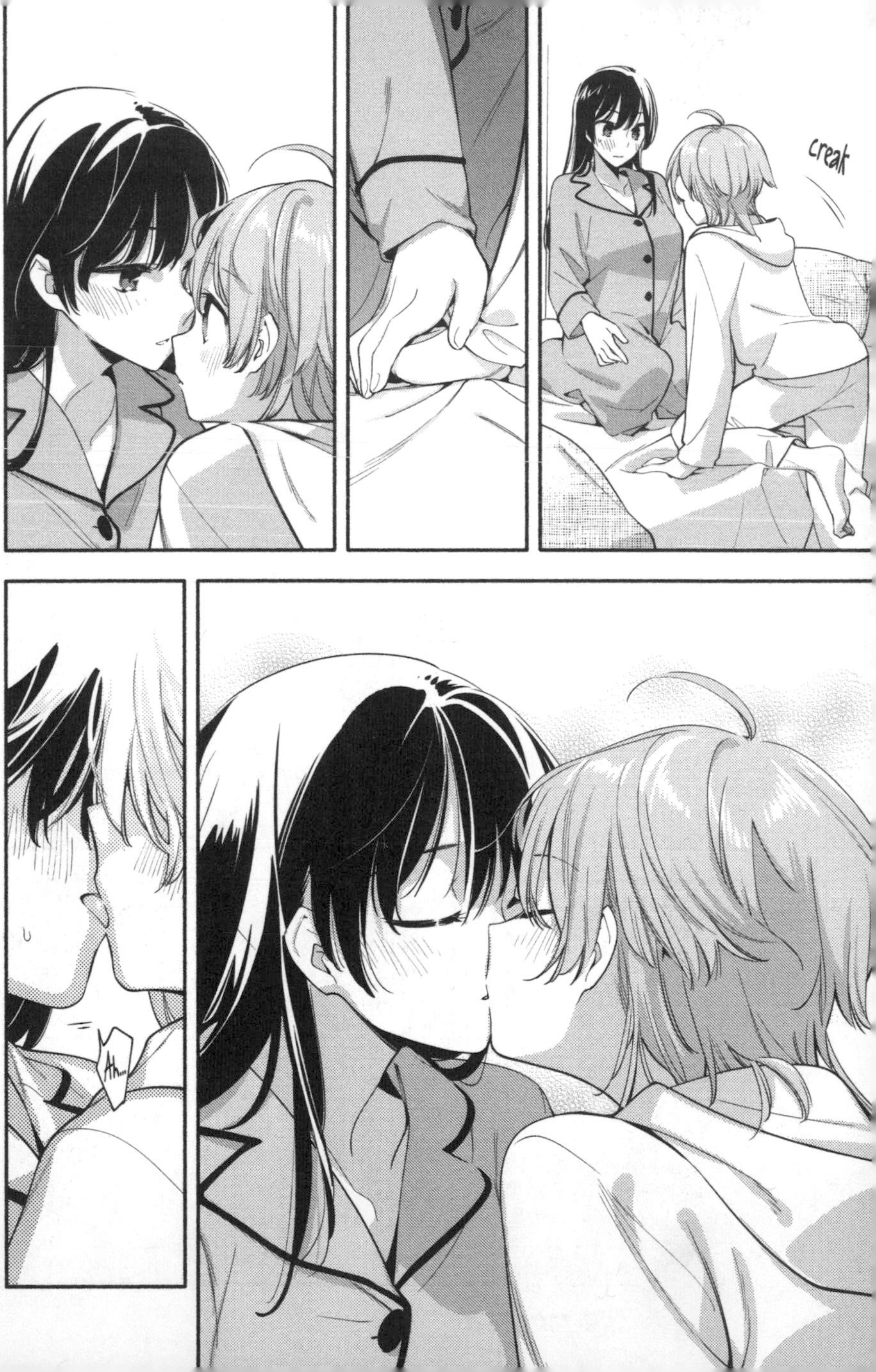
creak
Ah...

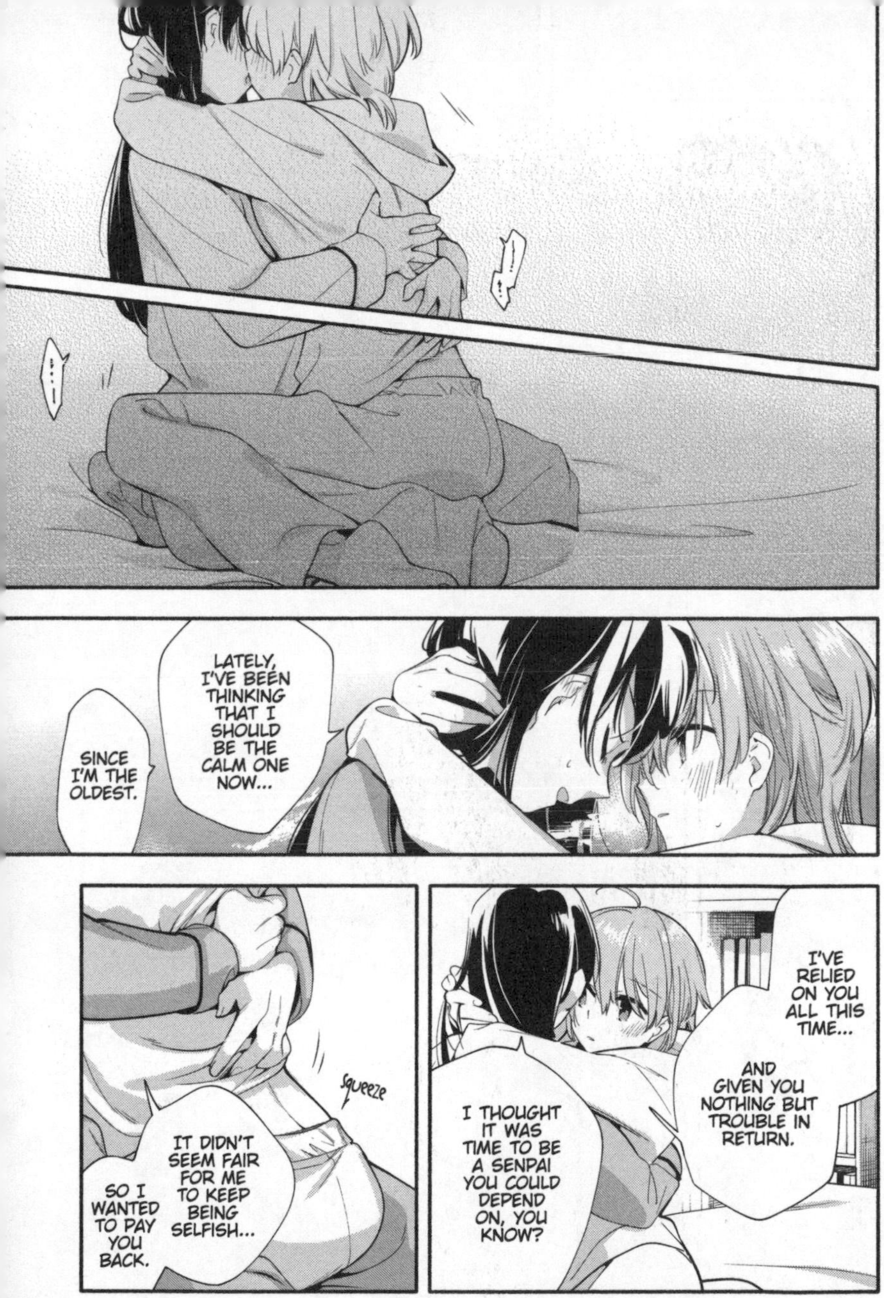
LATELY, I'VE BEEN THINKING THAT I SHOULD BE THE CALM ONE NOW...
SINCE I'M THE OLDEST.
I'VE RELIED ON YOU ALL THIS TIME...
AND GIVEN YOU NOTHING BUT TROUBLE IN RETURN.
I THOUGHT IT WAS TIME TO BE A SENPAI YOU COULD DEPEND ON, YOU KNOW?
squeeze
IT DIDN'T SEEM FAIR FOR ME TO KEEP BEING SELFISH...
SO I WANTED TO PAY YOU BACK.

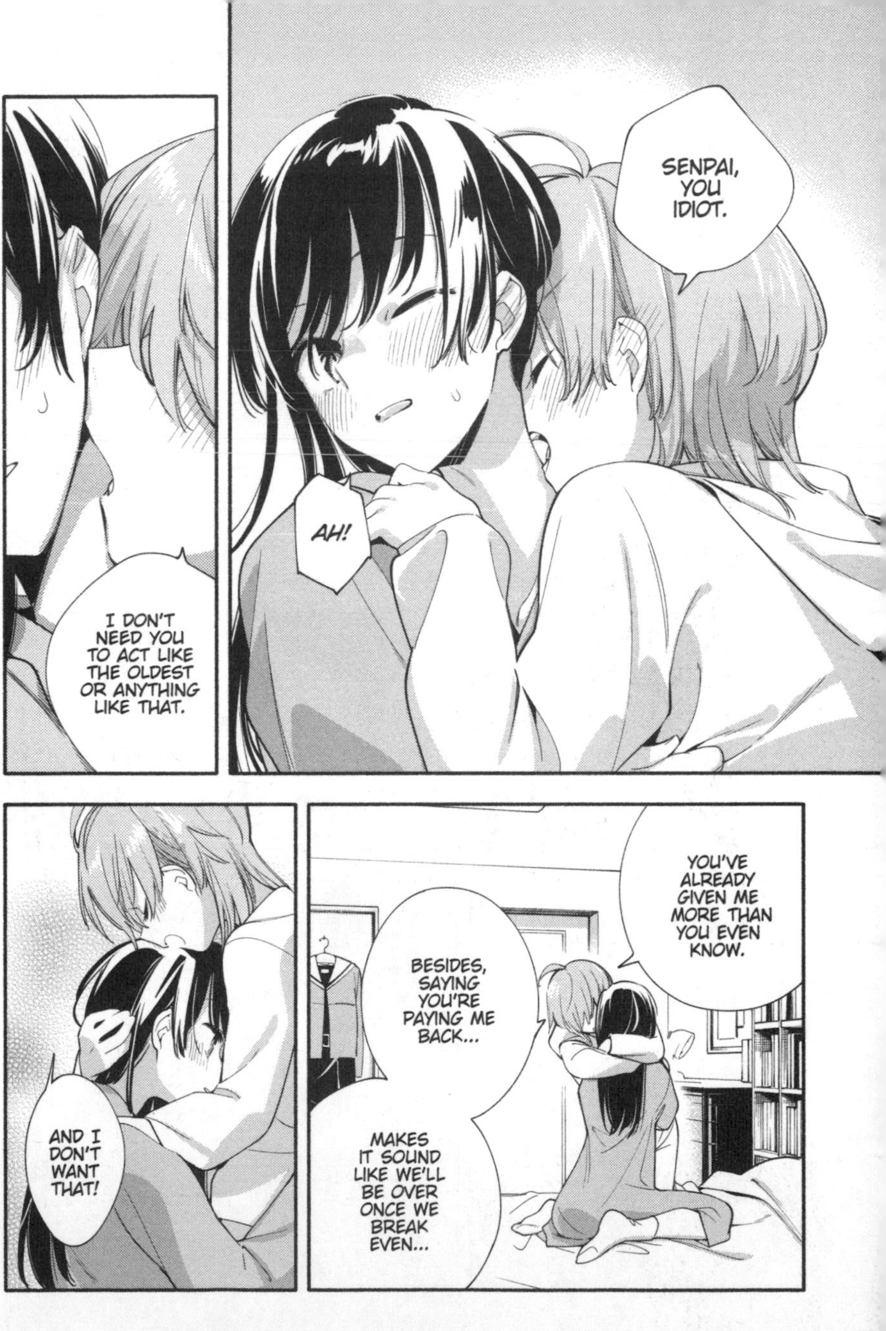
SENPAI, YOU IDIOT.
AH!
I DON'T NEED YOU TO ACT LIKE THE OLDEST OR ANYTHING LIKE THAT.
YOU'VE ALREADY GIVEN ME MORE THAN YOU EVEN KNOW.
BESIDES, SAYING YOU'RE PAYING ME BACK...
MAKES IT SOUND LIKE WE'LL BE OVER ONCE WE BREAK EVEN...
AND I DON'T WANT THAT!

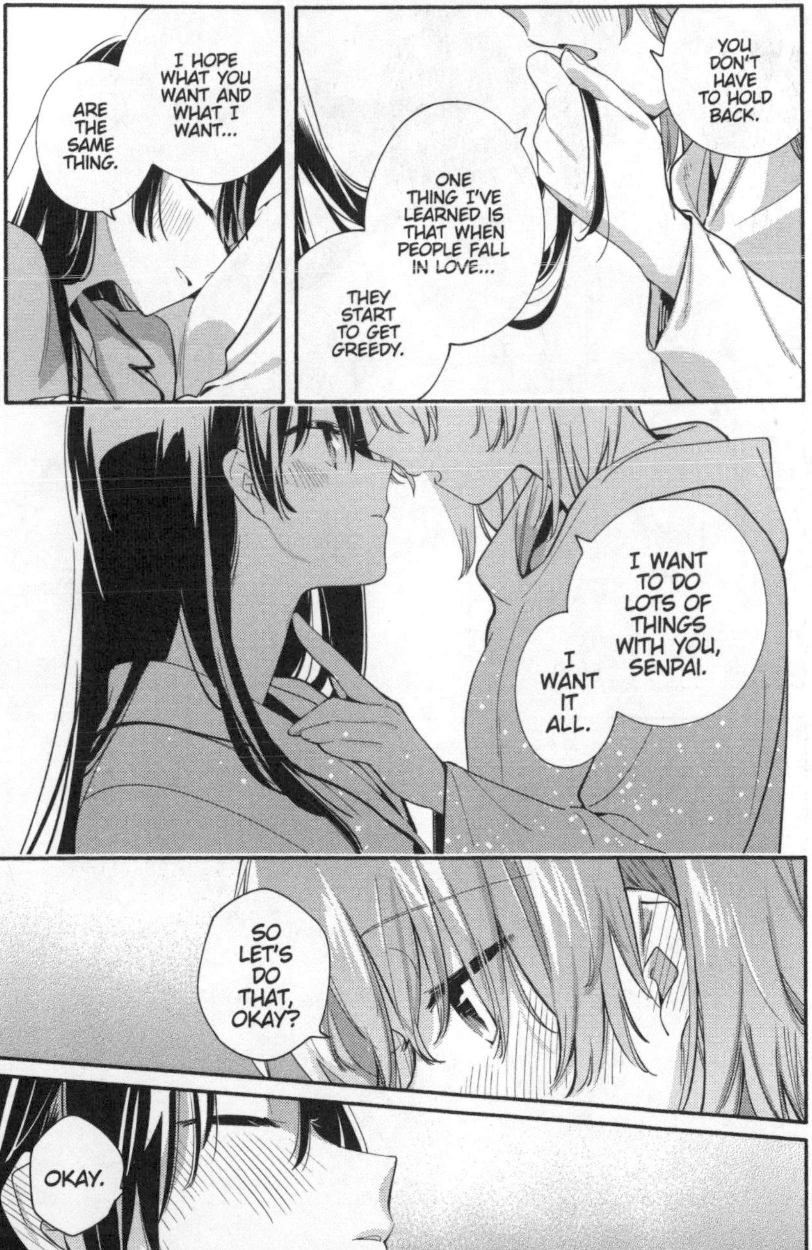
YOU DON'T HAVE TO HOLD BACK.
ONE THING I'VE LEARNED IS THAT WHEN PEOPLE FALL IN LOVE...
THEY START TO GET GREEDY.
I HOPE WHAT YOU WANT AND WHAT I WANT...
ARE THE SAME THING.
I WANT TO DO LOTS OF THINGS WITH YOU, SENPAI.
I WANT IT ALL.
SO LET'S DO THAT, OKAY?
OKAY.

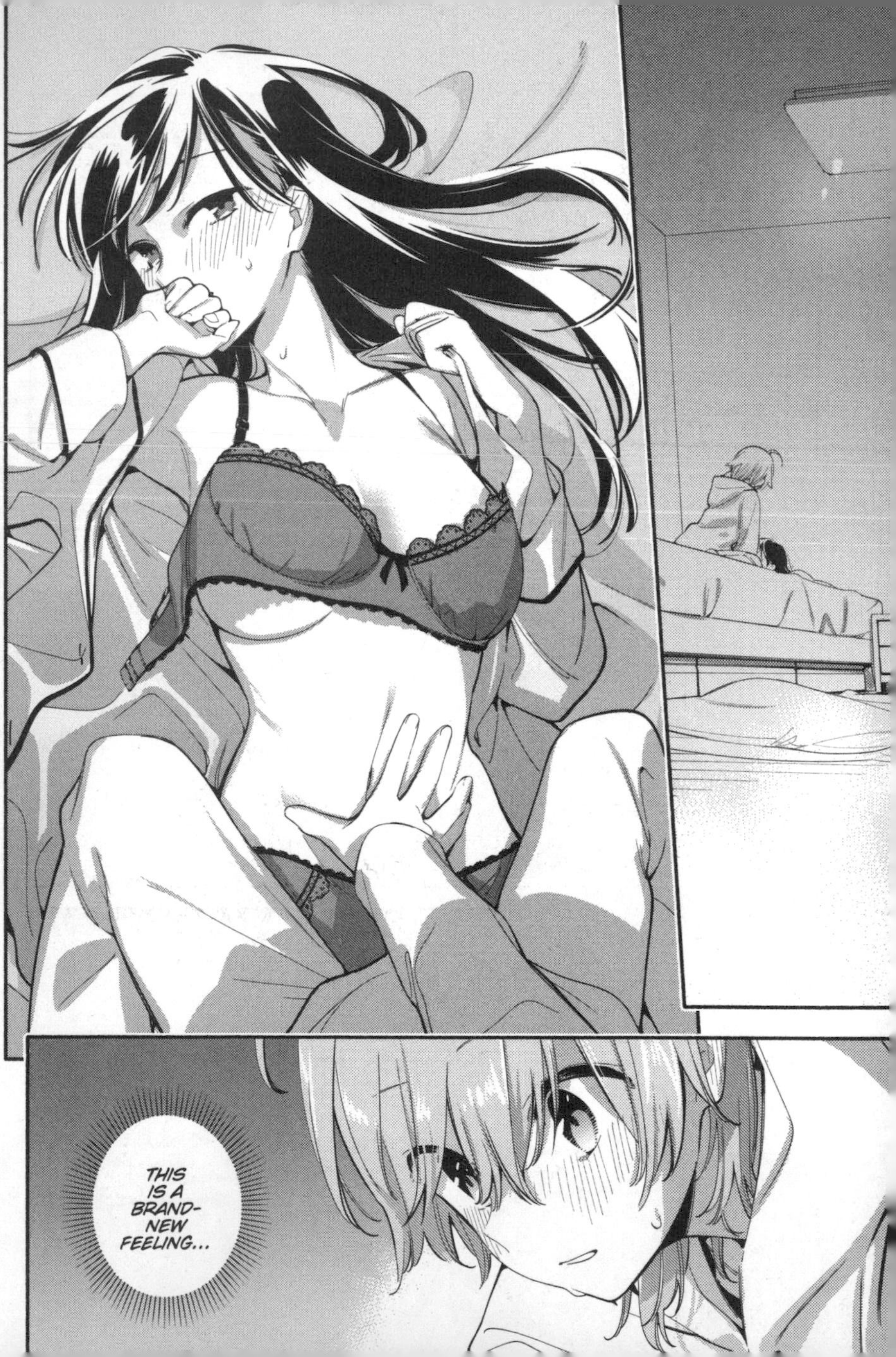
THIS IS A BRAND-NEW FEELING...

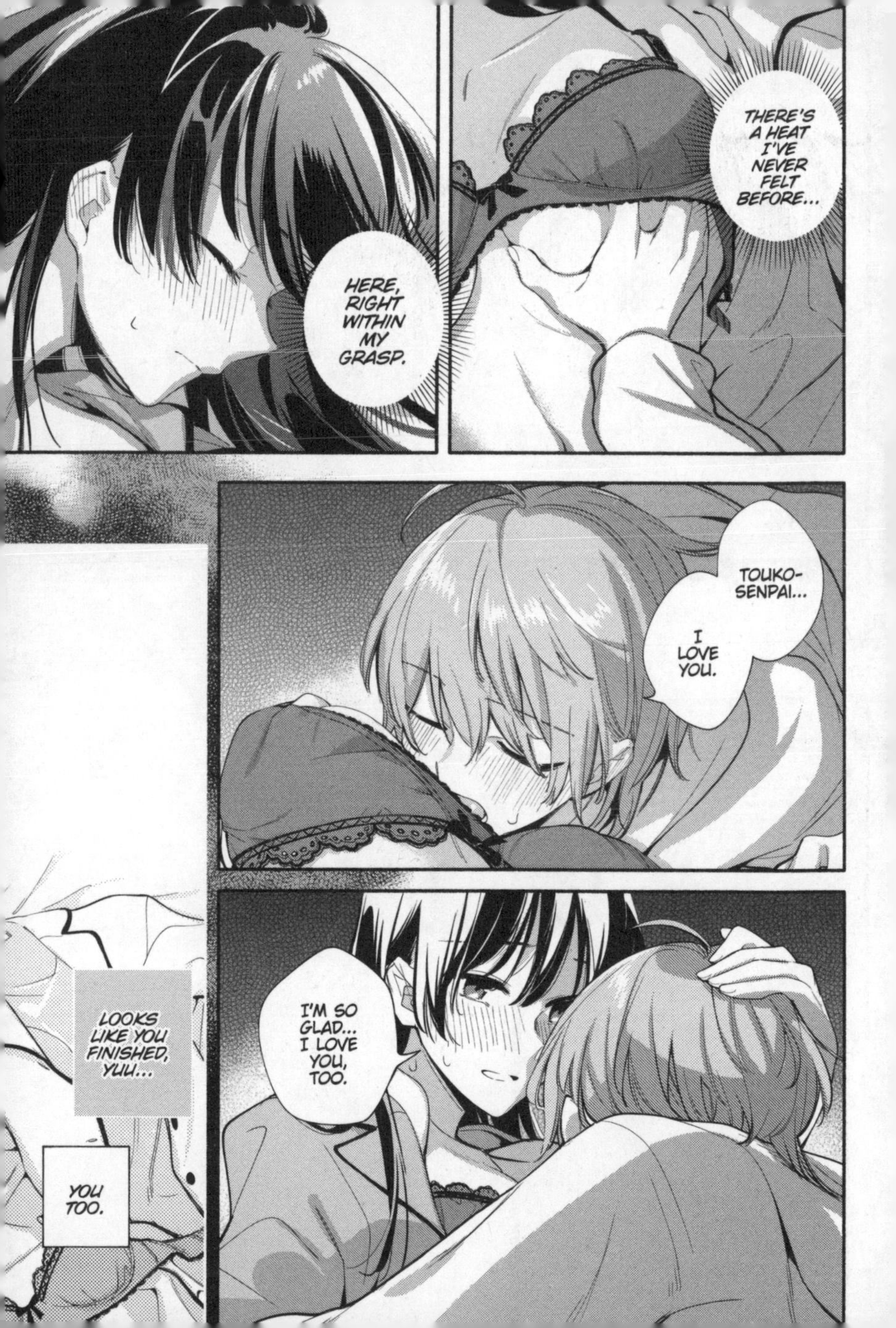
THERE'S A HEAT I'VE NEVER FELT BEFORE...
HERE, RIGHT WITHIN MY GRASP.
TOUKO-SENPAI...
I LOVE YOU.
I'M SO GLAD... I LOVE YOU, TOO.
LOOKS LIKE YOU FINISHED, YUU...
YOU TOO.

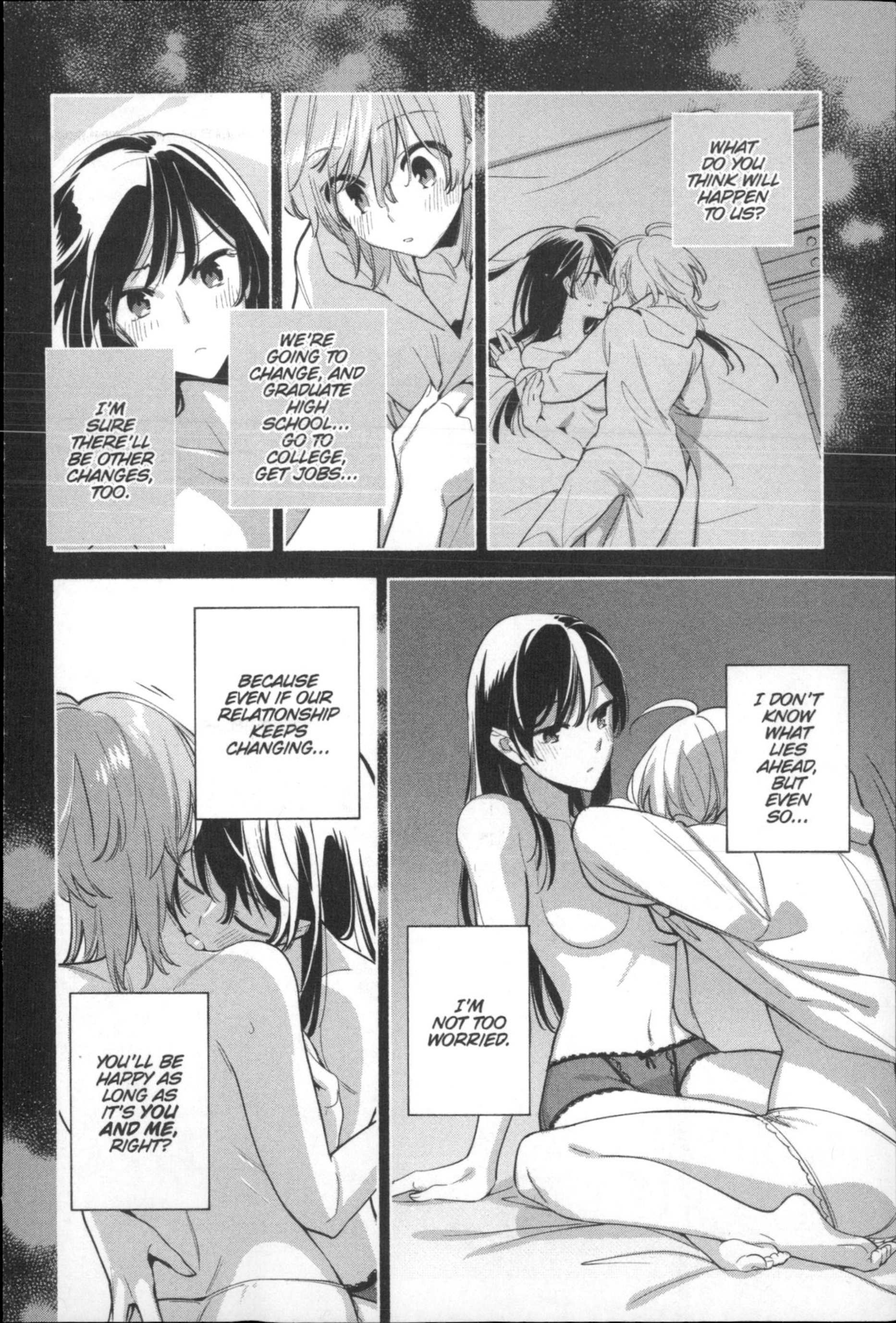
WHAT DO YOU THINK WILL HAPPEN TO US?
WE'RE GOING TO CHANGE, AND GRADUATE HIGH SCHOOL... GO TO COLLEGE, GET JOBS...
I'M SURE THERE'LL BE OTHER CHANGES, TOO.
I DON'T KNOW WHAT LIES AHEAD, BUT EVEN SO...
I'M NOT TOO WORRIED.
BECAUSE EVEN IF OUR RELATIONSHIP KEEPS CHANGING...
YOU'LL BE HAPPY AS LONG AS IT'S YOU AND ME, RIGHT?

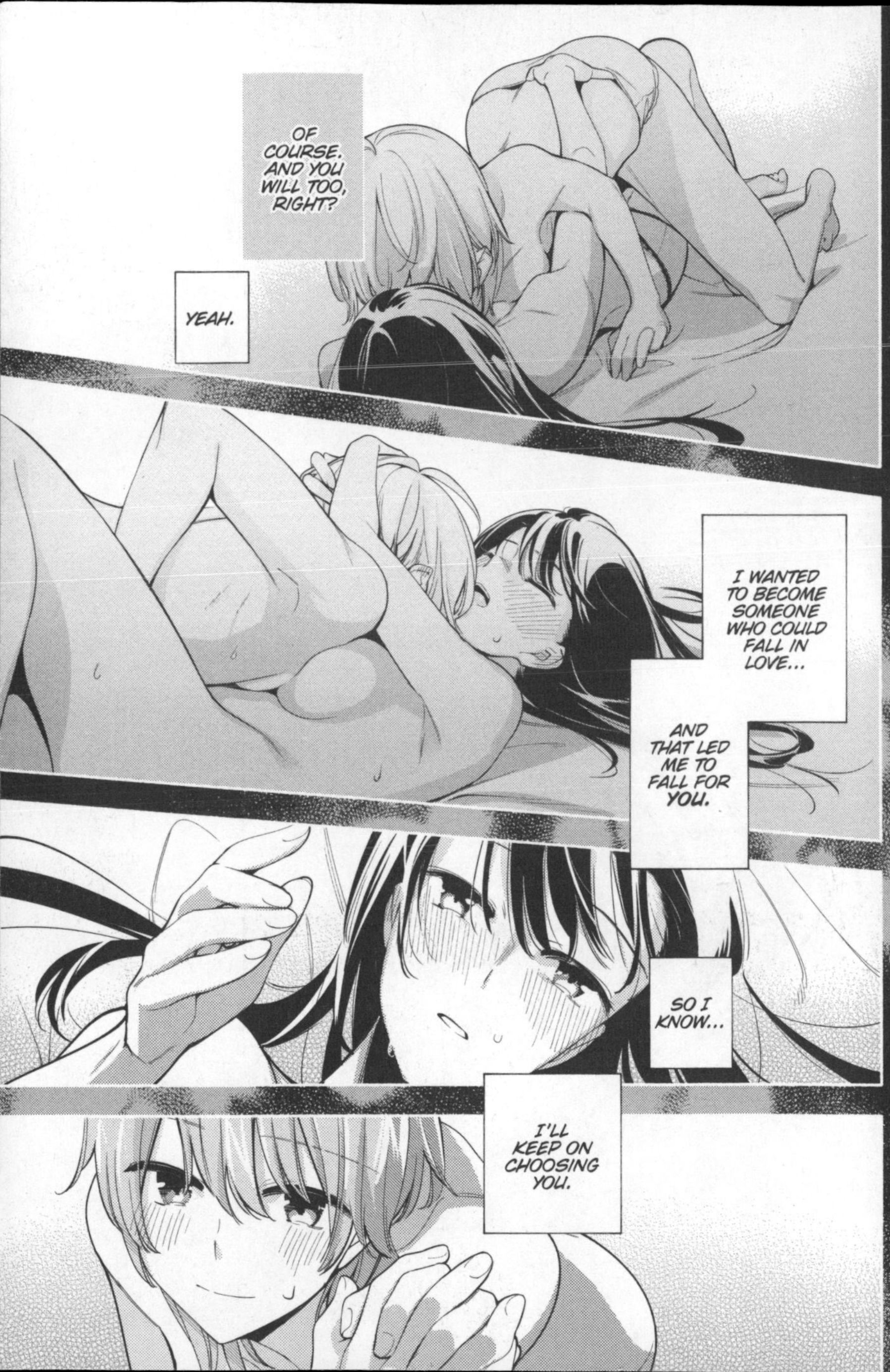
OF COURSE. AND YOU WILL TOO, RIGHT?
YEAH.
I WANTED TO BECOME SOMEONE WHO COULD FALL IN LOVE...
AND THAT LED ME TO FALL FOR YOU.
SO I KNOW...
I'LL KEEP ON CHOOSING YOU.

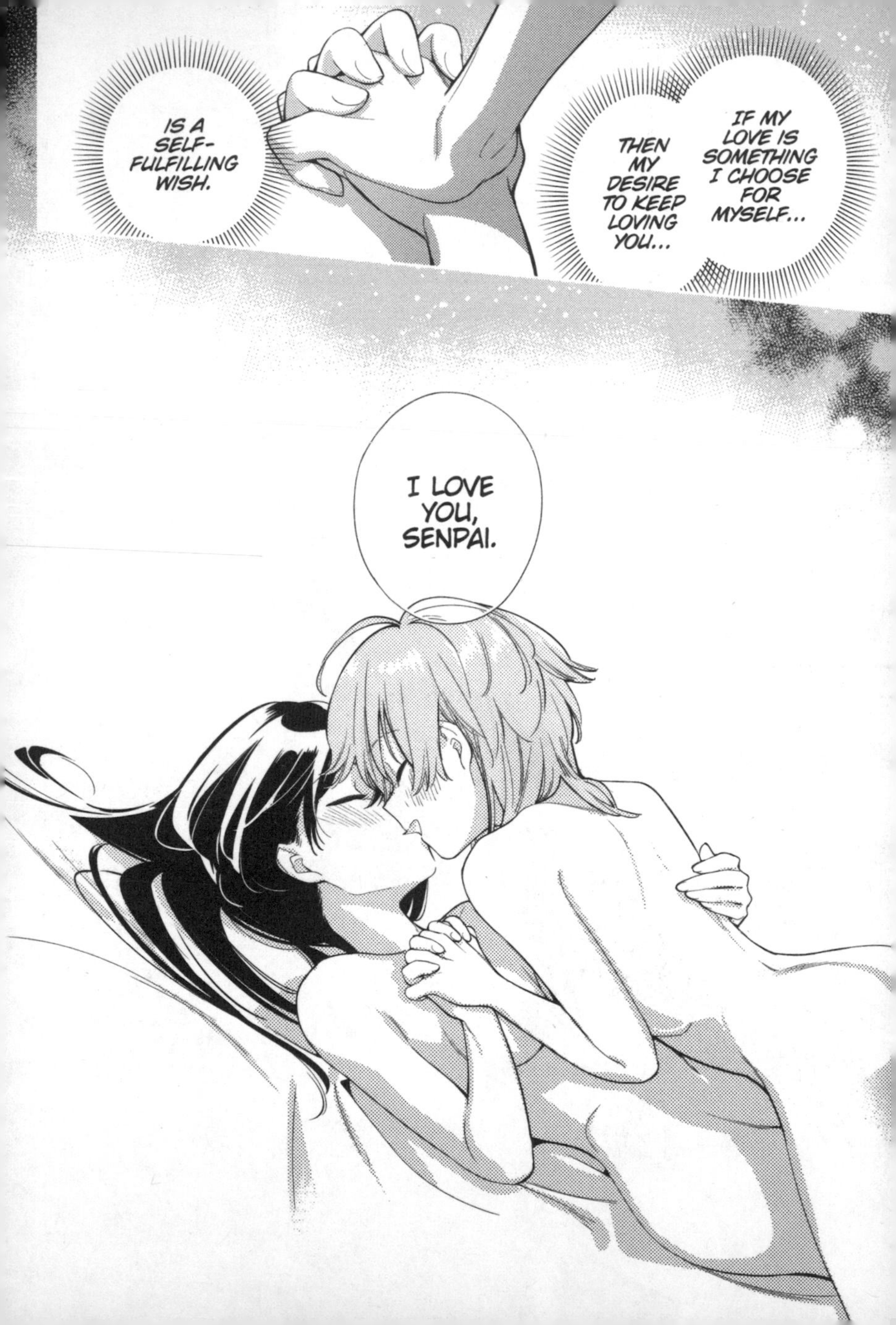
IF MY LOVE IS SOMETHING I CHOOSE FOR MYSELF...
THEN MY DESIRE TO KEEP LOVING YOU...
IS A SELF-FULFILLING WISH.
I LOVE YOU, SENPAI.

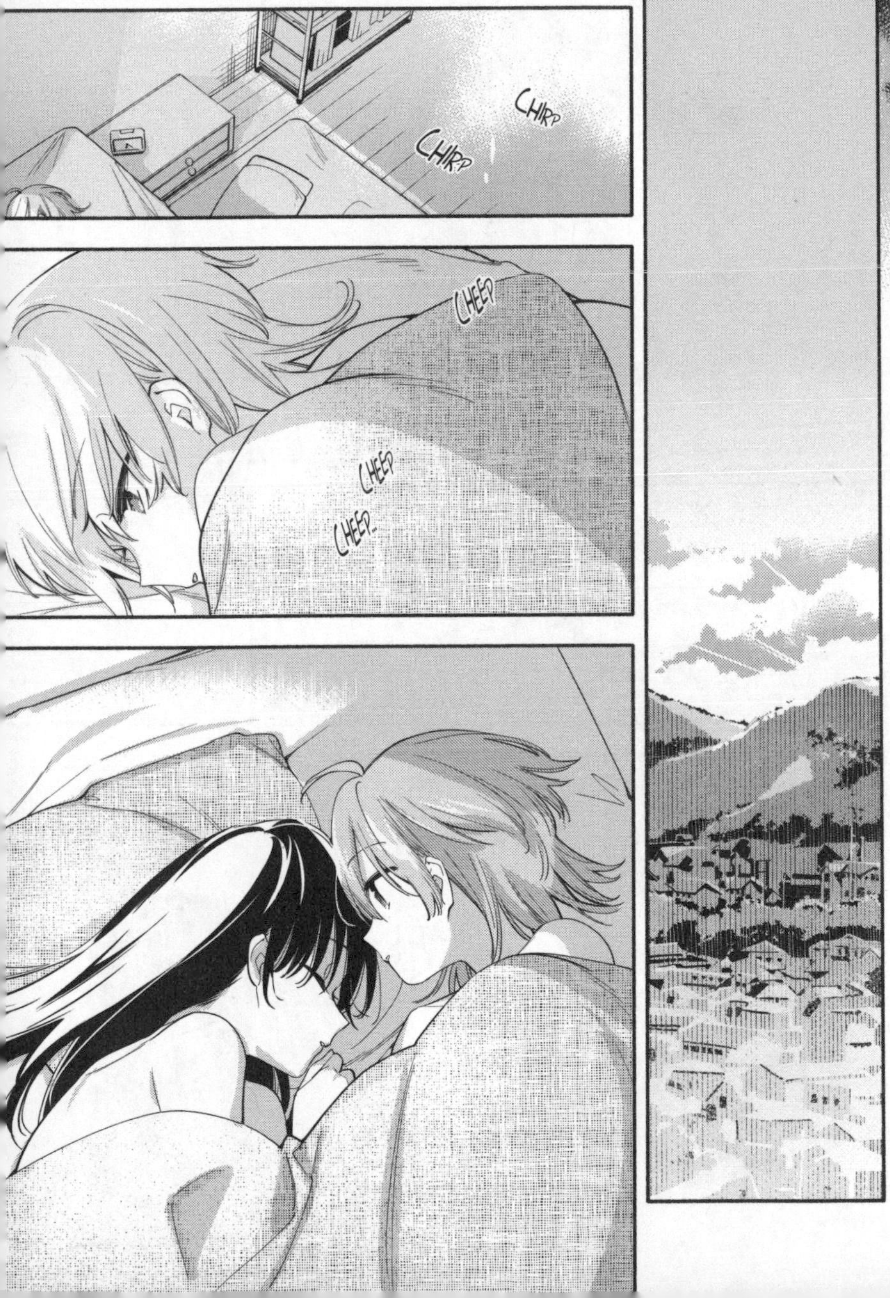
CHIRP
CHIRP
CHEEP
CHEEP
CHEEP...

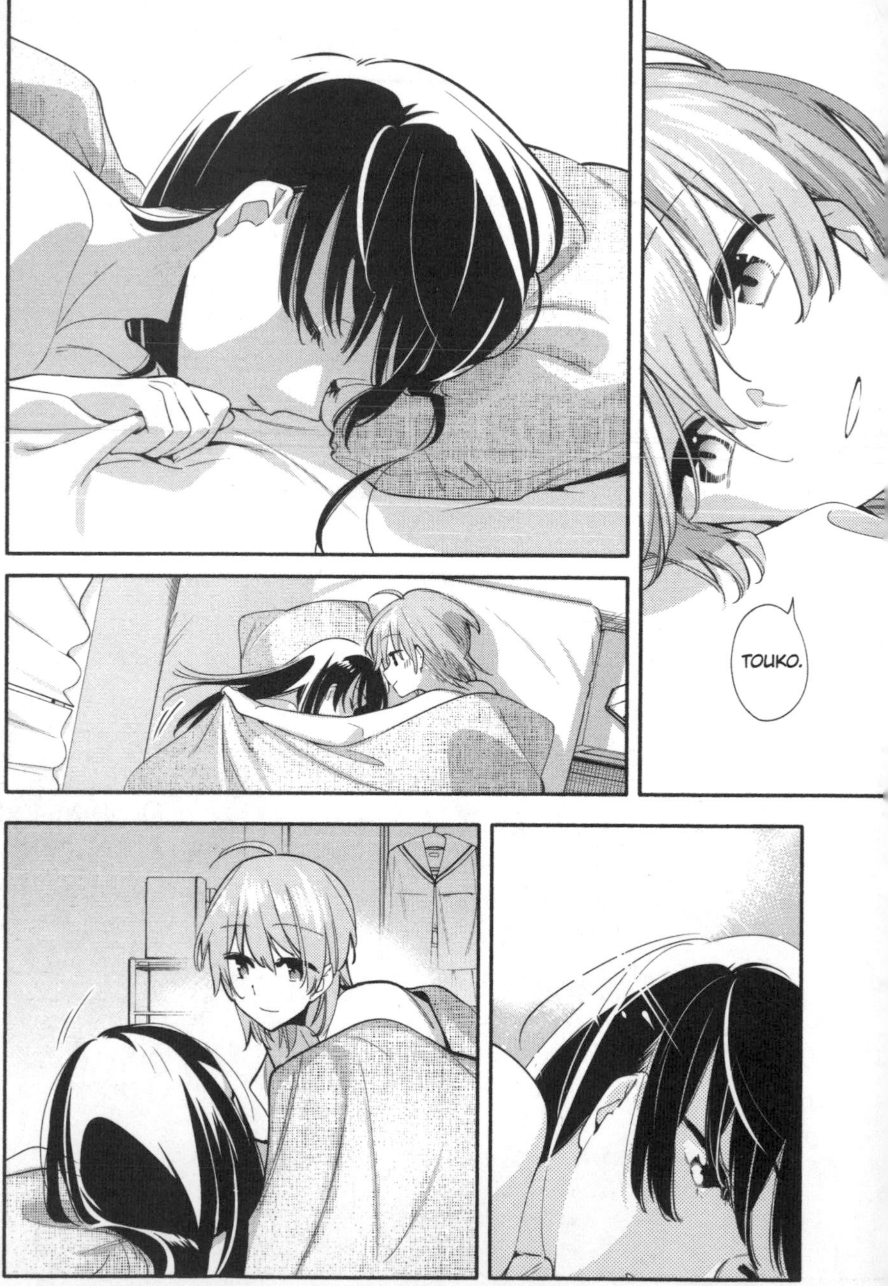
TOUKO.

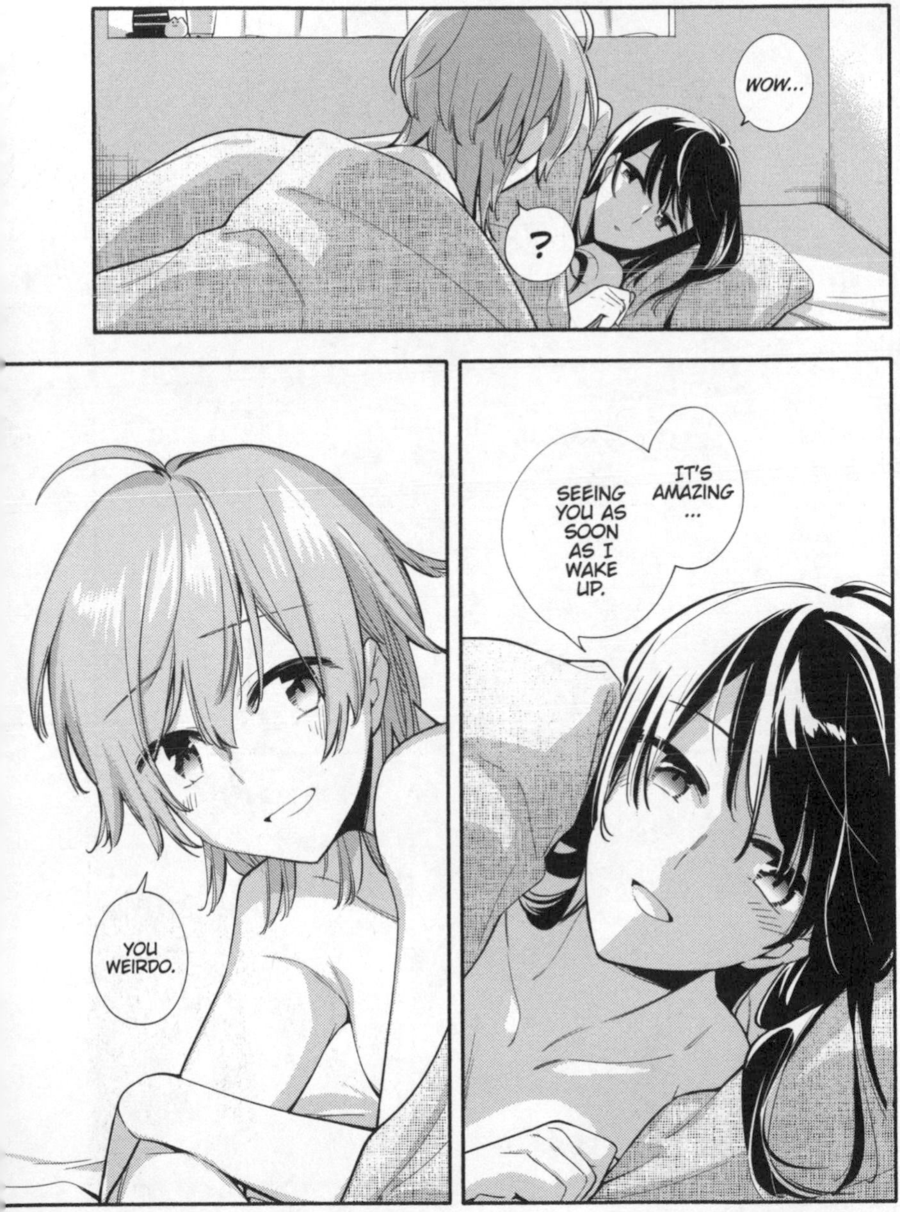
WOW...
?
IT'S AMAZING... SEEING YOU AS SOON AS I WAKE UP.
YOU WEIRDO.

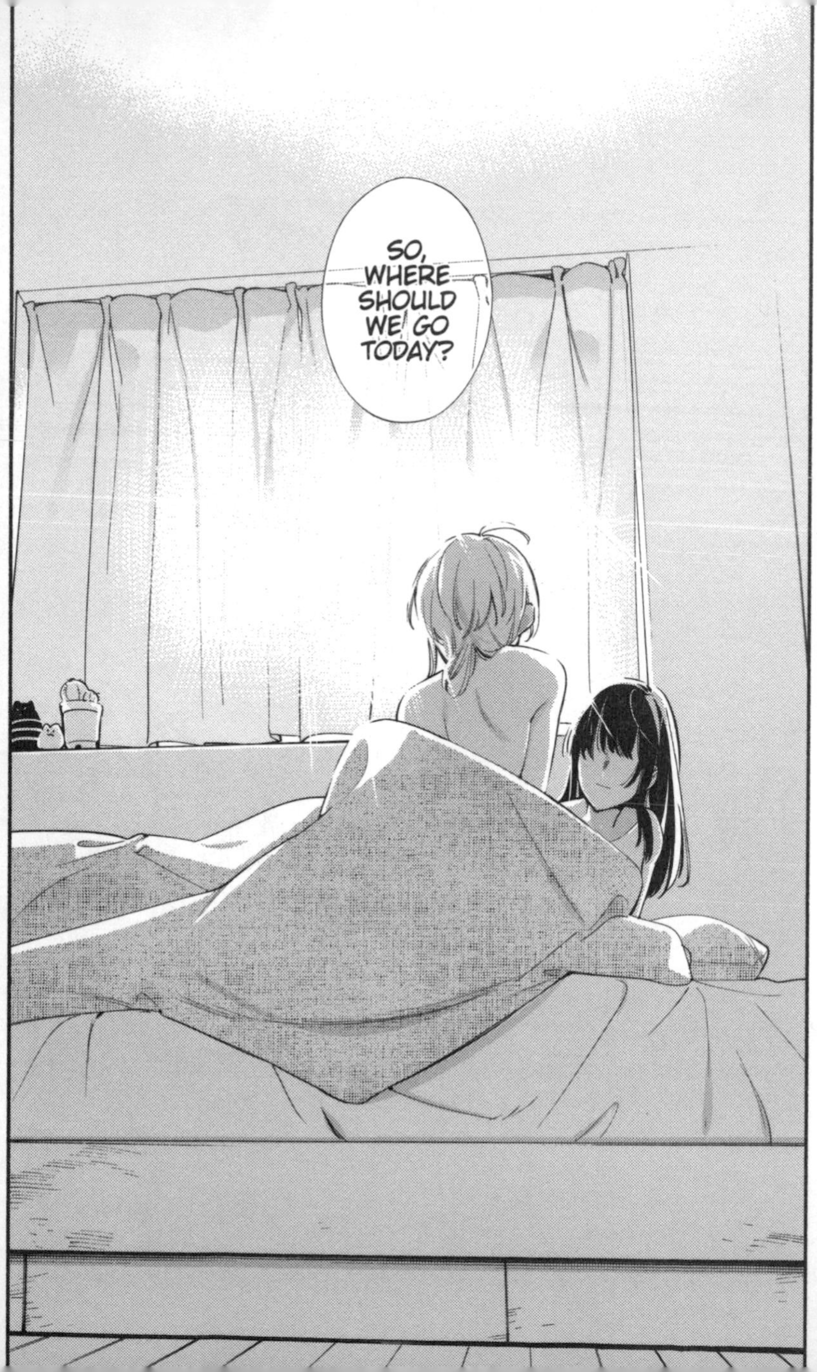
SO, WHERE SHOULD WE GO TODAY?

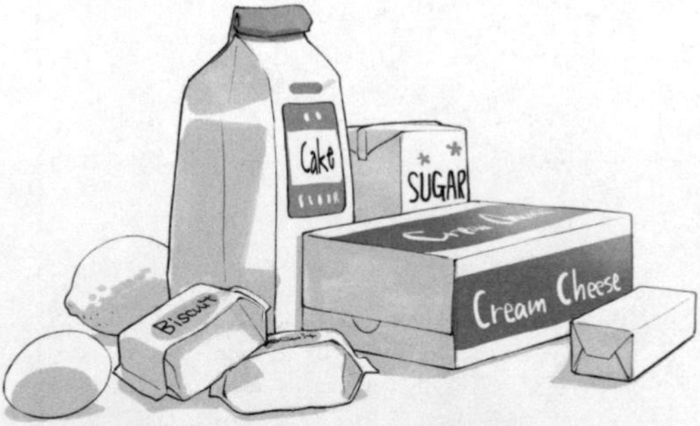
Cake
SUGAR
Cream Cheese
Biscuit

(Bloom Into You)

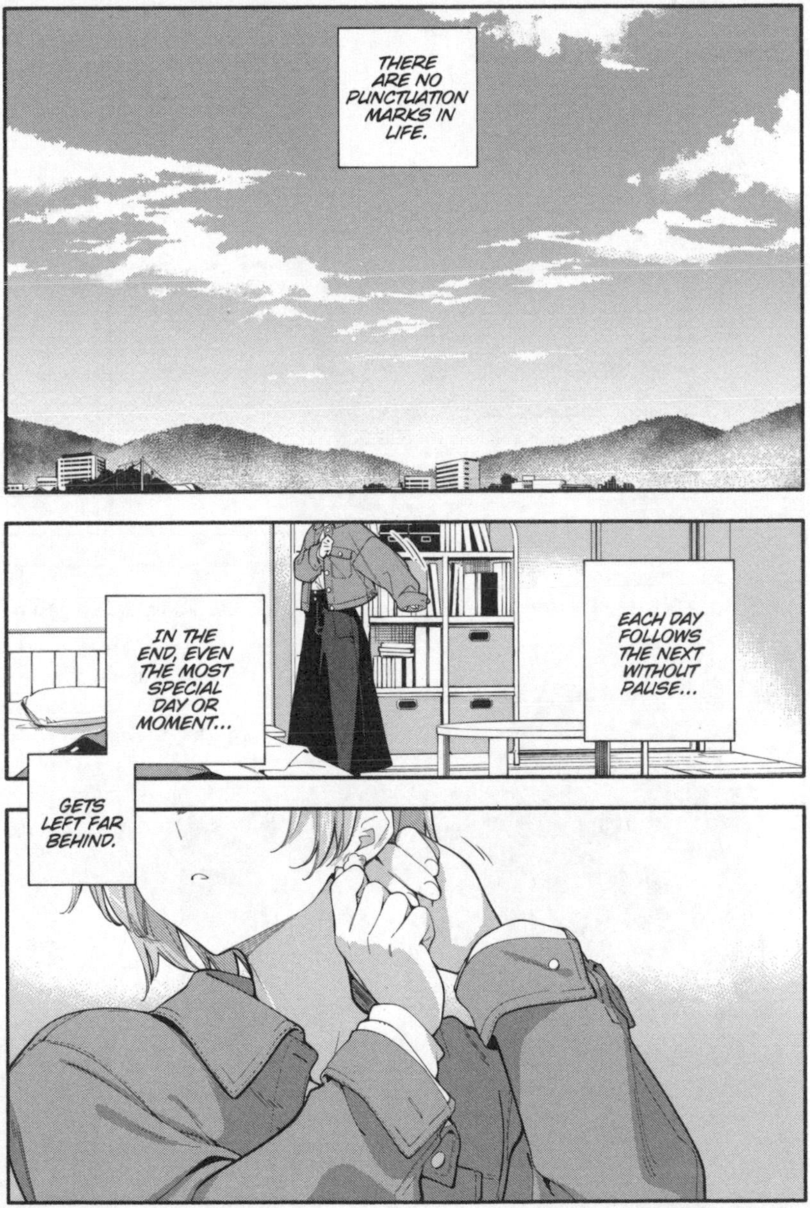
THERE ARE NO PUNCTUATION MARKS IN LIFE.
EACH DAY FOLLOWS THE NEXT WITHOUT PAUSE…
IN THE END, EVEN THE MOST SPECIAL DAY OR MOMENT…
GETS LEFT FAR BEHIND.

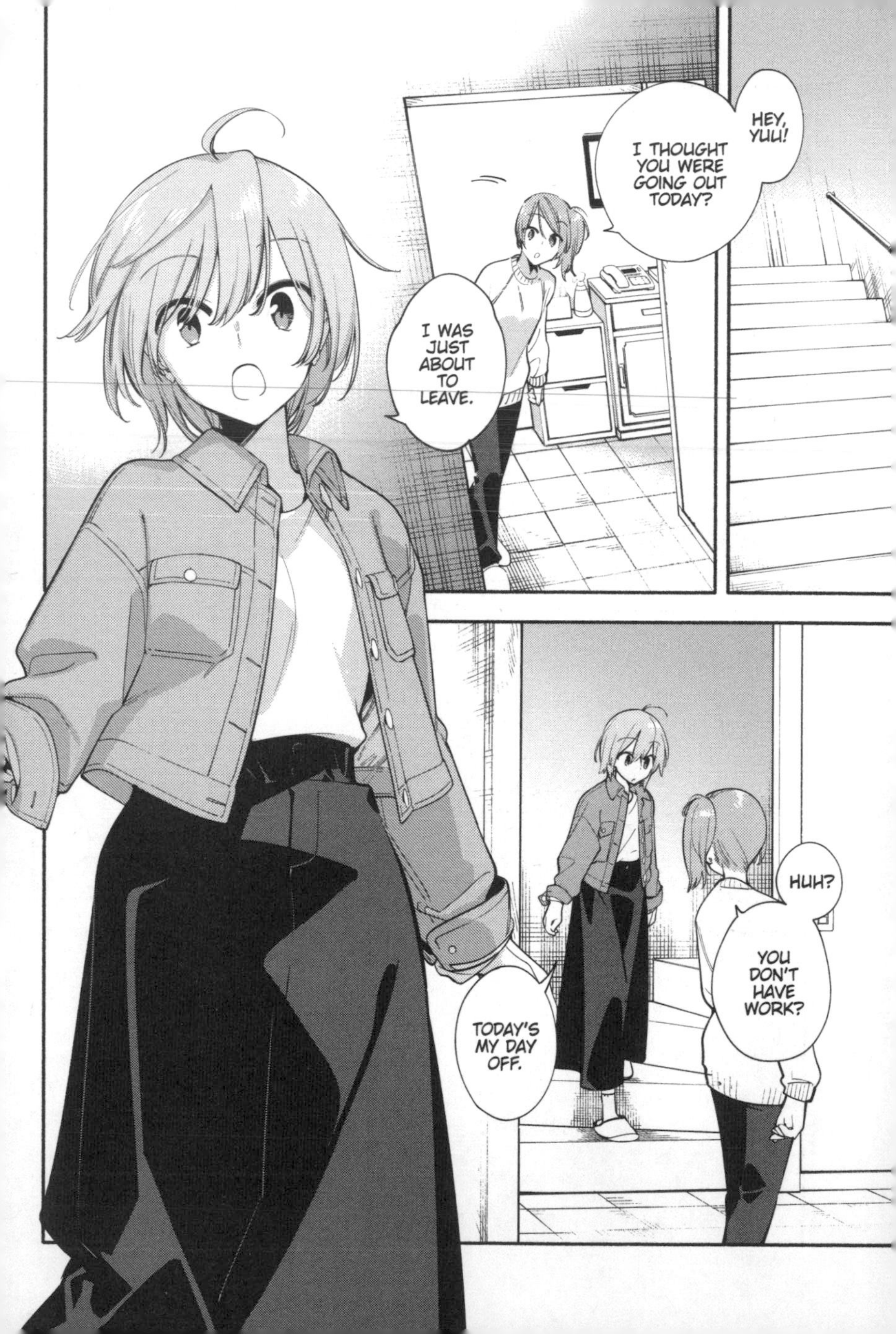
HEY, YUU!
I THOUGHT YOU WERE GOING OUT TODAY?
I WAS JUST ABOUT TO LEAVE.
HUH?
YOU DON'T HAVE WORK?
TODAY'S MY DAY OFF.

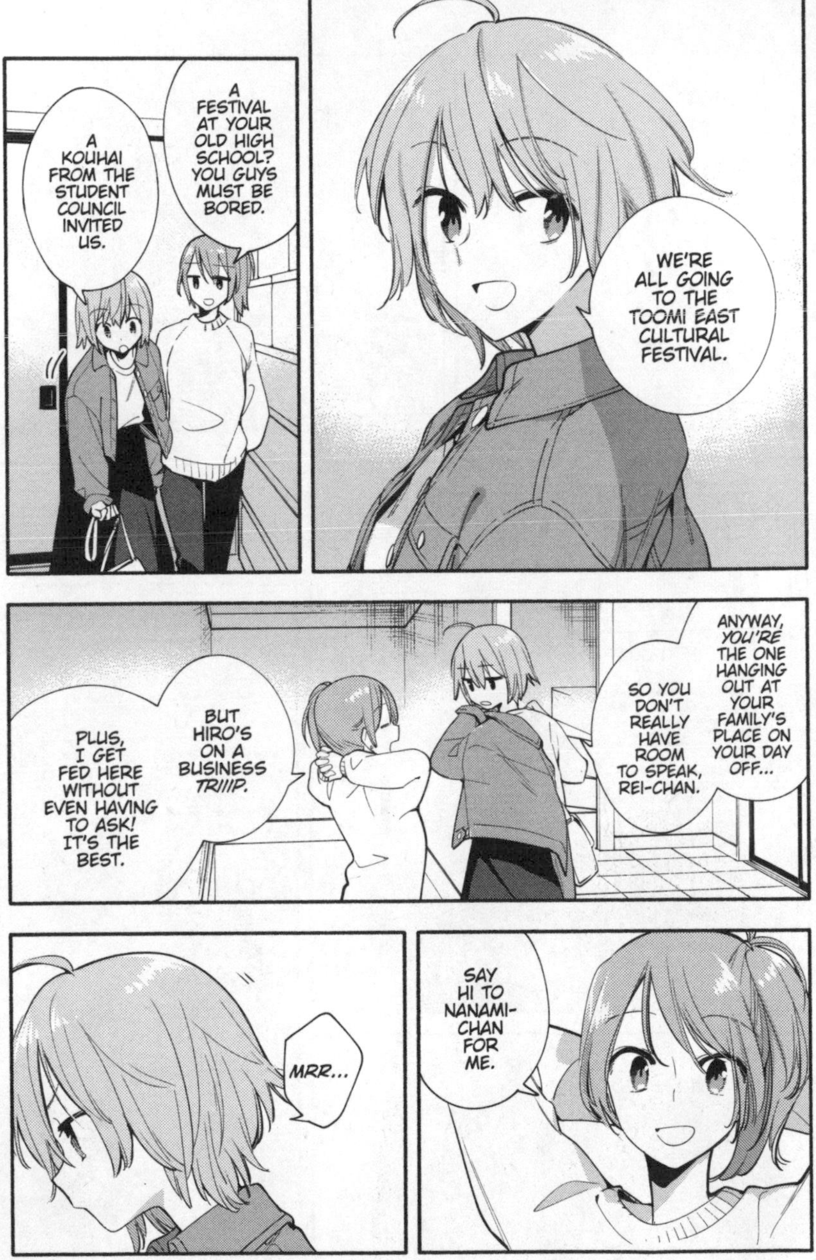

WE'RE ALL GOING TO THE TOOMI EAST CULTURAL FESTIVAL.
A FESTIVAL AT YOUR OLD HIGH SCHOOL? YOU GUYS MUST BE BORED.
A KOUHAI FROM THE STUDENT COUNCIL INVITED US.
ANYWAY, *YOU'RE* THE ONE HANGING OUT AT YOUR FAMILY'S PLACE ON YOUR DAY OFF...
SO YOU DON'T REALLY HAVE ROOM TO SPEAK, REI-CHAN.
BUT HIRO'S ON A BUSINESS *TRIIIP*.
PLUS, I GET FED HERE WITHOUT EVEN HAVING TO ASK! IT'S THE BEST.
SAY HI TO NANAMI-CHAN FOR ME.
MRR...

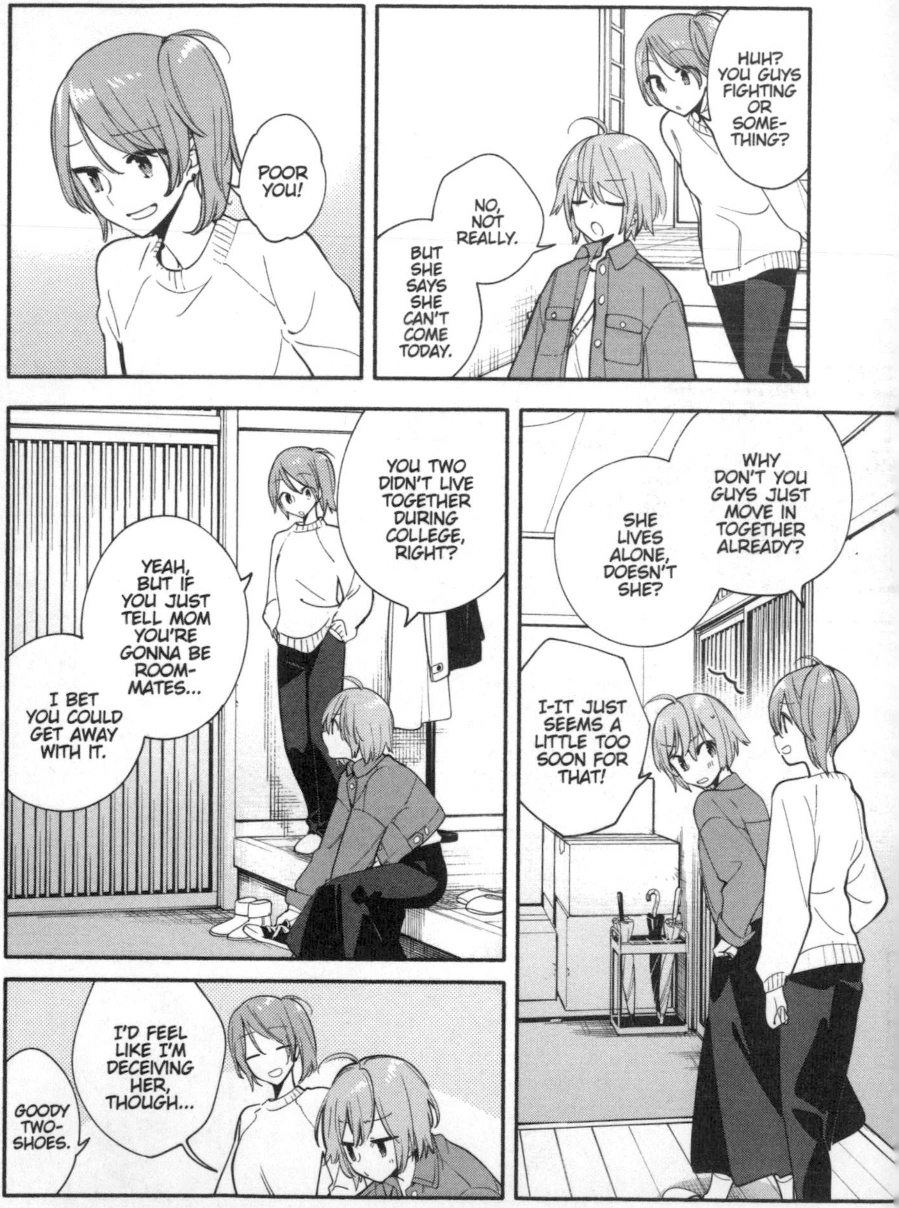
HUH? YOU GUYS FIGHTING OR SOME-THING?
NO, NOT REALLY.
BUT SHE SAYS SHE CAN'T COME TODAY.
POOR YOU!
WHY DON'T YOU GUYS JUST MOVE IN TOGETHER ALREADY?
SHE LIVES ALONE, DOESN'T SHE?
I-IT JUST SEEMS A LITTLE TOO SOON FOR THAT!
YOU TWO DIDN'T LIVE TOGETHER DURING COLLEGE, RIGHT?
YEAH, BUT IF YOU JUST TELL MOM YOU'RE GONNA BE ROOM-MATES...
I BET YOU COULD GET AWAY WITH IT.
I'D FEEL LIKE I'M DECEIVING HER, THOUGH...
GOODY TWO-SHOES.

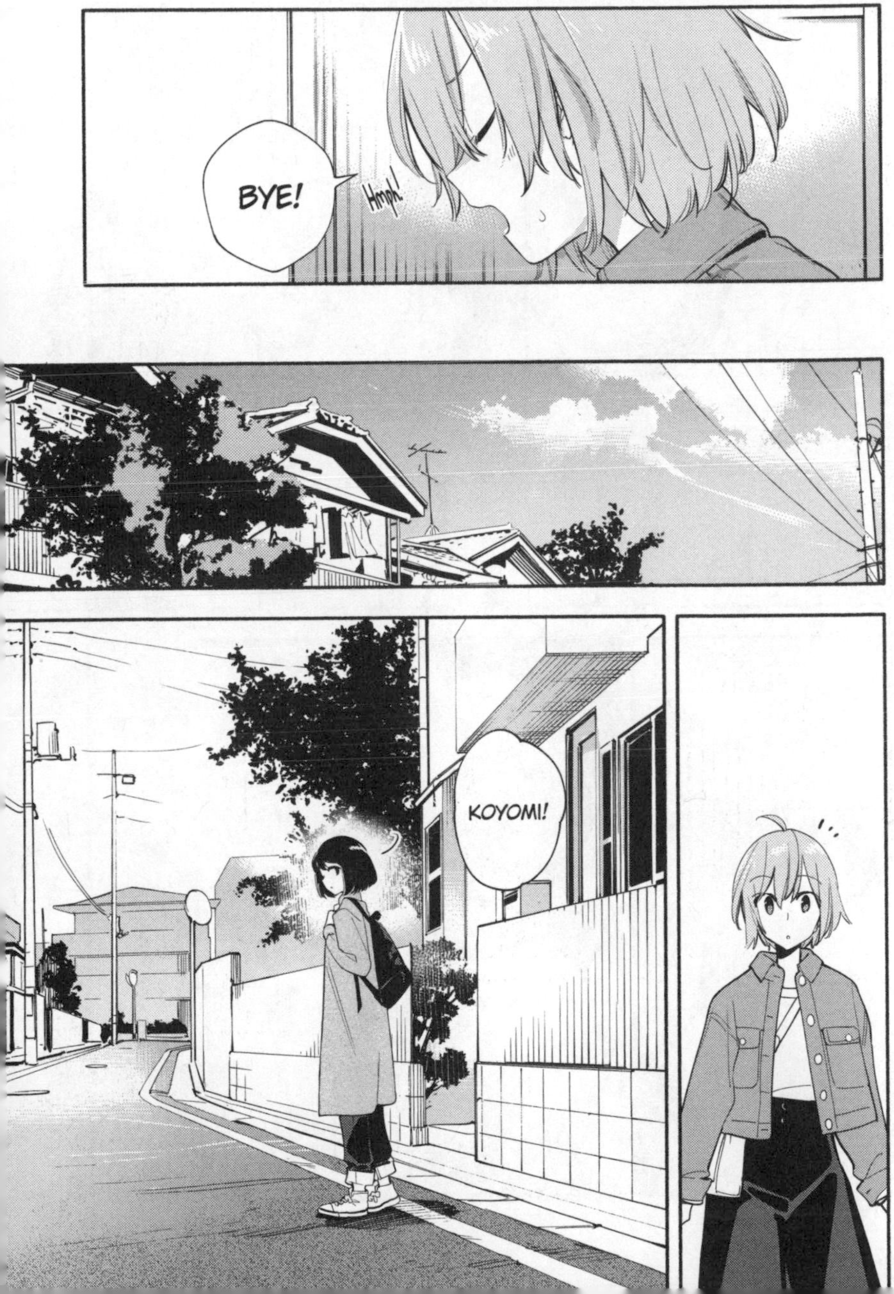
Hmph!
BYE!
KOYOMI!

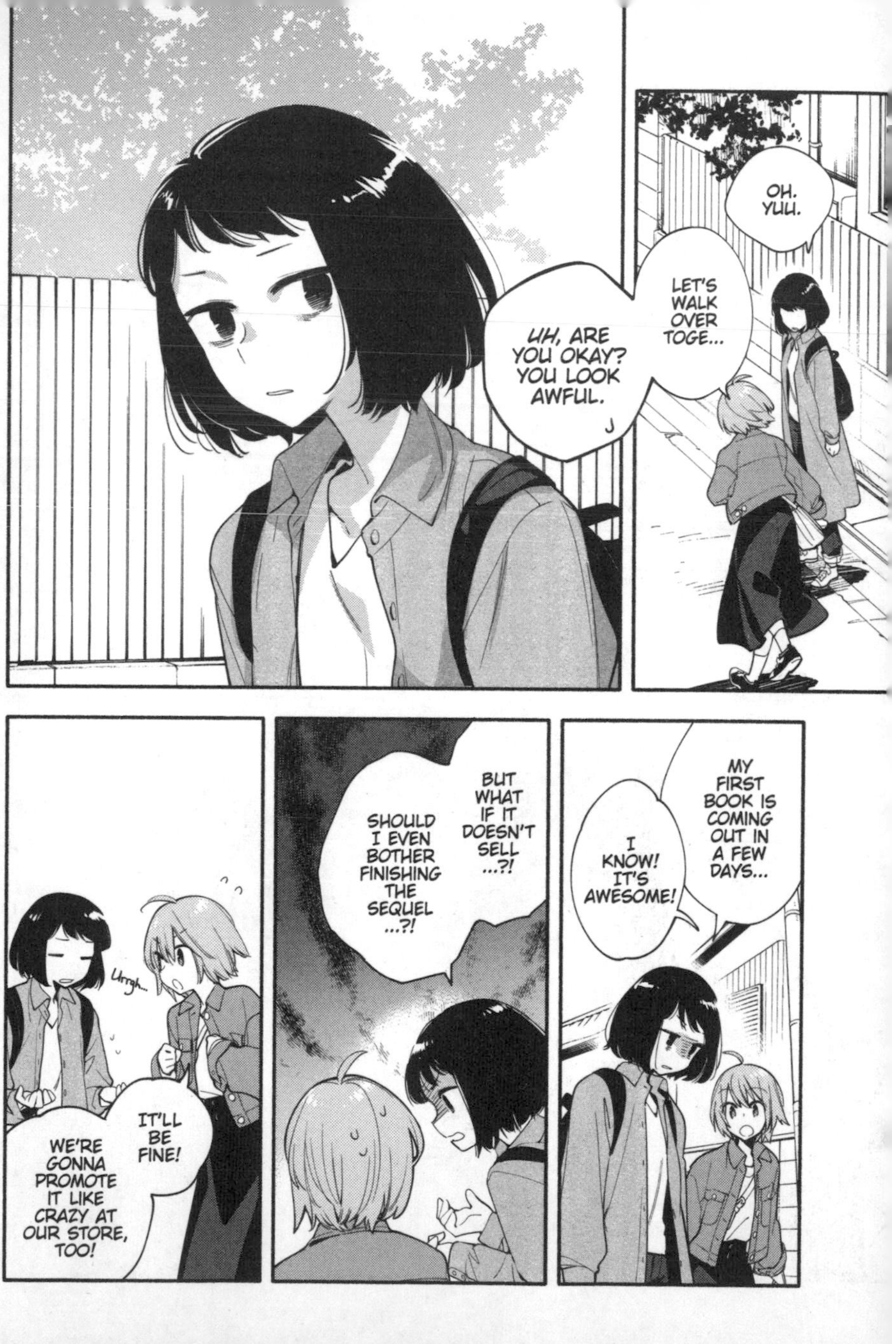
OH. YUU.
LET'S WALK OVER TOGE...
UH, ARE YOU OKAY? YOU LOOK AWFUL.
MY FIRST BOOK IS COMING OUT IN A FEW DAYS...
I KNOW! IT'S AWESOME!
BUT WHAT IF IT DOESN'T SELL ...?!
SHOULD I EVEN BOTHER FINISHING THE SEQUEL ...?!
Urrgh...
IT'LL BE FINE!
WE'RE GONNA PROMOTE IT LIKE CRAZY AT OUR STORE, TOO!

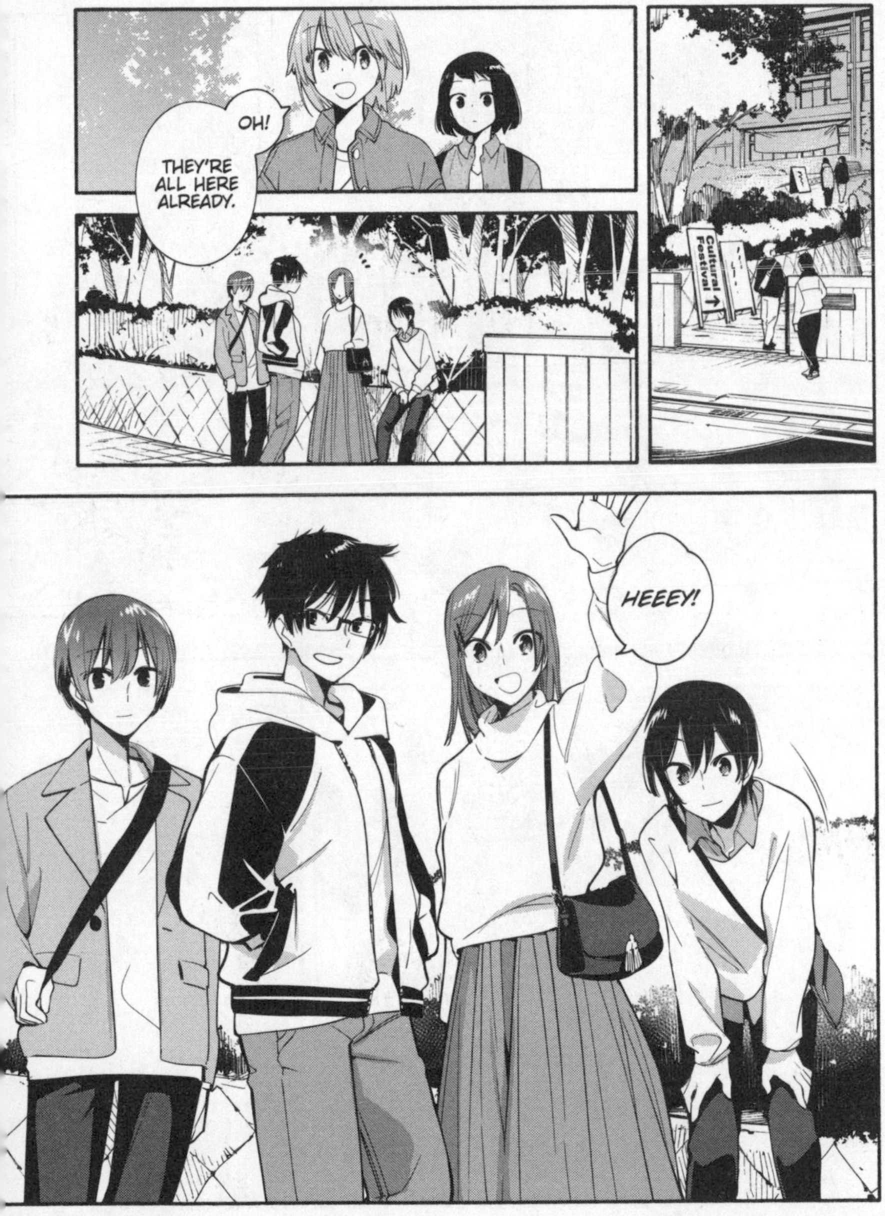
Cultural Festival
OH!
THEY'RE ALL HERE ALREADY.
HEEEY!

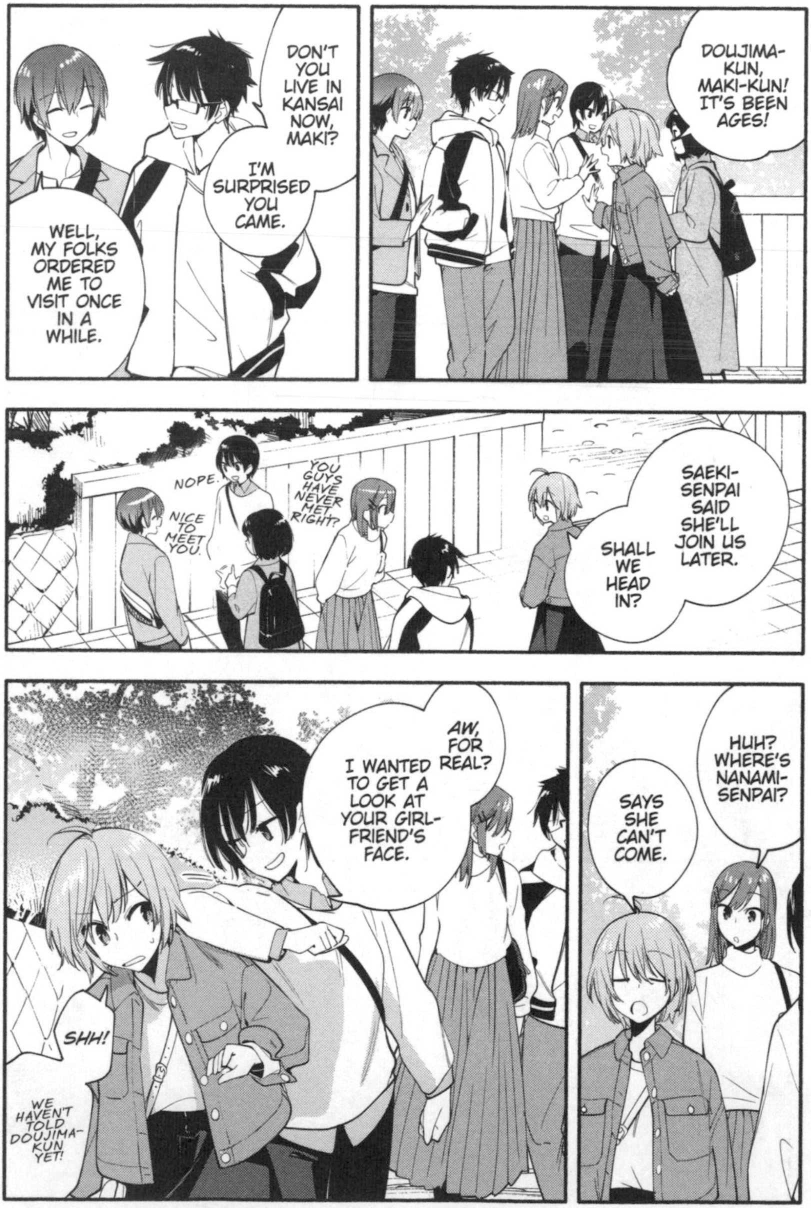
DOUJIMA-KUN, MAKI-KUN! IT'S BEEN AGES!
DON'T YOU LIVE IN KANSAI NOW, MAKI?
I'M SURPRISED YOU CAME.
WELL, MY FOLKS ORDERED ME TO VISIT ONCE IN A WHILE.
SAEKI-SENPAI SAID SHE'LL JOIN US LATER.
SHALL WE HEAD IN?
YOU GUYS HAVE NEVER MET RIGHT?
NOPE.
NICE TO MEET YOU.
HUH? WHERE'S NANAMI-SENPAI?
SAYS SHE CAN'T COME.
AW, FOR REAL?
I WANTED TO GET A LOOK AT YOUR GIRLFRIEND'S FACE.
SHH!
WE HAVEN'T TOLD DOUJIMA-KUN YET!

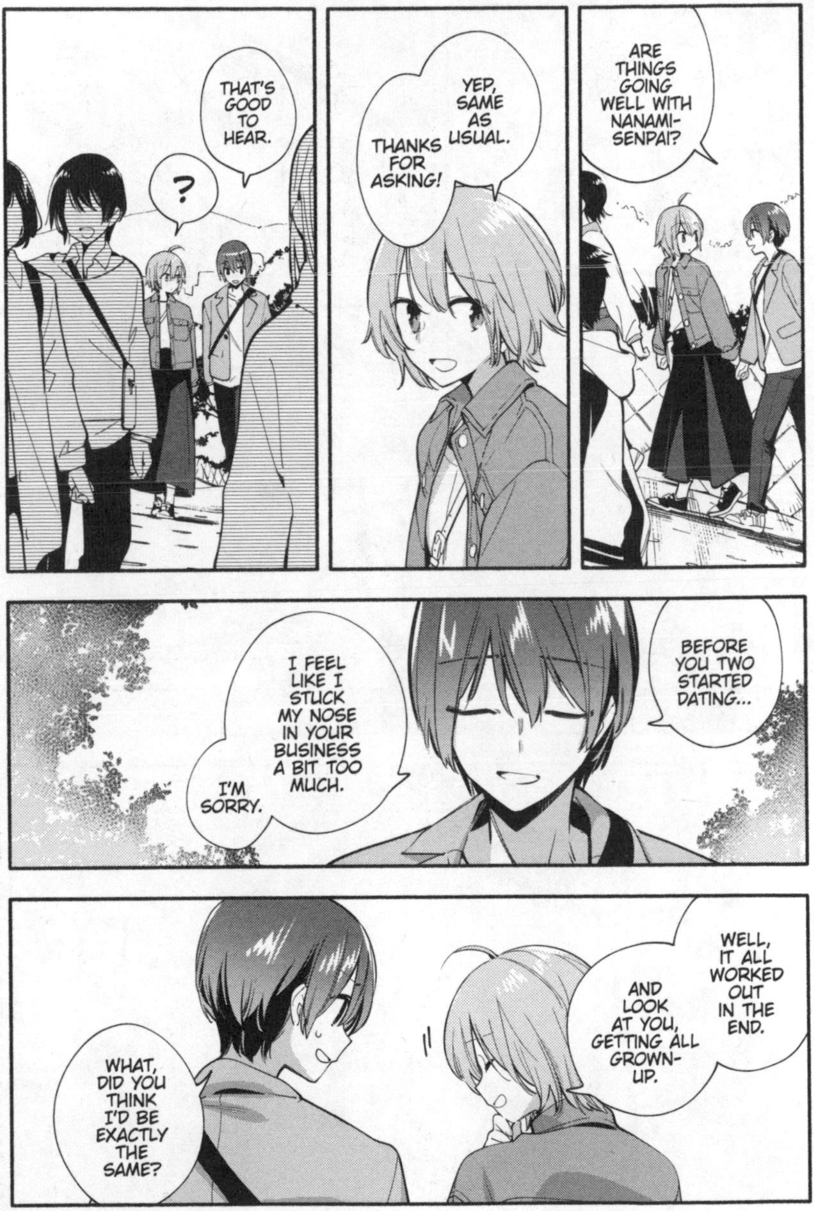
ARE THINGS GOING WELL WITH NANAMI-SENPAI?
YEP, SAME AS USUAL.
THANKS FOR ASKING!
THAT'S GOOD TO HEAR.
?
BEFORE YOU TWO STARTED DATING...
I FEEL LIKE I STUCK MY NOSE IN YOUR BUSINESS A BIT TOO MUCH.
I'M SORRY.
WELL, IT ALL WORKED OUT IN THE END.
AND LOOK AT YOU, GETTING ALL GROWN-UP.
WHAT, DID YOU THINK I'D BE EXACTLY THE SAME?

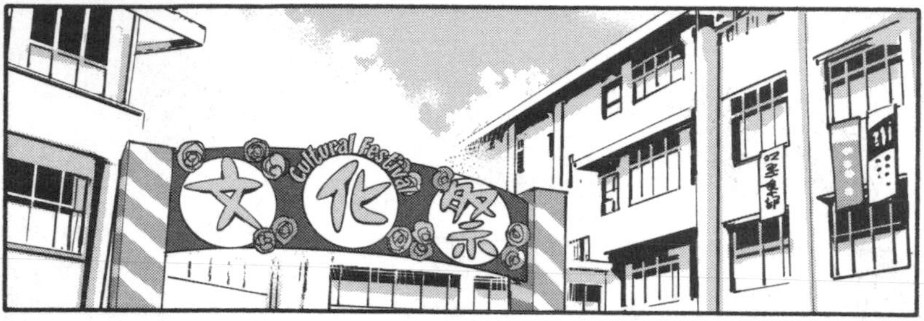
Cultural Festival
文化祭
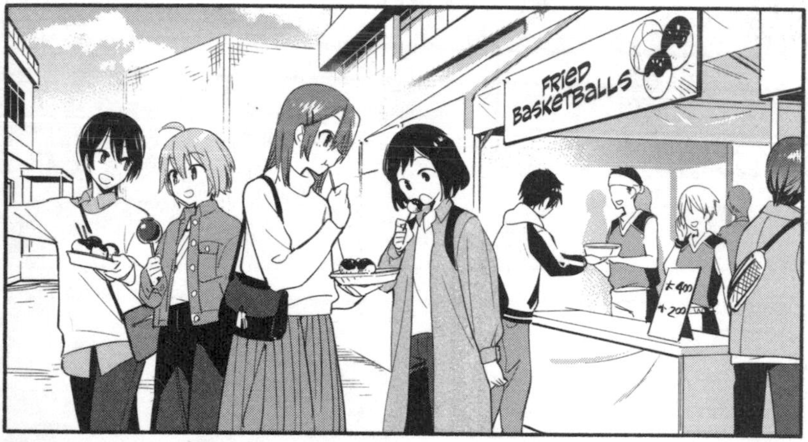
FRIED BASKETBALLS
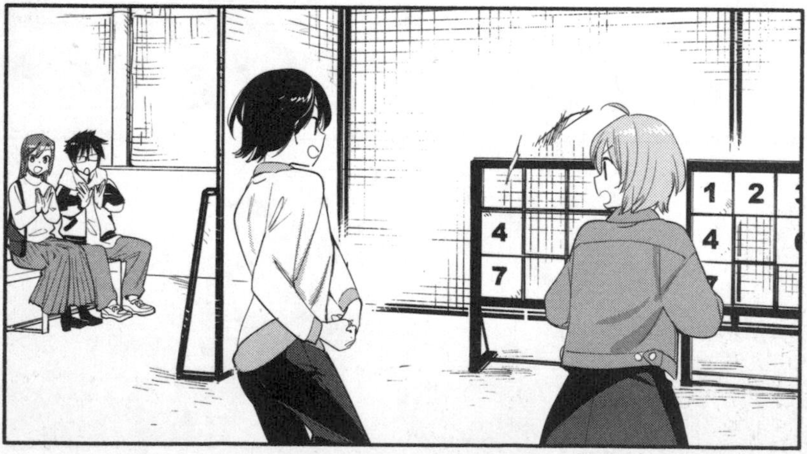

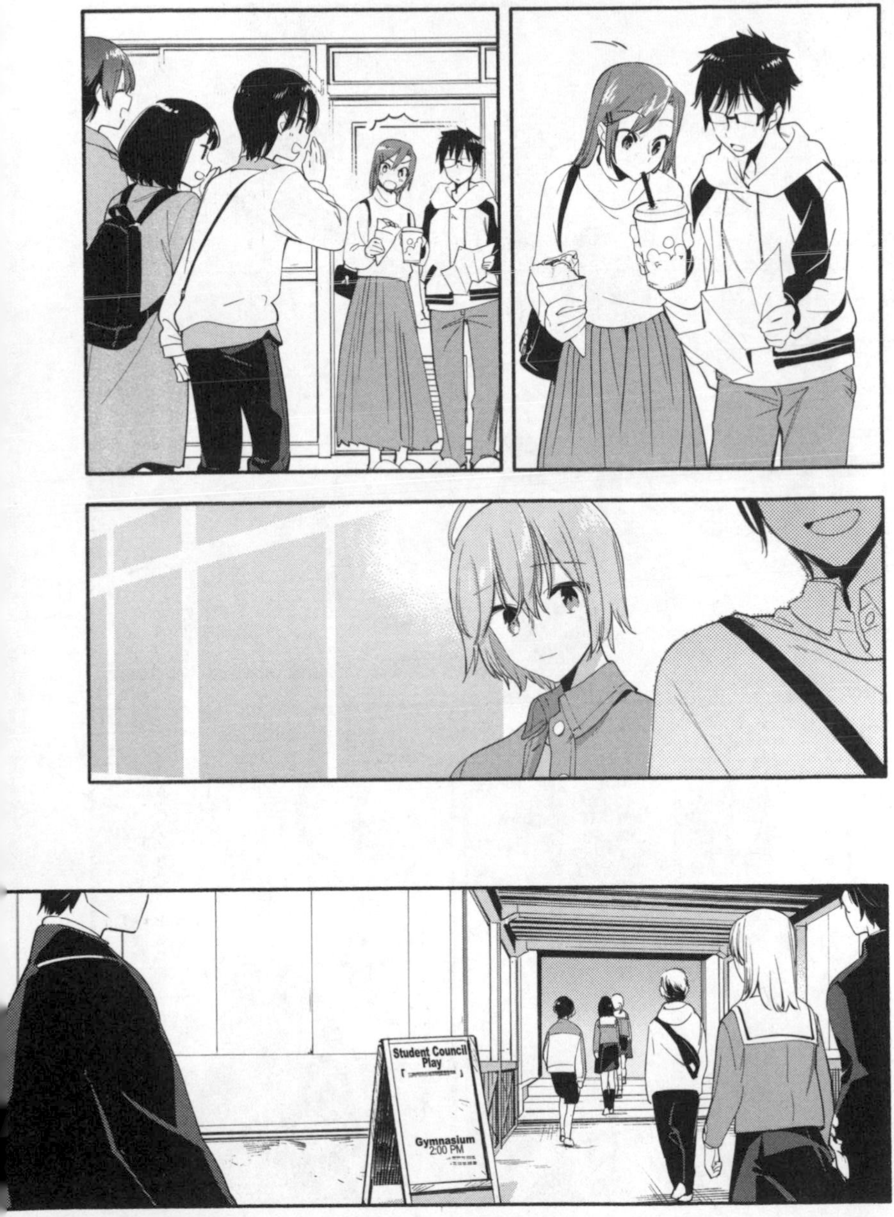
Student Council Play
Gymnasium
2:00 PM

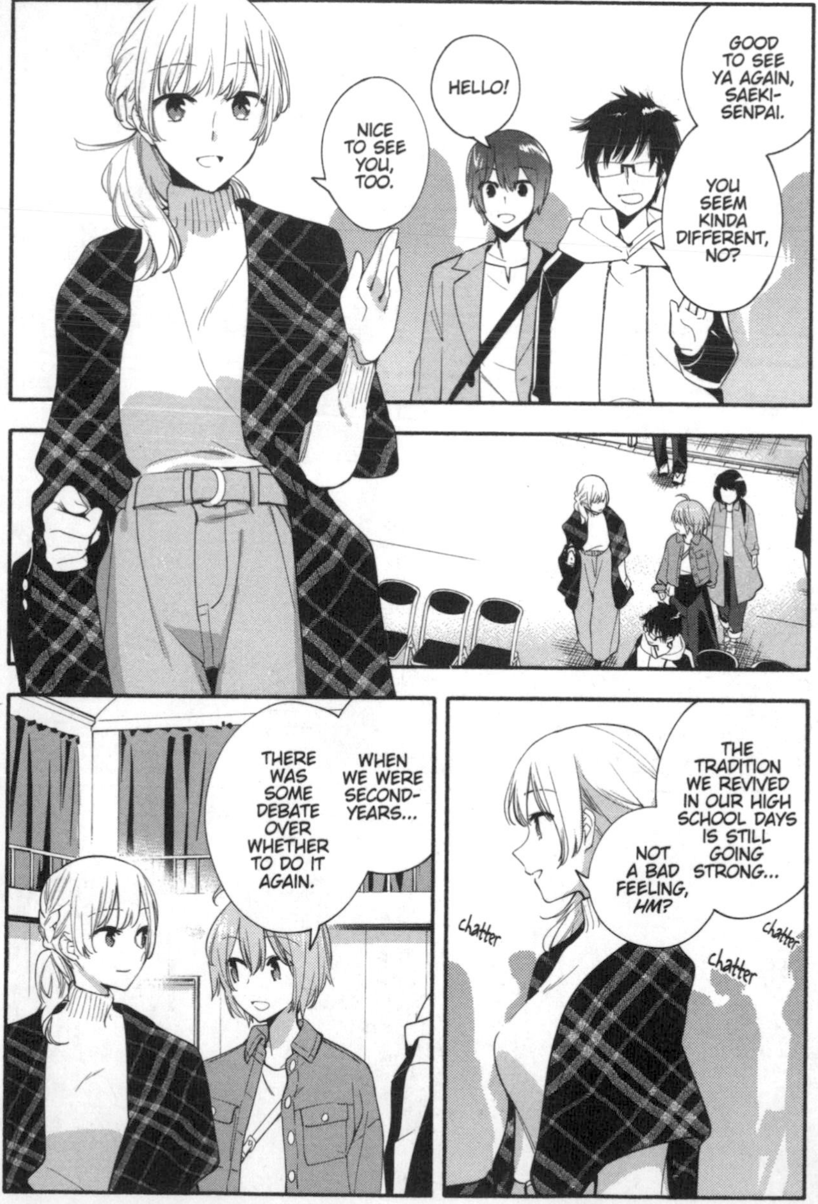
GOOD TO SEE YA AGAIN, SAEKI-SENPAI.
YOU SEEM KINDA DIFFERENT, NO?
HELLO!
NICE TO SEE YOU, TOO.
THE TRADITION WE REVIVED IN OUR HIGH SCHOOL DAYS IS STILL GOING STRONG...
NOT A BAD FEELING, HM?
chatter
chatter
chatter
WHEN WE WERE SECOND-YEARS...
THERE WAS SOME DEBATE OVER WHETHER TO DO IT AGAIN.

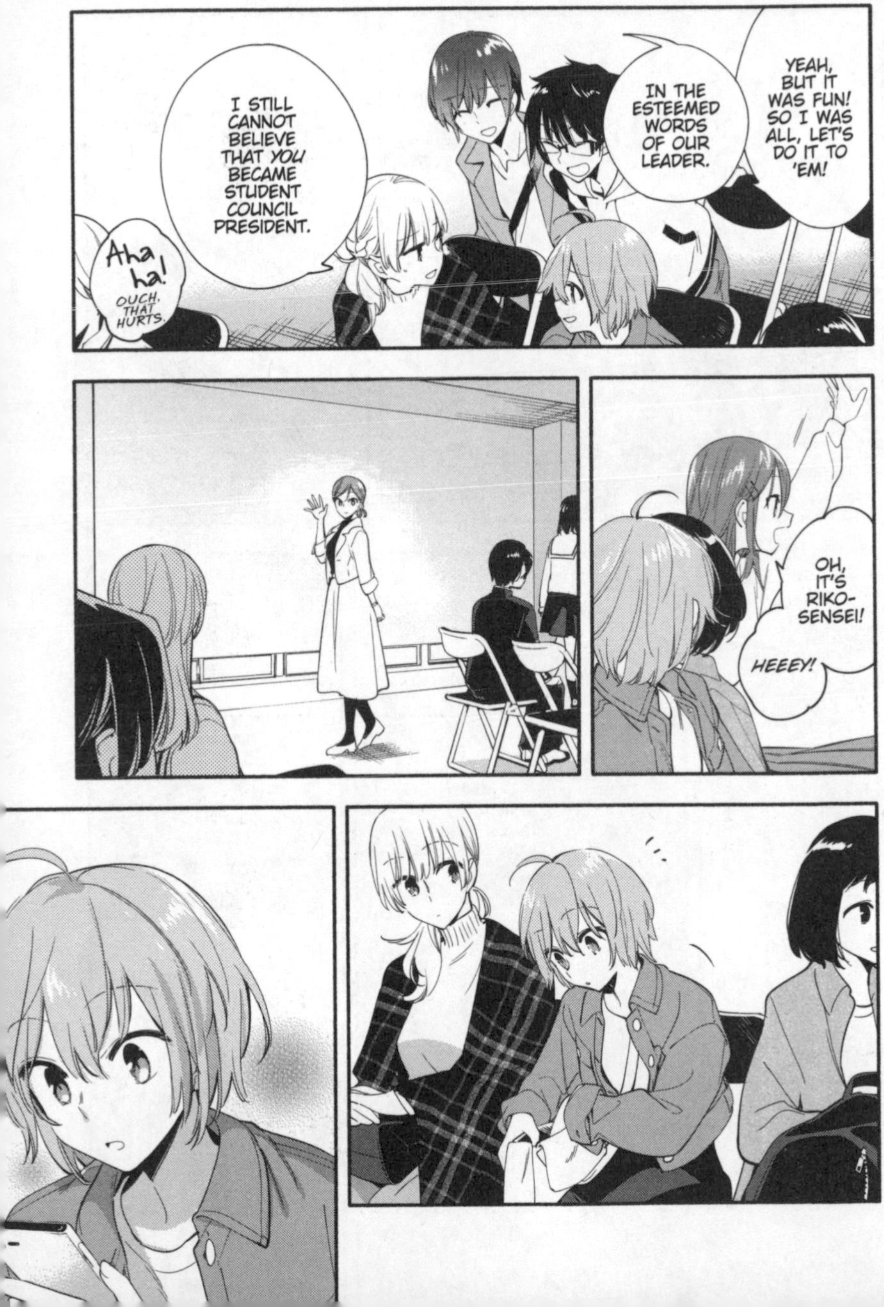
YEAH, BUT IT WAS FUN! SO I WAS ALL, LET'S DO IT TO 'EM!
IN THE ESTEEMED WORDS OF OUR LEADER.
I STILL CANNOT BELIEVE THAT *YOU* BECAME STUDENT COUNCIL PRESIDENT.
Aha ha!
OUCH, THAT HURTS.
OH, IT'S RIKO-SENSEI!
HEEEY!

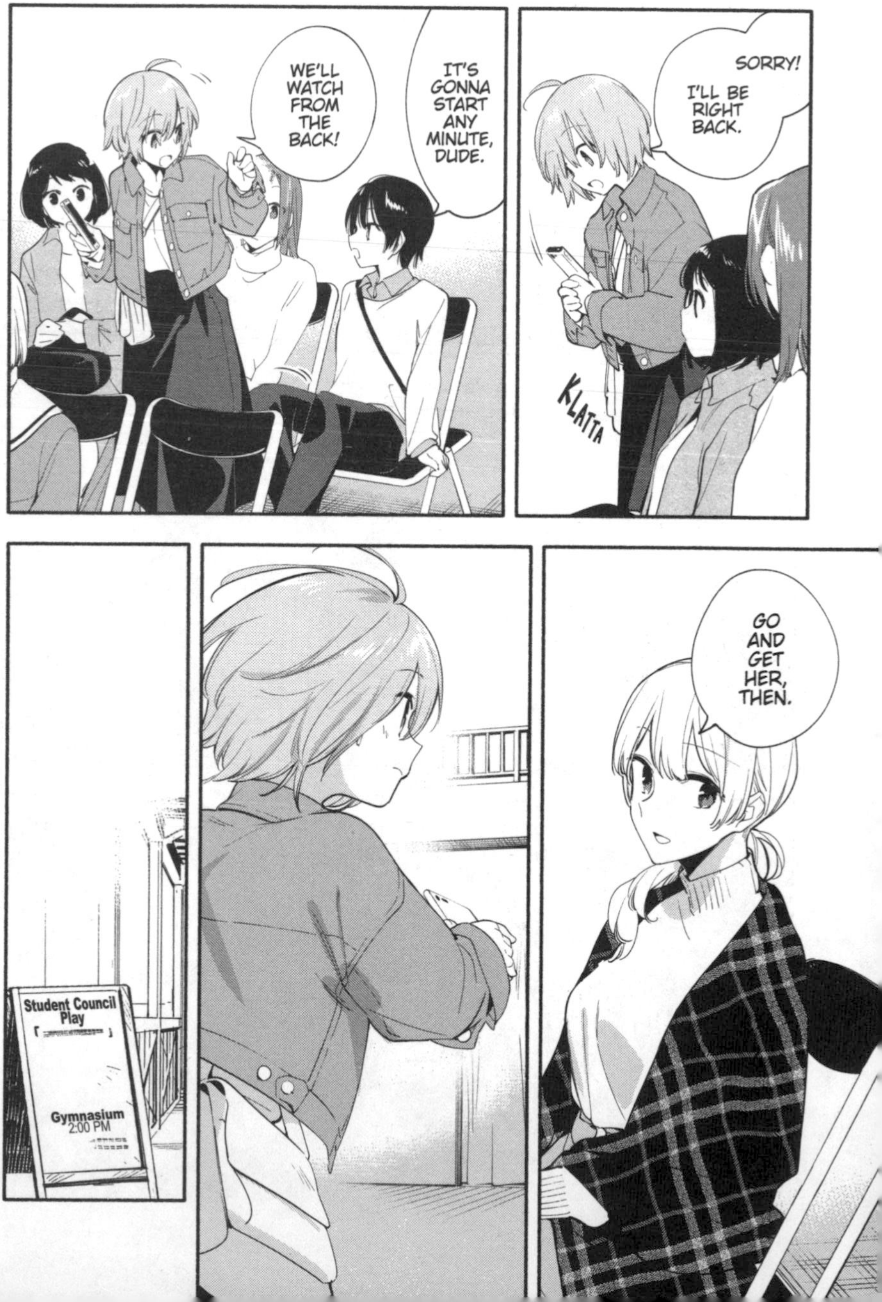
SORRY!
I'LL BE RIGHT BACK.
KLATTA
IT'S GONNA START ANY MINUTE, DUDE.
WE'LL WATCH FROM THE BACK!
GO AND GET HER, THEN.
Student Council Play
Gymnasium 2:00 PM

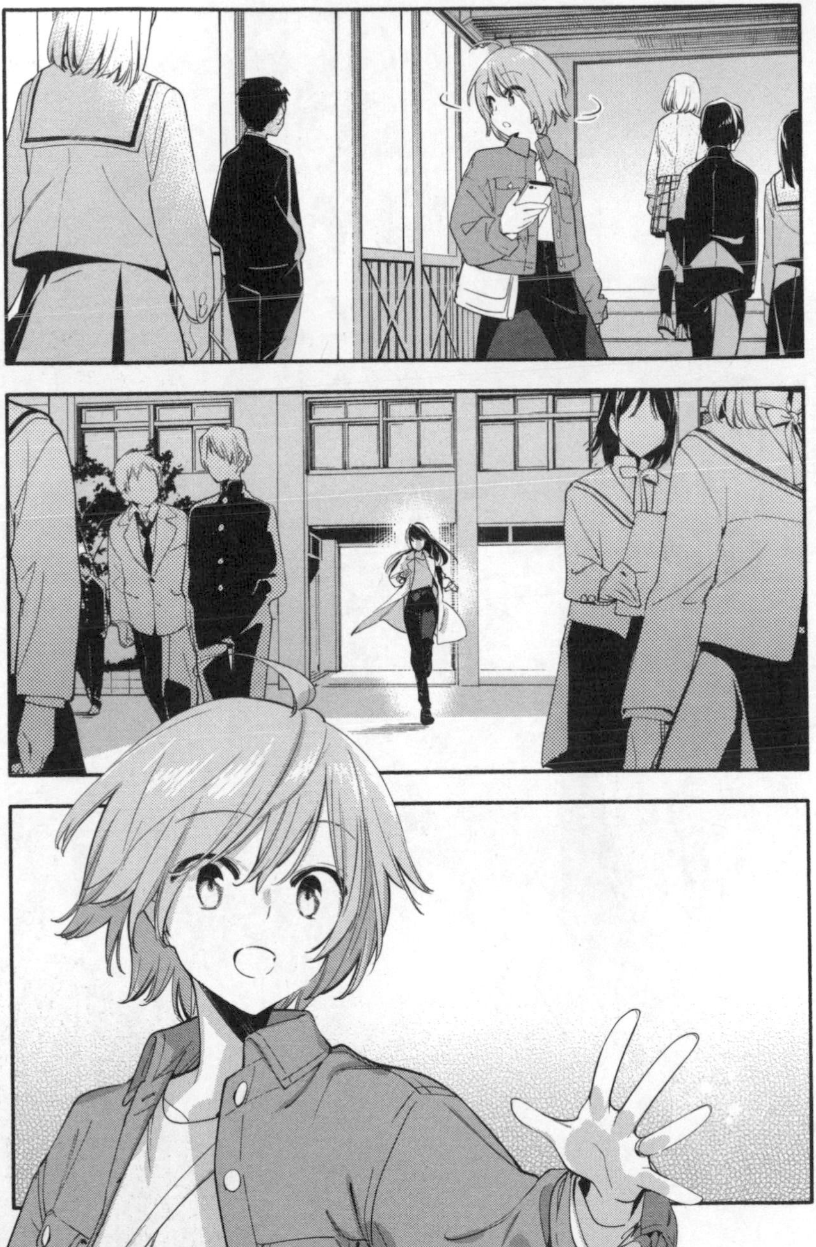

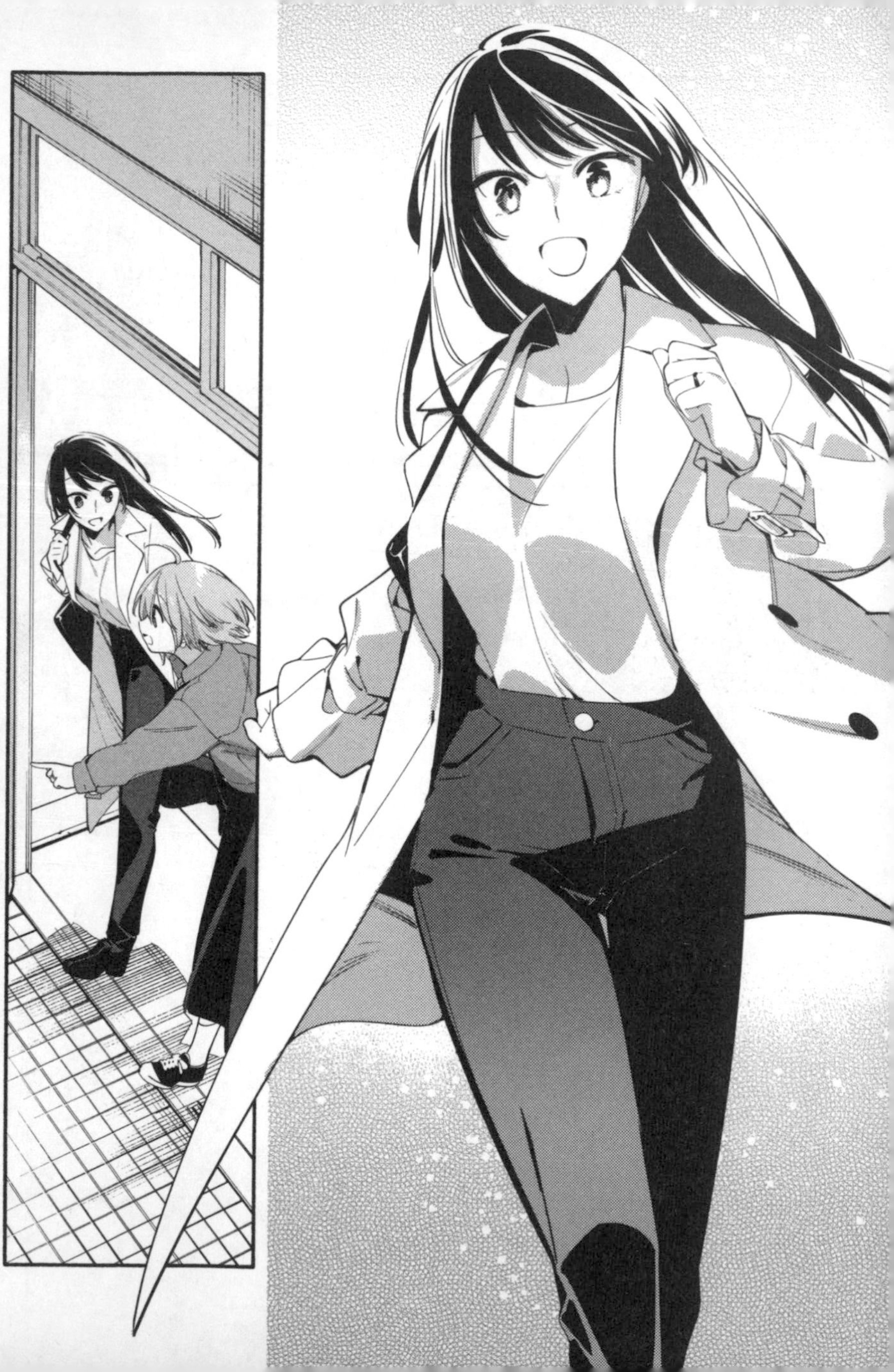

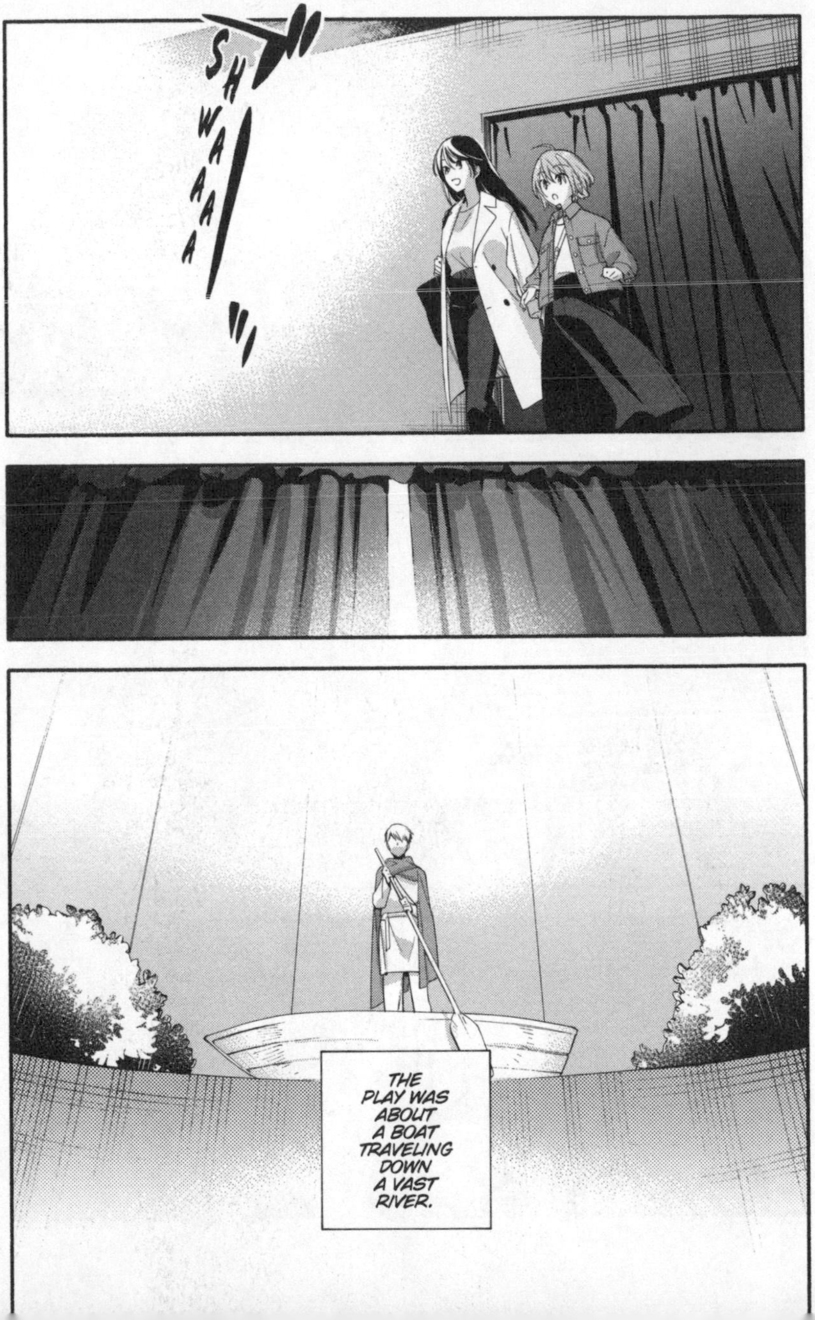
SHWAAAAA
THE PLAY WAS ABOUT A BOAT TRAVELING DOWN A VAST RIVER.

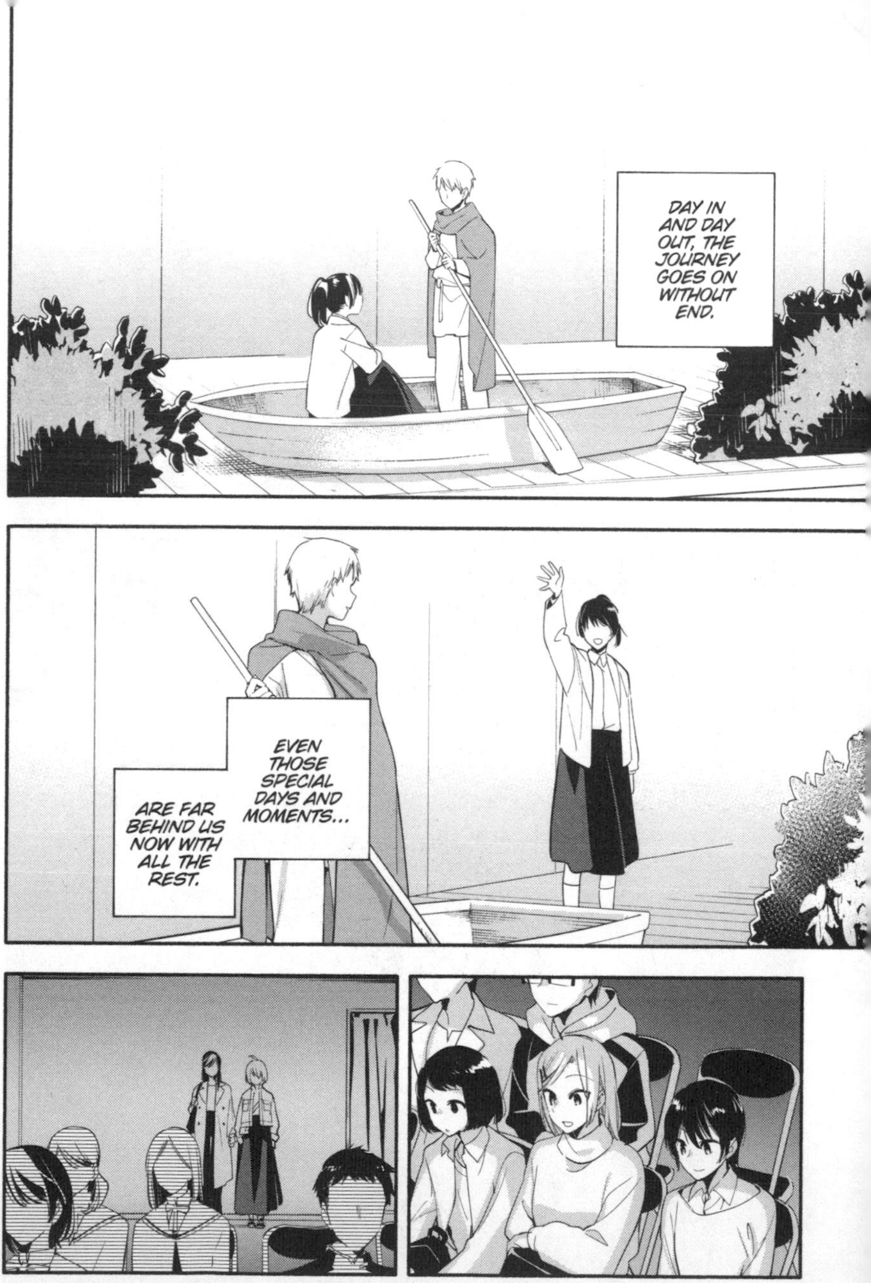
DAY IN AND DAY OUT, THE JOURNEY GOES ON WITHOUT END.
EVEN THOSE SPECIAL DAYS AND MOMENTS...
ARE FAR BEHIND US NOW WITH ALL THE REST.

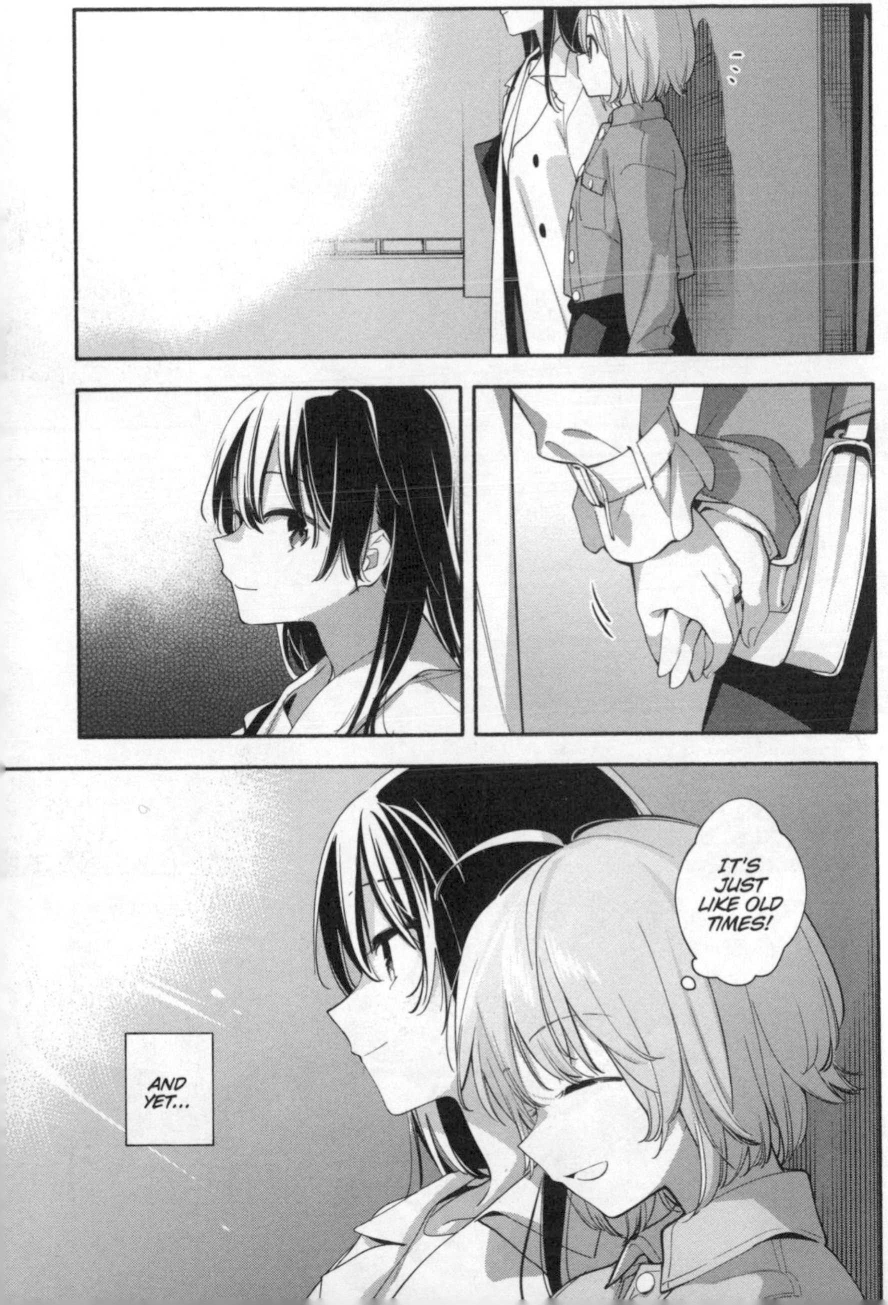
IT'S JUST LIKE OLD TIMES!
AND YET...

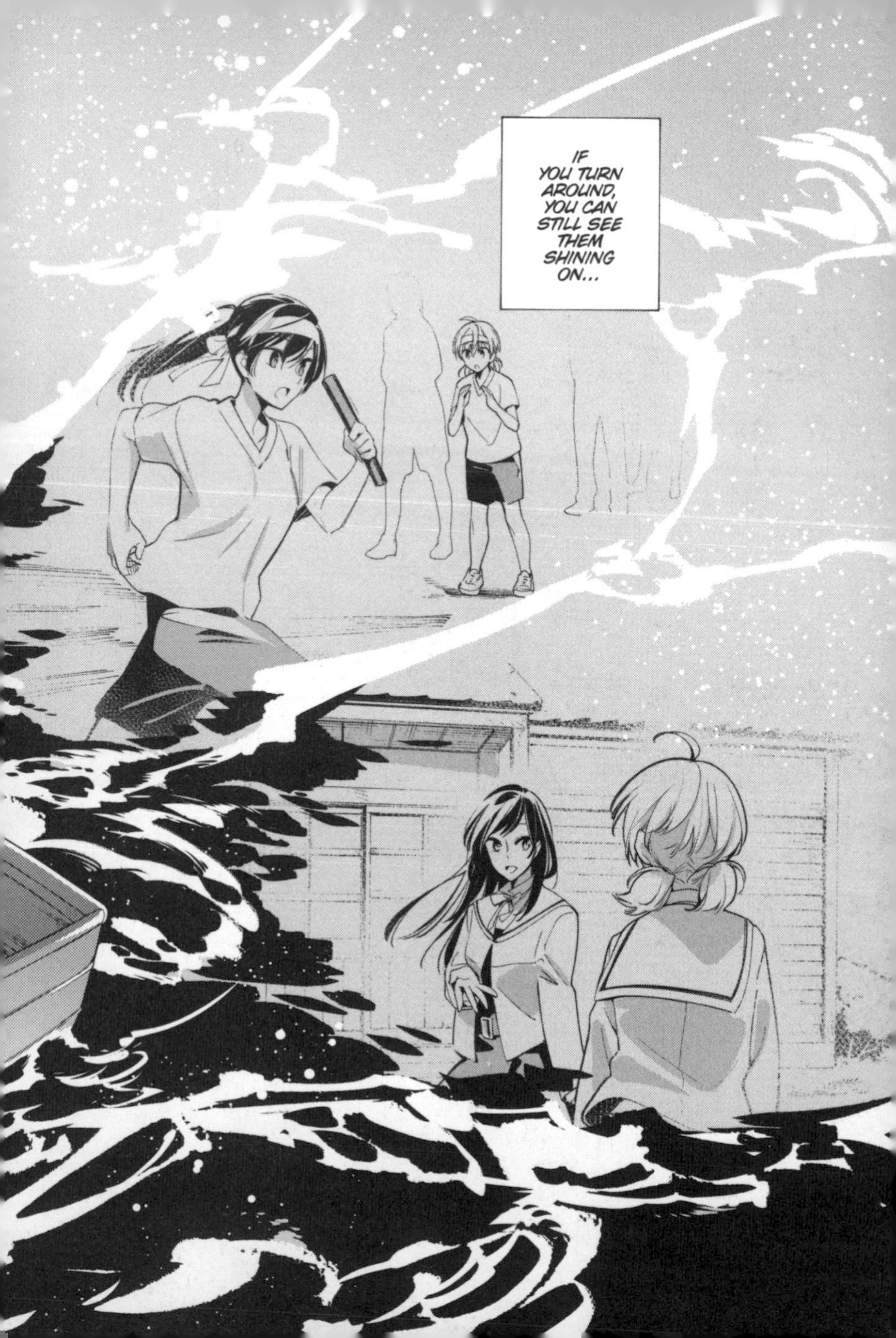
IF YOU TURN AROUND, YOU CAN STILL SEE THEM SHINING ON...

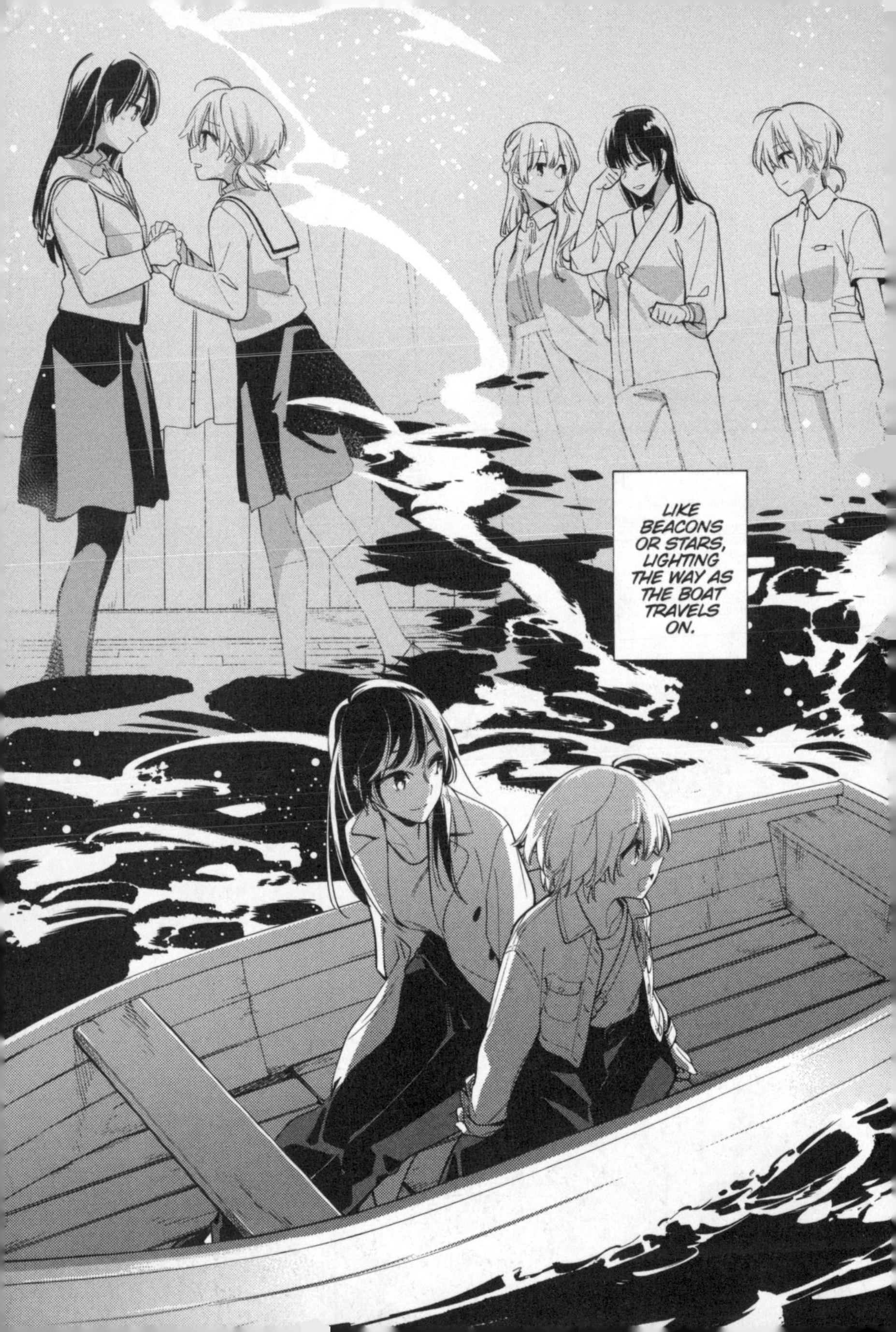
LIKE BEACONS OR STARS, LIGHTING THE WAY AS THE BOAT TRAVELS ON.

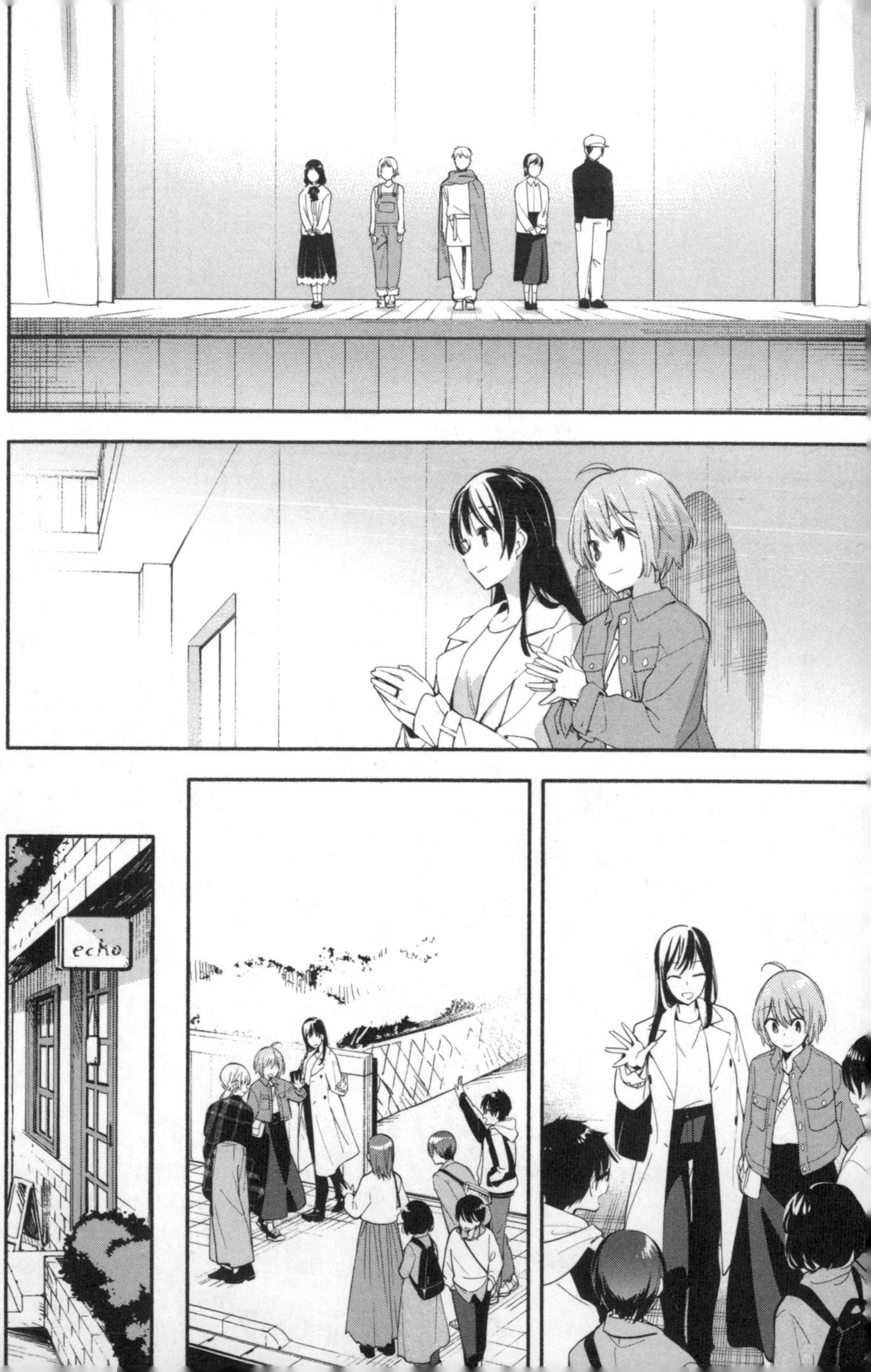
echo

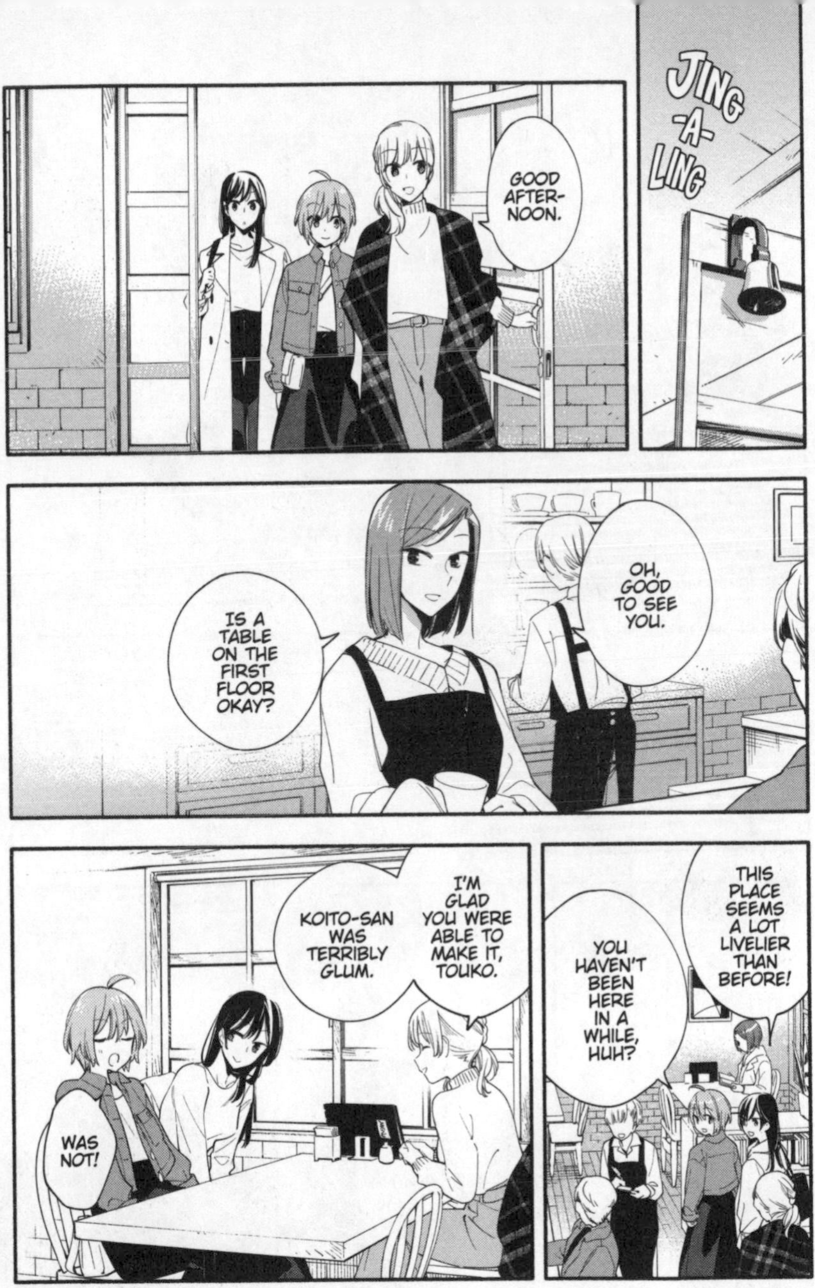
JING-A-LING
GOOD AFTER-NOON.
OH, GOOD TO SEE YOU.
IS A TABLE ON THE FIRST FLOOR OKAY?
THIS PLACE SEEMS A LOT LIVELIER THAN BEFORE!
YOU HAVEN'T BEEN HERE IN A WHILE, HUH?
I'M GLAD YOU WERE ABLE TO MAKE IT, TOUKO.
KOITO-SAN WAS TERRIBLY GLUM.
WAS NOT!

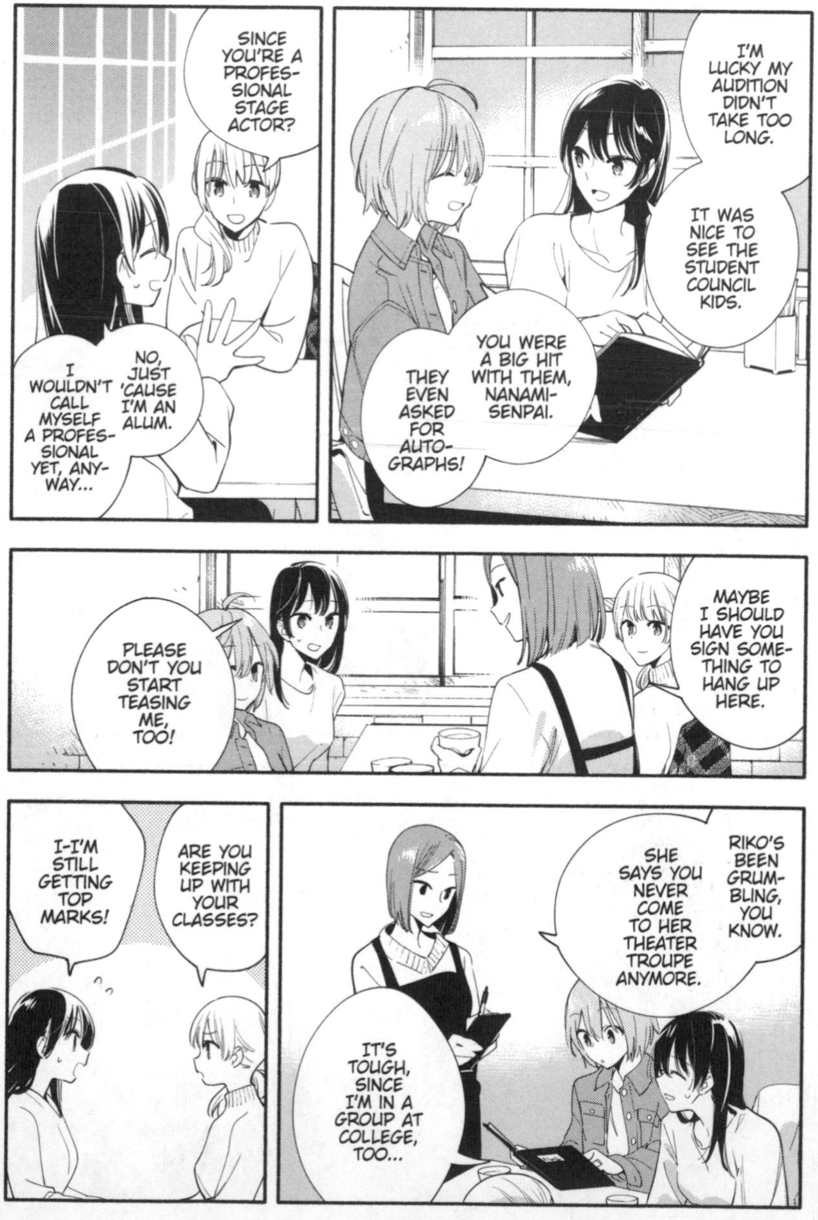
I'M LUCKY MY AUDITION DIDN'T TAKE TOO LONG.
IT WAS NICE TO SEE THE STUDENT COUNCIL KIDS.
YOU WERE A BIG HIT WITH THEM, NANAMI-SENPAI.
THEY EVEN ASKED FOR AUTOGRAPHS!
SINCE YOU'RE A PROFESSIONAL STAGE ACTOR?
NO, JUST 'CAUSE I'M AN ALUM.
I WOULDN'T CALL MYSELF A PROFESSIONAL YET, ANYWAY...
MAYBE I SHOULD HAVE YOU SIGN SOMETHING TO HANG UP HERE.
PLEASE DON'T YOU START TEASING ME, TOO!
RIKO'S BEEN GRUMBLING, YOU KNOW.
SHE SAYS YOU NEVER COME TO HER THEATER TROUPE ANYMORE.
IT'S TOUGH, SINCE I'M IN A GROUP AT COLLEGE, TOO...
ARE YOU KEEPING UP WITH YOUR CLASSES?
I-I'M STILL GETTING TOP MARKS!

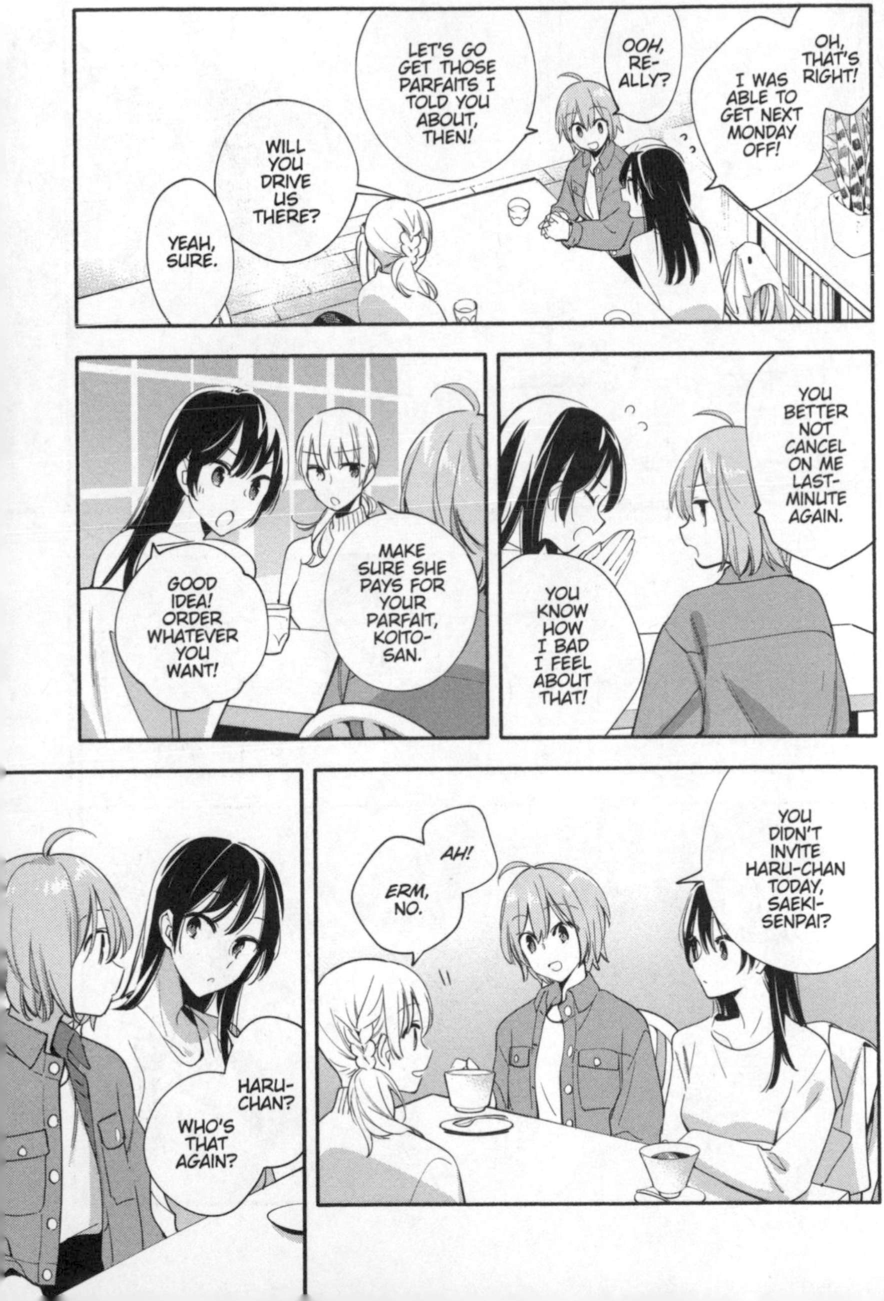
OH, THAT'S RIGHT! I WAS ABLE TO GET NEXT MONDAY OFF!
OOH, RE-ALLY?
LET'S GO GET THOSE PARFAITS I TOLD YOU ABOUT, THEN!
WILL YOU DRIVE US THERE?
YEAH, SURE.
YOU BETTER NOT CANCEL ON ME LAST-MINUTE AGAIN.
YOU KNOW HOW I BAD I FEEL ABOUT THAT!
MAKE SURE SHE PAYS FOR YOUR PARFAIT, KOITO-SAN.
GOOD IDEA! ORDER WHATEVER YOU WANT!
YOU DIDN'T INVITE HARU-CHAN TODAY, SAEKI-SENPAI?
AH!
ERM, NO.
HARU-CHAN? WHO'S THAT AGAIN?

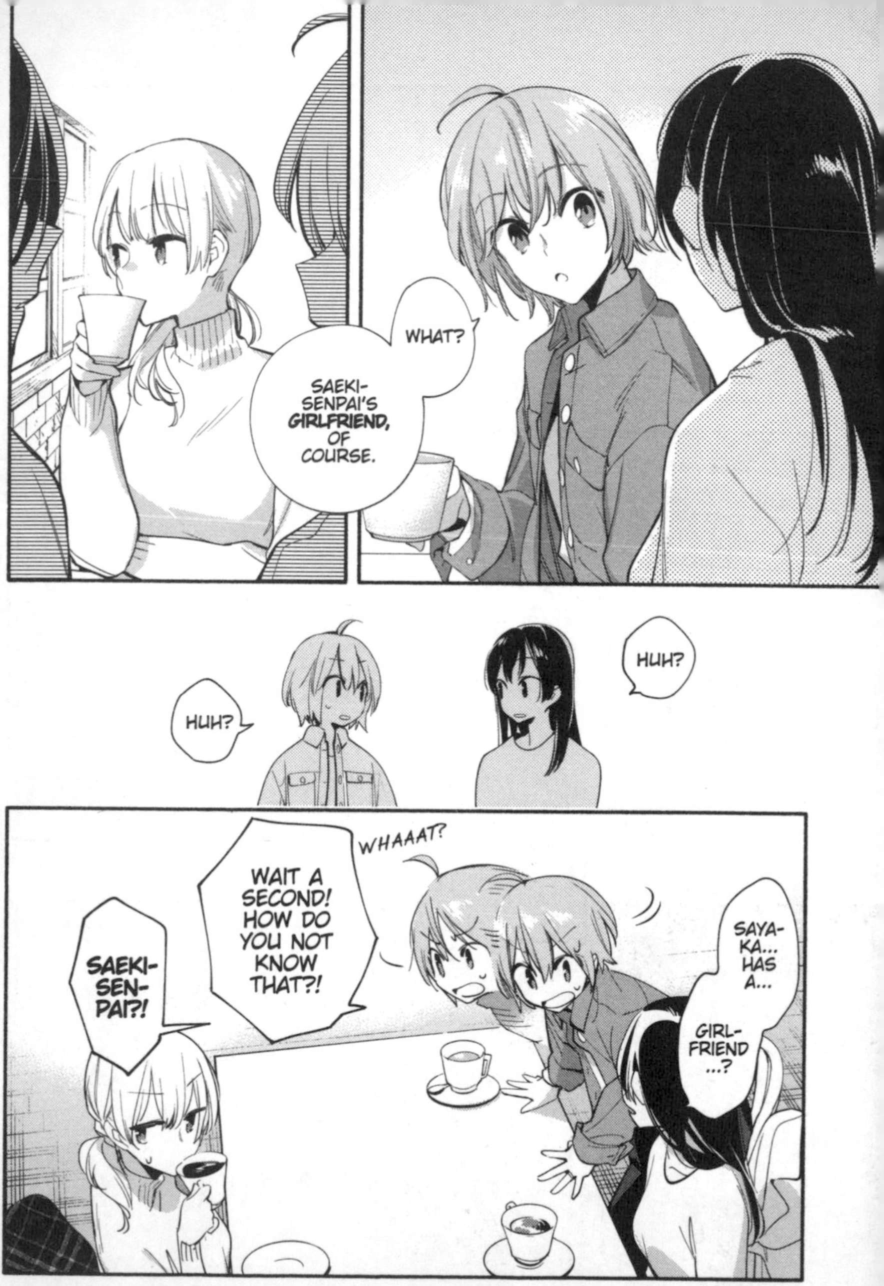
WHAT?
SAEKI-SENPAI'S **GIRLFRIEND,** OF COURSE.
HUH?
HUH?
WHAAAT?
SAYA-KA... HAS A...
GIRL-FRIEND ...?
WAIT A SECOND! HOW DO YOU NOT KNOW THAT?!
SAEKI-SEN-PAI?!

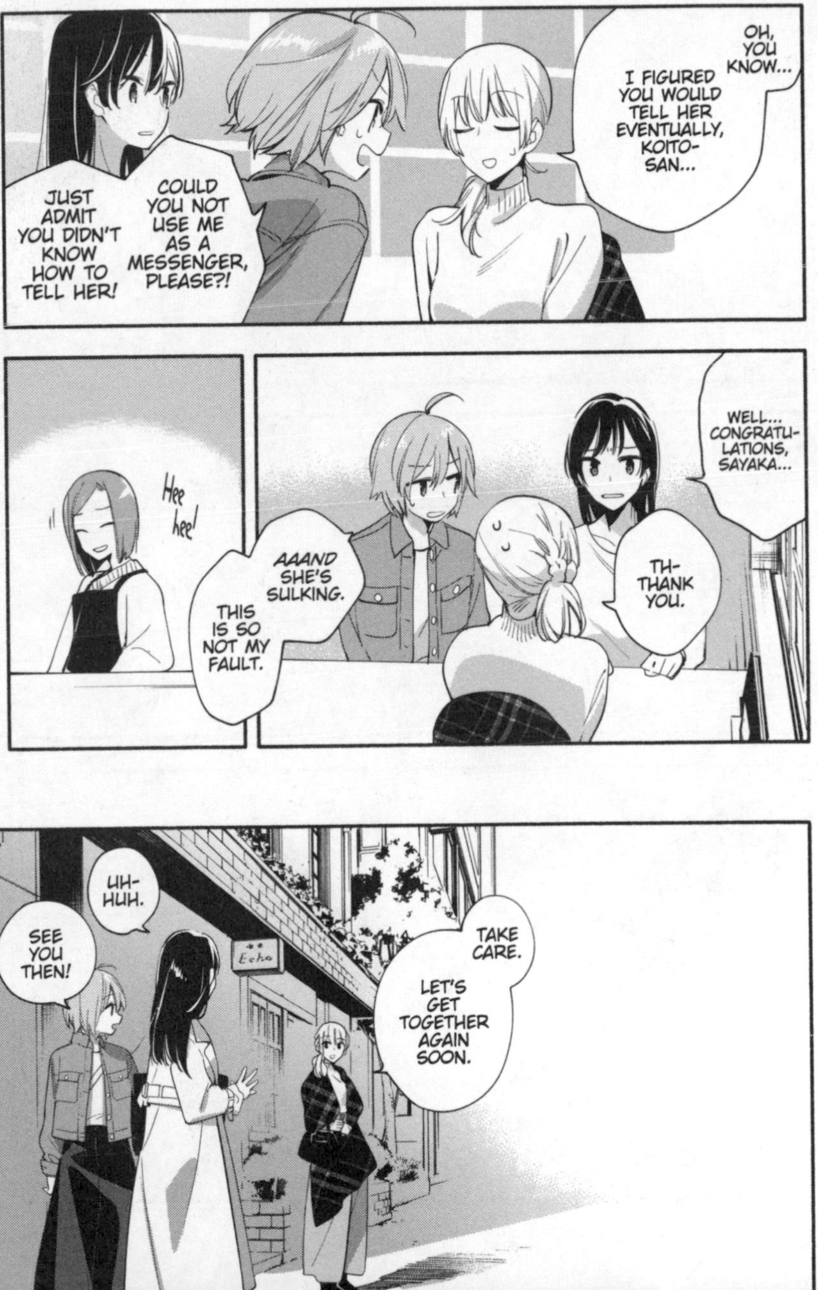
OH, YOU KNOW...
I FIGURED YOU WOULD TELL HER EVENTUALLY, KOITO-SAN...
COULD YOU NOT USE ME AS A MESSENGER, PLEASE?!
JUST ADMIT YOU DIDN'T KNOW HOW TO TELL HER!
WELL... CONGRATULATIONS, SAYAKA...
TH-THANK YOU.
AAAND SHE'S SULKING.
THIS IS SO NOT MY FAULT.
Hee hee!
TAKE CARE.
LET'S GET TOGETHER AGAIN SOON.
UH-HUH.
SEE YOU THEN!
Echo

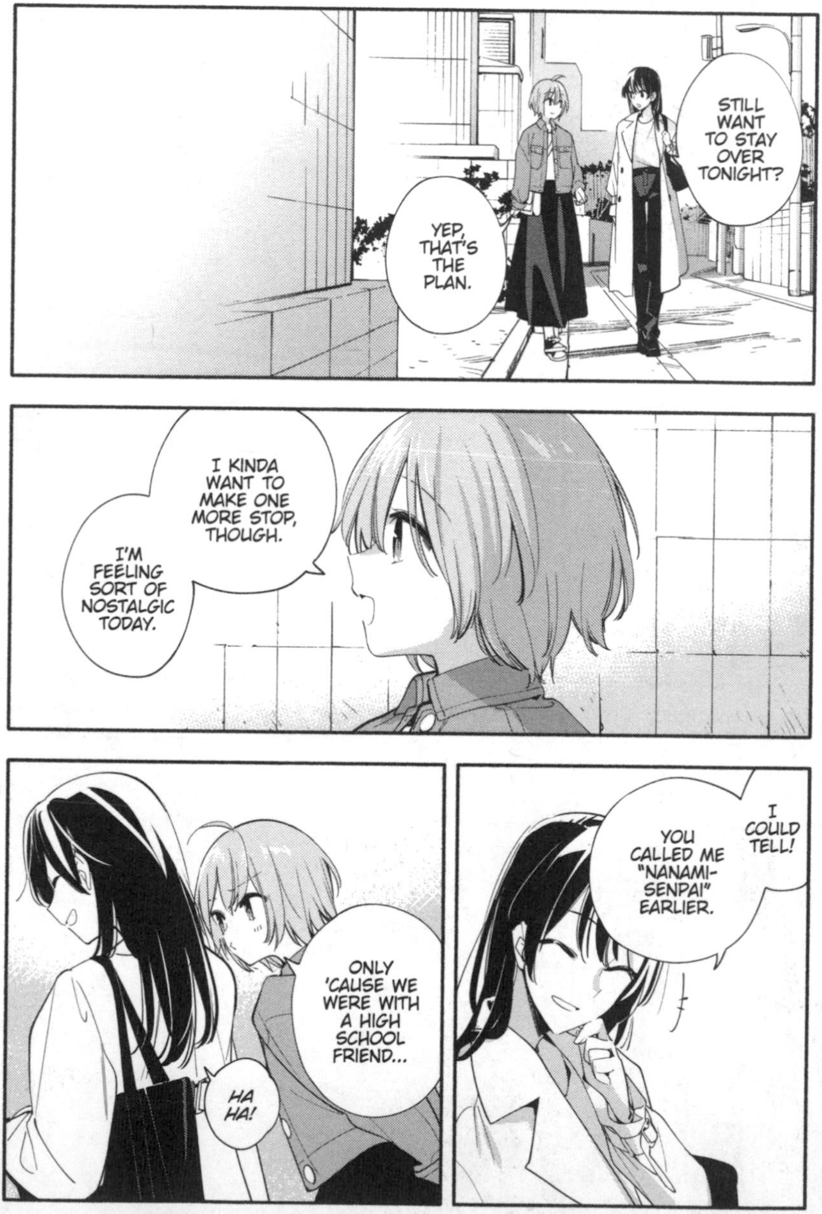
STILL WANT TO STAY OVER TONIGHT?
YEP, THAT'S THE PLAN.
I KINDA WANT TO MAKE ONE MORE STOP, THOUGH.
I'M FEELING SORT OF NOSTALGIC TODAY.
I COULD TELL!
YOU CALLED ME "NANAMI-SENPAI" EARLIER.
ONLY 'CAUSE WE WERE WITH A HIGH SCHOOL FRIEND...
HA HA!

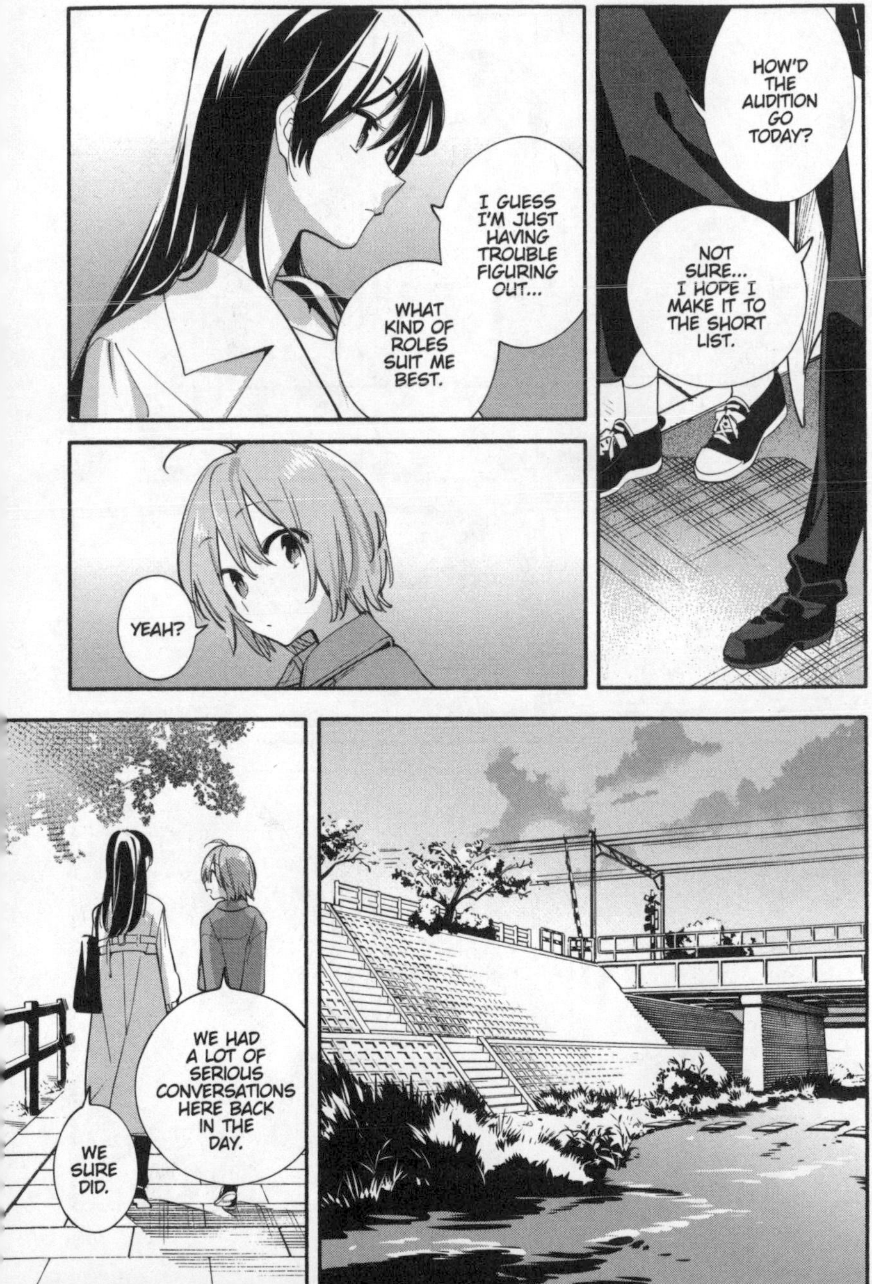
HOW'D THE AUDITION GO TODAY?
NOT SURE... I HOPE I MAKE IT TO THE SHORT LIST.
I GUESS I'M JUST HAVING TROUBLE FIGURING OUT...
WHAT KIND OF ROLES SUIT ME BEST.
YEAH?
WE HAD A LOT OF SERIOUS CONVERSATIONS HERE BACK IN THE DAY.
WE SURE DID.

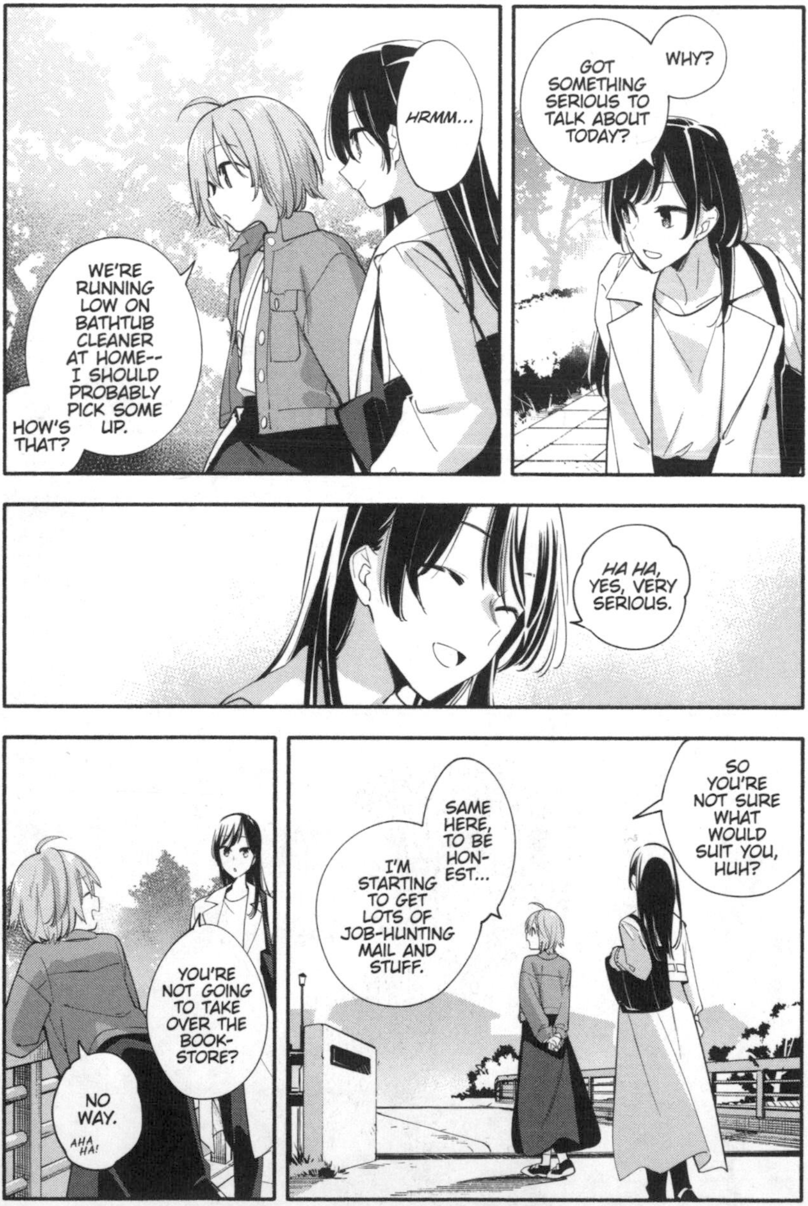
WHY?
GOT SOMETHING SERIOUS TO TALK ABOUT TODAY?
HRMM...
WE'RE RUNNING LOW ON BATHTUB CLEANER AT HOME-- I SHOULD PROBABLY PICK SOME UP.
HOW'S THAT?
HA HA, YES, VERY SERIOUS.
SO YOU'RE NOT SURE WHAT WOULD SUIT YOU, HUH?
SAME HERE, TO BE HON-EST...
I'M STARTING TO GET LOTS OF JOB-HUNTING MAIL AND STUFF.
YOU'RE NOT GOING TO TAKE OVER THE BOOK-STORE?
NO WAY.
AHA HA!

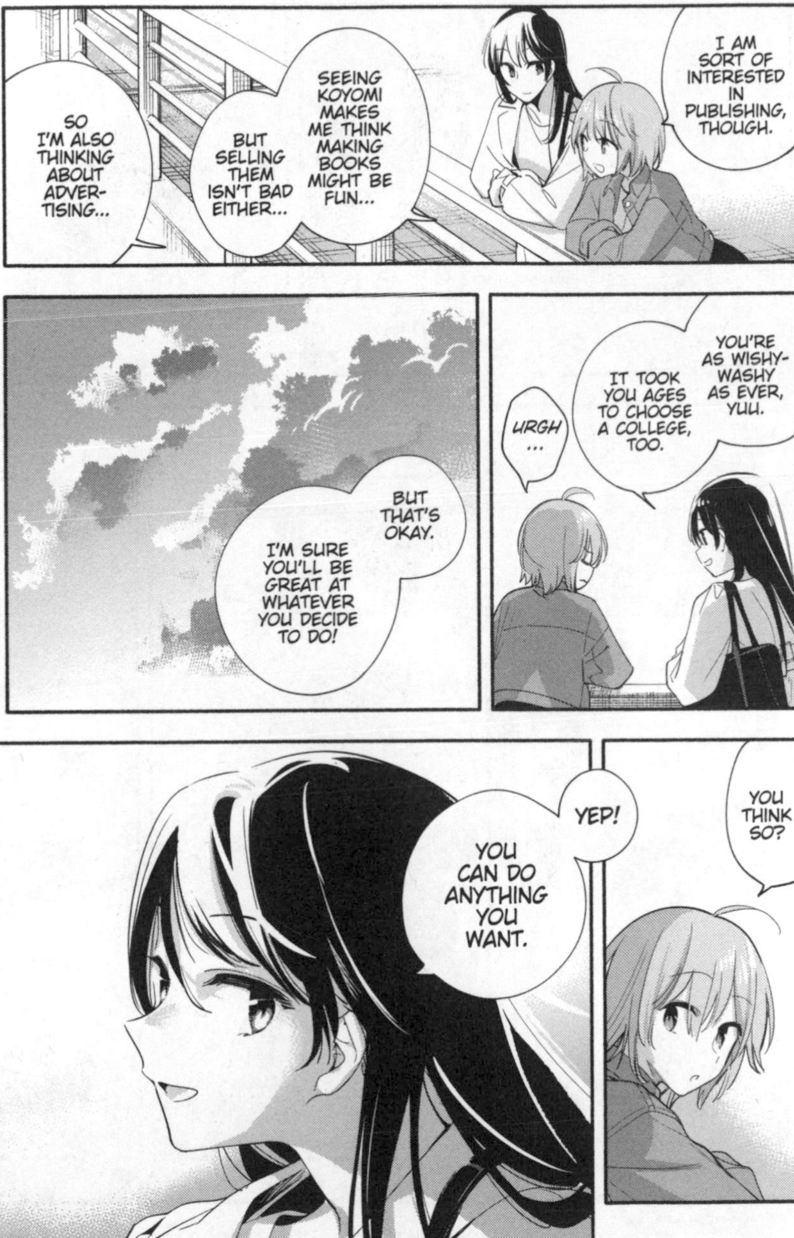
I AM SORT OF INTERESTED IN PUBLISHING, THOUGH.
SEEING KOYOMI MAKES ME THINK MAKING BOOKS MIGHT BE FUN...
BUT SELLING THEM ISN'T BAD EITHER...
SO I'M ALSO THINKING ABOUT ADVER-TISING...
YOU'RE AS WISHY-WASHY AS EVER, YUU.
IT TOOK YOU AGES TO CHOOSE A COLLEGE, TOO.
URGH...
BUT THAT'S OKAY.
I'M SURE YOU'LL BE GREAT AT WHATEVER YOU DECIDE TO DO!
YOU THINK SO?
YEP!
YOU CAN DO ANYTHING YOU WANT.

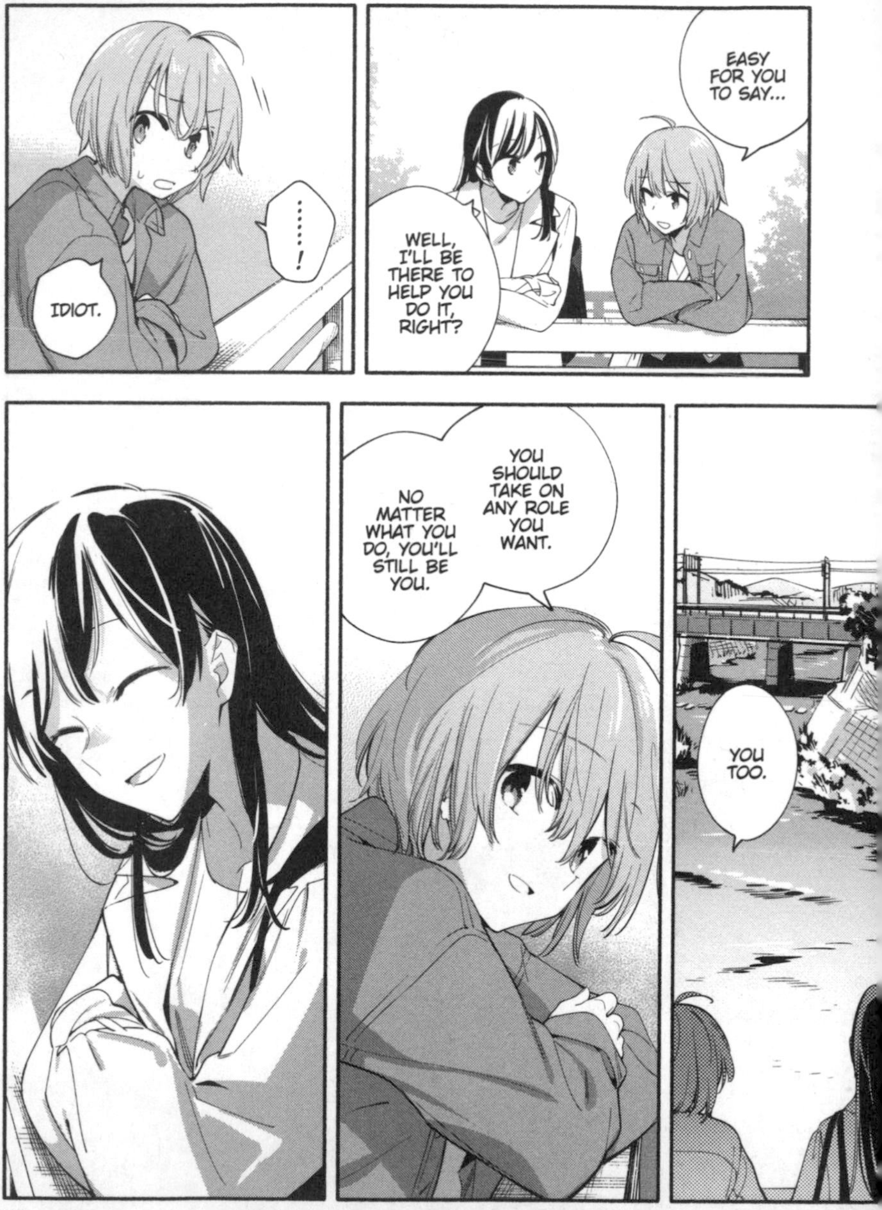
EASY FOR YOU TO SAY...
WELL, I'LL BE THERE TO HELP YOU DO IT, RIGHT?
......!
IDIOT.
YOU TOO.
YOU SHOULD TAKE ON ANY ROLE YOU WANT.
NO MATTER WHAT YOU DO, YOU'LL STILL BE YOU.

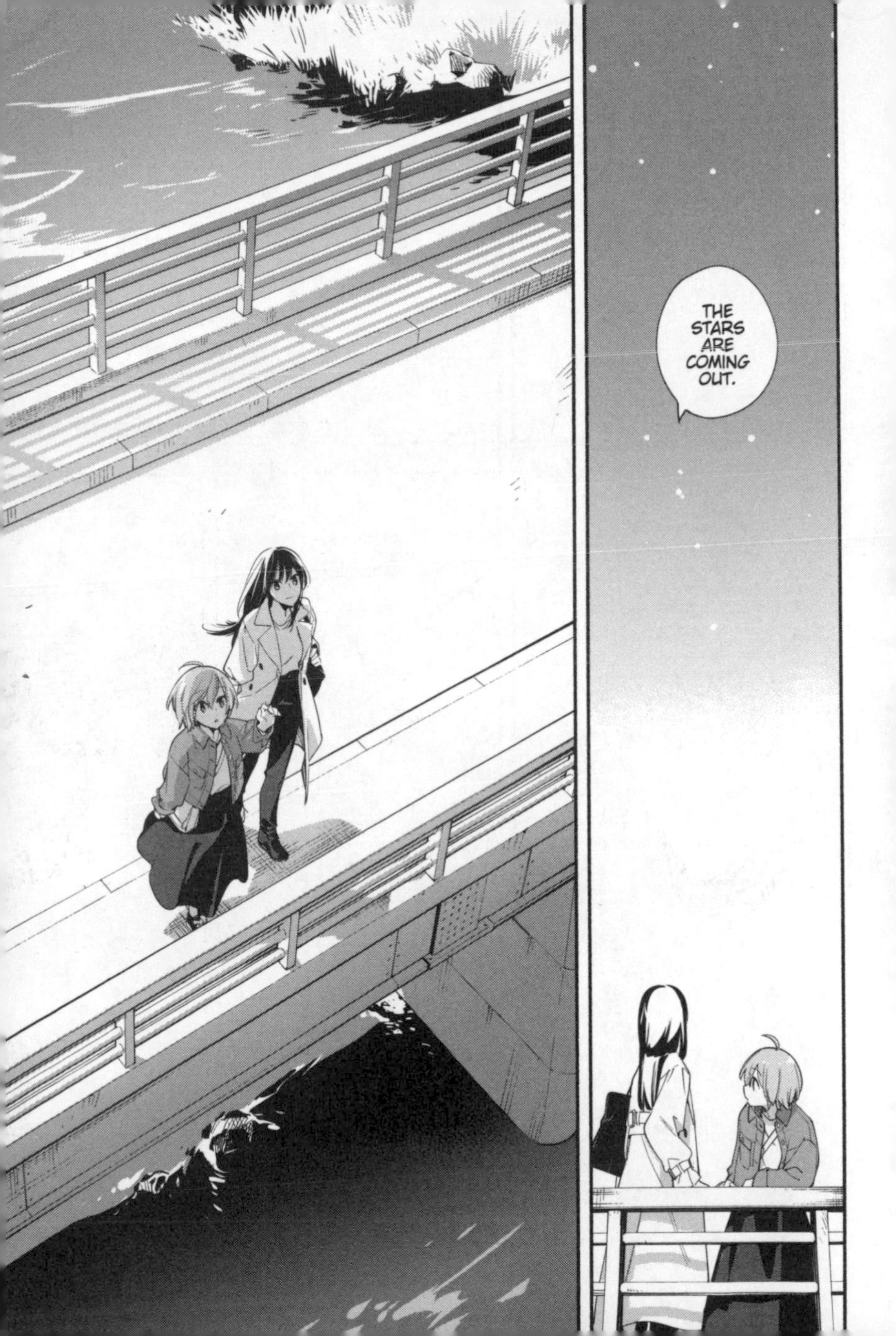
THE STARS ARE COMING OUT.

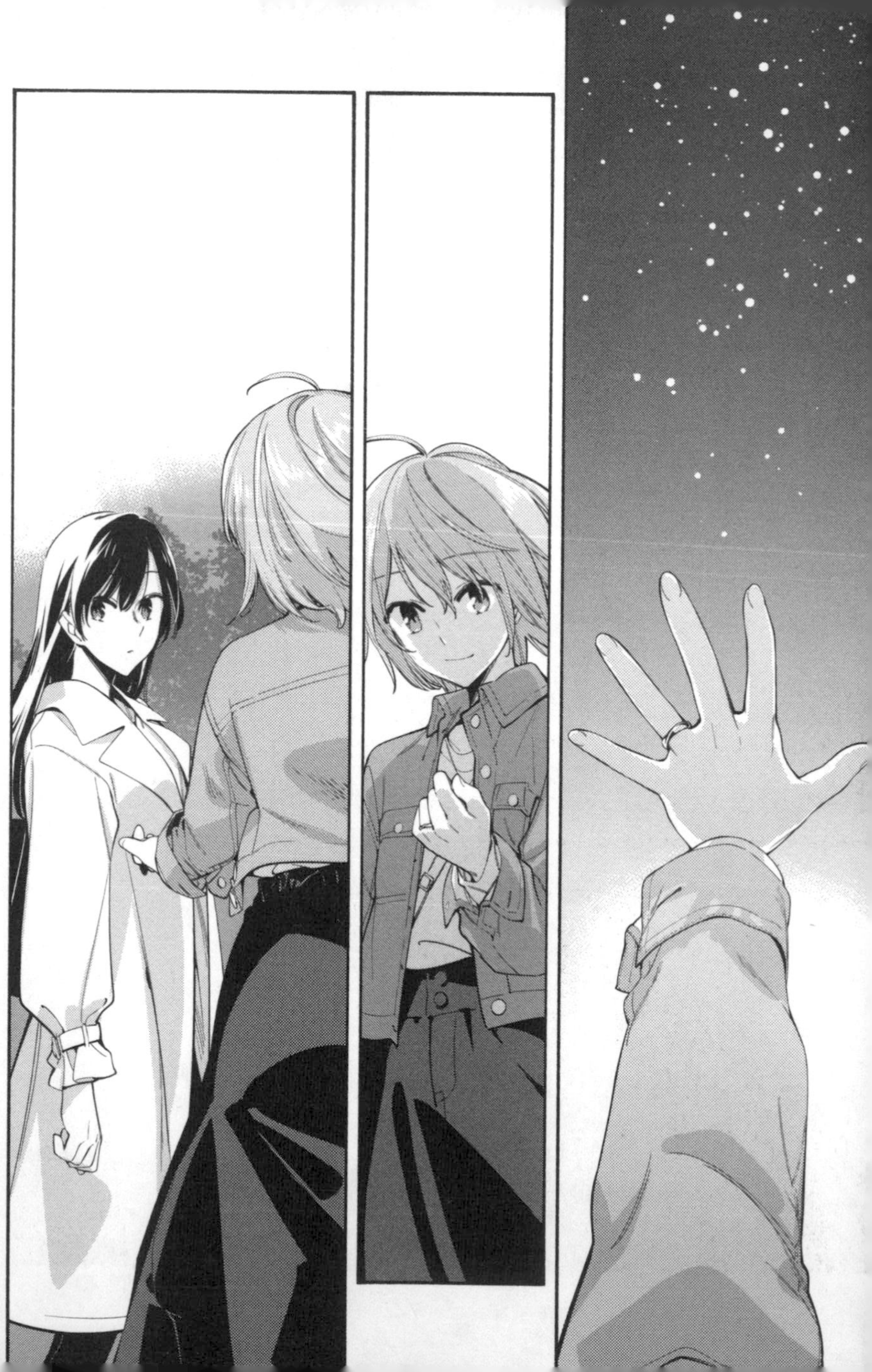

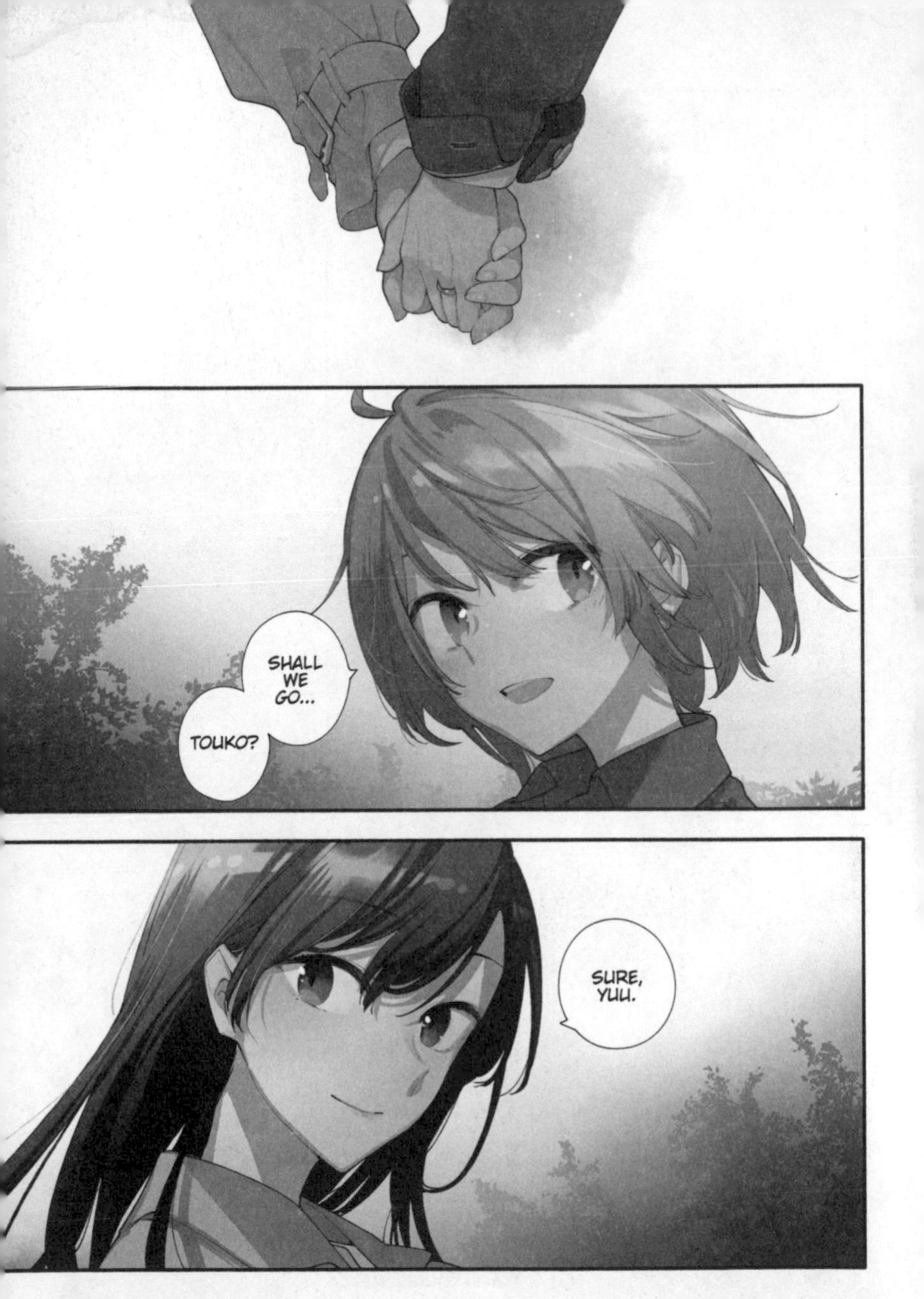
SHALL WE GO...
TOUKO?
SURE, YUU.

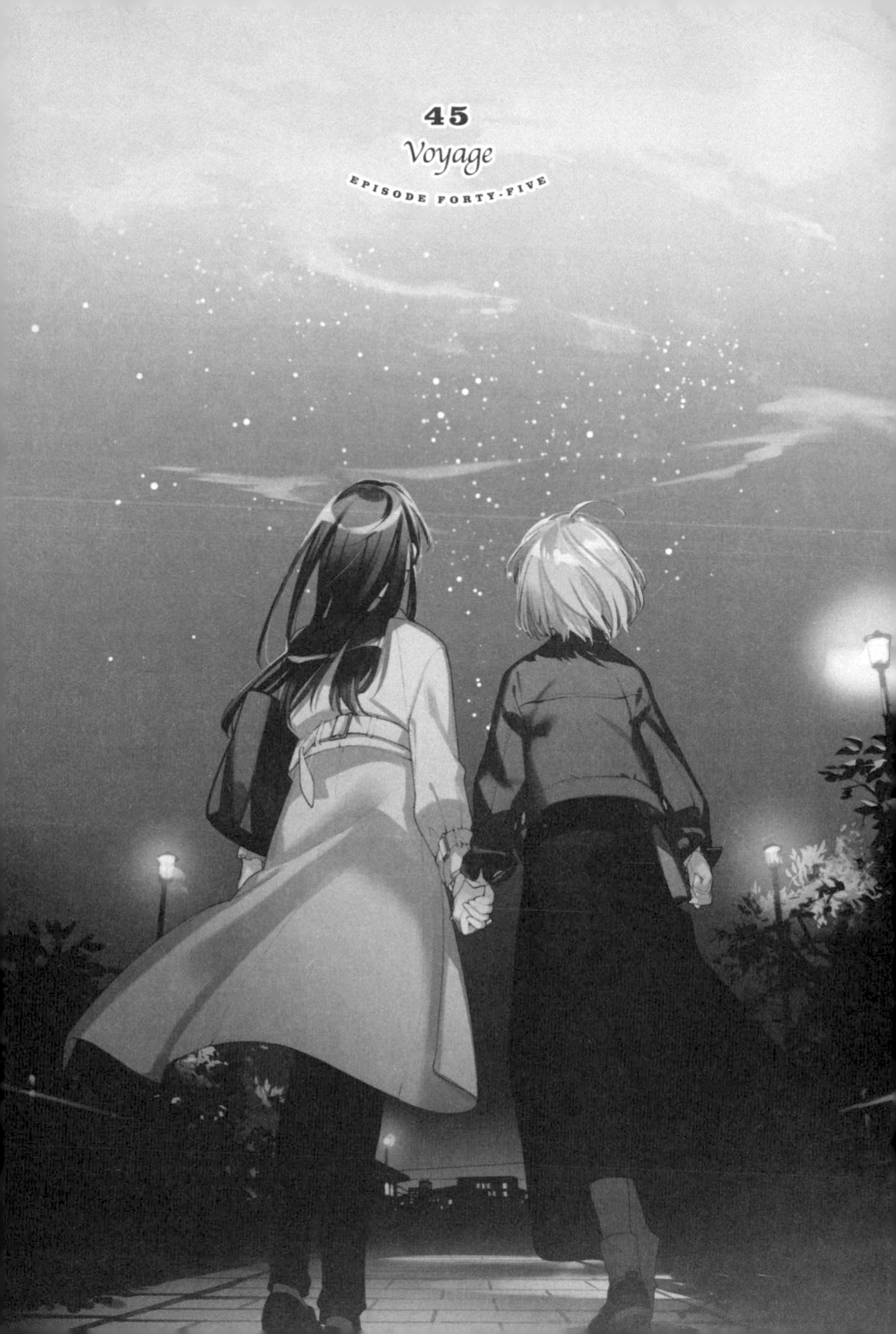
45
Voyage
EPISODE FORTY-FIVE

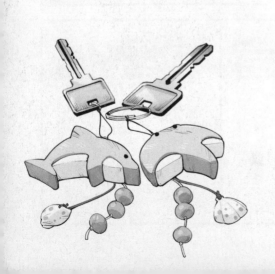

AFTERWORD MANGA

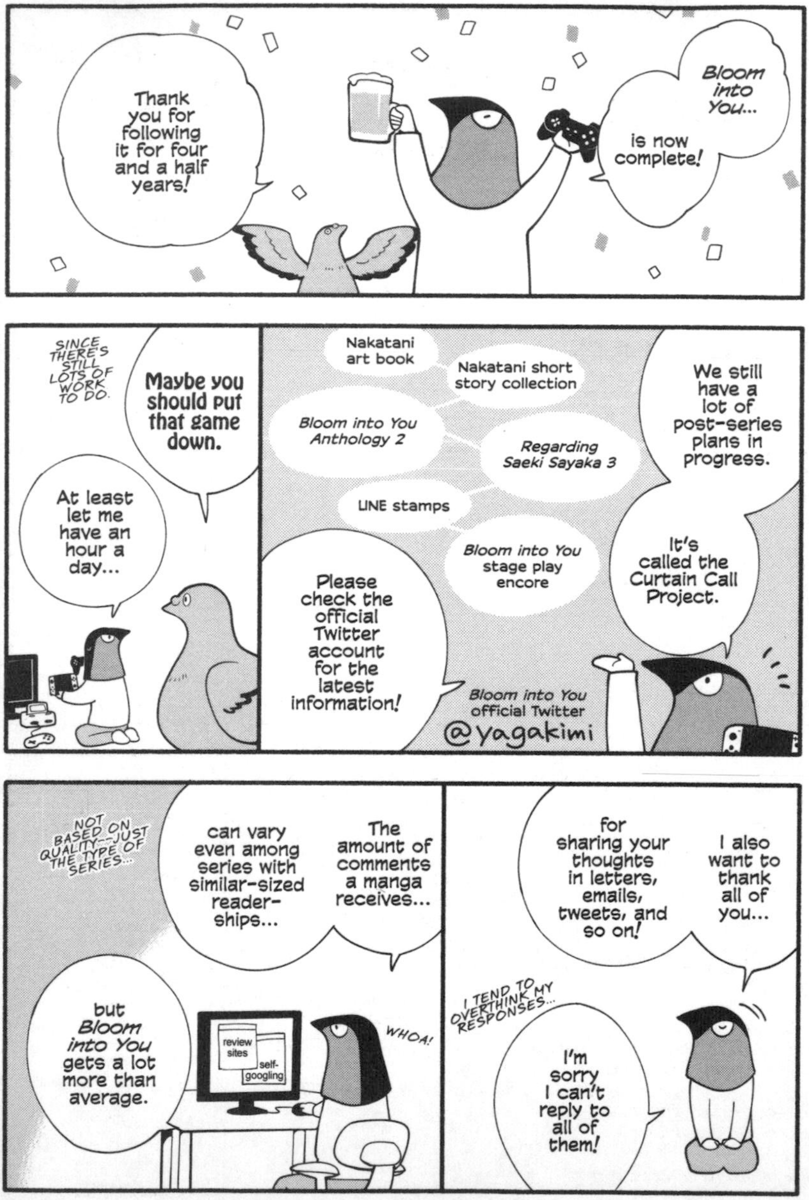
Bloom into You...
is now complete!
Thank you for following it for four and a half years!
We still have a lot of post-series plans in progress.
Nakatani art book
Nakatani short story collection
Bloom into You Anthology 2
Regarding Saeki Sayaka 3
LINE stamps
Bloom into You stage play encore
It's called the Curtain Call Project.
Please check the official Twitter account for the latest information!
Bloom into You official Twitter
@yagakimi
Maybe you should put that game down.
SINCE THERE'S STILL LOTS OF WORK TO DO.
At least let me have an hour a day...
I also want to thank all of you...
for sharing your thoughts in letters, emails, tweets, and so on!
I TEND TO OVERTHINK MY RESPONSES...
I'm sorry I can't reply to all of them!
The amount of comments a manga receives...
can vary even among series with similar-sized readerships...
NOT BASED ON QUALITY--JUST THE TYPE OF SERIES...
review sites
self-googling
WHOA!
but Bloom into You gets a lot more than average.

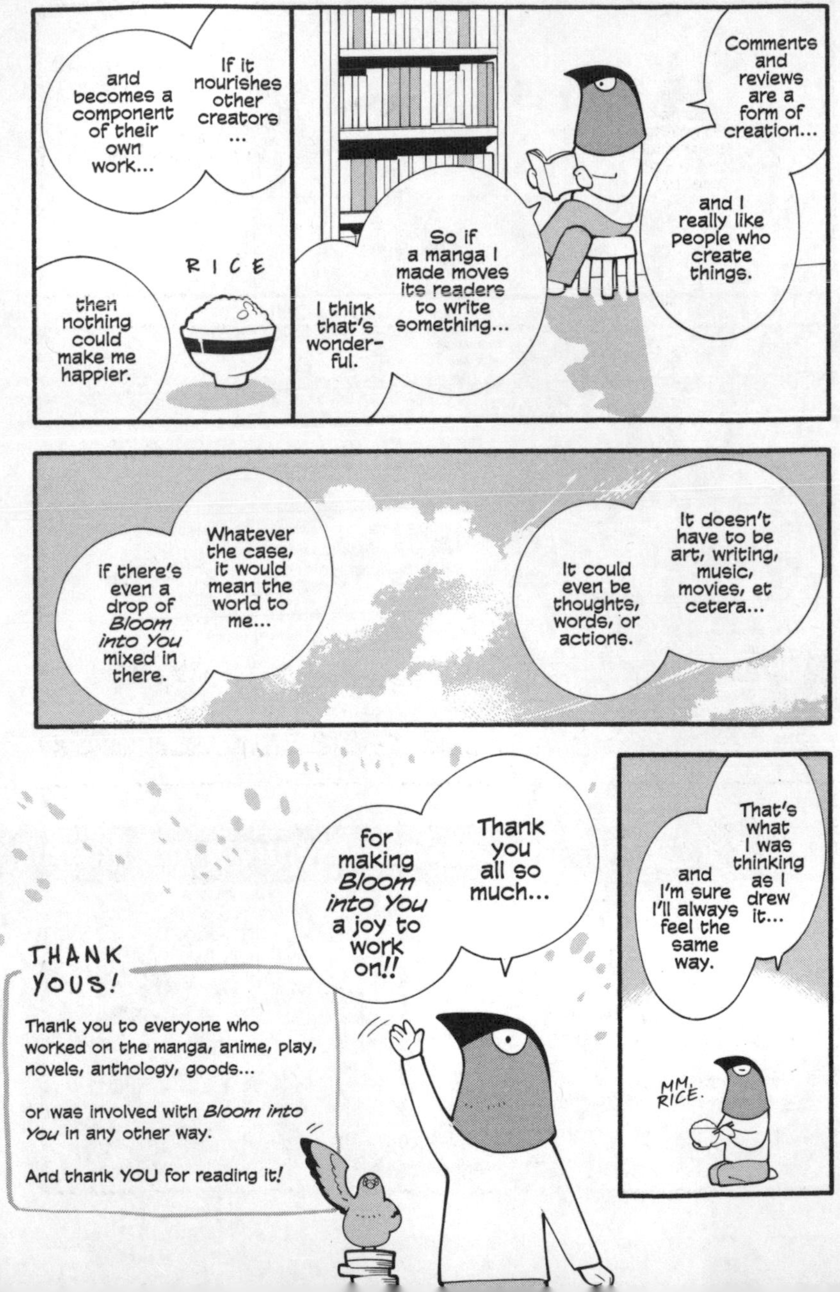
Comments and reviews are a form of creation...
and I really like people who create things.
So if a manga I made moves its readers to write something...
I think that's wonderful.
If it nourishes other creators...
and becomes a component of their own work...
RICE
then nothing could make me happier.
It doesn't have to be art, writing, music, movies, et cetera...
It could even be thoughts, words, or actions.
Whatever the case, it would mean the world to me...
if there's even a drop of *Bloom into You* mixed in there.
That's what I was thinking as I drew it...
and I'm sure I'll always feel the same way.
MM. RICE.
Thank you all so much...
for making *Bloom into You* a joy to work on!!
THANK YOUS!
Thank you to everyone who worked on the manga, anime, play, novels, anthology, goods...
or was involved with *Bloom into You* in any other way.
And thank YOU for reading it!

SEVEN SEAS ENTERTAINMENT PRESENTS

Bloom into You

mrya
9·20

story and art by NAKATANI NIO   VOLUME 8

TRANSLATION
Jenny McKeon

ADAPTATION
Jenn Grunigen

LETTERING AND RETOUCH
CK Russell

LOGO DESIGN
KC Fabellon

COVER DESIGN
Nicky Lim

PROOFREADER
Danielle King

PREPRESS TECHNICIAN
Rhiannon Rasmussen-Silverstein

PRODUCTION MANAGER
Lissa Pattillo

MANAGING EDITOR
Julie Davis

ASSOCIATE PUBLISHER
Adam Arnold

PUBLISHER
Jason DeAngelis

BLOOM INTO YOU VOL. 8
YAGATE KIMI NI NARU Vol.8
© Nakatani Nio 2019
First published in Japan in 2019 by KADOKAWA CORPORATION, Tokyo.
English translation rights arranged with KADOKAWA CORPORATION, Tokyo.

No portion of this book may be reproduced or transmitted in any form without
written permission from the copyright holders. This is a work of fiction. Names,
characters, places, and incidents are the products of the author's imagination
or are used fictitiously. Any resemblance to actual events, locales, or persons,
living or dead, is entirely coincidental.

Seven Seas press and purchase enquiries can be sent to Marketing Manager
Lianne Sentar at press@gomanga.com. Information regarding the distribution
and purchase of digital editions is available from Digital Manager CK Russell
at digital@gomanga.com.

Seven Seas and the Seven Seas logo are trademarks of
Seven Seas Entertainment. All rights reserved.

ISBN: 978-1-64275-746-0

Printed in Canada

First Printing: August 2020

10 9 8 7 6 5 4 3 2 1

READING DIRECTIONS

This book reads from *right to left*, Japanese style.
If this is your first time reading manga, you start
reading from the top right panel on each page and
take it from there. If you get lost, just follow the
numbered diagram here. It may seem backwards at
first, but you'll get the hang of it! Have fun!!

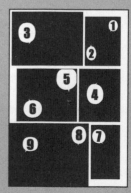